THE BEST PLACES
TO BUY A HOME IN FRANCE

edited by

Joe Laredo

SURVIVAL BOOKS • LONDON • ENGLAND

First published 2003
Reprinted 2003

Survival Books Limited, 1st Floor, 60 St James's Street
London SW1A 1ZN, United Kingdom
☎ +44 (0)20-7493 4244, 🖹 +44 (0)20-7491 0605
✉ info@survivalbooks.net
🖳 www.survivalbooks.net

British Library Cataloguing in Publication Data.
A CIP record for this book is available from the British Library.
ISBN 1 901130 12 6

Printed and bound in Finland by WS Bookwell Ltd

ACKNOWLEDGEMENTS

My sincere thanks to all those who contributed to the publication of this book, in particular Kerry Laredo for design and layout, Dennis Kelsall (Milestones) for superb photographs, Trevor Yorke and Lucy-Jane Cypher (Publisher and Editor respectively, *Living France*) for superb photographs and valuable information, John Evans (Eclipse Overseas) for information on Normandy and Brittany, Miranda Neame (Editor, *The News*) for help in finding knowledgeable writers, Sarah Cooper-Williams for extensive research on the south-west, Paul Owen and Stephanie Basibé (VEF) and Nicholas Smallwood (French Property Shop) for information on the property market in the south-west, Chris Rankin (Bordeaux British Community) for useful contacts, Marilyn Riley (President, Americans in Toulouse) for information about obtaining foreign products, Alison Monnier for information about Brittany, and Jean-Noël Brunet, Pamela Cooley, Françoise Labarbe, Petra Lugtig and the staff of the Conseil régional de l'Auvergne and the Conseil général du Lot for their help with Chapter 4. Finally, a special thank-you to Jim Watson for the superb cover, cartoons, illustrations and maps.

What Readers and Reviewers

When you buy a model plane for your child, a video recorder, or some new computer gizmo, you get with it a leaflet or booklet pleading 'Read Me First', or bearing large friendly letters or bold type saying 'IMPORTANT – follow the instructions carefully'. This book should be similarly supplied to all those entering France with anything more durable than a 5-day return ticket. It is worth reading even if you are just visiting briefly, or if you have lived here for years and feel totally knowledgeable and secure. But if you need to find out how France works then it is indispensable. Native French people probably have a less thorough understanding of how their country functions. – Where it is most essential, the book is most up to the minute.

Living France

We would like to congratulate you on this work: it is really super! We hand it out to our expatriates and they read it with great interest and pleasure.

ICI (Switzerland) AG

Rarely has a 'survival guide' contained such useful advice. This book dispels doubts for first-time travellers, yet is also useful for seasoned globetrotters – In a word, if you're planning to move to the USA or go there for a long-term stay, then buy this book both for general reading and as a ready-reference.

American Citizens Abroad

It is everything you always wanted to ask but didn't for fear of the contemptuous put down – The best English-language guide – Its pages are stuffed with practical information on everyday subjects and are designed to complement the traditional guidebook.

Swiss News

A complete revelation to me – I found it both enlightening and interesting, not to mention amusing.

Carole Clark

Let's say it at once. David Hampshire's *Living and Working in France* is the best handbook ever produced for visitors and foreign residents in this country; indeed, my discussion with locals showed that it has much to teach even those born and bred in l'Hexagone. – It is Hampshire's meticulous detail which lifts his work way beyond the range of other books with similar titles. Often you think of a supplementary question and search for the answer in vain. With Hampshire this is rarely the case. – He writes with great clarity (and gives French equivalents of all key terms), a touch of humour and a ready eye for the odd (and often illuminating) fact. – This book is absolutely indispensable.

The Riviera Reporter

Have Said About Survival Books

What a great work, wealth of useful information, well-balanced wording and accuracy in details. My compliments!

Thomas Müller

This handbook has all the practical information one needs to set up home in the UK – The sheer volume of information is almost daunting – Highly recommended for anyone moving to the UK.

American Citizens Abroad

A very good book which has answered so many questions and even some I hadn't thought of – I would certainly recommend it.

Brian Fairman

A mine of information – I may have avoided some embarrassments and frights if I had read it prior to my first Swiss encounters – Deserves an honoured place on any newcomer's bookshelf.

English Teachers Association, Switzerland

Covers just about all the things you want to know on the subject – In answer to the desert island question about the one how-to book on France, this book would be it – Almost 500 pages of solid accurate reading – This book is about enjoyment as much as survival.

The Recorder

it's so funny – I love it and definitely need a copy of my own – Thanks very much for having written such a humorous and helpful book.

Heidi Guiliani

A must for all foreigners coming to Switzerland.

Antoinette O'Donoghue

A comprehensive guide to all things French, written in a highly readable and amusing style, for anyone planning to live, work or retire in France.

The Times

A concise, thorough account of the DOs and DON'Ts for a foreigner in Switzerland – Crammed with useful information and lightened with humorous quips which make the facts more readable.
American Citizens Abroad

Covers every conceivable question that may be asked concerning everyday life – I know of no other book that could take the place of this one.

France in Print

Hats off to *Living and Working in Switzerland*!

Ronnie Almeida

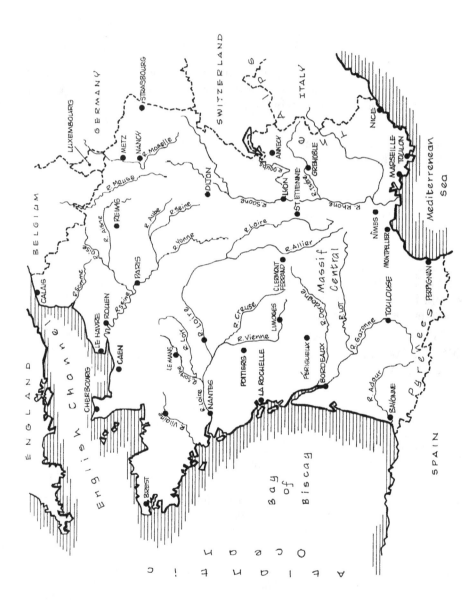

CONTENTS

ABOUT THE AUTHORS

Wanda Glowinska-Rizzi (Chapter 4)

Wanda was born in London of a Polish father and an Irish mother, has a French-Italian husband and has lived in Creuse since 1995. She's a translator and English teacher and presents a local radio programme. This is her first work for Survival Books.

Michael Keyte (Chapter 3)

Michael was born in Warwickshire in England, but married a Parisian and has been living in Gironde since 1995. He contributes regularly to *The News* and is particularly interested in French history and cooking. This is his first work for Survival Books.

Beverly Laflamme (Chapter 8)

Born and raised in the USA, Beverly has been living and working in the Ile-de-France for eight years and has had an active role in a number of Paris-based expatriate groups. She's the author of *Living and Working in Holland, Belgium and Luxembourg* and has also contributed to *Living and Working in Germany*, *Living and Working in France* and *Buying a Home in France* (all Survival Books).

Joe Laredo (Chapters 1, 2 & 5)

Joe has been living and working in Normandy since mid-2001, when he moved from his native Surrey (England). He's the author of *Living and Working in Ireland* and *Buying a Home in Ireland* and has contributed to *Living and Working in France* and *Buying a Home in France* as well as editing a number of other titles for Survival Books.

Richard Whiting (Chapters 6, 7 & 9)

Originally from Sussex in England, Richard has been living in the south of France for 20 years and has travelled throughout most of the coastal area, first as a sales representative and, more recently, as an estate agent's consultant. He now translates French property magazines and is also the English translator for the bi-lingual annual *Guide Horus* selection of best restaurants in Provence-Côte d'Azur. This is his first work for Survival Books.

IMPORTANT NOTE

Readers should note that the laws and regulations concerning buying property in France aren't the same as in other countries and are liable to change periodically. I cannot recommend too strongly that you always check with an official and reliable source (not always the same) and take expert legal advice before paying any money or signing any legal documents. Don't, however, believe everything you're told or read – even, dare I say it, herein!

To help you obtain further information and verify data, useful addresses and references to other sources of information have been included in all chapters and in Appendices A to C. You're particularly advised to read *Buying a Home in France* and *Living and Working in France* by David Hampshire (Survival Books).

EDITOR'S NOTES

- Property prices should be taken as estimates only, although they were mostly correct at the time of publication.

- His/he/him also means her/she/her (please forgive me ladies). This is done to make life easier for both the reader and (in particular) the author, and isn't intended to be sexist.

- All spelling is (or should be) British English and not American English.

- Warnings and important points are shown in **bold** type.

- The following symbols are used in this book: ☎ (telephone), ▤ (fax), 🖳 (Internet) and ✉ (e-mail).

- Lists of **Useful Addresses**, **Further Reading** and **Useful Websites** are contained in **Appendices A**, **B** and **C** respectively.

- For those unfamiliar with the Metric system of weights and measures, imperial conversion tables are included in **Appendix D**.

- A map of France showing the regions and departments and a map of the high-speed train (*TGV*) network are included in **Appendix E**, and a map showing the major cities and geographical features is on page 6. Maps of each region and sub-region showing the major towns and places of interest and the major airports and ports are included in the relevant chapters.

- **Appendix F** contains a rating of the 100 largest towns in France, with information taken from a survey published in January 2002 by *Le Point* magazine.

INTRODUCTION

If you're planning to buy a home in France but aren't sure where you would like to live, or just wish to compare towns in your chosen area – this is **THE BOOK** for you! The purpose of *The Best Places to Buy a Home in France* is to provide you with the information necessary to help you choose the most appropriate region or town **to satisfy your family's requirements**. Most important of all, it will help you to avoid buying a home in the wrong area and having to uproot yourself after a few years.

France offers something for everyone, but where should *you* buy *your* home? Perhaps you wish to live on an island off Brittany or in Corsica. Or maybe you fancy a home in one of France's many coastal regions, such as the Côte d'Azur, Normandy or Vendée. Or you may hanker after the fast pace of life in a French city such as Paris, Nice or Toulouse. With so many inviting regions and towns to choose from it can be a difficult decision, particularly as the climate, lifestyle and cost of property can vary considerably from region to region, and even within a region.

Where you buy a property in France will depend on a range of factors, including your preferences, your financial resources and, not least, whether you plan to work. If you intend to look for employment or start a business, you must live in an area that allows you the maximum scope. On the other hand, for a holiday home accessibility may be the key factor, and for a retirement home, the proximity of amenities and services.

For many people, choosing the location for a home in France has previously been a case of pot luck. However, with a copy of *The Best Places to Buy a Home in France* to hand you'll have a wealth of priceless information at your fingertips – information derived from a variety of sources, both official and unofficial, not least the hard-won experiences of the authors, their friends, colleagues and acquaintances. This book will also reduce your risk of making an expensive mistake that you may bitterly regret later and help you to make informed decisions and calculated judgements, instead of costly mistakes and uneducated guesses (forewarned is forearmed!). **Not least, it will save you money and repay your investment many times over.**

Buying a home in France is a wonderful way to make new friends, broaden your horizons and revitalise your life, and it also provides a welcome bolt-hole to recuperate from the stresses and strains of modern life. I trust this book will help you choose the most appropriate area and smooth your way to many happy years in your new home in France, secure in the knowledge that you've made the right decision.

Bon courage!

Joe Laredo (Editor)
November 2002

Conques – The Dordogne

1.

WHY BUY A HOME IN FRANCE?

Judging by its record 73 million visitors annually, France is the world's most popular country. Its premier tourist destinations, such as the Côte d'Azur, Dordogne, Loire Valley and Brittany, are among the world's favourite holiday-home and retirement destinations, and France is becoming increasingly popular among those looking to move permanently abroad. Many thousands of Europeans have settled in France, particularly Britons (over half a million of them have homes there and some 65,000 live there permanently), and in several villages foreign residents actually outnumber locals!

There are many excellent reasons for buying a home in France, although it's important to ask yourself *exactly* why you want to buy a home there. For example, are you primarily looking for a sound investment or do you plan to work or start a business in France? Are you seeking a holiday or retirement home? If you're seeking a second home, will it be mainly used for long weekends or for lengthier stays? Do you plan to let it to offset the mortgage and running costs? If so, how important is the property income? You need to answer these and many other questions before deciding on the best (and most appropriate) place to buy a home in France.

Often buyers have a variety of reasons for buying a home in France; for example, many people buy a holiday home with a view to living there permanently or semi-permanently when they retire. If this is the case, there are many more factors to take into account than if you're 'simply' buying a holiday home that you will occupy for just a few weeks a year (when it's usually wiser not to buy at all!). If, on the other hand, you plan to work or start a business in France, you will be faced with a completely different set of criteria. An increasing number of people live in France and work in another European country (e.g. neighbouring England, Belgium, Luxembourg, Germany, Switzerland and Italy), commuting back and forth by road, rail or air.

Property values in France generally increase at an average of less than 5 per cent a year or in line with inflation (with no increase in real terms). In some fashionable resorts and developments, however, prices rise faster than average, although this is usually reflected in much higher purchase prices. For example, prices increased by over 20 per cent per annum in some parts of the Côte d'Azur in the late 1990s and early 21st century. Generally, however, there's a stable property market in most of France, which acts as a discouragement to speculators wishing to make a 'fast buck', particularly when you consider that capital gains tax can wipe out much of the profit made on the sale of a second home. Bear in mind that you must also recover the costs associated with buying a home when you sell; these are particularly high in France.

ADVANTAGES & DISADVANTAGES

There are both advantages and disadvantages to buying a home in France, although for most people the benefits far outweigh any drawbacks. France has many attractions: much of the country enjoys a sunny and warm climate all year round, with over 300 days of sunshine annually and high temperatures in southern areas; access to your French home from home has never been easier or cheaper, especially from the UK, thanks mainly to the proliferation of low cost flights offered by airlines such as Buzz and Ryanair, but also to an increase in the number of cross-Channel ferries, the introduction of new routes and even new operators and the widespread freezing of ferry prices; France's motorway network is second to none (although expensive to use) and is constantly being improved, and most regions can now be reached by motorway; Europe's fastest trains (*TGV*) not only serve an increasing number of major towns and cities, but also link with a Europe-wide network via the new hub at Lille, and the government has recently 'ordered' the (nationalised) railway operators to compete with the low-cost airlines, so lower train fares can be expected.

France is famous for its huge variety of cultural and leisure activities, and the French people, although not renowned for their friendliness and hospitality, are generally welcoming to foreigners who make the effort to integrate. The standard of living is generally high and the cost of living reasonable by Western European standards, including very good value homes (if you avoid fashionable areas). Although prices have risen in many popular areas of France in recent years, property remains far cheaper than its equivalent in the UK, for example, with the bonus that it's often accompanied by generous amounts of land. A modest €75,000 (£50,000/$75,000) will buy you a small modern house or a large property in need of renovation in Normandy or Brittany, Limousin or Poitou-Charentes, a one-bedroom apartment on the Côte d'Azur or even a (tiny) studio flat in Paris, while for €150,000 (£100,000/$150,000) you can purchase a detached, three-bedroom house in Dordogne or Provence or an extensive property with acres of land in many other parts of the country. Those with a few hundred thousand euros to spend can stretch to a *maison de maître*, a *manoir*, a *châteaux* or even an entire hamlet (*hameau*), which in remote areas such as the Cévennes or the departments of Lozère and Ardèche in the south-east, can be picked up for €500,000 or less (you can even find them in Nord-Pas-de-Calais) – ideal if you really want to get away from the neighbours!

Among the many other advantages of buying a home in France are good rental possibilities (in many areas), good local tradesmen and services (particularly in resort areas), fine food and wine (some would argue, the best in the world) at reasonable prices, a relaxed pace of life in rural areas, one of the world's best healthcare systems, plenty of open space, and some of the most beautiful scenery in Europe all around you. When buying property in France, you aren't simply buying a home but a lifestyle, and in terms of quality of life, the country has few equals.

Naturally, there are also a few disadvantages, including the high purchase costs associated with buying a home in France, unexpected renovation and restoration costs (if you don't do your homework), a high rate of burglary in some areas, overcrowding in popular tourist areas during the peak summer season, traffic congestion and pollution in many towns and cities, and the expense of getting to and from France if you own a holiday home there and don't live in a nearby country with good air connections.

CHOOSING THE REGION

France is a huge country (the largest in western Europe) with a vast array of landscapes, including low-lying areas in the north and west, mountains in the centre, east and south-east, forests, farmland and wetlands. Unlike most Western countries, France is still largely rural. Some 25 per cent of the population lives in rural areas, a percentage which has hardly changed in half a century, and average population density is among the lowest in Europe at around 100 people per km² (260 per mi²). Paris has a population of almost 11 million, Lyons 1.6 million, Marseilles 1.4 million and Lille 1.1 million. Only five other cities (Toulouse, Bordeaux, Nantes, Strasbourg and Nice) have more than half a million inhabitants, while there are over 32,600 French villages with fewer than 1,000 inhabitants.

You can choose complete isolation in Lozère in the Massif Central, authentic French village life almost anywhere, an expatriate community where you will live among your own countrymen and other foreigners, such as those in Dordogne and parts of Provence, and an area where you can enjoy the best of both worlds. You may prefer the hustle and bustle of city life, mountain living in the Alps or the Pyrenees, nautical life in Brittany with some of the world's best sailing on your doorstep, or mixing it with the jet-set on the Côte d'Azur.

France is the only country in Europe that has three distinct climatic zones: maritime along the west and north-west coast (and making its influence felt as far inland as the departments of Dordogne, Lot, Tarn and Tarn-et-Garonne), continental in central and eastern areas, and Mediterranean in the south-east and in Corsica, with a mountain climate in the Alps, Pyrenees, Massif Central and Vosges and numerous micro-climates making certain areas warmer, drier, wetter or colder than you might expect. The Alps and Pyrenees experience extremes of weather, and there can be violent winds and storms in the south and north-west.

France is a world unto itself, and deciding where to live can be difficult and the choice overwhelming. For many people their choice is based on previous holidays, friends' recommendations, accessibility or simply an area's reputation. However, how do you know whether an area is a good investment and what you can expect to get for your money? Where can you find expatriate services, good hospitals or plenty of sports and leisure facilities? Which areas and resorts are busy in summer and which offer a more relaxed way of life? What are the local roads and public transport system like? Which areas are easily accessible by air and sea?

This book has been written to help answer these questions by providing comprehensive information about the most popular areas among foreign homebuyers in France and giving an accurate picture of what everyday life is *really* like in a certain area. The 'best' place to live in France obviously depends on your preferences and it's impossible to specify a best location for everyone. The aim of this book is to identify the positive and possible negative aspects of each of the selected areas in order to help you to choose the part of France that suits you and your family best.

It would be impossible in a book this size to describe in detail every part of France, so we've focused on the most popular locations with foreign homebuyers and have divided these into seven areas, each of which includes one or more of the 22 named regions of France (see map on page 394). Each of these areas is dealt with in a separate chapter, starting in the north and moving around the country anti-clockwise to end with Paris and the Ile-de-France. A final chapter summarises the advantages and disadvantages of the other parts of France and lists sources of further information.

● Chapter 2: Normandy and Brittany

● Chapter 3: the west coast

● Chapter 4: Dordogne, Lot and the Auvergne and Limousin

● Chapter 5: the south-west

● Chapter 6: the Mediterranean coast

● Chapter 7: the Alps

● Chapter 8: Paris and the Ile-de-France

● Chapter 9: other areas

Each of the main chapters examines an area in detail with a description of the most popular towns and villages, the advantages and disadvantages of living there, the climate, regional language (if any), crime rate and cost of living, local services and amenities, communications by air, sea, road and public transport, planned developments, employment prospects and the property market, including typical homes, the availability and cost of rental accommodation, and the average prices of different kinds of property and land. For those considering buying a property in or near a major town, a rating of the 100 largest towns in France (derived from a nationwide survey published by *Le Point* magazine in January 2002) is included in **Appendix F**.

Note that prices change continually and those quoted in this book were accurate in mid-2002. Properties in traditionally popular places, such as Provence (see page 210), Dordogne (see page 130) and Brittany (see page 36), will probably always show a steady increase in value, as it's unlikely that these regions will lose their appeal to foreign (and particularly British) buyers, but there are other parts of France waiting in the wings that could soon (and suddenly) increase in popularity and where prices could therefore jump dramatically. These include the department of Mayenne (see page 95), Aveyron and Gers (see pages 169 and 168), the Auvergne and Limousin regions (see pages 133 and 134), Burgundy (see page 341) and the Roussillon coast (see page 210). Note also that, although budget airlines have recently made acessible previously remote parts of France, such services are notoriously fickle and it isn't wise to buy in a particular area purely because it's served by cheap flights; airlines create and cancel routes at the drop of a hat and you could be left stranded.

Once you've decided on a preferred region or area, you must consider the type of home you want to buy and the kind of location which will best suit you.

LOCATION

The most important consideration when buying a home anywhere is usually its location – or as the old adage goes, the *three* most important considerations are location, location and location! A property in a reasonable condition in a popular area is likely to be a better investment than an exceptional property in a less attractive location. There's usually no point in buying a dream home in a terrible location. France offers almost everything that anyone could want, but you must choose the right property in the right place. **The wrong decision regarding location is one of the main causes of disappointment among foreigners who purchase property in France.**

There are many points to consider regarding the location of a home, and you should take into account the present and future needs of all family members in relation to the following factors:

Climate: You should bear in mind both the winter and summer climate of your chosen region, the average daily amount of sunshine, the rainfall and wind conditions, as well as the position of the sun relative to a property. The orientation or aspect of a building is vital, and if you want morning or afternoon sun (or both) you must ensure that balconies, terraces and gardens are facing the right direction (take a compass when house hunting).

Natural Phenomena: Check whether an area is liable to natural disasters such as storms, floods or forest fires. If a property is located near a waterway, it may be expensive to insure against floods (or flash floods), which are a threat in some areas. Note that in areas with little rainfall there may be frequent droughts, water restrictions and high water bills.

Noise: Noise can be a problem in some parts of France, although the French are generally considerate neighbours. You should ensure that a property isn't located next to a busy road, industrial plant, commercial area, building site, discotheque, night club, bar or restaurant (where revelries may continue into the early hours). Look out for objectionable neighbouring properties and check whether nearby vacant land has been zoned for commercial activities. In rural areas, make sure your neighbours don't have noisy dogs or a cockerel. In some resorts, many properties are second homes and are let short-term, which means you may have to tolerate boisterous holiday-makers as neighbours throughout the year (or at least during the summer months). In towns, traffic noise, particularly from motorcycles, can continue all night!

Tourists: Bear in mind that if you live in a popular tourist area, i.e. almost anywhere on the Mediterranean coast, you will be inundated with tourists in the summer. They won't just jam the roads and pack the beaches and shops, but will also occupy your favourite table at your local bar or restaurant (heaven forbid!). Bear in mind that while a 'front-line' property sounds attractive and may be ideal for short holidays, it isn't always the best solution for permanent residence. Many beaches are hopelessly crowded in the peak season, streets may be smelly from restaurants and fast food outlets, parking will be impossible, services stretched to breaking point and the incessant noise may drive you crazy. You may also have to tolerate water shortages, power cuts and sewage problems. Some people prefer to move inland to higher ground, where it's less humid, you're isolated from the noise and can also enjoy excellent views. On the other hand, getting to and from hillside properties can be difficult, and the often poorly-maintained roads (usually narrow and unguarded) are for sober, confident drivers only.

Community: Do you wish to live in an area surrounded by other expatriates from your home country (as you will almost inevitably be in some parts of Provence and Dordogne) or as far away from them as possible? If you wish to integrate with the local community, you should avoid the foreign 'ghettos' and choose a French village or an area or development with mainly local inhabitants. However, unless you speak fluent French or intend to learn it, you should think twice before buying a property in a village, although residents who take the time and trouble to integrate into the local community are invariably warmly welcomed. If you're buying a permanent home, it's important to check on your prospective neighbours, particularly when buying an apartment. For example, are they noisy, sociable or absent for long periods? Do you think you will get on with them? **Good neighbours are invaluable, particularly when buying a second home in a village.**

On the other hand, if you wish to mix only with your compatriots and don't plan to learn French, living in a predominantly foreign community will be ideal. Note, however, that some towns in popular tourist areas are inhabited largely by second homeowners and are like ghost towns for most of the year. In these areas, many facilities, businesses and shops are closed outside the main tourist season, when even local services such as public transport and postal collections may be severely curtailed.

Town or Country: Do you wish to be in a town or do you prefer the country? Inland or by the sea? How about living on an island? Life on an island is more restricted and remote, e.g. you cannot jump into your car and drive to Lyons or Paris or 'pop' over the border into Andorra, Spain, Italy or Switzerland. Bear in mind that if you buy a property in the country you will have to tolerate poor (or non-existent) public transport, long travelling distances to a town of any size, solitude and remoteness, and the high cost and amount of work involved in the upkeep of a country house and garden. You may not be able to walk to the local shop for fresh bread or to the local bar for a glass of your favourite tipple, or have a choice of restaurants on your doorstep. In a town or large village, the weekly market will be just around the corner, the doctor and chemist's close at hand, and if you need help or run into any problems, your neighbours will be near by.

On the other hand, in the country you will be closer to nature, will have more freedom (e.g. to make as much noise as you wish) and possibly complete privacy, e.g. to sunbathe or swim *au naturel*. Living in a remote area in the country will suit those looking for peace and quiet who don't want to involve themselves in the 'hustle and bustle' of town life (not that there's a lot of this in French rural towns). If you're seeking peace and quiet, make sure that there isn't a busy road or railway line nearby or a local church within 'DONGING' distance. Note, however, that many people who buy a remote country home find that the peace of the countryside palls after a time and they yearn for the more exciting city or coastal life. If you've never lived in the country, it's wise to rent before buying. Note also that while it's cheaper to buy in a remote or unpopular location, it's usually much more difficult to find a buyer when you want to sell.

Garden: If you're planning to buy a country property with a large garden or plot, bear in mind the high cost and amount of work involved in its upkeep. If it's a second home, who will look after the house and garden when you're away? Do you want to spend your holidays mowing the lawn and cutting back the undergrowth? Do you want a home with a lot of outbuildings? What are you going to do with them? Can you afford to convert them into extra rooms or guest accommodation?

Employment: If you will be working in France, how secure is your job or business and are you likely to move to another area in the near future? Can you find other work in the same area, if necessary? If there's a possibility that you will need to move in a few years' time, you should rent a home or at least buy one that will be relatively easy to sell so that you can recoup the cost. You should consider also your partner's and children's actual or possible job requirements.

Schools: What about your children's present and future schooling? What is the quality of local schools? Note that even if your family has no need or plans to use local schools, the value of a home may be influenced by the quality and location of schools.

Services: What local health and social services are provided? How far is the nearest hospital with an emergency department? Are there English-speaking doctors and dentists and private clinics or hospitals in the area?

Shopping: What shopping facilities are provided in the neighbourhood? How far is it to the nearest large town with good shopping facilities, e.g. a super/hypermarket? How would you get there if your car was out of commission? Note that many rural villages are dying and have few shops or facilities, and they aren't usually a good choice for a retirement home.

Sports & Leisure Facilities: What is the range and quality of local leisure, sports, community and cultural facilities? What is the proximity to sports facilities such as beaches, golf courses, ski resorts and waterways? Bear in mind that properties in or close to ski and coastal resorts are considerably more expensive, although they also have the best letting potential. If you're a keen skier, you may want to be close to the Alps or the Pyrenees, although there are smaller skiing areas in other regions.

Transport: Is proximity to public transport or access to a motorway important? Don't believe all you're told about the distance or travelling times to the nearest airport, railway station, motorway junction, beach or town, but check for yourself.

Parking: If you're planning to buy in a town or city, is there adequate private or free on-street parking for your family and visitors? Is it safe to park in the street? Note that in French cities it's important to have secure off-street parking if you value your car. Parking is a problem in cities and most large towns, where private garages or parking spaces are unobtainable or expensive. Traffic congestion is also a problem in many towns and tourist resorts, particularly during the high season. Bear in mind that an apartment or townhouse may be some distance from the nearest road or car park. How do you feel about carrying heavy shopping hundreds of metres to your home and possibly up several flights of stairs? If you're planning to buy an apartment above the ground floor, you may wish to ensure that the building has a lift.

Crime Rate: What is the local crime rate? In many resort areas the incidence of burglary is high, which also results in more expensive home insurance. Check the crime rate in the local area, e.g. burglaries, stolen cars and crimes of violence. Is crime increasing or decreasing? Note that professional crooks love isolated houses, particularly those full of expensive furniture and other belongings that they can strip bare at their leisure. You're much less likely to be the victim of thieves if you live in a village, where crime is virtually unknown – strangers stand out like sore thumbs in villages, where their every move is monitored by the local populace.

Administration: Is the local council well run? Unfortunately many are profligate and simply use any extra income to hire a few more of their cronies or spend it on grandiose schemes. What are the views of other residents? If the municipality is efficiently run, you can usually rely on good local social and sports amenities and other facilities. In areas where there are many foreign residents, the town hall may have a foreign residents' department.

This book will provide you with answers to many of the above questions. However, although the information about each area is comprehensive and up-to-date, it isn't intended as a substitute for personal research.

RESEARCH

It's essential to spend time looking around your areas of interest. If possible, you should visit an area a number of times over a period of a few weeks, both on weekdays and at weekends, in order to get a feel for the neighbourhood (it's better to walk than to drive around). A property seen on a balmy summer's day after a delicious lunch and a few glasses of *vin de pays* may not be nearly so attractive on a subsequent visit *sans* sunshine and the warm inner glow. If possible, you should also visit an area at different times of the year, e.g. in both the summer and winter, as somewhere that's wonderful in summer can be forbidding and inhospitable in winter (or vice versa if you don't like extreme heat). This is particularly important when choosing a holiday resort, which may be bustling and lively during the summer months but deserted in winter. If you're planning to buy a winter holiday home, you should view it in the summer, as snow can hide a multitude of sins! In any case, you should view a property a number of times before deciding to buy it. If you're unfamiliar with an area, most experts recommend that you rent for a period before buying. This is particularly important if you're planning to buy a permanent or retirement home in an unfamiliar area. Many people change their minds after a period and it isn't unusual for buyers to move once or twice before settling down permanently.

Before looking at properties, it's important to have a good idea of the type of property you want and the price you wish to pay, and to draw up a short list of the areas and towns of interest. Most importantly, make a list of what you want and don't want – if you don't do this, you're likely to be overwhelmed by the number of properties to be viewed. You should consider a property's proximity to your place of work, schools, bars and restaurants, countryside or towns, shops, public transport, beaches, swimming pools, entertainment, sports facilities, etc. If you buy a country property, the distance to local amenities and services could become a problem, particularly if you plan to retire to France. If you live in a remote rural area, you will need to be much more self-sufficient than if you live in a town. Don't forget that France is a BIG country and if you live in a remote area you will need to use the car for everything (which will increase your cost of living).

If you wish to live near a particular town, airport or facilities, such as a beach, sports or other amenities, obtain a large scale map of the area and decide the maximum distance you will consider travelling. Mark the places that you've seen on the map, at the same time making a list of the plus and minus points of each property. If you use an estate agent, he will usually drive you around and you can then return later to the properties that you like best at your leisure (provided you've marked them on your map!). Note, however, that agents may be reluctant to give you the keys to visit a property on your own.

A number of companies organise 'discovery tours' of various regions of France, on which you can get a feel for an area and the type and prices of properties and maybe see a few properties that are available, although these tours aren't cheap and you may prefer to arrange your own itinerary. For example, in the USA there's International Living Discovery Tours, 235NE 4th Avenue, Ste 102, Delray Beach, FL#33483, USA (☎ 561-243 6276 or 800-926 6575 toll free, ✉ tours@internationalLiving.com), and in the UK KBM Consultancy, Tawny Barn, Downs Mill, Frampton Mansell, Stroud, Glos. GL6 8JX (☎ 08700-113141, 💻 www.kbmconsultancy.com), whose 'Immotours' currently cover only Normandy and Brittany.

IMPORTANT NOTE

Unless you know exactly what you're looking for and where, it's best to rent a property until you're familiar with an area. As when making all major financial decisions, it's never wise to be too hasty. Many people make expensive (even catastrophic) errors when buying homes abroad, usually because they do insufficient research and are in too much of a hurry, often setting themselves ridiculous deadlines, such as buying a home during a long weekend break or a week's holiday. Not surprisingly, most people wouldn't dream of acting so rashly when buying property in their home country! It isn't uncommon for buyers to regret their decision after some time and wish they'd purchased a different property in a different region (or even in a different country!).

The decision to purchase property, retire or relocate to France (or any other country) should only be taken after careful consideration and extensive research. You should also consider learning French, particularly if you intend to live in France permanently, although there are a few parts of France where the *lingua franca* is English. There are numerous books about France (see **Appendix B**), including *Buying a Home in France* and *Living and Working in France*, written by David Hampshire and published by Survival Books, which are packed with important information about property purchase and daily life in France. **Note that the cost of investing in a few books or magazines (and other research) is tiny compared with the expense of making a big mistake.** Numerous websites (see **Appendix C**) also provide free information about France.

Jim Watson

Vitré–Brittany

Normandy and Brittany have long been popular areas for foreign buyers, particularly the British on account of the regions' accessibility and similar climate and countryside, as well as their historical and cultural kinship. Like Britain, Normandy was invaded by the Vikings – 200 years before the Normans themselves invaded Britain – and it was part of England in the early Middle Ages (the Queen is still 'Duke of Normandy'!). Britain in French is 'big Brittany' to distinguish it from the French region, which was founded by Cornish settlers fleeing Anglo-Saxon invaders in the fifth century. They took their language with them (curiously, Breton survives but Cornish doesn't) and remain proudly Celtic. It wasn't until 1532 that Brittany officially became part of France. There are also more recent cultural ties between the two regions and Britain, with twinnings (e.g. Rennes with Exeter, Honfleur with Sandwich in Kent, and the department of Calvados with Devon) and frequent cross-Channel exchanges. There's even the unlikely *hot dog Breton*, a sausage in a pancake, and Breton whisky, distilled at Lannion! In a wide-ranging survey of the 100 largest towns in France published in January 2002, *Le Point* magazine rated three towns in this area – Caen (14), Rennes (35) and Vannes (56) – among the country's top twelve; according to the criteria selected by us, Vannes rates as the country's second-best town to live in, Quimper the fourth-best and Rennes tenth (see **Appendix F**).

Normandy

Normandy (*La Normandie*) contains the departments of Calvados (14), Eure (27), Manche (50), Orne (61) and Seine-Maritime (76) and is officially divided into two areas: Upper Normandy (*Haute-Normandie*) to the east, comprising the departments of Eure and Seine-Maritime, and Lower Normandy (*Basse-Normandie*) to the west. Upper Normandy, which covers an area of around 12,500km² (5,000mi²), has a population of around 1.7 million, and Lower Normandy (17,600km²/7,000mi²) a population of around 1.4 million. This relatively recent (1972) administrative division, however, has neither a historical nor a geographical basis. Historically, Upper and Lower Normandy were separated by the Seine, which now runs roughly along the dividing line between the departments of Eure and Seine-Maritime in Upper Normandy.

Geographically, Normandy can be said to be divided into three areas: the eastern 'plains' (roughly corresponding to Upper Normandy), interrupted by the Seine valley; the western *bocage*, a landscape of fields and hedges resulting from 19th century methods of dairy farming; and a central area divided vertically between plains to the west of the river Orne and *bocage* to the east. (Confusingly, the word *bocage* is used to describe both the area south-west of Caen and any similar landscape in Normandy or France as a whole.) Within the central area, south of Caen, is 'Swiss Normandy' (*La Suisse normande*), so called because of its similarity to the Swiss landscape, with deep gorges and rocky peaks, although the highest point, Mont Pinçon, is only 365m (120ft) above sea level.

Normandy was originally divided into 'lands' (*pays*), many of which are still referred to and even marked on maps (although they often straddle departments and even the division between Upper and Lower Normandy), e.g. the Pays d'Argentan, Pays du Houlme and Pays du Perche in Orne, the Pays d'Auge (around Caen), the Pays de Bray (near the border with Picardy), the Pays de Caux (a largely rural and agricultural area between Rouen and Dieppe), the Pays d'Ouche (between Bernay and Verneuil-sur-Avre) and the Pays du Vexin normand in north-east Eure.

Demographically, Upper Normandy is more urbanised and Paris-influenced (the department of Eure in particular is said to be in the shadow of the capital), Lower Normandy more rural and 'traditional'. The three largest towns in Normandy are Rouen (population around 400,000), the administrative capital of Upper Normandy, Caen (117,000), the administrative capital of Lower Normandy and Le Havre (193,000), other major towns including Dieppe, Evreux, Les Andelys, Lisieux, Pont-Audemer, Verneuil-sur-Avre and Yvetot (see **Major Towns & Places of Interest** on page 41).

Normandy is noted for its lovely countryside and wide variety of scenery, including lush meadows, orchards, rivers and brooks, quiet country lanes, and over 600km (370mi) of coastline (100km/60mi of which were the scene of the D-Day landings in June 1944). Some 30 per cent of Upper Normandy is grassland and 50 per cent of Lower Normandy (the highest percentage in France); the north-west of Calvados is known as the Bessin – land of grass, milk and marshes. A further 45 per cent of Upper Normandy and 30 per cent of Lower Normandy is arable land.

Normandy is a rich agricultural region, producing meat, milk, butter, cheese (most famously Camembert, but also numerous other cheeses, including Livarot, Neufchâtel and Pont l'Evêque), apples, cider and calvados – a spirit distilled from apple juice (Upper Normandy is sometimes referred to as 'calvaland'). It's also renowned for its cuisine, with local specialities including shellfish dishes (Calvados is a major shellfish producer) and apple tart. Normandy is an important maritime centre, with no fewer than 50 ports along its coast, including Cherbourg-Octeville, Dieppe, Fécamp, Granville, Le Havre, Honfleur, Port-en-Bessin and Tréport, as well as the major inland ports of Rouen and Caen.

Normandy has four regional *parcs naturels* – Boucles de la Seine Normande (between Rouen and Le Havre), Marais du Cotentin et du Bessin (north of Saint-Lô on the Cotentin peninsula), Perche (east of Alençon, in Orne, stretching into Eure-et-Loir), Normandie-Maine (west of Alençon) – and three areas of marshland: around the mouth of the Vire in Manche (where the Parc régional du Cotentin et du Bessin is Europe's largest 'wetland'), around the mouth of the Orne in Calvados and around the mouth of the Seine in Seine-Maritime.

Normandy has long been popular with the British for holidays and second homes, particularly in and around the Channel ports and resorts. With the exception of Nord-Pas-de-Calais and Picardy, it's the most accessible region from Britain via the ports of Caen, Cherbourg-Octeville, Dieppe and Le Havre. Coastal property is relatively expensive (homes with a sea view command a steep premium) and prices increase the closer you get to Paris (Parisians weekend on the Normandy coast). Honfleur has a surfeit of British residents and Deauville is packed with chic Parisians, and both are very expensive. On the other hand, there are still bargains to be found (particularly for British buyers) and relatively undiscovered parts, especially in the department of Orne.

Calvados (14): Possibly named after the rocky ridge ('*calvadorsa*') between the Orne and Vire rivers, Calvados has given its name to the apple brandy made throughout Normandy but particularly in this department. The department is divided vertically by the Orne, which meets the sea at Ouistreham after passing through Caen. The departmental capital of Calvados and the administrative capital of Lower Normandy and the region's second-largest town, Caen, is famous for its stone (used to build the Tower of London and Canterbury Cathedral). The eastern part of the coast is known as the 'Floral Coast' (*Côte fleurie*) and the western part the 'Mother-of-Pearl Coast' (*Côte de Nacre*). Calvados attracts some 5 million tourists each year, mostly to the coast and particularly to the beaches where the Allied landings took place in 1944 (four of which are in Calvados and one, 'Utah Beach', in Manche) and to see the famous tapestry in Bayeux (incidentally the first town in France to be liberated from the Nazis). The beaches are long, sandy and gently shelving but less attractive than those of western Manche (see below).

The area south of Caen known as *La Suisse normande*, on account of its thickly wooded hills and few rocky outcrops by the river Orne, and the area around Falaise, with its vast, flat corn fields, are atypical of Normandy, although attractive in their different ways. On the other hand, for many, the eastern part of of the department, known as the Pays d'Auge (bounded roughly by Pont-l'Evêque in the north, Orbec in the east, Vimoutiers in the south and Saint-Pierre-sur-Dives in the west), is the quintessential Normandy, with its lush green fields of dappled cows, apple orchards and half-timbered houses. This is where the best cider and the best cheeses come from: Camembert, Livarot and Pont-l'Evêque are all made here and you can follow the *Route du Cidre*, linking Cambremer, Beuvron-en-Auge, Bonnebosq and Beaufour-Druval, and the *Route du Fromage* (no longer signposted), including the cheese museums at Livarot and Saint-Pierre-sur-Dives. Another tourist route running through the department is the *Route des Traditions* in the *bocage*.

Eure (27): Like many French departments, Eure is named after the river which flows through it, and it boasts some of the most beautiful river scenery in Normandy, along the Andelle, Iton, Risle and Seine as well as the Eure itself. Eure has no coastline (unless you count 12km/7.5mi of the Seine estuary east of Honfleur), although it's within easy reach of the beaches of Calvados and Seine-Maritime. Despite being the closest part of Normandy to Paris, it's the region's most wooded department, the largest forest being the Forêt de Lyons, which covers over 6,500 hectares (15,500 acres), in the north-east. Eure's capital is the historic town of Evreux, but it's Monet's house and garden at Giverny (near Vernon) which is the department's principal tourist attraction.

Manche (50): Named after the English Channel, known to the French as 'the Sleeve' (*la Manche*) on account of its shape, Manche has more farms, cattle and horses than almost any other department in France and is the country's biggest producer of oysters as well as a major producer of mussels, meat, carrots, leeks, cauliflower, parsley, cider apples, apple juice, calvados and *pommeau* (a mixture of apple juice and calvados). In contrast to Eure, the department is France's least forested area, although the comparative lack of trees is compensated for by the many hedgerows that characterise the *bocage*, considered by many to be the most attractive rural scenery in Normandy. Manche has 330km (200mi) of coastline and its northern part, known as the Cotentin peninsula, has sea on three sides, where the tide is said to come in faster than a galloping horse. The west coast boasts Normandy's finest beaches – long, sandy and gently sloping – backed by a string of attractive resorts (popular with the French in summer). Less than 50km (30mi) off the west coast of Manche lie the Channel Islands (known to the French as *les Iles anglo-normandes*), as well as the French Iles Chausey, of which there are around 50, although only one is inhabited – by around 100 people. (The islands can be reached from Granville in Manche and from Saint-Malo in neighbouring Ille-et-Vilaine – see below.) In the extreme west of the department, on the border with Brittany, is the Mont Saint-Michel, once a place of religious pilgrimage but now Manche's principal tourist attraction (and one of the most popular in France).

Orne (61): Another department named after its principal river (which has its source just north of Alençon), Orne has around 25,000 hectares (60,000 acres) of forest, including the 7,000ha (17,000 acre) Forêt des Andaines, and contains the 235,000ha (565,000 acre) Normandie-Maine 'natural park' in the south. The department also boasts some 2,000km (1,250mi) of horse riding trails, and the Perche area (east of Argentan) is renowned for horse breeding and racing (the *percheron* is reputed to be the world's best draught horse); Haras du Pin, the French national stud, is located here. Orne has no coastline, but is within easy reach of the beaches of Calvados and Manche. A speciality of the department is pear cider (*poiré*), which is made principally in the area around Passais.

Seine-Maritime (76): As its name suggests, the Seine meets the sea in this department, at Le Havre, having been joined by the Andelle, Epte, Eure and Iton, among other tributaries. Seine-Maritime has an attractive coast known as the 'Alabaster Coast' (*Côte d'Albâtre*) with chalk cliffs up to 100m (330ft) high between Dieppe and Le Havre. Seine-Maritime's (and Upper Normandy's) capital, Rouen, the largest city in north-western France (it was once the country's second-largest city after Paris), is one of the department's major tourist attractions, along with the Bénédictine factory at Fécamp and the town of Honfleur, Normandy's answer to Saint-Tropez, which attracts 3.5 million visitors annually.

Brittany

Brittany (*La Bretagne*) is the westernmost region of France (and Europe) and comprises the departments of Côtes-d'Armor (22), Finistère (29), Ille-et-Vilaine (35) and Morbihan (56). Brittany has some 3,000km (1,875mi) of Atlantic coast – over 25 per cent of the French coastline. The west coast is characterised by dramatic cliffs and rock formations, the north by attractive coves and tiny harbours, and the south has wide estuaries and long, sandy beaches. Brittany is popular with sailors, although the sea is not without its dangers – all those who die at sea are supposed to meet in the Baie des Trépassés ('Bay of the Departed') near Douarnenez, from where they're ferried to a mythical island of the blessed! More than a third of French lighthouses are in Brittany – most of them in Finistère. The inland region, known as the *Argoat* ('land of woods'), is almost flat; only two ridges and a solitary peak rise above 250m (800ft), although the Bretons call them mountains – the Montagnes noires (Black Mountains), the Monts d'Arrée (Arée Mountains) and the Montagne de Locronan. Inland Brittany is also largely agricultural, unspoiled (some would say rather barren) and scenic, with delightful wooded valleys, lakes and moors.

In contrast with Normandy, however, Brittany is 55 per cent arable land and only 15 per cent grassland. Vegetables and fruit are the two main agricultural products, and the department of Ille-et-Villaine was France's biggest cider producer until the mid-20th century (when there were over 300 varieties of cider apples; today there are fewer than 100). The average Breton is reputed to drink over 300 litres of cider per year! Brittany is also a major producer of pork, poultry, milk and fish, as well as seaweed, which is used in food additives, fertilisers and cosmetics. Cancale is reputed to be a gastronomic Mecca, and the entire region is a paradise for seafood lovers.

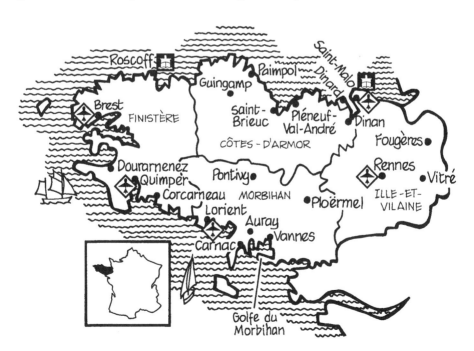

Local culinary specialities include *crêpes* and *galettes* (different types of pancake used for sweet and savoury fillings respectively), *cotriade*, a sort of paella without the rice (the Breton equivalent of *bouillabaisse*) and *cervoise*, a beer reputed to be the favourite drink of the Gauls (or Vikings, according to which history you read).

Brittany's population is just under 3 million and the regional capital, Rennes, is its largest city, having just over 200,000 inhabitants. The next largest town is Brest with around 155,000. Other main towns include Dinan, Dinard, Lorient, Quimper, Saint-Brieuc, Saint-Malo, Vannes and Vitré. The local people (Bretons) are of Celtic origin with a rich maritime tradition and a unique culture (preserved mainly in the more isolated west). Proud and independent (they claim that Brittany is a country apart), they even have their own language which has been revived in recent years (see page 49). Rennes University is a centre of Breton studies. Like Ireland, Brittany is a land of legend and folklore – the jagged coastline is said to have been carved out by the giant Gargantua, and the Forest of Broceliande is claimed to have been the hide-out of the Arthurian sorcerer Merlin. Traditional Breton costume is still worn on special occasions, one of the most colourful of which is the *Fête des Filets bleus* ('Festival of the Blue Nets') held in the fishing village of Concarneau in August.

Brittany is popular with both holidaymakers and second homebuyers, particularly the British, on account of its sea connections via the ports of Roscoff and Saint-Malo, and the nearby Normandy ports of Caen and Cherbourg-Octeville. In fact, there has been an 'invasion' of British buyers in recent years, which has pushed up property prices but also helped to regenerate many previously moribund rural areas. Property is expensive on the coast, particularly around Quimper and Bénodet (an area known as the Pays Bigouden), and very expensive on the islands (many of which are inhabited by rich Parisians and French celebrities). The triangle of land between Dinan, Dinard and Saint-Malo is also popular, which is reflected in relatively high prices. The interior is quieter and cheaper (nowhere in Brittany is more than an hour's drive from the coast), although the extreme west coast of Finistisère is also good value.

Côtes-d'Armor (22): The Côtes-d'Armor (Armor meaning 'land of the sea') includes the majority of the north coast of Brittany, as well as several islands – most notably the Sept-Iles, the oldest nature reserve in France (the Ile Rouzic has the country's richest 'collection' of wildlife). The department has some 6,000ha (15,000 acres) of forest, and the coastal area is farmed mainly for vegetables. The coastline itself is noted for fine beaches nestling between cliffs. The department's principal town is Saint-Brieuc, and there are many attractive fishing ports along the coast.

Finistère (29): Finistère, which translates as 'Land's End', includes the westernmost point in mainland Europe and more lighthouses than any other part of France. The department's west coast consists mainly of high cliffs, whereas the north coast is lined with dunes. The white, sandy beaches south of Quimper are among the finest in Brittany, and La Torche offers some of the best surfing in France. There are a dozen islands (all of them bird sanctuaries) off Finistère between Le Conquet and Ouessant, and another group of islands, l'Archipel des Glenan, off the southern coast. Brest and Quimper, the departmental capital, are the two principal towns, and there are attractive resorts, such as Benodet, La Forêt-Fouesant and Pont-Aven (painted by Gaugin), as well as lots of pretty fishing villages, including Le Guilvines, Lesconil, Loctudy and Saint-Guénolé.

Ille-et-Vilaine (35): The easternmost department of Brittany, Ille-et-Vilaine (named after its principal rivers) borders Manche in Normandy, and Loire-Atlantique and Mayenne in Pays-de-la-Loire (see **Chapter 3**). Although it has the shortest coastline (70km/45mi) of any Brittany department, it includes the major resorts of Dinard and Saint-Malo. The so-called 'Emerald Coast' (*Côte d'Emeraude*) is dotted with cliffs, dunes and sandy beaches, Dinard boasting some of the highest tidal variations in Europe. Inland, there's a varied landscape including the Forêt de Paimpont, where King Arthur is believed (by the French) to have encountered Merlin (little of the original forest remains), and the 7,000ha (17,500 acre) Forêt de Brocéliande.

Morbihan (56): The southernmost department of Brittany, Morbihan (meaning 'little sea' in Breton) has an almost Mediterranean micro-climate with 'exotic' flora and fauna. Its 500km (300mi) coastline includes numerous bays (most notably the Golfe du Morbihan with its 60 islands), estuaries (principally the Etel) and offshore islands (including the Ile de Groix, Ile d'Houat, Ile d'Hoëdic and Belle-Ile-en-Mer, the largest of the Breton islands). The coast is lined with dunes, the longest of which extends for 8km (5mi) at Erdeven, and Morbihan has the largest number of coastal water mills in France; a Brittany invention, these were in use until as recently as the 1960s. Morbihan is famous for containing the world's greatest concentration of standing stones and also has over 250km (155mi) of navigable river and canal and some 50 *sites naturels*, including three nature reserves. Morbihan is the most visited department in Brittany, with over 3 million visitors per year, and 25 per cent of its summer activity is tourism-related.

ADVANTAGES & DISADVANTAGES

Both Normandy and Brittany are largely unspoiled and rural with beautiful countryside, fine (mostly sandy) beaches, pretty villages and attractive properties. All of Normandy and most of Brittany are readily accessible by ferry from the UK, and parts of Normandy are within easy reach of the Paris airports. The many attractions of Paris (see **Chapter 8**) are also accessible from most parts of Normandy, there's plenty to see and do in both regions and the coast is never far away. Both regions are noted for their excellent food, particularly seafood, and everything you buy, eat and drink (except wine) is likely to be produced locally. Normandy is known as an artistic region, having inspired numerous writers, including Corneille, Flaubert, Gide, Maupassant, Maurois, Prévert and Proust, and painters, including Boudin, Braque, Dufy, Léger, Millet, Poussin and Monet, who made his home at Giverny near Vernon in Eure and captured the region's ever-changing light in his series paintings.

There are also disadvantages to buying a home in Normandy or Brittany. The weather is poor for France: it's often wet and (particularly in Brittany) windy, and summer temperatures are moderate. There are few direct international flights to airports in Normandy or Brittany, so the regions aren't readily accessible from countries other than the UK, with the exception of the departments of Eure and Seine-Maritime, which are within reach of the Paris airports. Even from Britain, Channel crossings become progressively longer the further west you go (see page 81), and western Brittany is a long drive from the nearest port, Saint-Malo. Much of Normandy was destroyed in the second world war and the vast majority of towns have been rebuilt in the last half-century, which means that there are few attractive old towns. The people of Normandy, who are descended from the Vikings (Normans means 'north men') have a reputation for being reserved, not to say secretive, although if you make an effort you will be rewarded by true and lasting friendships. Bretons, by contrast, are reputed to be more outgoing and progressive.

Although property generally is less expensive than on the west coast or in the South of France, for example, prices have been rising steadily in recent years and bargains are few and far between. However, it's still possible to buy a habitable property for €50,000, a restoration project for €20,000 or a 1,000m^2 plot for €5,000, provided you aren't looking to live in a popular area.

'Green' towns include Caen (14), Saint-Brieuc (22) and Saint-Malo (35), where there's over 40m^2 of green space for every inhabitant (in contrast with Vannes (35), which offers less than 3m^2 per inhabitant), and parts of Ille-et-Vilaine enjoy a lower mortality rate (from all causes) than almost any other part of France. (On the other hand, the rates of alcohol-related illnesses and suicides in Brittany are particularly high!) No fewer than 22 of the area's beaches and 28 of its marinas – the majority in Côtes-d'Armor, Manche and Morbihan – have been awarded a 'blue flag' by the Foundation for European Education and Environment (see 🖳 www.pavillonbleu.com), but almost as many beaches have earned a 'black flag' from the Surfrider Foundation Europe, which draws attention to what it considers to be unacceptable levels of pollution (see 🖳 www.surfrider-europe.org): one each in Ille-et-Vilaine and Manche, two in Calvados, three in Morbihan, four in the Côtes-d'Armor and no fewer than seven in Finistère. Large stretches of the Finistère coast have recently been affected by a toxic seaweed called Dinophysis, and foul-smelling weed has also affected beaches in the Côtes-d'Armor, particularly in the summer but also in spring. In addition, some of Brittany's rivers are reckoned to contain unacceptably high levels of chemical and animal waste.

Prospective buyers may also like to note that Normandy has three of France's 20 nuclear power stations: two on the northern coast of Seine-Maritime – at Penly between Dieppe and Tréport, and at Paluel between Dieppe and Fécamp – and one in Manche at Flamanville on west coast of the Cotentin peninsula. Manche also has a nuclear waste reprocessing plant at La Hague on the northern tip of the Cotentin peninsula. There are no nuclear power stations in Brittany.

MAJOR TOWNS & PLACES OF INTEREST

Calvados (14)

Calvados's capital, Caen (pop. 117,000), was largely destroyed in the second world war but still boasts two medieval abbeys, an ancient castle and an impressive cathedral, as well as a prestigious university and several parks (even a 'prairie'!). Calvados boasts several fashionable resorts along the *Côte Fleurie*, including Cabourg (smart but unpretentious), Deauville (with its famous *Promenade* rivalling that of Nice – well, almost), Honfleur (with its picturesque harbour), Houlgate and Trouville. These are favourite locations among Parisians (and even Normans) for second homes. Less popular but equally attractive are the resorts of Arromanches and Port-en-Bessin further west.

Other main towns include Lisieux (24,000), a university town which boasts one of the world's largest churches – a place of pilgrimage – but is otherwise unprepossessing, Bayeux (pop. 15,400), one of Normandy's most attractive towns, having largely escaped destruction during the second world war, and boasting the famous tapestry depicting the Norman conquest of England (which attracts almost half a million visitors annually), Vire (13,900), a rather unattractive industrial town which prides itself on its cultural activities, and Falaise (8,800), largely destroyed in the war but sympathetically reconstructed and boasting the castle where William the Conqueror was born, Hérouville-Saint-Clair (24,400). Also attractive are the smaller towns of Orbec, with its long main street of timbered buildings, and Saint-Pierre-sur-Dives, with an ancient abbey and a famous market. Beuvron-en-Auge is the department's prettiest village and the only really 'touristy' place in the Pays d'Auge, and there are other attractive villages, including Beaumais, east of Falaise, and Clécy in the *Suisse normande*.

Côtes-d'Armor (22)

The department's principal town is Saint-Brieuc (pop. 49,000), founded by the Welsh monk Brieuc in 482AD, with its imposing cathedral. Other towns of interest include Dinan (11,900), one of Brittany's finest medieval towns and a major tourist attraction, Guingamp (8,000), another town of historic and architectural as well as religious interest (it's the site of an annual pilgrimage in July), Paimpol (7,900) with its attractive harbour, Plouha (4,400), boasting Brittany's highest cliffs (104m/340ft), Pleumeur-Bodou (3,800) with its nearby leisure parks, and Pléneuf-Val-André (3,700) with its magnificent beaches and traditional fishing harbour at Dahouët. There are also many beach resorts, including Perros-Guirec, Saint-Cast and Trégastel, and fishing ports, including Binic and Saint-Quay-Portrieux. The Côtes-d'Armor boasts no fewer than six *'petites cités de caractère'*, including Jugon-les-Lacs, an ancient fortress town surrounded by rivers and lakes, Portrieux with its wash houses and triangular 'squares', Quintin with its attractive *château* and other historic buildings, and Tréguier with its pretty streets and magnificent cathedral – one of the finest in Brittany.

Eure (27)

Eure's capital is the historic town of Evreux (pop. 54,000), a dynamic business centre with an attractive town centre and cathedral. Other main towns include Vernon (25,000) on the Seine with its magnificent Château de Bizy and nearby business centre of Saint-Marcel, Louviers (19,000), former textile centre on the Eure with an attractive cathedral, Bernay (11,600), with its attractive wood-beamed houses, the town recently relieved of traffic by the diversion of the N138, Gisors (11,100), with attractive streets, cathedral and castle, Les Andelys (9,300), dominated by Richard the Lionheart's Château Gaillard, and the 'new town' of Val-de-Reuil (14,000), France's newest commune created in the 1970s to attract business people away from Paris but now inhabited largely by African immigrants and featuring a nearby high-security prison! The A13 motorway and main railway line from Paris run (more or less parallel) through Eure (see **Communications** on page 80), the former being something of a rat run for Parisians dashing to and from the coast for weekends and holidays. The department's principal tourist attraction is Monet's house and garden at Giverny (near Vernon) and one of its prettiest villages is Le Bec-Hellouin near Brionne. Eure also boasts France's smallest *mairie* at Saint-Germain-de-Pasquier, north-west of Louviers, measuring just 10m^2!

Finistère (29)

The department's capital and the ancient capital of *Cornouaille* is the magnificent medieval town of Quimper (pop. 67,000) on the river Jet, the oldest city in Brittany with a splendid Gothic cathedral and a relaxed atmosphere, although Brest (156,000) is by far the largest town in Finistère, as well as easily the second-largest in Brittany after the capital Rennes. Other major towns and places of interest include Concarneau (19,400), which claims to be France's 'biggest' fishing port in terms of the number of boats (230), fishermen (1,600) and fish caught (around 30,000 tonnes per year), Morlaix (16,000) on the *Côte de Granit rose* ('Pink Granite Coast') with its impressive viaduct, jumble of lanes and unique 'lantern houses', Douarnenez (15,800), actually four villages with three harbours, Locronan, a *'petite cité de caractère'* often used as a film set (and rated one of France's most beautiful villages, along with Le Faou and l'Ile-de-Sein), Moëlan-sur-Mer with its beautiful coastal walks, Carhaix-Plouguer (8,000), Brittany's geographical and cultural centre, Châteaulin (5,800), Plouguerneau (5,600), with its varied coastline and the tallest stone lighthouse in Europe, Pont-Aven (3,000) with its artistic heritage, and the deliaghtful nearby port of Doelan. The coast of Finistère is dotted with fishing villages, including Le Guilvines, Lesconil, Loctudy and Saint-Guénolé.

Ille-et-Vilaine (35)

Brittany's historic capital, 2,000 year-old Rennes (pop. 212,500), which lies at the confluence of the Ille and Vilaine rivers, is one of the department's four *'villes d'art'*, the others being Fougères (21,800), whose castle is reckoned to be one of the finest in Europe, with a nearby 1,500ha (3,700 acre) forest, Saint-Malo (52,700) and Vitré (15,900), the 'gateway to Brittany' and one of the finest medieval towns in the region. Other towns and places of interest include Redon (10,500), at the confluence of Brittany's two largest rivers, the Oust and the Vilaine, Cancale, famous for its oysters, Dinard (10,400), considered to be one of Europe's finest seaside resorts (when the sun shines!), Dol, Lamballe, Paimpont (1,400), with its fine abbey, and Ille-et-Vilaine's three *'petites cités de caractère'*: Bécherel, with its many bookshops and *château* known as the 'Breton Versailles', Châteaugiron (5,500), with its magnificent fortress, and Combourg, whose castle is one of the finest in Brittany. The coastal towns of Saint-Malo and Dinard and the area inland as far as Dinan (22) – i.e. the area around the Rance estuary – are the most popular with homebuyers.

Manche (50)

The department's largest town (and the second largest urban area in Lower Normandy after Caen) is Cherbourg-Octeville (the two towns were officially united in 1999), France's second-busiest port after Calais, with a total population of around 120,000, but the departmental capital and also the national capital of horse-breeding and riding is Saint-Lô, whose population is only 21,500. Manche's third-largest town is Equeurdreville-Hinneville with 18,600 inhabitants, Tourlaville has 18,000, and a further 54,000 people live in the region surrounding Coutances (11,500), which boasts a magnificent cathedral and several fine churches but is otherwise rather lacking in charm.

Other main towns include the water-sports centre of Tourlaville (pop. 17,900), Granville (13,500), the 'Monaco of the North' with its marina and beaches, and Avranches (9,200), near Mont-Saint-Michel and the main road from Caen into Brittany, although itself also somewhat charmless. There's a number of attractive resorts on the west coast, including Portbail and Barneville-Carteret. The pretty port of Barfleur, on the east coast, is where William the Conqueror launched the Norman conquest of England, and nearby Saint-Vaast-la-Hougue, with its food shops and fish restaurants, is a favourite among 'yachties'. Inland, Bricquebec, with its medieval castle, is one of Manche's most impressive towns, but Manche's principal tourist attraction is the Mont Saint-Michel, which attracts some 3 million visitors per year, despite being overcrowded and expensive (it's packed with over-priced cafés, restaurants and tourist junk shops – you can even buy Mont Saint-Michel air in cans!).

Morbihan (56)

Morbihan's capital is Vannes (pop. 55,000), an ancient town and residence of the former Dukes of Brittany. Other major towns include the modern town of Lorient (59,200), so named because of its trade with the far east, Pontivy (15,000), with its attractive medieval streets, Hennebont (13,400), a *'cité d'art'* with its medieval walls, Auray (10,900), a historic and attractive town with a pretty port, Ploërmel (7,500), and smaller towns include Arradon, a popular sailing resort on the Golfe du Morbihan, Arzon, which faces both the Atlantic and the Golfe du Morbihan, Carnac, with beautiful beaches and the famous megalithic site nearby (see below), Erdeven, with 8km (5mi) of dunes (and naturist beach), Josselin, with a splendid castle overlooking the river Oust, Lizio and Malestroit (the last three *'petites cités de caractère'*), Penestin-sur-Mer, an attractive seaside resort, Port-Louis, a lively seaside resort, Rhuys, Rochefort-en-Terre, reckoned to be one of France's most beautiful villages, Suscinio with its impressive castle and La Trinité-sur-Mer, Brittany's 'yachtie' centre.

Morbihan boasts an abundance of islands, many of which can be reached by boat from the mainland, including Belle-Ile-en-Mer (20km/13mi long, 4,900 inhabitants), the largest French island in the Atlantic, with its impressive fortress at Le Palais and rocks painted by Monet, l'Ile d'Arz (3km/2mi long) with its lovely old houses and many sailing schools, l'Ile de Groix (8km/5mi long with 2,500 inhabitants) with its mild microclimate, l'Ile d'Hoëdic (2.5km/1.5mi long with 125 inhabitants), a botanist's paradise, l'Ile d'Houat (5km/3mi long with 400 inhabitants, swollen to 1,000 in summer) with its beautiful sandy beaches and few cars, and l'Ile aux Moines (6km/4mi long), perhaps the most beautiful island in Morbihan.

Morbihan's famous standing stones, spread over some 40 separate sites, are linked by the *Route des Mégalithes*. Carnac is the world's largest megalithic site, where there are reckoned to be 2,792 stones, extending for more than 1km; a further 1,000 have been counted in a great arc between Erdeven and Plouharnel. Locmariaquer boasts the world's largest 'standing' stone (it's actually horizontal), weighing around 300 tonnes, and the nearby Musée Miln-le-Rouzic has world's largest collection of megalithic artefacts (around half a million) dating back to 450,000BC.

Orne (61)

Orne's capital is Alençon (pop. 31,000), famous for its lace and, until its recent closure, Moulinex, one of Normandy's largest employers (Alençon used to be known as 'Moulinexland'). Other main towns include Flers (17,600), 'capital' of the *bocage* and the mechanical engineering centre of Lower Normandy, Argentan (17,400), largely industrial but at the heart of horse-riding country, L'Aigle (9,300) on the river Risle, and Mortagne-au-Perche (4,900), historic 'capital' of the Perche area. One of the most attractive smaller towns is Domfront, which boasts a medieval town centre, and Saint-Cénéri-le-Gérei, west of Alençon, is considered to be one of France's prettiest villages. The department's main tourist attractions are the national stud, Haras du Pin, at Pin-au-Haras, east of Argentan (described as 'the Versailles of the horse'!), and Camembert, where the eponymous cheese is supposed to have been 'invented' in 1791 by one Marie Harel.

Seine-Maritime (76)

The departmental and regional capital is the city of Rouen, where Joan of Arc was Martyred, with its magnificent cathedral, painted by Monet. Other main towns and places of interest (most of them also featuring in Monet's paintings) include the busy port and industrial town of Le Havre (pop. 193,000), one of Europe's major ports and petrol refineries, Dieppe (35,700), France's oldest seaside resort with one of its longest bathing beaches, Mont-

Saint-Aignan (21,800), the fishing port of Fécamp (21,500), home to the Bénédictine liqueur distillery housed in a 'Disney' fantasy of a building, Elbeuf (16,900) near Rouen by the Seine, and Etretat on the coast with its spectacular cliff arches.

POPULATION

The population of Normandy is around 3.1 million (1.7 million in Upper Normandy 1.4 million in Lower Normandy) and that of Brittany 2.9 million, divided as shown below. Each department covers a similar area, i.e. 5,500 to 6,000km² (2,200 to 2,400mi²), which means that population figures also indicate population density. The populations of both Normandy and Brittany are growing at an above the average rate for France. Both Caen (14) and Rennes (35) have a very high proportion of students (around 25 per cent) among their populations, whereas the percentage of students in other towns is low, e.g. 6 per cent in Quimper (29), 5 per cent in Le Havre (76) and a mere 2 per cent in Saint-Malo (35). For populations of smaller towns, see **Major Towns & Places of Interest** above.

Normandy

Upper Normandy is one of the most densely populated areas of France with 140 people per km² (55 per mi²) compared with the national average of just over 100 (40 per mi²). It has a relatively young population (over 30 per cent are under 20) and a higher than average birth rate, although the population is growing more slowly and therefore ageing more rapidly than the national average. Paris is gradually 'overflowing' along the Seine valley, and Eure is the fastest growing department (at 0.57 per cent or around 3,000 people per annum). Around 30 per cent of the population of Upper Normandy lives within 25km (15mi) of the centre of Rouen.

Some 45 per cent of the population of Lower Normandy is concentrated around the towns of Alençon, Argentan, Caen, Cherbourg-Octeville, Flers, Lisieux and Saint-Lô, and the region's population is expected to rise by around 45,000 in the next 20 years before beginning to decline. The population of Orne is already in gradual decline (30 per cent of the population is over 60), whereas that of Calvados, which is attracting people, particularly those in their early 20s, from neighbouring departments, is expected to continue to increase until around 2030. The population of Manche is fairly stable, although it has lost around 16,000 people between the ages of 20 and 30 and gained half as many elderly people in the last decade.

Calvados (14): Total population 600,000, of which 4,600 are non-French EU citizens (including over 1,200 Portuguese), 1,100 Algerians, 1,000 Turks, 900 Moroccans and 3,000 other nationalities. The capital Caen has 117,000 inhabitants but 60 per cent of the department's population live in the Caen area, including nearby Hérouville-Saint-Clair – the department's second-largest urban area with 24,400 inhabitants. Almost 30 per cent of Calvados's population is under 19. The next largest towns are Lisieux (24,000 inhabitants), Mont-Saint-Aignan (21,800), Bayeux (15,400) and Vire (13,900).

Eure (27): Total population 540,000 – a similar average density to Brittany's Côtes-d'Armor – of which almost 5,000 are non-French EU citizens (including over 2,750 Portuguese), 2,500 Moroccans, 2,000 Turks, 1,700 Algerians and 4,400 other nationalities. The capital Evreux has 54,000 inhabitants and Vernon, the department's second-largest town, 25,000. The next largest towns are Louviers (19,000 and a further 40,000 in the surrounding area), Val-de-Reuil (14,000, including a high proportion of African immigrants), Bernay (11,600) and Gisors (11,100).

Manche (50): The second-least densely populated department in Normandy or Brittany, with a total population of 470,000 and the lowest proportion of foreign residents, with 1,800 non-French EU citizens, 700 Moroccans, 340 Turks and 1,200 other nationalities. The department's largest town (and the second-largest urban area in Lower Normandy after Caen) is Cherbourg-Octeville with a total population of around 120,000, the departmental capital Saint-Lô having only 21,500. Manche's third-largest town is Equeurdreville-Hinneville with 18,600 inhabitants, Tourlaville has 18,000, and a further 54,000 people live in the region surrounding Coutances (11,500).

Orne (61): The most sparsely populated department in Normandy or Brittany, with a total population of 300,000, of which almost 2,000 are non-French EU citizens (including over 750 Portuguese), 1,900 Turks, 1,100 Moroccans, 1,700 Algerians and 1,600 other nationalities. Orne has few large towns; the capital Alençon has just 31,000 inhabitants. The next largest towns are Flers (17,600) and Argentan (17,400).

Seine-Maritime (76): By far the most densely populated department in either region, with a total population of 1.24 million, of which 8,500 are non-French EU citizens (including over 4,500 Portuguese and almost 1,000 Italians), 6,900 Algerians, 6,400 Moroccans, 1,600 Turks, 1,300 Tunisians and over 8,000 other nationalities. Over 40 per cent of the population lives in and around the capital Rouen, which has seen an influx of students since the opening of the new university science faculty in 2001. The next largest towns are Le Havre (193,000 inhabitants), Dieppe (35,700) and Elbeuf (16,900).

Brittany

Around 2.9 million people live in Brittany, whose population is growing at slightly above the national average rate (Vannes in Morbihan has the fastest growing population of any major town in France). The department of Ille-et-Vilaine attracts half of Brittany's immigrants. Over two-thirds of the population live in urban areas (an increase of 20 per cent in the last decade), and the capital Rennes (35) and its surrounding area, the country's third-fastest growing urban area, has over half a million inhabitants. Brest (29) is the only other town in Brittany with more than 67,000 inhabitants. Brittany has a generally young population, 35 per cent of people being under 25. It's predicted that the population of Brittany will continue to increase over the coming decades, although at a slower rate.

Côtes-d'Armor (22): The least densely populated department in Brittany, with a total population of 540,000 – similar to that of Eure in Normandy – and the lowest proportion of foreign residents in Brittany, with over 3,000 non-French EU citizens (including almost 800 Portuguese), 500 Moroccans, 300 Turks and 1,300 other nationalities. The capital and only large town in the department is Saint-Brieuc, which has 49,000 inhabitants (100,000 including suburban areas). The next largest towns are Lannion (19,350), Dinan (11,900), Guingamp (8,000) and Paimpol (7,900). The Côtes-d'Armor has the oldest population in Brittany, averaging 41, with a high proportion of retired people, especially in rural areas along the coast. Saint-Brieuc has the department's youngest population.

Finistère (29): Total population 850,000, of which over 4,000 are non-French EU citizens (including almost 1,600 Portuguese), 850 Moroccans, 750 Turks and 2,500 other nationalities. The largest town is Brest with 156,000 inhabitants, followed by the departmental capital Quimper with 67,000. The next largest towns are Concarneau (19,400), Morlaix (16,000) and Douarnenez (15,800). Finistère has the most static population in Brittany: over one in three people were born in the department, although three-quarters of immigrants to the department in the last decade have come from outside Brittany. Finistère also has the region's highest proportion of one-person households (around 35 per cent). Brest and the surrounding area has the youngest population.

Ille-et-Vilaine (35): The most densely populated department in Brittany, with a total population of 870,000, of which almost 4,000 are non-French EU citizens (including almost 1,200 Portuguese), 1,900 Moroccans, 1,250 Turks and 5,500 other nationalities. The capital Rennes has 212,500 inhabitants and attracts a large mobile population, mainly because of its university. The next largest towns are Saint-Malo (52,700), Fougères (21,800), Vitré (15,900), Redon (10,500) and Dinard (10,400). The population of Ille-et-Vilaine is the youngest in Brittany, averaging under 37.

Morbihan (56): Total population 640,000, of which 2,600 are non-French EU citizens, 1,100 Turks and 2,000 other nationalities. The department's largest town is Lorient 59,200 inhabitants, and the capital is Vannes has 55,000. The next largest towns are Pontivy (15,000), Hennebont (13,400) and Auray (10,900). Morbihan has the most rapidly ageing population of the four Breton departments, as many young people leave the department to study or work.

LANGUAGE

Although French is spoken throughout Normandy and Brittany, as throughout the rest of France, Breton is also spoken in parts of Brittany. Linguistically, Breton belongs to the Brittonic branch of the Insular Celtic family, the Continental branch (Gaulish, Galatian, etc.) being extinct. As a Brittonic language, Breton is close to Welsh (they became separate languages from the 16th century) and is parent to Scottish Gaelic, Irish Gaelic and Manx, although speakers of those languages won't understand much Breton (or vice versa). It was Cornish settlers who introduced their language to Brittany between the third and fifth centuries and, although Cornish has now died out, Breton survives and, like Gaelic, is currently enjoying something of a revival.

There are estimated to be around 600,000 Breton speakers, most of them in the west of Brittany, i.e. throughout Finistère and in the western part of Côtes-d'Armor and Morbihan, but also in Rennes (in Ille-et-Vilaine) and Nantes, which used to be the capital of Brittany, but is now in the Pays-de-la-Loire region (see **Chapter 3**). Although less than half as many use the language regularly, a recent opinion poll suggested that almost 90 per cent of Bretons would like the language to be preserved. Breton is taught in four *collèges*, one *lycée* and around 30 primary schools run by an organisation called Diwan. These bi-lingual schools were introduced in late 1970s and teach only in Breton until CE1 level (age 7–8), when French is introduced (for this reason, there is opposition to them being incorporated into the state system). The number of children educated at Diwan schools is increasing by 15 to 20 per cent annually, and around 9,000 adults enrol in Breton classes every year. Around 10 per cent of the books published in Brittany are in Breton, most of them for children, and there are Breton periodicals (including the monthly *Bremañ*. Local stations of Radio France allocate a certain amount of time to Breton-language programmes, and there are Breton programmes on television in the western half of Brittany as well as plans to introduce a bilingual TV channel called *Breizh*. There are bi-lingual road signs on all major roads and in some towns (e.g. Lorient and Quimper) in the Côtes-d'Armor and Finistère regions.

It isn't necessary to learn Breton in order to integrate into the local community, although being able to get your tongue round a few words and phrases (being related to Welsh, Breton is one of the world's most complicated languages!) will undoubtedly facilitate the process.

CLIMATE

Normandy and Brittany are among the wettest areas of France, at least in terms of the number of days of rain (up to 155 days per year in the extreme west of Brittany) if not in terms of total annual rainfall (which is higher in mountainous areas). The wettest months are usually November and December, with up to 150mm (6in) of rain per month, and the driest May and June, with around 50mm (2in) per month, although January has the most rainy days (20 on average) and it's rare to have more than a week without some rain at any time of year. There can be frost from October to April but snow rarely falls. Average summer temperatures are among lowest in France, although the regions can experience very hot spells (over 30°C). Annual sunshine hours vary between over 2,000 in Vannes (56) and under 1,700 in Rouen (76). Those used to a British climate will find the weather similar in many respects, although noticeably warmer even than southern England at most times of year and (slightly) less changeable.

Normandy

Although known (by the French) as 'the chamber pot of France', Normandy is less wet and windy than Brittany, which shelters it from the Atlantic. The weather is generally damp and mild and the barometer rarely strays far either side of 'variable' (Normandy's climate has been described as 'nuances of bad weather'). However, the weather is highly changeable and it's rare to have more than a few days of similar conditions; a hot, sunny spell can unexpectedly give way to cold, wet, windy weather. Generally, the further west you go, the wetter the weather. The so-called 'rotten land' (*Lande pourrie*) around Mortain in southern Manche has the highest rainfall in Normandy (over 1,200mm/47in per year), the most frequent frosts (50 to 60 days compared with only 10 in Landes-de-la-Hague on the Cotentin peninsula) and the most likelihood of snow.

Other wet areas are the Cotentin peninsula and the area to the north-east of Le Havre. Eure has the region's driest, most continental climate and most clearly defined seasons, and the extreme south-east of the department is one of driest areas in France, with less than 800mm (30in) of rain per year. Normandy is also frequently (and often densely) shrouded in fog in the mornings, although it usually clears by midday. (Curiously, most of the locals believe that England is more or less permanently fog-bound!) The table below shows the number of hours' sunshine and number of days' rainfall in selected towns in the region.

Town	Sunshine Hours	Days' Rainfall
Caen (14)	1,764	123
Le Havre (76)	1,788	125
Rouen (76)	1,687	131

Brittany

Brittany's has a generally maritime climate, being exposed to the Atlantic on three sides. It's the wettest part of France in terms of the number of days' rainfall per year (Brest is France's rainiest town with rainfall on 155 days per year). The weather can be stormy in winter, although summers are usually warm and pleasant. The north-west coast is somewhat milder, as it's influenced by the Gulf Stream, and Finistère boasts the '*Ceinture dorée*' ('Golden Belt'), whose climate allows farmers to grow over half of France's vegetables.

The southern coast enjoys a warm micro-climate. Vannes (and indeed the whole of the coastal area from Quimper to La Baule in Loire-Atlantique) has as much sunshine as Toulouse (over 2,000 hours per year), relatively little rainfall and average maximum summer daily temperatures of around 22°C (72°F); parts of Morbihan are sufficiently 'Mediterranean' to support flora normally seen in the south of France. Coastal areas generally have little frost – only around a dozen days a year (no more than the Côte d'Azur). Inland areas are often misty. The table below shows the number of hours' sunshine and number of days' rainfall in selected towns in the region.

Town	Sunshine Hours	Days' Rainfall
Saint-Brieuc (22)	1,795	130
Brest (29)	1,749	155
Quimper (29)	1,749	146
Rennes (35)	1,851	115
Saint-Malo (35)	1,853	128
Vannes (35)	2,024	131

COST OF LIVING

The cost of living in Normandy and Brittany is around average for France. Fresh food is particularly good value, much of it being produced locally, although supermarket prices vary considerably according to the chain (the Leclerc chain, which has dozens of stores in the area, was recently found to be the cheapest nationally). Inevitably, the cost of most items is higher in rural areas, although the difference isn't marked. Property taxes and water prices vary considerably from commune to commune (as they do throughout France) without any definable pattern, rates being set by local rather than national or regional authorities.

CRIME RATE & SECURITY

Crime rates in Brittany and Normandy are around average for France (see below) with 80 to 90 reported crimes per 1,000 population per year in most major towns. 'Safest' city is Saint-Brieuc (22) with 72.5 crimes, and least safe are Rennes and Saint-Malo (35) with around 94 crimes. Although the crime rate in Quimper (29) is around average, it increased by over 25 per cent between 1998 and 2000. It should also be noted that there are five high-risk factories in the Le Havre area.

General: The crime rate in France as a whole is similar to that found in most western European countries, although (according to statistics for the year 2000 based on reported crimes of all types) lower than Britain's, with 61 reported crimes per thousand inhabitants per year compared with 72 in the UK. As elsewhere in Europe, juvenile crime is on the increase (and at an increasingly low age); it accounts for around 20 per cent of all criminal arrests and juveniles are estimated to cause around 35 per cent of street crimes and 25 per cent of crimes of assault and battery. Theft accounts for around 65 per cent of French crime, although the incidence of burglary is much lower than in the UK, for example, where there are 31 burglaries per thousand inhabitants per year compared with France's 12.

Most violent crime takes place in certain regions of Paris and its suburbs (see page 295), cities and major towns near the Mediterranean (see page 224) and Strasbourg (see page 346). In general, however, foreigners aren't targeted more (or less) than French people by criminals. The government elected in June 2002 has vowed to reduce crime levels and had already taken several steps to achieve this aim by September 2002.

Although crime rates are generally lower in rural areas, between the months of September and January you should beware of hunters, as some 50 people die each year in hunting accidents in France (mainly the hunters themselves!). Great care should be taken if you go walking in remote areas and you should look out for signs that display the word *chasse* (hunting).

AMENITIES

Sports

There's a wealth of sporting facilities and opportunities in Normandy and Brittany, including the following:

Watersports: Brittany is one of France's premier regions for watersports, sailing in particular. Morbihan has no fewer than 115 marinas offering moorings for 7,500 boats (Port Crouesty near Arzon and La Trinité-sur-Mer are among Brittany's largest marinas, each with over 1,000 berths) as well as two natural watersports areas in the Golfe du Morbihan and the Baie de

Quiberon – the latter noted for its constant winds. There are at least 40 marinas in the Côtes-d'Armor, and many more in Finistère, including Brest (the region's largest) and Morlaix (one of the largest harbours on the English Channel), and in Morbihan. There are also numerous sailing schools, including over 50 in Morbihan, where La Trinité-sur-Mer is home to Brittany's largest sailing school, and L'Aber Wrac'h on the west coast, where thousands of Parisian children have been initiated into the joys of boating.

There's also a considerable amount of boating and other activity on Brittany's many rivers, lakes and canals. In the Côtes-d'Armor, for example, there are over 40 sailing schools (including ten using traditional boats), over 30 canoe/kayak clubs, 13 diving clubs, 350km (220mi) of navigable river and estuary, 3,000km (1,870mi) of fishable river bank and 26 lakes for fishing (notably the 400ha/1,000 acre Lac de Guerlédan). Another large lake for watersports and fishing is the Lac au Duc (250ha/620 acres) near Ploërmel (56). There's canoeing on the Nantes-Brest canal and fishing on the 245km (155mi) Canal d'Ille-et-Rance et la Vilaine (35), where three boat hire companies and two excursion companies operate. There's even white-water rafting on the Hyères river near Carhaix-Plouguer (29).

In Normandy, there are marinas at Cabourg, Caen, Courseulles-sur-Mer, Deauville, Dives-sur-Mer, Grandcamp-Maisy, Le Havre, Honfleur, Isigny-sur-Mer, Merville-Franceville, Ouistreham, Trouville (14), Agon-Coutainville, Barfleur, Barneville-Carteret, Carentan, Cherbourg-Octeville (France's most popular marina for visiting yachtsmen with 15,000 boats passing through it every year), Dielette, Fermanville, Flamanville, Goury, Granville, Omonville-la-Rogue, Port-Bail, Quineville, Regneville-sur-Mer, Saint-Vaast-La-Hougue, Tourlaville (50), Dieppe, Fécamp (where an annual multihull race is held and where the marina is due to be extended), Le Havre, Saint-Aubin-lès-Elbeuf, Saint-Valery-en-Caux and Le Tréport (76). There are sailing schools all along the coast.

Inland, there are numerous watersports parks in both regions, including those at Lisieux, Pont-l'Evêque, Vire (and one at Falaise due to open in 2003) (14), Guerlédan, Jugon-les-Lacs, Port Gelin (22), La Bonneville-sur-Iton, Brionne, Grosley-sur-Risle, Léry-Poses, Toutanville (27), Chênedet near Fougères (35), Granville, which boasts the third-largest sailing school in France, Saint-Martin-d'Aubign, Tourlaville (50), Baud, Grandchamp, Ploërmel, Priziac and on the 400ha (1,000 acre) Lac de Guerlédan (56), Alençon, La Ferté-Macé, Le Mêle-sur-Sarthe, Rabodanges, Saint-Evroult Notre-Dame-du-Bois (61), Cany-Barville, Jumièges, Longroy-Gamaches, Montville, Saint-Aubin-le Cauf and Tourville-la-Rivière (76). There's also canoeing/kayaking and rowing on many rivers in both regions.

For those who like sailing without getting wet, there's sand-sailing (*char à voile*), which is particularly popular on the long, sandy beaches of Calvados, Manche and Morbihan.

Walking, Cycling & Horse Riding: Normandy and Brittany are ideal regions for those who enjoy walking, cycling or horse riding. Ille-et-Vilaine, for example, has 1,200km (750mi) of marked walks, 500km (300mi) of mountain bike trails and over 25 equestrian centres. Brittany as a whole has 3,000km (1,875mi) of coastline and 3,700km (2,300mi) of hiking trails. The Perche area (in eastern Orne) has over 2,000km (1,250mi) of horse riding trails, there are over 50 riding schools and equestrian centres in the Côtes-d'Armor, almost as many in Ille-et-Vilaine, a further 70 in Calvados; in Normandy's *bocage* there are some 6,000 areas dedicated to horse riding.

Golf: Golf is popular in both regions, where there are over 65 courses, including the spectacular Golf de Pléneuf-Val-André (22) and Champ de Bataille at Le Neubourg (27). The table below lists the number of courses in each department. Information (in both French and English) on how to find courses, the cost of a round (which varies between €15 and €50), etc. is available via the Internet (💻 www.backspin.com). Another useful website for golfers is 💻 www.golf.com.fr.

Department	No. of Courses
Calvados	3 x 9 holes, 5 x 18 holes, 5 x 27 holes
Côtes-d'Armor	3 x 9 holes, 5 x 18 holes
Eure	2 x 9 holes, 4 x 18 holes
Finistère	3 x 9 holes, 3 x 18 holes, 1 x 27 holes
Ille-et-Vilaine	2 x 9 holes, 4 x 18 holes, 3 x 27 holes
Manche	5 x 9 holes, 1 x 18 holes
Morbihan	1 x 9 holes, 5 x 18 holes, 1 x 27 holes
Orne	3 x 9 holes, 1 x 18 holes
Seine-Maritime	7 x 18 holes

Fishing & Hunting: There are literally hundreds of locations for fishing in both regions, on rivers, lakes and the sea. There are also hunting clubs and associations in many towns and even in some villages. Each department has a hunters' federation (*Fédération départemental des Chasseurs/FDC*), which can tell you how and where you can get your licence and what associations or clubs exist in the department. To find the address and telephone number of the nearest *FDC* either look in the yellow pages or consult the government website (💻 www.oncf.gouv.fr/org/index.htm).

Other Sports: Most towns have a municipal swimming pool, and a new pool is planned for Vire (14), as well as a new sports complex for Louviers (27). There's a 20,000 seat sports stadium in Caen (14), and a large stadium is planned for Darnétal (76). In a 19th century *château* near Verneuil-sur-Avre

(27) is Center Parcs, a sporting and holiday centre (frequented mainly by over-stressed Parisians). There are many other sporting facilities in both regions, including rock climbing in Eure, Ille-et-Vilaine, Manche, Morbihan and Orne, diving in the Côtes-d'Armor, Ille-et-Vilaine and Manche, bungee jumping into the Souleuvre river in Calvados (plunge through 60m/650ft of air **and** 4m/13ft of water!), hot-air ballooning in Orne, and paragliding and hang-gliding in Calvados (organised by the discouragingly named Association Icare!).

Leisure

There's no shortage of leisure facilities in Normandy and Brittany. Brittany alone boasts over 300 listed sites and 1,000 historic monuments, including some of the world's most important megalithic remains, particularly in Morbihan (see page 41), but also in the Côtes-d'Armor and Ille-et-Vilaine, where there are some 300 megalithic monuments, Saint-Just being the most important site. Normandy is home to one of France's premier attractions, the Mont Saint-Michel (although the Bretons believe it should be theirs!). There are numerous other castles, *châteaux* and manor houses in both regions, some of which can be visited and others merely admired from without.

For nature lovers, there are four bird sanctuaries in the Côtes-d'Armor, as well as some 60 ports from where you can take boat trips to island bird reserves. There are also bird sanctuaries in Calvados and a spectacular nature reserve in Yeun Elez (29). Those in need of relaxation could try a little balneology (also known as thalassotherapy): Deauville, Luc-sur-Mer, Ouistreham and Trouville (14) have establishments offering seaweed baths – the *infusion de varech* (less-appealingly called 'bladderwrack' in English) is recommended by connoisseurs – and there are also centres in Dinard and Saint-Malo (35), Granville (50), Bagnoles-de-l'Orne (61) and throughout the Côtes-d'Armor and Morbihan. (For a list of all centres offering treatment, go to 🖥 www.thalasso-france.com.) Or, of course, you can simply laze on the beach (only two of the nine departments in Normandy and Brittany have no coastline) – weather permitting!

Theatres & Concert Halls: In Normandy, there are theatres in Evreux and Val-de-Reuil (27), Dieppe, Eu (recently opened), Fécamp, Le Havre and Petit-Quevilly, near Rouen (76), Cherbourg-Octeville (50) and Alençon, Bagnoles-de-l'Orne, Domfront and Flers (61), concert halls in Evreux (27), Equeurdreville-Hainneville (50), Alençon, Cléon, Le Havre and Sotteville-lès-Rouen (76), and major local orchestras and ensembles include the Big Band Christian Garros (Rouen), L'Ensemble (the regional orchestra of Lower Normandy, based at Caen), Maitrise de Caen (sacred music), Orchestre de Caen (the regional conservatory orchestra), Orchestre Léonard de Vinci (which performs concerts and operas at the Rouen Opera) and Orchestre régional des jeunes de Haute-Normandie (Rouen). The Theatre des Arts in Rouen stages modern dance, classical music and opera as well as plays, and there are other venues which host a variety of cultural events in Caen, Hérouville-Saint-Clair (14), Elbeuf, Grand-Quevilly near Rouen, Le Havre, Mont-Saint-Aignan, Rouen, Saint-Etienne-du-Rouvray and Saint-Valéry-en-Caux (76).

In Brittany, the principal concert and other performance venues are the Carré magique in Lannion (22), the Centres culturels in Pont-l'Abbé, Morlaix (29), Cesson-Sévigné, Fougères, Liffré, Mordelles, Rennes and Vitré (35), the centre at Rennes being brand new, and the Palais des Arts in Vannes (56), with other venues in Brest, Douarnenez (29) and Saint-Jacques-de-la-Lande (35). There are theatres in Dinan, Guingamp, Saint-Brieuc (22), Brest, Morlaix, Quimper (29) and Redon and three in Rennes (35), which also boasts an opera house and a national dance centre.

Festivals: The regions' many festivals and other cultural events include a variety of music festivals: avant-garde, blues, classical, jazz, medieval, rock, and traditional music; Brittany is especially renowned for its music festivals, which include the Festival Saint-Loup (August) in Guingamp, the festival of sea songs (August) in Paimpol, the Artrock festival (June) and *Jazz dans les feuilles* (September) in Saint-Brieuc (22), *Les Tombées de la Nuit* (July), Rock'n Solex (August) and *Les Transmusicales* (December) in Rennes (35), *Le Pont du Rock* (July) in Malestroit and an opera festival (July/August) in Belle-Ile-en-Mer (56), a jazz festival (June) in Blainville-Crevon (76). *Octobre en Normandie* is an extensive festival of music and dance in Rouen, Le Havre and other towns in Normandy throughout October. Ille-et-Vilaine claims to be the 'home' of the accordion (especially the Pays de Fougères area), and the annual *Fête de la Bouëze* (which in French has nothing to do with drinking!) in June attracts 200 to 300 players. There are also many traditional Breton festivals, particularly in Finistère, including the *Festival de Cornouaille* (July) in Quimper, in which some 4,000 people take part. One of the largest, however, is the *Festival interceltique* (August) in Lorient (56), which involves some 4,500 performers.

There are also many film, drama, dance, and literary festivals, most notable among the last being the Brittany Book Fair (August) in Carhaix-Plouguer, the maritime book fair (April) in Concarneau and the book fairs (Easter and August) in Bécherel (35). There are traditional fishermen's festivals in Honfleur, Livarot (14), Concarneau (29), Granville (50), Le Havre, Saint-Valéry-en-Caux, Veules-les-Roses and Veulettes (76), apple festivals in late September in several towns and villages, a chestnut festival (October) in Redon (35) and an oyster festival (April) on the Rhuys peninsula (56), and 'horse days' throughout Calvados in the autumn. Other events include a balloon festival in Balleroy (14) in June, medieval festivals in Deauville (14) in August and in Rudepont (27) in April, the Joan of Arc

Festival in Rouen (76) in May, and a spectacular procession of tall ships up the Seine as far as Rouen every four years (the next one is in 2004). Brittany is known for its religious festivals (*pardons*), one of the biggest being the pilgrimage to Locronan in honour of Saint Ronan, known as *la Grande Troménie*, which takes place every six years (the next isn't due until 2008), and there are village festivals throughout the region from spring to late autumn.

Museums & Galleries: The regions' major museums and galleries include the Musée de Normandie in Caen (14) with 80,000 artefacts tracing the region's history, the Breton museum in Rennes (35), fine arts museums in Caen (14), with a major collection of paintings and engravings displayed in William the Conqueror's castle, Brest and Quimper (29), Rennes (35) and Rouen (76), where there's a particularly good collection of Impressionist paintings, and local history museums at Saint-Brieuc (22), Caen and Evreux (27), Saint-André-de-Bohon and Saint-Lô (50), Alençon (61), Le Havre and Rouen (76). Modern art galleries include Artothèque in Caen, Cherbourg-Octeville (50) and Sotteville-lès-Rouen, the Centre culturel de Cherbourg-Octeville, Galerie Hélène Lemarque in Rouen, Centre d'Art contemporain in Hérouville-Saint-Clair (14), the Château de Vascoeil (which also houses the permanent Musée Michelet), the Palais Bénédictine at Fécamp, and SPOT at Le Havre.

In Calvados, Manche and Orne, there's a number of museums commemorating the D-Day landings and the Battle of Normandy, e.g. at Arromanches, Bayeux, Caen (where the Mémorial de Caen/Musée pour la Paix contains an illustrated history of the 20th century), Falaise, Ranville (the first French village to be liberated), Saint-Laurent-sur-Mer, Tilly-sur-Mer, Ver-sur-Mer and Vierville-sur-Mer (14), Avranches, Azeville, Cherbourg-Octeville, Quinéville, Sainte-Marie-du-Mont and Sainte-Mère-l'Eglise (50), and L'Aigle and Montormel (61), as well as numerous military cemeteries.

There are also many specialist museums in the two regions, covering subjects as diverse as balloons, granite, posters, seaweed, bicycles, monastic life, cider, witchcraft, fire-fighting equipment and childhood. Of particular note are the museum of *haute couture* in Granville (50), in the house where Christian Dior was born, and the lace museums in Alençon and Argentan (61). There are also several museums dedicated to horses, and the national stud at Pin-au-Haras (61) and the stud at Hennebont (56) are major tourist attractions. For those who like to sample the local produce, the Bénédictine factory at Fécamp (76) is worth a detour, and of course you can visit cheese, cider and calvados-making factories to your heart's (and stomach's) content!

Parks, Zoos & Theme Parks: There's a wealth of zoos, aquariums and theme parks in Normandy and Brittany, including the following:

● Aquarium de la Pointe-du-Raz in Audierne (29): unusual sea creatures;

● Aquarium de Saint-Malo (35): mysteries of the sea;

- Aquarium intra-muros de Saint-Malo (35): freshwater fish;
- Aquarium marin de Trégastel (22): Breton sea life;
- Aquarium de Vannes (56): tropical and other fish;
- Aventure Parc in Quelneuc (56): activity park;
- Bel Air Land in Landudec (29): various children's activities;
- Canyon Park in Epretot (76): amusement park for young children;
- Le Cerza in Herminal-les-Vaux (14): wild animals in 'natural' surroundings;
- Cité de la Mer in Cherbourg-Octeville (50): museum of the sea, including an aquarium, bathyscaphe and nuclear submarine;
- Cobac Parc in Lanhélin (35): leisure park with aquatic and land-based attractions;
- Cosmopolis in Pleurmeur-Bodou (22): scientific park incorporating a planetarium and telecommunications museum;
- Domaine de Branfère between Vannes and La Roche-Bernard (56): zoological and botanical park with almost 2,000 animals, including many endangered species;
- Driver's Club in Deauville (14): vehicles of all kinds (including boats) to drive;
- Ecomusée in Hennebont (35): 19th century history brought to life;
- L'Estran in Dieppe (76): museum/aquarium depicting the history of the sea and seafaring;
- Festyland in Bretteville-sur-Odon (14): 'historical' theme park;
- La Galopette in Hanvec (29): activities for children and adults;
- Le Jardin aux Papillons in Vannes (56): butterfly park;
- La Maison de la Mer in Courseulles-sur-Mer (14): cold-water fish and shellfish;
- Natur'Aquarium in Trouville (14): 60 aquariums;
- Le Naturospace in Honfleur (14): tropical butterflies;
- Océanopolis in Brest (29): everything to do with the sea;
- Parc animalier du Quinquis in Clohars-Carnoët (29): wild animals and plants;
- Parc de Branféré in Le Guerno (56): exotic animals and plants;
- Parc de Préhistoire de Bretagne in Malansac (56): including life-size dinosaurs;

- Parc Zoologique de Champrepus in Villedieu-les-Poeles (50): wildlife park;

- Parc Zoologique de Clères (76): botanical garden with 1,200 species of bird;

- Parc Zoologique de Pont-Scorff (56): endangered species;

- Port Musée de Douarnenez (29): floating maritime museum;

- Souterroscope des Adroisières in Caumont-l'Eventé (14): caves;

- Tolysland in Tosny (27): amusement park;

- Tropical Parc in Saint-Jacut-les-Pins (56): tropical plants and landscapes;

- Zoo de Jurques (14): 500 animals;

- Zoo Loisirs in Tinteniac (35): zoo and water park.

Casinos: Somewhat surprisingly, the greatest concentration of casinos in France outside Alpes-Maritimes and Var on the Côte d'Azur is to be found in Calvados and Seine-Maritime in Normandy, where there are no fewer than 17 casinos: at Bagnoles-de-l'Orne, Cabourg, Deauville, Houlgate, Luc-sur-Mer, Ouistreham, Saint-Aubin-sur-Mer, Trouville and Villers-sur-Mer (14), and Dieppe, Etretat, Fécamp, Forges-les-Eaux, Saint-Valéry-en-Caux, Le Tréport, Veulettes-sur-Mer and Yport (76), with a new casino soon to open in Le Havre. There are also four casinos in Manche: at Agon-Coutainville, Cherbourg, Granville and Saint-Pair-sur-Mer. Brittany has almost as many: at Fréhel, Pernos-Guirec, Pléneuf-Val-André and Saint-Quay-Portrieux (22), Bénodet, Plouescat and Roscoff (29), Dinard and Saint-Malo (35), and Arzon, Carnac and Quiberon (56). Details of all casinos and what they offer are available via the Internet (e.g. 🖳 www.journaldescasinos.com – partly in English).

Libraries: Normandy's main libraries are to be found at Caen, Rouen, Ranville (14), Evreux (27), Saint-Lô (50), Alençon, Mont-Saint-Aignan (61) and Mont-Saint-Aignan (76). Brittany's major libraries are in Plerin (22), Landivisiau, Quimper (29), Rennes (35), Caudon, Pontivy and Vannes (56). There are also university libraries at Caen (14), Brest (29), Rennes (35), Le Havre and Rouen (76).

English-language Cinema & Theatre

The best place to see films in their original language (*version originale/VO*) is Rennes (35), where no fewer than three cinemas occasionally show *VO* films, including the Ciné TNB Salle Louis Jouvet, where more *VO* films are shown than anywhere else in Brittany or Normandy. The next best department for Anglophone cinema-goers is Finistère, where there are four cinemas showing *VO* films; the worst is the Côtes-d'Armor, which has none. In all other departments, there's at least one cinema regularly or occasionally showing films in *VO*, as listed below:

● Caen (14): Cinéma Lux;

● Hérouville-Saint-Clair (14): Café des Images;

● Evreux (27): Ciné Zénith;

● Le Neubourg (27): Le Viking;

● Brest (29): Le Studio;

● Douarnenez (29): Le Club;

● Quimper (29): Le Chapeau Rouge;

● Roscoff (29): Le Sainte-Barbe;

● Redon (35): Le Manivel;

● Rennes (35): L'Arvor, Ciné TNB Salle Louis Jouvet and Le Gaumont;

● Cherbourg-Octeville (50): Club 6;

● Lanester (56): Ciné Stars;

● Quistembert (56): Iris;

● Mortagne-au-Perche (61): L'Etoile.

A useful website for finding out what films are on in a given area, which also indicates whether the films are being shown in the original language, is 🖥 www.cinefil.com. There's an annual British Film Festival in October in Dinard (35) (🖥 www.festivaldufilm-dinard.com) and an annual American cinema festival in Deauville (14) in early September.

There's little English-language theatre in the area. The *Scène nationale* in Dieppe (76) has an annual festival (in April) of plays in English called 'Too Much' and occasionally stages productions in English during the rest of the season, as do the Théâtre d'Evreux (27) and Le Volcan in Le Havre (76).

Shopping Centres & Markets

There are major shopping centres in Caen (14), Paimpol (22), Evreux, Louviers and Vernon (27), Brest and Quimper (29), Rennes (35), Barentin, Bolbec, Dieppe, Le Havre, Rouen and Yvetot (76). The largest retail park in Normandy is at Tourville-la-Rivière near Rouen, where there are reputed to be 59 super and hypermarkets.

As in other parts of France (and Europe), small shops are gradually giving way to supermarkets, hypermarkets and retail parks. In Lower Normandy, for example, some 35 per cent of small shops have disappeared since 1980, and there's now one grocer for every four communes with under 250 inhabitants compared with one in every small commune 20 years ago. Only the *bocage* region around Flers, Mortain and Saint-Lô has managed to retain a high proportion of small shops. In most other rural areas, the average person must travel 7km (4mi) to find a shop selling anything other than bread and newspapers.

Nevertheless, small and large towns still have their daily or weekly markets – some consisting of just one or two stalls, others dozens – and there are traditional 'fairs' between May and November in Manche. The Tuesday market in Hennebont (56) is one of best known in the region, and the market in La Guerche-de-Bretagne (35), which has been running every Tuesday since 1121AD(!), is reckoned to be one of the 'great' markets of France. The weekly markets in Bayeux, Saint-Pierre-sur-Dives (14) and Bricquebec (50) are also highly recommended. In Bécherel (35), there's a monthly book market, and Les Andelys (27) boasts France's second-largest *foire à tout* (after Lille) in mid-September, with around 10km (6mi) of stalls. Lists of local markets are available from tourist offices, town halls, etc. (e.g. the leaflet *Mon Marché en Basse-Normandie* for Lower Normandy).

Foreign Food & Products

There are few specialist foreign product shops, although most supermarkets (and particularly Carrefour) stock a few foreign items, such as American hamburger buns, British-style bread, marmalades and sauces (e.g. HP), Australian wines, and foreign spirits (e.g. Scotch and Bourbon), Dutch and Greek cheeses and Italian pasta. In towns with a high proportion of immigrants, there's a usually number of shops selling North African products (e.g. in Val-de-Reuil in Eure). There's an English bookshop in Rouen (76), the ABC Book Shop (☎ 02.35.71.08.67), and La Bouquinerie du Centre in Rennes (35) stocks many second-hand English-language novels and children's books.

General: UK chains found in France include The Body Shop, Burton and Habitat (originally British but now 'standard modern' in appearance). Regrettably, Marks and Spencer have closed their shops in France. Specialist English and Chinese furniture shops are found in most cities. The CityVox website (🖳 www.cityvox.com) provides details of shops selling foreign products in selected cities in France. English, Scottish, Irish, American, Australian and many other countries' goods can also be ordered via the Internet (see **Appendix C**) – a good idea which could prove expensive if you have a craving for baked beans or peanut butter and jelly sandwiches! Delivery (by expatshopping) takes around a week by UPS, and the carriage charge for a 20kg (45lb) parcel is around €15.

English-language books can be ordered from any of the established web-based booksellers such as Amazon, whose French affiliate (⌨ www.amazon. fr) normally carries a selection of English-language titles that can be shipped anywhere in France overnight. Orders from the UK (⌨ www.amazon.co.uk) take three or four days to arrive in the Paris area and normally incur a small shipment fee. An alternative to Amazon is WH Smith (⌨ www.whsmith. co.uk). Ordering books by post from the USA can take as long as six weeks, combined with high shipping costs and the risk that you'll be charged 19.6 per cent VAT on the invoiced value of your package (including the shipping costs) when it arrives.

Restaurants & Bars

As in other parts of France, there's no shortage of bars and restaurants in Normandy and Brittany, and tourist towns are positively overflowing with them. However, in rural areas and even in many towns, most bars close at around 20.00 and are frequented largely by men. Restaurants vary from bistrot-style, serving salads, *crêpes* and snacks, and café-style, serving a set menu for around €10, to exclusive establishments with menus costing up to €100. (Rouen boasts four Michelin-starred restaurants, including the two-star Restaurant Gill, specialising in fish, on the quai de la Bourse.)

In rural areas, an alternative to a restaurant is the *ferme auberge*, a working farm offering simple home-cooking using local produce. The Normandy Tourist Board (see **Useful Addresses** on page 87) publishes a leaflet called *Bienvenue à la Ferme en Normandie*, which lists *fermes auberges*. In the towns, there are also Chinese restaurants, pizzerias and fast-food outlets such as MacDonald's and Quick. Orne boasts one of France's few vegetarian hotels and restaurants, run by an English couple, at Ticheville, south-east of Vimoutiers (☎ 02.33.36.95.84); the hotel is open all year but the restaurant only during the summer.

SERVICES

Services generally have become more centralised in the last 20 years, although to a lesser extent in Manche, while in some areas where the population is ageing (e.g. in Orne), health services have become more widespread.

International & Private Schools

There are no international schools in either region (the nearest is the Ecole internationale de Lille) and just two private schools with facilities for English-speaking pupils: in Normandy, the Ecole des Roches in Eure (BP 710, 27130

Verneuil-sur-Avre, ☎ 02.32.60.40.0, 🖳 www.ecoledesroches.com) has French as a Foreign Language department in both its *école maternelle/ primaire* and *collège/lycée*, for pupils spending a year or two in France who wish to continue studying towards Cambridge, SAT or TOEFL exams (and obtain a *Diplôme d'Etudes de Langue française* or *Diplôme approfondi de Langue française*) or those settling permanently who need to be progressively integrated into the French curriculum; in Brittany, the Lycée privé mixte Sainte-Geneviève in Ille-et-Vilaine (14, rue Genguené, BP546, 35006 Rennes, ☎ 02.99.65.10.08, 🖳 http://ecole.wanadoo.fr/stegenevieve35) accepts pupils from the age of 11 for periods of as little as a month.

Language Schools

Language lessons are offered by a number of public and private bodies in the area, including those listed below. Language courses are also offered by local Chambres de Commerce et d'Industrie and Centres culturels.

- CEFA Normandie in Lisieux (14);
- A Breath of French Air in Montviette (14);
- Ecole des Roches in Verneuil-sur-Avre (27) – see above;
- Centre international d'Etudes des Langues (CIEL Brest) in Le Relecq-Kerhoun (29);
- Action Langues vivantes in Rennes (35);
- Langue et Communication in Rennes (35);
- Maison des Langues in Rennes (35);
- University of Rennes (35);
- Centre d'Etudes des Langues in Saint-Malo (35);
- Inlingua Normandy in Le Petit-Quevilly near Rouen (76);
- Alliance française in Rouen (76).

Details of the above schools can be found on 🖳 www.europa-pages.com. The French Consulate in London (see **Appendix A**) publishes a booklet called *Cours de français Langue étrangère et Stages pédagogiques du français Langue étrangère en France*, which includes a comprehensive list of schools and organisations providing French language courses throughout France.

Hospitals & Clinics

In Normandy, there are major hospitals in Aunay-sur-Odon, Bayeux, Equemauville, Falaise, Lisieux, Pont-l'Evêque, Trouville, Vire (14), Bernay,

Evreux (a new one is planned for nearby Cambolle), Gisors, Mortagne-au-Perche, Saint-Sébastien-de-Morsent, Verneuil-sur-Avre, Vernon (27), Avranches, Carentan, Cherbourg-Octeville, Coutances, Granville, Saint-Hilaire-du-Harcouët, Saint-Lô, Valgnes (50), Aigle, Alençon, Argentan, Domfront, la Ferté-Macé, Flers (61), Darnétal, Dieppe, Elbeuf, Fécamp, Le Havre, Lillebonne, Mont-Saint-Aignan and Montivilliers (76). In Brittany, there are main hospitals in Lannion and Saint-Brieuc (22), Brest, Landernau and Quimper (29), Antrain, Dinard and Rennes (35), and Pontivy, Ploermel and Vannes (56).

There are teaching hospitals (*Centre hospitalier universitaire/CHU*) in Brest, Caen, Rennes and Rouen, where all services and medical procedures are available, and the Groupe hospitalier du Havre is the largest non-teaching hospital in France, with over 2,000 beds. All five rated among the top 50 hospitals in France in a survey published in August 2002 by *Le Point* magazine (Caen 16th, Rennes 18th, Rouen 24th, Brest 36th and Le Havre 47th). The *CHU* in Rouen is Upper Normandy's second-largest employer with 1,300 medical staff and comprises the Charles Nicolle, Bois-Guillaume, Satin-Julien and Oissel hospitals as well as the Boucicaut retirement home. There are also specialist clinics and hospitals in many towns, with a particularly large number in Rouen (76). A full list of hospitals and clinics, including details of specialisms, can be found at ▣ www.chu-rouen.fr/ssf/hopfr.html.

Doctors & Dentists

Brittany is well provided with doctors, Ille-et-Vilaine in particular having a high number of doctors per 100,000 inhabitants (around 160 general practitioners and 150 specialists). Normandy, on the other hand, has below the national average number of GPs and specialists per 100,000 inhabitants: fewer than 143 GPs and 95 specialists in all departments except Calvados and Seine-Maritime, which have a higher than average proportion of doctors. Nevertheless, it's usually easy to find and register with a doctor, many of whom speak some English (there's no list of English-speaking doctors in the area). The same applies generally to dentists, who in some cases share group practices with doctors.

Tradesmen

There's no list of English-speaking tradesmen in the area, although several advertise their servies in magazines such as *French Property News* and newspapers such as *The News* (see **Appendix B**) and others can be found by word-of-mouth. French tradesmen are unlikely to speak much English but are generally reliable.

English-language Radio

There's no local radio in English, but it's possible to receive BBC Radio 4 on long wave (198) in some parts of the area. BBC Radio 1, 2, 3, and 4 can be received on your television via the Astra satellite, and you can listen to recordings of radio programmes on Radio 1, 2, 3, 4, 5, 6 and 1Extra on your computer via the Internet (go to ⌨ www.bbc.co.uk/radio/aod/index.shtml). The World Service is on 648MW, as well as on short wave (for frequency details, go to ⌨ www.bbc.co.uk/worldservice/schedules/frequencies/eurwfreq.shtml) and via the Astra satellite. Local music stations broadcast 60 per cent non-French language songs, most of which are in English. (They're obliged to play at least 40 per cent French music, but rarely exceed this proportion, as even French people prefer to listen to English songs!)

English-language Press

In larger towns it's possible to find major international newspapers such as *The International Herald Tribune*, the *Guardian* and the *European Financial Times* on the day of publication (although not normally before breakfast). The only local English-language periodical is *Normandie & South of England Magazine* (330, rue Valvire, BP414, 50004 Saint-Lô, ☎ 02.33. 77.32.70, ⌨ www.normandie-magazine.fr), a bimonthly current affairs magazine in French and English. There are also two English-language periodicals published in France and distributed nationally, *The News* (monthly) and *France Review* (bimonthly) (see **Further Information** on page 87 and **Appendix A**).

Consulates & Embassies

Both Normandy and Brittany are covered by the British Embassy and Consulate in Paris (see page 314), although information can also be obtained (often far more easily!) from the consulates in Bordeaux (see page 190), Lille (☎ 03.20.12.82.72), Lyons (☎ 04.72.77.81.70) and Marseilles (see page 235). There's an American Presence Post in Brittany (30, quai Duguay-Trouino, 350000 Rennes, ☎ 02.23.44.09.60). For details of the US Embassy and Consulate in Paris, see page 314.

Churches

Churches in the following towns hold regular services in English:

● Caen (14) – Chapelle de la Miséricorde;

● La Chapelle-Caro (56);

- Dinard (35) – Saint Bartholomew;
- Guénin (56) – Interdenominational Church of Saint Andrew;
- Guerlesquin (29);
- Le Havre (76) – Bethel Baptist Church;
- Ploërmel (35) – Maison Mère des Frères de la Mennais;
- Rouen (76) – All Saints.

There are also a few churches near campsites in Brittany where English services are held during the summer months only, including:

- Bénodet (29) – RC church by quayside, Port de la Plaisance;
- Carnac (56) – La Chapelle de la Congrégation;
- Névez (29) – Sainte Thumette Parish Church.

Further details of English-language services can be obtained from Revd Roger Fray, 14a, Le Lesnot, 56460 La Chapelle-Caro (☎ 02.97.74.97.93). Those in southern Brittany may be able to attend services in Loire-Atlantique (see page 150). The Intercontinental Church Society in the UK publishes a *Directory of English-Speaking Churches Abroad* (see **Appendix A**).

There are mosques in Hérouville-Saint-Clair (14), Châteaudun, Evreux, Gaillon, Louviers (27), Brest, Quimper (29), Rennes (35), Cherbourg-Octeville (50), Lorient, Vannes (56), Candher, Elbeuf, Le Havre and Rouen (76); details can be found on 🖳 http://mosquee.free.fr. There are only two synagogues in the area: in Deauville (14) and Rouen (76). Details can be found on 🖳 www.pagesjaunes.fr (enter 'Synagogues' in the first box and the name of the town).

Clubs

There are no English-language clubs in either region, although those in Upper Normandy may be able to access clubs in the Ile-de-France (see page 315). For French speakers, the Accueil des Villes françaises (AVF), a French organisation designed to welcome newcomers to an area, is an option (there's often at least one fluent English-speaker in each group). There are at least 25 AVF groups in Normandy – in Bayeux, Caen, Honfleur, Lisieux, Vire (14), Evreux, Louviers, Le Vaudreuil, Verneuil-sur-Avre, Vernon (27), Cherbourg-Octeville, Granville (50), Alençon, Flers (61), Bonsecours, Dieppe, Eu, Fécamp, Fontaine-la-Mallet, Le Havre, Le Mesnil-Esnard, Mont-Saint-Aignan, Montivilliers, Notre-Dame-de-Gravenchon and Rouen (76) – and 29 in Brittany: in Lannion, Loudeac, Paimpol, Saint-Brieuc (22), Bannalec, Bigouden, Brest, Concarneau, Crozon, Guipavas, Landerneau, Loperhet,

Moelan-sur-Mer, Morlaix, Plougastel, Quimper, Roscoff, Saint-Pol-de-Léon (29), Cesson-Sévigné, Dinard, Fougères, Rennes, Saint-Malo, Vannes (35), Auray, Baden, Lorient, Ploemeur and Ploermel (56). The AVF website (🖥 www.avf.asso.fr) includes a directory (*annuaire*) of local groups by department as well as an online form for contacting your local AVF before you move to the area. Listings indicate whether information and services are available in English or other languages. Other sources for clubs in the area are *The News* (see **Appendix B**) and the English-speaking church (see above).

PROPERTY

The popularity of Normandy and Brittany, particularly among British buyers, means that the demand for properties exceeds the supply. There was a spate of house building in the 1980s in Upper Normandy, when the number of houses grew three times as fast as the population, mainly on account of Parisians (and others) building and buying second homes in the area, particularly in Eure (and especially the western part of the department). The rate of increase slowed in the 1990s, to around 1 per cent per year. House building in Brittany enjoyed a boom in 1999 and 2000, when the number of houses increased by around 5 per cent per year, but the rate has since slowed to around 1 per cent. However, the demand for new properties in Brittany is still high, especially in coastal areas, where second homes represent almost 10 per cent of the property market. (In some communes, there are over 100 second homes per km².)

The most popular areas in Normandy are those within a short drive of the Channel ports (i.e. Caen, Cherbourg, Dieppe and Saint-Malo), particularly the southern half of the Cherbourg peninsula, and the coast of Calvados near Deauville and Honfleur. In Brittany, the area around Dinan, Dinard and Saint-Malo is especially popular. This is reflected in relatively high prices, which have caused buyers to look further west along the coast of the Côtes-d'Armor and into Finistère. If there are bargains to be found, they're in central Brittany and the extreme west of Finistère and in the department of Orne in Normandy, which is among the least popular parts of the area.

The demand for holiday accommodation in Brittany in particular is as great as anywhere in France, so second homebuyers have little difficulty in letting their properties and can usually cover their mortgage payments through rental income.

Typical Homes

Normandy is famous for its half-timbered *colombage* houses (often simply referred to as '*style normand*'), which are either original (with real timbers and much sought-after) or modern imitations (with wooden facings on breezeblock). *Colomage* houses often feature a protruding roof known as a *queue* or *cul de geai* ('jay's tail' or 'bottom') at one end and some are thatched (traditionally with irises growing along the apex of the roof!), which are generally considerably more expensive. Another typical house found in both Normandy and Brittany is the *longère* – as its name suggests, a long, straight, single storey building (although often with added bedrooms in the roof).

Among the most popular homes in Brittany are the characteristic Breton cottage, built mainly of granite with a slate roof. As with the Norman *colombage*, there are many modern imitations (known as '*néo-breton*'). Equally prevalent throughout both regions are stone and brick houses, often rather plain but sometimes in flamboyant 'gothic' style and sometimes with a distinctive glass 'porch' above the front door. Houses are often built end-on to the street and surrounded by high stone walls and solid gates to ensure privacy. Almost every house in Normandy is adorned with geraniums in window boxes, and hydrangeas, irises and hollyhocks are common in gardens throughout the area. Many modern houses are without any particular stylistic features – simply four white walls and a roof, often semi-bungalow with one or two rooms in the roof (called *chambres mansardées*). Modern homes are often raised on earth mounds with a basement (*sous-sol*) as large as the ground floor and incorporating a garage.

Cost of Housing

The demand for homes in Normandy and Brittany has led to a steady overall increase in prices in recent decades, with sharp rises in certain parts. Brittany in particular has experienced steep price rises, especially on islands, where property has increased in value by 300 per cent in 15 years. A 100m² house with a sea view on the island of Bréhat off Paimpol, for example, can cost up to €450,000, and similar properties on islands such as Moines and Arz in the Golfe de Morbihan can fetch up to €600,000. (Houses in need of renovation are cheaper, but restoration costs on islands can be 30 per cent higher than on the mainland.) Elsewhere, prices are more reasonable, although the days when you could pick up a habitable farmhouse for £20,000 ($/€30,000) are gone.

Of the major towns in the area, Brest (29) boasts the lowest average prices for older properties, while the highest average prices are to be found in Saint-Malo (35). The table below gives average prices per m² for older properties in all the major towns in Normandy and Brittany:

Town	Average Price per m² (€)
Caen (14)	955
Saint-Brieuc (22)	920
Brest (29)	760

Quimper (29)	885
Rennes (35)	1,190
Saint-Malo (35)	1,425
Vannes (56)	1,215
Le Havre (76)	975
Rouen (76)	1,075

Note, however, that average property prices aren't always a reliable indication of the relative price of similar properties in different towns, as one town may have a preponderance of cheaper or more expensive properties. The tables below give an indication of price ranges for different types of property in the nine departments of Normandy and Brittany, although it should be borne in mind that, as elsewhere, location has a significant effect on the value of property; a home with a sea-view, for example, can command a 100 per cent premium (indicated by the upper end of price ranges). Where there are no figures, this indicates that there are few if any properties of that type in the relevant department or area.

Apartments

Most apartments are of course to be found in the main cities and towns, where older apartments tend to be more expensive than modern apartments. Rouen has the cheapest new apartments of any of the main cities surrounding Paris (Amiens, Reims, Troyes, Orléans, Le Mans) – around 25 per cent of the price of Parisian apartments.

Department/Area	Size (m^2)	No. of Bedrooms	Price (€)
Calvados			
Caen	25	Studio	25,000
	50	1	65,000
	70	2	100,000
	90	3	100,000–230,000
Coast	25	Studio	20,000–50,000
	50	1	75,000–120,000
	70	2	110,000–150,000
	90	3	140,000–220,000
Inland	25	Studio	20,000–30,000
	90	3	60,000–100,000

Côtes-d'Armor

Saint-Brieuc	25	Studio	20,000–45,000
	50	1	50,000–100,000
	70	2	50,000–130,000
	90	3	50,000–140,000
Coast	25	Studio	70,000–80,000
	50	1	75,000–100,000
	70	2	100,000–150,000
	90	3	115,000–160,000
Inland	25	Studio	15,000–30,000
	50	1	60,000
	70	2	95,000
	90	3	125,000

Eure

Evreux	25	Studio	25,000–55,000
	50	1	50,000–90,000
	70	2	80,000–115,000
	90	3	80,000–165,000
Elsewhere	25	Studio	25,000–50,000
	50	1	45,000–85,000
	70	2	60,000–115,000
	90	3	75,000–160,000

Finistère

Brest	25	Studio	30,000–40,000
	50	1	45,000–70,000
	70	2	50,000–90,000
	90	3	55,000–100,000
Quimper	25	Studio	20,000–35,000
	50	1	40,000–90,000
	70	2	60,000–100,000
	90	3	85,000–105,000
Coast	25	Studio	40,000

Inland	25	Studio	20,000–30,000
	50	1	25,000–55,000
Ille-et-Vilaine			
Rennes	25	Studio	20,000–50,000
	50	1	80,000–120,000
	70	2	90,000–150,000
	90	3	90,000–220,000
Coast	25	Studio	35,000–60,000
	50	1	90,000–125,000
	70	2	120,000–200,000
	90	3	135,000–300,000
Inland	25	Studio	40,000–45,000
	50	1	40,000–90,000
	70	2	85,000–140,000
	90	3	115,000–180,000
Manche			
Cherbourg-Octeville	25	Studio	25,000–40,000
	50	1	30,000–70,000
	70	2	35,000–80,000
	90	3	60,000–115,000
Coast	25	Studio	55,000
	50	1	65,000
	70	2	100,000
	90	3	105,000–175,000
Inland	25	Studio	30,000
	50	1	35,000
	70	2	50,000
	90	3	75,000–90,000
Morbihan			
Vannes	25	Studio	30,000–55,000
	50	1	45,000–95,000
	70	2	75,000–110,000

	90	3	105,000–130,000
Coast	25	Studio	55,000–95,000
	50	1	55,000–125,000
	70	2	70,000–185,000
	90	3	90,000–225,000
Inland	25	Studio	35,000–55,000
	50	1	40,000–90,000
	70	2	45,000–130,000
	90	3	80,000–210,000

Orne

Alençon	25	Studio	30,000-40,000
	50	1	45,000–60,000
	70	2	50,000–75,000
	90	3	55,000–80,000
Elsewhere	25	Studio	15,000–30,000
	50	1	25,000–70,000
	70	2	40,000–90,000
	90	3	65,000–105,000

Seine-Maritime

Rouen	25	Studio	25,000–45,000
	50	1	45,000–80,000
	70	2	65,000–90,000
	90	3	90,000–115,000
Le Havre/Coast	25	Studio	30,000–70,000
	50	1	45,000–75,000
	70	2	55,000–115,000
	90	3	85,000–200,000
Inland	25	Studio	25,000–50,000
	50	1	35,000–55,000
	70	2	45,000–75,000
	90	3	65,000–90,000

Houses

Gardens range from around 400m^2 for a town house (sometimes as much as 600m^2, sometimes virtually nothing) to several hectares for a farmhouse in the country, where the average plot is around 2,000m^2 (half an acre). However, plot size has little direct bearing on the cost of a property and is therefore ignored in the tables below, which compare house prices in main cities and towns with those in coastal and inland areas (where appropriate).

Department/Area	No. of Bedrooms	Price (€)
Calvados		
Caen	2	85,000–115,000
	3	100,000–250,000
	4	135,000–325,000
	5	200,000–550,000
Coast	2	55,000–130,000
	3	65,000–150,000
	4	85,000–195,000
	5	175,000–500,000
Inland	2	35,000–100,000
	3	125,000–200,000
	4	160,000–250,000
	5	185,000–300,000
Côtes-d'Armor		
Saint-Brieuc	4	130,000
	5	175,000–300,000
Coast	2	75,000–300,000
	3	130,000–400,000
	4	180,000–500,000
	5	210,000–550,000
Inland	2	50,000–125,000
	3	105,000–190,000
	4	120,000–300,000
	5	125,000–500,000

Eure	2	100,000–150,000
	3	130,000–220,000
	4	175,000–260,000
	5	220,000–400,000
Finistère		
Brest	2	110,000–160,000
	3	125,000–190,000
	4	130,000–220,000
	5	135,000+
Quimper	2	80,000
	3	135,000
	4	145,000
	5	160,000
Coast	2	110,000–175,000
	3	130,000–215,000
	4	155,000–280,000
	5	185,000–380,000
Inland	2	110,000–180,000
	3	120,000–265,000
	4	130,000–285,000
	5	155,000–400,000
Ille-et-Vilaine		
Rennes	2	135,000
	3	175,000–260,000
	4	195,000–425,000
	5	250,000–500,000
Coast	2	100,000
	4	230,000–335,000
Inland	2	50,000–160,000
	3	60,000–260,000
	4	150,000–280,000
	5	195,000–300,000

Manche

Saint-Lô	3	140,000
	4	120,000–200,000
Cherbourg-Octeville	2	55,000–65,000
	3	80,000–200,000
	4	120,000–200,000
	5	120,000–200,000
Coast	2	110,000–120,000
	3	105,000–145,000
	4	135,000–185,000
	5	140,000–200,000
Inland	2	50,000–135,000
	3	105,000–175,000
	4	105,000–200,000
	5	145,000–400,000

Morbihan

Vannes	3	180,000–275,000
	4	185,000–400,000
	5	220,000–550,000
Coast	2	105,000–240,000
	3	150,000–300,000
	4	200,000–350,000
	5	400,000–500,000
Inland	2	55,000–185,000
	3	100,000–260,000
	4	140,000–350,000
	5	165,000–450,000

Orne

	2	70,000–175,000
	3	80,000–200,000
	4	135,000–250,000
	5	185,000–400,000

Seine-Maritime

Rouen	2	100,000
	3	100,000–155,000
	4	180,000–240,000
	5	240,000–265,000
Le Havre	2	90,000–130,000
	3	100,000–200,000
	4	110,000–215,000
	5	115,000–270,000
Coast	2	80,000–185,000
	3	125,000
Inland	2	90,000–120,000
	3	100,000–200,000
	4	165,000–250,000
	5	215,000–300,000

Properties for Restoration

Despite what estate agents might tell you, there are still plenty of properties to restore in Normandy and Brittany, although you should always check whether there a problems associated with a property (e.g. whether it's in an area liable to flooding or whether there's a complicated inheritance situation associated with it). The following examples will give those looking for a property to restore an idea of the prices they can expect to pay in the various departments.

Type	Location	Size (m²)	Rooms	Price (€)
Apartment	Rennes (35)	50	3-room	30,000
House	Calvados	-	2-bed	20,000–40,000
House	Calvados	100	3-bed	85,000
House	Côtes-d'Armor	210	-	50,000
Longère	Côtes-d'Armor	400	-	105,000
House	Eure	80	2-bed	45,000
House	Finistère	-	2-bed	25,000–70,000
House	Finistère	-	4-bed	120,000

Longère	Ille-et-Vilaine	100	-	100,000
Longère	Ille-et-Vilaine	200	-	65,000
House	Manche	90	2-bed	80,000
House	Manche	160	3-bed	110,000
Longère	Manche	140	-	130,000
Farmhouse	Manche	180	2-bed	130,000
House	Morbihan	35	-	60,000
House	Orne	80	2-bed	70,000
Longère	Orne	120	-	100,000
House	Seine-Maritime	350	4-bed	135,000

Land

Building land is available in all areas, although it isn't plentiful. Prices vary enormously according to location and whether main services are connected. Land in or near a small village, where there's no mains drainage, can be bought for less than €5 per m², whereas land with connections to all services, including electricity and telephone, near a town can cost as much as €100 per m². Plots range from around 400m² to several hectares, the average plot being between 1,000 and 3,000m² and costing between €10,000 and €40,000. Most local estate agents sell building plots (*terrains à bâtir* or *terrains constructibles*).

Rental Accommodation

Apartments: Apartments are available for long-term rent in all departments, although few have more than three bedrooms (in Rennes and Cherbourg, there are few with more than two). The majority of rental apartments are to be found in the principal towns in each department (except in Côtes-d'Armor, where the few available apartments are spread among several towns, and Morbihan, where the majority are in Lorient), and few are available elsewhere. Price ranges for these towns (and the department of Côtes-d'Armor) are shown below.

Town (Department)	No. of Bedrooms	Monthly Rental (€)
Caen (14)	Studio	225–350
	1	300–400
	2	375–600
	3	450–800

Côtes-d'Armor	Studio	250–400
	1	300–500
	2	400–550
	3	500–600
Evreux (27)	Studio	300–400
	1	300–500
	2	500–700
	3	700–1,100
Brest (29)	Studio	250–350
	1	300–500
	2	350–550
	3	500–650
Rennes (35)	1	325–450
	2	450–600
Cherbourg-Octeville (50)	Studio	125–200
	1	225–400
	2	350–450
Lorient (56)	Studio	250–300
	1	300–400
	2	400–550
	3	400–650
Alençon (61)	Studio	200
	1	225–350
	2	350–500
	3	400–700
Rouen (76)	Studio	150–350
	1	200–500
	2	350–650
	3	600–1,000

Houses: Rented houses are less common than apartments, and very few are to be found in or near the main towns. The table below gives an indication of the rental prices for houses in each department.

Department	No. of Bedrooms	Monthly Rental (€)
Calvados	2	350+
	3	400–750
	4	500–900
	5	600–1,000
Côtes-d'Armor	2	300–500
	3	400–600
	4	600–650
Eure	2	400–550
	3	650–800
	4	700–1,250
Finistère	3	550–800
	4	650+
	5	700+
Ille-et-Vilaine	3	700–1,000
	4	700–1,100
	5	750–1,100
Manche	2	450–550
	3	500–800
	4	550+
Morbihan	3	500–650
	4	600–950
Orne	2	300–550
	3	400–600
	4	500–700
	5	700+
Seine-Maritime	2	350–500
	3	400–750
	4	650–1,200
	5	900–1,500

COMMUNICATIONS

Air

There are several airports in Normandy and Brittany with links to Paris and other major French cities as well as a few European cities, including London (Stansted), although international services tend to be unreliable – in the sense that they're started and terminated at short notice (for example, Buzz started a Rouen/Stansted service in March 2002 and cancelled it the following September!). The services listed below were in operation in September 2002. Airports are shown on the maps at the beginning of this chapter.

● Brest-Guipavas (☎ 02.98.32.01.03) 10km (6mi) north-east of the city: daily flights to London Stansted (Buzz) as well as to Bordeaux, Lyons, Nantes and Paris (Air France);

● Caen 'Carpiquet' (☎ 02.31.71.20.10) 7km (4mi) west of the city: daily flights to London Stansted (Buzz);

● Dinard-Pleurtuit-Saint-Malo (☎ 02.99.46.18.46) 5km (3mi) south-east of Dinard: daily flights to London Stansted (Ryanair);

● Le Havre (☎ 02.35.54.65.00, 🖳 www.havre.aeroport.fr) 5km (3mi) north-west of the city: daily flights to Lyons;

● Lorient-Lann-Bihoué (☎ 02.97.87.21.50) 9km (5mi) west of Lorient: daily flights to Paris CDG (Air France);

● Quimper 'Cornouaille', (☎ 02.98.94.30.30) 8km (5mi) west of Quimper: daily flights to Paris Orly (Air France);

● Rennes 'Saint-Jacques' (☎ 02.99.29.60.00, 🖳 www.rennes.aeroport.fr) 8km (5mi) south-west of Rennes: daily flights to Clermont-Ferrand, Paris (CDG and Orly) and Lyons;

● Rouen-Boos 'Vallée de Seine' (☎ 02.35.79.41.00, 🖳 www.rouen. aeroport.fr) at Boos, 10km (6mi) south-east of the city: daily flights to Lyons.

Major airports in Normandy and Brittany are shown on the maps at the beginning of this chapter. Other airports accessible from Upper Normandy are Charles de Gaulle and Orly in Paris (see page 323) and Beauvais (in the department of Oise in Picardy ☎ 03.44.11.46.66), which offers flights to Dublin, Shannon, Glasgow (Ryanair ☎ 03.41.11.41.41, 🖳 www.ryanair. com), Gothenburg, Stockholm, Malmo (Goodjet) and Parma (Ciaofly). Nantes airport (in Loire-Atlantique, ☎ 02.40.84.80.00) is well placed for southern Brittany (see page 122). Details of all French airports and their services can be found on 🖳 www.aeroport.fr.

Sea

Normandy is well provided with ports accessible from England. Furthest east (and therefore offering the shortest and usually cheapest crossing) is Dieppe (76), followed by Le Havre (76), Caen (14) and Cherbourg-Octeville (50), France's second busiest port for cross-channel traffic after Calais, with 1.5 million passengers per year. Brittany has only two major ports: Saint-Malo (35), connecting with Portsmouth in England, and Roscoff (29), connecting with Plymouth in England and Cork in Ireland. The details below were correct in September 2002 (prices are return fares for a standard car with four passengers in July).

- Newhaven-Dieppe (Hoverspeed, ☎ 0870-240 8070, 🖳 www.hoverspeed. com): two or three ferries daily throughout the year (4 hours) plus two or three Super Seacats March to September (2 hours); from £130 to £200 for up to five days, £200 to £330 for more than five days (the lower prices apply if you book before 30th November the year before!);

- Portsmouth-Le Havre (P&O Portsmouth, ☎ 0870-242 4999, 🖳 www.po portsmouth.com): three crossings daily throughout the year; 5 hours 30 minutes daytime or 8 hours night time; from £150 to £320 for up to five days; from £220 to £385 for more than five days (depending on time of travel; overnight crossings most expensive);

- Portsmouth-Cherbourg (P&O Portsmouth): three crossings daily throughout the year; 5 hours daytime or 8 hours night time; from £150 to £320 for up to five days; from £220 to £385 for more than five days (depending on time of travel; overnight crossings most expensive)

- Portsmouth-Caen (Brittany Ferries, ☎ 0870-536 0360, 🖳 www.brittany-ferries.co.uk): up to three crossings daily; 6 hours; £340;

- Poole-Cherbourg (Brittany Ferries): up to three crossings daily by standard ferry (4 hours 15 mins) and daily crossing by fast ferry (70 minutes); £265;

- Portsmouth-Saint-Malo (Brittany Ferries): daily crossing; 8 hours 45 minutes; £460;

- Plymouth-Roscoff (Brittany Ferries) up to three crossings daily; 6 hours; £400;

- Cork-Roscoff (Brittany Ferries) 15.30 from Cork arrives 07.00, midnight from Roscoff arrives 13.00 (local times); £900! (Note that the introduction of a new, larger and faster ferry is due to allow twice as many sailing per week and reduce the sailing time to 10 hours; it isn't clear whether this will also reduce prices.)

There are also local ferry services from Morbihan to the many offshore islands, including Belle-Ile-en-Mer (1 hr), l'Ile d'Hoëdic (1 hr 30 mins) and l'Ile d'Houat (1 hr). The islands in the Golfe de Morbihan can be reached by boat from Quiberon (daily all year) as well as from Lorient and Vannes (in summer only), from where there are also services to the l'Ile d'Arz and the Ile de Groix (45 mins from Lorient).

Public Transport

Trains: Normandy and Brittany are well connected by rail to Paris and, in the case of Brittany, to south-western France, but only Brittany is on the *TGV* network. There's a main line (not *TGV*) from Paris Saint-Lazare to Le Havre (76) via Vernon, Gaillon, Val-de-Reuil (27), Oissel, Rouen, Yvetot and Bréauté-Beuzeville (76), although services to the Vernon, Gaillon, Val-de-Reuil and Oissel are infrequent. Some trains stop at a few smaller towns along the way. (There has been talk of upgrading this line to accommodate high-speed trains, but as Le Havre is less than two hours from Paris by ordinary train, it's unlikely to happen.) There are also ordinary train services from Paris Saint-Lazare to Cherbourg-Octeville (50) via Evreux, Bernay (27), Lisieux, Caen, Bayeux (14), Carentan and Valognes (50). Journey time to Cherbourg varies between three and three-and-a-half hours depending on the number of stops en route. Again, some trains also stop at smaller towns. To get to Dieppe or Le Tréport (76), you must change at Rouen.

The *TGV* runs from Paris Montparnasse via Vitré to Rennes (35), from where there are two lines: one to Brest (29) via Lamballe, Saint-Brieuc, Guingamp, Plouaret (22) and Morlaix (29), and one to Quimper (29) via Vannes and Lorient (56). The latter line also runs south to Nantes in Loire-Atlantique. There are 20 trains a day from Paris to Rennes (just over two hours), 8 from Paris to Brest and 11 from Paris to Quimper (both journeys just under four-and-a-half hours). It's also possible to travel by *TGV* from Quimper to Bordeaux without changing, although there's only one train a day and the route is rather circuitous. For details of the *TGV* network, see map in **Appendix E**. Other major towns and smaller towns in Brittany are linked by local trains.

Trams & Undergrounds: Several towns in Normandy and Brittany have recently built tramways, including Caen and Hérouville-Saint-Clair (14), both of which began operating in 2002, and Rouen (76). Rouen's tramway (called *métrobus*) runs partly underground from the city centre to the southern suburbs along two routes and to the western suburbs. Rennes (35) has an 'underground' railway (parts of it are elevated!) called the VAL.

Buses: All large towns have bus services, which run from the centre to the suburbs. However, these services tend to finish early in the evening. There are also some bus services between towns, particularly during rush hours and to link with train arrivals and departures. In rural areas, however, bus services (apart from school buses) can be few and far between or non-existent, and a car is often essential.

Roads

Major roads in Normandy and Brittany tend to run roughly from east to west, with the exception of the N137 from Saint-Malo south via Rennes (35) to Nantes (in Loire-Atlantique). Brittany has no motorways except the 45km (28mi) stretch of the A58 north-east of Rennes, but there are many dual-carriageways, most of them radiating from Rennes, including the recently completed A84 north-eastwards to Avranches and on to Caen (14), which has greatly improved communications between the Channel ports and Brittany's capital, the N157 eastwards, which becomes the A11 to Paris at the border with Mayenne, and the N12 north-westwards to Saint-Brieuc (22). The N164, which leaves the N12 just west of Rennes, runs due west through the centre of Brittany to Châteaulin (29). There's also a major road running more or less around the coast, from the Normandy/Brittany border (near Avranches) to Brest (N176/12) and from Brest via Quimper and Vannes to Nantes (N165), all of which is dual-carriageway.

Normandy has several motorways, principally the A13 from Paris to Caen (14) via Rouen (76), with a branch (A131) leading to Le Havre (76). The new A29, which links Upper and Lower Normandy, leaves the A13 south of Le Havre, passes close to Honfleur (14), crosses the A131 and continues in an arc, via Yvetot (76), to join the A28 coming out of Rouen north-east towards Abbeville in Somme; here the A28 joins the A16 from Paris to Boulogne, Dunkerque and on to Belgium. (The A28 north-east of Rouen and south of Alençon are due to be linked in a major motorway construction project – see **Planned Developments** below.) There's also a short section of motorway north from Rouen towards Dieppe (76), becoming the N27 where it crosses the A29 (around half way to Dieppe). The A13 is a particularly busy route, especially in summer, when Parisians race to the coastal resorts of Calvados for the weekends. Perhaps for this reason, it's one of the most expensive toll roads in France.

Other major roads tend to radiate from Rouen, including the N31 (east towards Beauvais in Oise), the N14 (south-east towards Pointoise in Val-d'Oise), the N15 (south to Vernon in Eure), the A154/N154 south to Evreux in Eure – only a short stretch is motorway) and the N138 (south-west to Alençon in Orne). The N13 from Paris runs parallel to the A13 until the Eure border and then west as far as Cherbourg-Octeville (50) via Evreux, Bernay (27), Lisieux, Caen and Bayeux (14). Alençon (61) is linked to Paris to the east by the N12, which is soon to be widened to four lanes, and Brittany to the west by the N12/176.

PLANNED DEVELOPMENTS

A number of improvements to local and regional communications are in the pipeline, including a major extension to the A28 motorway, which currently ends at Rouen, as far as Alençon (61). Work started in 2002 and is due to finish in 2005 at a cost of over €750 million. The new road will pass near the towns of Brionne, Harcourt (27), Orbec (14), Gacé, Le Merierault and Sées (61). Another project is the upgrading to a motorway of the N29 from the A16 near Amiens (in Somme) to the A28 near Neuchâtel-en-Bray (27), and Cherbourg-Octeville is to be linked by 2004 to the motorway network (A13 and A84); these two roads are themselves to be linked near Saint-Lô (50), which is to be bypassed. The N158 near Argentan (61) and the N12 through Perche (61) are to be widened to four lanes, and Mortagne-au-Perche and Bayeux (14) are also to be bypassed (the latter road due to be built between 2003 and 2010). No new motorways are planned for Brittany, but many local roads are being improved and a new road linking Lorient (56) and Carhaix-Plouguer (29) will greatly improve access to this part of Finistère and assist Carhaix's expansion.

A project that is already well under way in Normandy is 'Port 2000' in Le Havre (76), involving the construction of a 1.4km (1mi) long quay plus improvements to rail and road connections, including an A29/A131 link. The ports of Caen, Honfleur and Rouen and the marina at Fécamp (76) are also in line for development. Le Havre has been officially designated a 'seaside resort' and Caen may be renamed 'Caen-sur-Mer'. Also on the leisure front, there are plans to enlarge the Mémorial de Caen museum, construct a library in Sotteville-lès-Rouen and open a *médiathèque* (audio-visual library) in Rouen, build a new sports and concert hall in Argentan (61), a new swimming pool in Vire (14) and an aquatic centre in Falaise (14) and a large stadium in Darnétal (76), and renovate the 'Circus Theatre' in Elbeuf (76). Bernay (27) is to see the restoration of its abbey and the creation of a cultural centre as part of a reconstruction of its town centre.

Other urban improvements are planned for Le Havre, whose northern and southern suburbs are due for redevelopment, and Rouen, where the station area and 'Heights' are to be developed in an attempt to attract businesses. Rouen is also awaiting an extension to its tramway (2003) and the development of the quays (2004–05). After the collapse of Moulinex (see below), Alençon (61) is to have two new business parks.

In Brittany's capital, Rennes, a massive new cultural centre is due to open in 2004, incorporating a science centre, the Musée de Bretagne, a 500-seat conference hall, the city's main public library, a book shop and a cafeteria. Elsewhere in the region, smaller developments are helping to regenerate rural areas that were until recently moribund, although there are still villages which are 'dying', and you should check on local prospects before choosing a place to buy a home.

EMPLOYMENT PROSPECTS

Employment across the two regions is varied, with 55 per cent of jobs service-related, 40 per cent in industry and 5 per cent in agriculture in Upper Normandy, 50 per cent services, 30 per cent industry and 20 per cent agriculture in Lower Normandy and a ratio of 65:15:20 in Brittany.

The service sector is the only one of the three to have created jobs since 1990 and it employs almost 700,000 people in Brittany. The principal service industries are tourism, which employs 36,000 in Lower Normandy, mostly in the Pays d'Auge, and 18,000 in Upper Normandy, and research. Brittany in particular is noted for technological innovation, with 12 technology transfer centres and around 3,000 full-time researchers (notably in electronics and communications). Some 60 per cent of French oceanographic research is carried out in Brest.

Industry in Normandy is centred around cars and accessories (employing over 30,000 people with major Renault and Peugeot/Citroën factories in Calvados and Seine-Maritime), petrochemical and chemical products (employing around 30,000 people; the region is France's leading area for refining, oils and additives, as well as a European leader in the manufacture of fertilizers and polymer production, especially in 'Chemical Valley' along the Seine near Le Havre), and electrical and electronic goods (employing around 20,000, although 15 per cent of these jobs were lost in January 2002 when Moulinex in Alençon went bankrupt).

Other important industries in Normandy include aeronautical and aerospace (the engines for the Ariane rocket are manufactured in Eure), ship building (especially in Le Havre and Cherbourg-Octeville, where nuclear submarines are constructed), mechanical and metallurgy (especially in Eure), printing (Herissey in Evreux is one of the five biggest printing companies in France), paper and paper products (especially along the Seine), IT and telecommunications (international companies include Hewlett Packard, IBM, Oracle and Rank Xerox, and Caen has a high-tech research centre), pharmaceuticals (especially in Eure, where companies include Aventis Pasteur and GlaxoSmithKline), plastics (Alençon is second-largest plastics industry centre in France), glass making and textiles.

Transport is big business in Upper Normandy, where it employs over 6 per cent of the workforce (compared with 4.5 per cent nationally) and the ports of Le Havre (Europe's second-largest port after Antwerp, it handles all the coffee consumed in France!) and Rouen (although inland, Europe's largest grain port) directly or indirectly employ over 3,000 people.

Brittany has less industry than Normandy. Under 200,000 people work in manufacturing industry (18 per cent of regional employment), the major sectors being cars, electronics, shipbuilding, armaments and communications, and a further 70,000 in the construction industry and 60,000 in food production. There are over 40,000 small craft and cottage businesses in Brittany, employing more than 80,000 people.

The main agricultural product in Upper Normandy is grain, followed by meat and milk, which account for only 20 per cent of output compared with 75 per cent in Lower Normandy, where agriculture is less diversified. In Brittany there are more than 60,000 farms employing over 100,000 people (10 per cent of the working population) and the region produces over half of French pork, half the country's poultry consumption and 20 per cent of its milk, as well as vast quantities of vegetables (over 90 per cent of French production of cauliflowers, 75 per cent of its artichokes and a high proportion of its beans, Brussels sprouts, cabbages, chicory, lettuces, peas, spinach and tomatoes) and fruit (apples, apricots, cherries, grapes, peaches, pears and plums). Fishing employs around 5,000 in Brittany, where over 50 per cent of France's fish are caught and 75 per cent of its shellfish produced, including up to 4,000 tonnes of *coquilles St-Jacques* per year. (The French hypermarket chain *Intermarché* even has its own fishing fleet in Lorient!) Brittany is also a major source of seaweed (over 650 species!), of which almost 100,000 tonnes are harvested annually for use in food additives, fertilisers and cosmetics but also in balneology.

After falling for several years, unemployment increased in late 2001 to 11.6 per cent in Brittany, 8.6 per cent in Lower Normandy (Calvados has the region's highest unemployment rate) and 10.9 per cent in Upper Normandy, although around 5,000 new businesses are created every year in Upper Normandy. In Lower Normandy, there has recently been a marked decline in agricultural and artisanal employment, while Brittany has recently enjoyed a surge in job creation and new business success; Saint-Malo (35) has by far the country's highest new business success rate. In a comparative survey of 100 major towns in France published in January 2002 by *Le Point* magazine, Rennes (35) was rated in second place behind Paris in terms of its attractiveness to workers, and Vannes (56) came eighth (see **Appendix F**). Until a decade ago, there was little in the way of employment prospects in Brittany outside the towns, but there are now opportunities throughout the region, especially in the building industry (including renovation work) but also in the tourist trade, which is enjoying an upturn, particularly in coastal areas. However, salaries tend to be low and many immigrants (especially Britons) are tempted to work 'on the black', which is of course illegal and punishable by large fines and even imprisonment.

The largest number of jobs in Upper Normandy are in the Rouen area (there's a large industrial zone to the west of the city), followed by Le Havre (one of Europe's largest petrol refining centres), Evreux, Vernon/Gaillon and Louviers in that order (the last three forming an employment triangle). Almost 30,000 people in Upper Normandy commute to work in the Ile-de-France. In Lower Normandy, jobs are centred around the towns of Alençon, Argentan, Caen, Cherbourg-Octeville, Flers, Lisieux and Saint-Lô. Job seekers in Normandy should contact Emploi Conseil in Rouen (☎ 02.35.07.52.95), the Fédération nationale des Associations d'Accueil et de Réinsertion sociale (FNARS) in Rouen (☎ 02.35.07.41.50), and Retravailler (which has offices in Caen, Evreux, Flers, Granville and Rouen). There are also offices of the international employment agencies ADECCO, ADIA and Manpower France in Normandy and Brittany. Jobseekers in Brittany should consult the two regional newspapers, *Ouest France* and *Le Télégramme* as well as local publications. For general information on finding a job in France, see *Living and Working in France* by David Hampshire (Survival Books). A list of companies in each department can be obtained from the French Chamber of Commerce in London (see **Appendix A**).

FURTHER INFORMATION

Useful Addresses

- Comité régional de Tourisme de **Normandie**, Le Doyenné, 14, rue Charles Corbeau, 27000 Evreux (☎ 02.32.33.79.00, 🖳 www.normandy-tourism.org)
- Comité régional du Tourisme de **Bretagne** (74bis, rue de Paris, 35000 Rennes, ☎ 02.99.36.15.15, 🖳 www.tourismebretagne.com)
- Comité départemental du Tourisme de **Calvados**, Place du Canada, 14054 Caen cedex 4 (☎ 02.31.27.90.30, 🖳 www.calvados-tourisme.com)
- Comité départemental du Tourisme des **Côtes-d'Armor**, 7, rue Saint-Benoît, BP 4620, 22046 Saint-Brieuc (☎ 02.96.62.72.00, 🖳 www.cotes darmor.com)
- Comité du Tourisme de l'**Eure**, boulevard Georges Chauvin, BP 367, 27003 Evreux (☎ 02.32.62.04.27, ✉ cdt-eure@wanadoo.fr)
- Comité départemental du Tourisme de **Finistère**, 11, rue Théodore-le-Hars, BP1419, 29104 Quimper (☎ 02.98.76.20.70, 🖳 www.finistere tourisme.com)
- Comité du Tourisme de l'**Ille-et-Vilaine**, 4, rue Jean-Jaurès, BP 60149, 35101 Rennes (☎ 02.99.78.47.47, 🖳 www.bretagne35.com)

- Comité départemental du Tourisme de la **Manche**, Maison du Département, route de Villedieu, 50008 Saint-Lô (☎ 02.33.05.98.70, 🖳 www.manchetourisme.com)

- Comité départemental du Tourisme du **Morbihan**, PIBS, Allée Nicolas Leblanc, BOP 408, 56010 Vannes (☎ 02.97.54.06.56, 🖳 www.morbihan. com)

- Comité départemental du Tourisme de l'**Orne**, 88, rue Saint-Blaise, BP 50, 61002 Alençon (☎ 02.33.28.88.71, ✉ orne.tourisme@wanadoo.fr)

- Comité départemental du Tourisme de la **Seine-Maritime**, 6, rue Couronné, BP60, 76420 Bihorel (☎ 02.35.12.10.10, ✉ seine.maritime. tourisme@wanadoo.fr)

- Skol Diwan Naoned (Diwan schools), 160 rue du Corps-de-Garde, 44100 Nantes (☎ 02.51.80.50.32)

Useful Publications

- **Le Tambour de Ville** – monthly guide to what's on in Rouen available from tourist offices

- **Normandie & South of England Magazine**, 330, rue Valvire, GP414, 50004 Saint-Lô (☎ 02.33.77.32.70, 🖳 www.normandie-magazine.fr) – bimonthly current affairs magazine in French and English

- **A Normandy Tapestry**, Alan Biggins (Kirkdale Books)

- **Selling French Dreams**, Alan Biggins (Kirkdale Books) – sequel to above

Useful Websites

🖳 www.anarvorig.com – general information about Brittany (An Arvorig was the ancient name of Brittany)

🖳 www.arts-et-culture.com – cultural information for Brittany

🖳 www.brittany-net.com – information on Brittany provided by the Brittany Network

🖳 www.french-at-a-touch.com/brittany_categorized_web_sites_a_-_g.htm – general information on Brittany and links to many other sites

🖳 www.normandydev.com – information and assistance for those wishing to set up business in Normandy

🖳 www.normandy-tapestry.com – Kirkdale Books' site (see above), with links to other Normandy sites

🖳 www.normandy.worldweb.com – general information on Normandy

Château de Chenonceau
~The Loire Valley

This chapter describes two administrative regions which lie on the Atlantic coast. Poitou-Charentes, covering an area of 25,809km^2 (10,066mi^2), is made up of four departments: Charente (16), Charente-Maritime (17), Deux-Sèvres (79) and Vienne (86). The Pays-de-la-Loire (32,082km^2/12,512mi^2) comprises five departments: Loire-Atlantique (44), Maine-et-Loire (49), Mayenne (53), Sarthe (72) and Vendée (85). The Loire is France's longest river (1,020km/628mi), with its source in the Vivarais mountains (south of Saint-Etienne in the department of Loire) and its outlet at Saint-Nazaire in Loire-Atlantique. It flows through the middle of the Pays-de-la-Loire, dividing the departments of Maine-et-Loire and Loire-Atlantique horizontally, and is fed by a number of important tributaries in the area, notably the Vienne (which flows through the department of the same name), the Thouet (which joins the Loire at Saumur), the Mayenne (which joins it at Angers), and the Sèvre Nantaise (which joins it at Nantes).

Note that the area covered by this chapter includes the western Loire valley but excludes the area in which are most of the great Loire *châteaux* (see page 340). The two regions together occupy the Atlantic coastal area between Brittany to the north and the Bordeaux vineyards to the south. Half of the west coast area is given over to arable land, the Pays-de-la-Loire consisting of 10 per cent woodland and 25 per cent grassland, while Poitou-Charentes is 15 per cent woodland and 20 per cent grassland; the remaining 20 per cent of the land in both regions is put to other uses, including urban areas.

In the last few thousand years, the sea has been receding along the west coast leaving a flat plain. Along the border between the two regions is land which has been reclaimed from the sea, known as the *Marais Poitevin* (Poitevin Marsh). Part of the Marsh hasn't been drained, however, and consists of a pattern of tree-lined canals between small fields used for market gardening and cattle rearing – an area known as '*la Venise verte*' ('Green Venice') and one of the most unusual landscapes in France. Further south, in Charente-Maritime, the sand and mud banks which are covered at high tide are France's biggest centre for the production of oysters and other shellfish. Elsewhere, the flat shore is used for drying out sea water in shallow pans to make salt. Both regions are also notable for their navigable rivers, including the Mayenne and the Charente, on which there's much boating activity.

Inland, in Vendée and Deux-Sèvres, there's gently rolling countryside with small fields, hedges, trees and woodlands called *le bocage* and similar to that found in parts of Normandy (see page 33). Further south, in Charente and Charente-Maritime, are gently rolling chalk hills covered with cognac vines, poultry farms and grazing for dairy herds, the wooded hilltops rising to over 160m (500ft). The area is also noted for the production of white wine and cognac as well as for heavy industry, with shipyards at Saint-Nazaire, and factories near La Rochelle.

Coastal areas benefit, of course, from tourism but, with increasing life expectancy in France, they attract more and more retired people, as well as foreigners. The department of Vendée in particular is attracting an increasing number of foreign homebuyers, and property prices are rising fast. In a survey of the 100 largest towns in France published in January 2002, *Le Point* magazine rated three towns in this area – Nantes (44), Angers (49) and La Roche-sur-Yon (85) – among the ten best to live in; according to the criteria selected by us, La Roche-sur-Yon is the best town in France to live in (despite having no museums, no Michelin-starred restaurants and only two historical monuments!), Laval third-best and Poitiers eighth (see **Appendix F**).

Pays-de-la-Loire

The locals say that the Loire is the only river in Europe which has never been tamed by dams. In dry summers, it weaves its way through banks of shingle which cover most of its bed but are covered after winter storms. Near the mouth of the river stands the great port of Nantes, which was once the capital of Brittany. This is the home of the Plantagenets, who by marrying the right heiresses became kings of an immense domain which spread from Scotland to the Pyrenees. The English Kings Henry II and Richard the Lionheart are buried at Fontevraud, near Saumur. (They weren't English, of course – none of them could speak a word – but clever, scheming French aristocrats!)

Along the coast to the west is the industrial town of Saint-Nazaire and beyond it several attractive and fashionable seaside resorts. Inland are the vineyards which produce the famous Muscadet and Rosé d'Anjou wines, and to the north the department of Mayenne, named after the river that runs into the Loire – an attractive area for boating as well as for walking and cycling.

The most easterly part of the region is Sarthe, which centres on Le Mans, notable not only for its 24-hour motor races but also for its spectacular cathedral. This part of the region is less than an hour from Paris by *TGV* or under two hours' drive by car and, with its fields, hedges and beech woodlands, is popular with Parisians, many of whom have second homes in the country.

On the southern part of the coast, much of Vendée is flat and windy (its symbol is a windmill). The department has a dark history of mass slaughter during the religious and revolutionary wars, but now the land is smiling, with its almost endless beaches, seaside resorts and fishing villages and a soft and sunny climate which encourages mimosa.

Poitou-Charentes

The Poitou-Charentes region is almost completely unspoiled with virtually no industry and is one of the most tranquil in France. Its long Atlantic coastline is noted for long, sandy beaches, marinas, golf courses and islands, which

make it an ideal summer holiday destination. Two large islands, the Ile de Ré and the Ile d'Oléron, with their pine-shaded beaches and superb shellfish, were connected by road bridges to the mainland a generation ago and have seen their populations grow rapidly as a result; camp sites have also proliferated. No cars are allowed on the smaller island of Aix, where Napoleon spent his last night in France before leaving for Saint-Helena. The marshes along the estuary of the Seudre have been converted into oyster beds with lines of thick wooden posts, on which mussels are also farmed.

Inland, the landscape is flat, particularly in Charente, and the land is used for mixed farming and livestock breeding, as well as for vineyards from which the wines are used to distil cognac. The region is crossed by the medieval routes used by pilgrims on their way to the shrine of Saint James at Compostella in Spain, a practice which is currently being revived. These routes were also used by the stone masons who built the region's many Romanesque churches, such as Saint Pierre at Aulnay (17). Other notable monuments include the 15th century church tower built by the English at Marennes (79), the fourth century baptistery in Poitiers (86)and the collection of 11th century frescos in the church at Saint-Savin (86), and there are numerous places of historical interest, including the fortified town of Brouage, abandoned as a port when the sea receded, the 17th century naval port of Rochefort which replaced it, and the Vieux Port at La Rochelle (all in 17). In contrast, present-day attractions include Futuroscope near Poitiers and what is reputed to be France's best zoo at La Palmyre (see **Leisure** on page 107).

Poitou-Charentes is a popular region with tourists, holiday homeowners and retirees, particularly British property buyers, many of whom favour the area around Cognac (16) and Saintes (17). There's a huge difference between the cost of property on the coast and inland, where homes are good value.

ADVANTAGES & DISADVANTAGES

The area generally enjoys a pleasant climate and a healthy lifestyle (both the Pays-de-la-Loire and Poitou-Charentes enjoy low mortality rates compared with most other regions of France). The Atlantic coast of Charente-Maritime in particular has an excellent micro-climate and is noted for its long hot summers and mild winters, although it can be very cold inland. The west coast boasts almost 30 resorts with 'blue flag' beaches and eight blue flag ports (see 🖳 www.pavillonbleu.com), although there are also a few 'black flag' beaches (considered unacceptably polluted by the Surfrider Foundation Europe – see 🖳 www.surfrider-europe.org): one at La Rochelle, two at Fouras and one at Aytré (17), one at Batz-sur-Mer near Le Pouliguen (44) and one on the Ile d'Yeu (85). La Rochelle (17) has the unusual distinction of having more cycle track per inhabitant than any other major town in France, as well as plenty of green space (over 53m^2 per inhabitant). Angoulême (16), Le Mans (72) and

La Roche-sur-Yon (85) are even greener but the prize for urban open space goes to Cholet (49) with almost 100m² per inhabitant.

Homes can also be found in charming villages and countryside, although properties in coastal areas and close to the large towns can command high prices and those in Vendée are currently rising by 30 per cent per year. The road system is good, however, so it's possible to live inland and travel to the beach for the day. On the other hand, prices rise again as you approach Paris, and in parts of Sarthe and northern Mayenne virtually all suitable week-end and holiday cottages have already been bought up by Parisians. Those wishing to settle into rural houses in the area and who cannot speak French should be warned that they may well fail to establish a satisfactory social life or new friends through English-speaking associations.

Access by air is restricted (only two airports offer flights from the UK, for example) and there are no ferry services to the west coast, but the area is well served by the *TGV* and road access to Poitou-Charentes is good via the A10 motorway from Paris, although it doesn't run through the department of Charente.

There's a nuclear power station in the area, south-east of Poitiers near Lussac-les-Châteaux (86), and another nearby – on the south bank of the Loire in the Parc naturel régional Loire-Anjou-Touraine near Avoine in the western part of Indre-et-Loire (37), around 10km (6mi) north-east of Fontevraud.

MAJOR TOWNS & PLACES OF INTEREST

Charente (16)

The departmental capital Angoulême (pop. 43,000) is dominated by the old town within its ramparts, which you can walk right around on foot (it's also used each September as the circuit for a vintage car race). The town has a splendid (although clumsily restored) Romanesque cathedral and is home to the Centre national de la Bande dessinée et de l'Image (National Cartoon and Illustration Centre), where you can find well known cartoon characters such as Astérix, Tintin and Flash Gordon, as well as to the Musée du Papier, celebrating the area's tradition of paper-making.

Cognac (pop. 19,500) gives its name to France's best-loved brandy and houses the distilleries of Hennesy, Martell and Rémy Martin, among others. (Many of the town's older buildings are covered by a black fungus which lives on the fumes of distillation!) The town is sited on the Charente river, which is navigable as far as the estuary beyond Rochefort (17) and offers idyllic boat trips and floating holidays.

Charente-Maritime (17)

The departmental capital La Rochelle (pop. 80,000) became an important port in the Middle Ages, especially under the Protestant Huguenots, who developed trade with Africa and both North and South America. There was much commerce with Quebec, and the huge paving slabs in the old town were brought back from there as ballast in sailing ships. The old town survives virtually unchanged, alongside the Vieux Port with its many seafood restaurants and cafés, although the city has become an important industrial centre, where for example high-speed trains are constructed. To the west is the modern port of La Pallice.

Rochefort (pop. 25,800) is another port, built by Colbert in the 17th century and with many elements of the original docks still intact, although they've recently been abandoned by the French navy. The 375 metre-long royal rope-winding works are now a museum and international maritime centre, and in one of the dry docks a faithful replica is being built of the frigate Hermione, which fought on the American side during the War of Independence. Behind the river front lies the town Colbert built, a little austere but with considerable charm, faithfully depicted by composer Michel Legrand in his musical film *Les Demoiselles de Rochefort*.

South of Rochefort and around 15km (9mi) into the flat marshland is Brouage, a medieval village later fortified by Vauban whose ramparts have survived in good condition. As the sea receded, its harbour became unusable and the naval port was moved to Rochefort. Brouage attracts many Canadian visitors, because it was the birthplace of Samuel de Champlain, the Protestant navigator who founded Quebec. South of Rochefort, at the mouth of the Gironde, lies Royan (17,000), almost totally destroyed by Allied bombs before its eventual liberation in April 1945 and rebuilt in the worst possible 'new-town' style. In July and August the town overflows with tourists and is best avoided.

Just to the north-west of Royan are the smaller coastal resorts of Pontaillac and Saint-Palais-sur-Mer, which were undamaged in the war and have kept their character. Inland, the town of Saintes (25,600) was the region's capital in Roman times and retains a Roman arch on the east bank of the Charente and the remains of a 20,000-seat arena. The Abbaye aux Dames was consecrated in 1047 and became an important Benedictine nunnery. Pons (4,450), south of Saintes, was on the route taken by pilgrims on their way to Compostella in northern Spain. The 12th century hospice built for them has been classified by UNESCO as a 'European Historic Monument', as has the stone vault which spans the road outside, where pilgrims could sleep under cover if they arrived after the hospice had closed for the night. Pons is dominated by a 30m (100ft) high dungeon, from whose roof there are fine views of the town and the surrounding picturesque countryside.

Still further south is Jonzac (4,200), a small market town well placed for exploring La Haute Saintonge, an area of rolling landscapes quite different from the department's coastal plain. The recently opened leisure centre Les Antilles (the French name for the Caribbean islands) has many facilities, such as shops, restaurant, health club and a fake Martinique village, all surrounding a huge covered swimming pool, which has an outdoor extension in summer adjoining the beach.

Loire-Atlantique (44)

Nantes (pop. 270,000), the departmental and regional capital, claims to be the most rapidly developing city in France, with a conurbation of over half a million people, France's largest refinery and the country's fourth-largest port, a university, and modern industries such as electronics and aviation. Situated astride the Loire, the town was the capital of Brittany until the revolution and still has the castle that belonged to the Dukes, although it isn't open to visitors. One of the city's most famous sons is Jules Verne, the first great science fiction writer and author of *Around the World in 80 Days* among many other novels. Around the Sainte Croix church is the medieval town, with narrow streets and timber-framed houses, and to the west, the elegant shopping arcade known as La Passage Pommeraye.

To the west, at the mouth of the Loire, Saint-Nazaire (pop. 65,000) is essentially a ship-building town, which started to develop when Scotsman John Scott started the first yard in 1862. Giant liners such as the Normandie and the France were built there, and the largest ever cruise ship, the Queen Mary 2, is now under construction. The town also boasts a vast new factory, used to build part of the fuselages of the Airbus A380. A few miles west of Saint-Nazaire is the little resort of Saint-Marc where Jacques Tati shot his classic comedy Les Vacances de Monsieur Hulot.

South of Saint-Nazaire is Pornic (pop. 12,000), a fishing village that has become a popular seaside resort, once frequented by Auguste Renoir and Gustave Flaubert but now overcrowded during July and August. West of Saint-Nazaire, La Baule-Escoublac (44,500), the west coast's answer to Saint-Tropez, is a resort created in the 19th century when the railway was built (the original station has been magnificently restored); thanks to the *TGV* service, it's now less than three hours from Paris. Along the whole of the gently curved beach (reckoned by some to be the finest in Europe) and promenade, on which beach babes compete for attention, is a 'cliff' of modern apartments costing up to half a million euros each. Behind them and among the pine trees are many large 19th and early 20th century villas.

Maine-et-Loire (49)

The departmental capital Angers (pop. 156,300), on the south bank of the river Maine near its confluence with the Loire, dates from Roman times and became the home of the Dukes of Anjou. One of them, Geoffrey V, used to wear a sprig of broom (*genêt*) in his headgear, and the family became known as the Plantagenets. The *château* became the home of Henry II of England, his wife Eleanor of Aquitaine, and sons Richard the Lionheart and King John; it was later given an immense outer wall, by Louis IX, which still stands, dominating the old town. In a specially built gallery is the rich and colourful 14th-century Apocalypse tapestry, over 100m (330ft) long and 6m (20ft) high. Nearby, in the old town, is the 12th and 13th century cathedral, with superb period stained glass.

Cholet (pop. 55,100), south-west of Angers, is a pleasant town which was almost completely destroyed during the savage civil war in 1793–94 between the royalists and the republicans, when Cholet was burnt and its inhabitants massacred. The traditional industry of weaving is celebrated in the textile museum, and the surrounding region, called the *Mauges*, is a delightful countryside, with hedges and trees, lakes, *châteaux* and their parks.

Saumur (30,500), east of Angers and Cholet, boasts a *château* dominating the town from the south bank of the Loire and has changed little since it was rebuilt in the 14th century. In the 18th century, the Marquis de Sade was locked away in Saumur's prison, which now houses three museums. The famous Saumur cavalry school moved to the town before the revolution, and in June 1940 some 800 under-equipped trainee officers put up a sustained resistance to the advancing German army. The area around Saumur is well known, of course, for its wines – less so for mushrooms, around 200,000 tonnes of which are produced each year in the 800km (500mi) of galleries in the cliffs along the river valley, which were originally stone quarries.

Mayenne (53)

The most northerly department in this area has Laval (pop. 50,700) as its capital. The town's castle was built in the 11th century and is claimed to be unique in France for having retained all its original defences. Around the castle are ancient houses. One of them was the birthplace of the primitive painter Douanier Rousseau, and the castle itself now houses a museum of naive art. The Port-Salut Abbey is 7km (4mi) south of the town at Entrammes, where the 13th century monastic church sells various produce but not, alas, the famous Port Salut cheese, which they stopped making some time ago.

The town of Mayenne (pop. 13,600), with its traditional industry of weaving furnishing fabrics, is of limited interest, although it's surrounded by attractive countryside. The Mayenne river has once again become navigable and its restored tow path offers a perfect cycle track 85km (53mi) long. There are Roman remains and an archaeological museum at nearby Jublains.

Sarthe (72)

The departmental capital Le Mans (pop. 146,000) is perhaps best known for its 24-hour car race. (In fact, there are several 24-hour races: one for motorbikes in April and one for heavy vehicles in October as well as races for different types of car in May.) The circuit is south of the town, between the N138 and the D139, and at its northern end is the Sarthe Automobile Museum. Le Mans' cathedral (where Geoffrey Plantagenet married William the Conqueror's granddaughter Mathilda) is a magnificent example of the French Gothic style, with its array of flying buttresses, and the interior is enriched with 16th century tapestries and 13th century stained glass windows. The unspoilt old town with its many historic houses boasts a wide choice of shops and restaurants.

Le Mans is situated on the river Sarthe, which gives its name to the department as well as to the town of Sablé-sur-Sarthe (pop. 12,500), where there are many 18th and 19th century houses. The town's *château*, built by the Colbert family, is now used by the national library as an annexe for book repair and rebinding. There are river cruises on the Sarthe and the charming countryside around the town is worth exploring.

Les-Deux-Sèvres (79)

Niort (pop. 59,500), the departmental capital, was a Roman town which prospered under the Plantagenets, who granted the town a charter and built a castle, completed by Richard the Lionheart. The outer defence wall has been demolished, but the massive dungeon stands proudly overlooking the town and the Sèvre Niortaise river below. In the 18th century, Niort specialised in tanning skins from Canada to make top quality chamois leather for gloves (as well as breeches for Napoleon's *Grande Armée*!). The town specialises in angelica, which is sold not only candied but also as *crème* and *liqueur d'angélique*. More significantly, Niort has attracted several mutual insurance companies since 1945, which have enlivened its economy.

Bressuire (pop. 19,300) was sacked by the Protestants during the religious wars, and again by the Republicans in 1793, but it has recovered and is famous for its major cattle markets and for France's only school for meat trade professionals. It's the centre of rich and picturesque countryside, known as the *bocage bressuirais*, used for cattle breeding and rearing. In many ways, the landscape is similar to that of the Dordogne (but you won't find *The Daily Telegraph* on sale here!).

Melle (4,000), south-east of Niort, is a green and florally decorated town that hides its origins as a centre for lead and silver mining (the royal silver mine and its tenth-century garden can be visited in summer) and for minting coins. The town was also once famous for mule breeding. Melle was on one of the main routes used by pilgrims heading for Compostella in Spain, who were welcomed in the church of Saint Hilaire, a superb example of the region's version of Romanesque and designated by UNESCO as a world heritage site.

Parthenay (10,500), north of Niort, was founded in 1020 on an outcrop of rock above the Thouet river, and the medieval town has kept its character. It also became an important staging town for pilgrims on their way to Compostella. It was for them that a local priest, Aimeri Picaud, wrote what is probably the world's oldest surviving guide book, the *Guide du Pèlerin*, indicating the best routes to take and the best places to eat, to pray and to find lodgings.

Vendée (85)

La Roche-sur-Yon (pop. 46,000), the departmental capital, was just a village until the Vendée department was created after the revolution and the village's central location prompted Napoleon to turn it into the prefecture (the event is celebrated by his equestrian statue in the Place Napoléon). The name of the village was changed to Napoléon-Vendée, then to Bourbon-Vendée in 1815, then back to Napoléon-Vendée under Napoleon III, and finally to La Roche-sur-Yon in 1870. Horse lovers may be interested in the local stud, one of France's largest, but otherwise there's little to interest visitors. Perhaps because of this, the town earns a top rating as a good place to live (see **Appendix F**).

Les Herbiers (pop. 14,000), north-east of La Roche, is a busy industrial town, where you can buy clothes straight from the factory. It's an excellent centre for touring Vendée's picturesque *haut bocage*. Around 10km (6mi) north-east of the town is one of France's major theme parks, Le Puy-du-Fou (see **Leisure** on page 107).

Les Sables-d'Olonne (15,500), south-west of La Roche, was once a whaling and fishing port, but the town benefited from the fashion for sea bathing, which arrived from England at the end of the Napoleonic wars, and the later arrival of the railway from Nantes, which brought middle-class visitors. A separate port for pleasure craft, Port-Olona, providing over 1,000 berths, was built in the 1960s and the town is now Vendée's chicest resort (and the finishing point of the Vendée-Globe single-handed round-the-world yacht race): its population is reckoned to increase in July and August to over 100,000 – you have been warned! Around 20km (13mi) east of Les Sables-d'Olonne is the pretty village of Jard-sur-Mer with its picturesque harbour, lovely beaches and delightful cliff-top walks through forests.

Other places of interest in Vendée include Apremont near Aizenay, a picturesque village clinging to the rocky sides of the Vie valley with the largest lake in Vendée (it even has a sandy beach), Mareuil-sur-Lay near Luçon, an attractive wine-producing town, Port-du-Bec near Beauvoir-sur-Mer on the Bay of Bourgneuf, nicknamed the 'Chinese port', Sallertaine near Challans, a delightful village on the canals full of artists and craftspeople, where exhibitions of local life are staged in the 12th-century church, Vouvant near La Châtaigneraie, one of France's most beautiful villages, and the area around the villages of Avrillé and Le Bernard, near Jard-sur-Mer, which is dotted with prehistoric stones.

Vienne (86)

Poitiers (pop. 83,500) is the departmental and regional capital and boasts France's oldest Christian building, the Saint Jean baptistery, built in the middle of the fourth century and full of archaeological relics. The town boasts some of France's finest examples of Romanesque architecture, especially Notre Dame la Grande. About 8km (5mi) north of the town is Futuroscope, France's scientific theme park, created by the Vienne department (see **Leisure** on page 107). The village of Saint-Savin, around 40km (25mi) east of Poitiers, is world famous for the 11th century wall and ceiling paintings in its church, which Malraux described as "the Sistine chapel of Romanesque art".

North of Poitiers is Châtellerault (pop. 34,000), a charming town with tree-lined avenues and the imposing Henry IV bridge, built four centuries ago, which crosses the river Vienne. Across it is the Manu, a disused arms factory rehabilitated to become a culture and leisure centre, and a museum of cars and motorbikes. To the north-west is Loudun (7,700), best known for the devils which are believed to have possessed the residents of the local nunnery. The priest found responsible for the sorcery was tortured and then burnt to death in 1634 in the main square of the town. (The story in full and repulsive detail is told by Aldous Huxley in *The Devils of Loudun*). The square tower which dominates the town was built in 1040 and offers splendid views from the top. Vienne also contains one of France's most beautiful villages, Angles-sur-l'Anglin.

Le Marais Poitevin

Known as the *marais desséché* (drained marshes), the Poitevin Marsh has been recovered from the sea, which has retreated along this part of the Atlantic coast. It was seen by Benedictine and Cistercian monks as the opportunity to create wealth, by digging drainage channels and building up dykes. In the 17th century, Dutch engineers were brought in, and by the time of the revolution the greater part of the area had been drained. The eastern part of the Marsh is subject to flooding at exceptional tides and after heavy rain. Although uniformly flat, it's picturesque, with canals running under arcades of willow, white poplar, ash and alder, market gardens on isolated and fertile plots, producing globe artichokes, onions, melons and courgettes, and fields for cereals and for grazing cattle and sheep. A 70,000ha (170,000 acre) area of the Marsh, which is due to become a regional park, has been dubbed '*La Venise verte*' ('Green Venice') and attracts many visitors, who take boat trips from points such as Arçais and Coulon on the Sèvre Niortaise river (79).

POPULATION

Poitou-Charentes has a population of just over 1.6 million (population density is just 63.5 people per km²), whereas the Pays-de-la-Loire, which is less than 30 per cent larger, has almost exactly twice as many inhabitants (over 100 people per km²) and its population is growing faster than the average for France, especially in the two coastal departments of Loire-Atlantique and Vendée. Nantes (44) has the second-fastest-growing population of any major town in France (after Vannes in Brittany), and that of La Roche-sur-Yon (85) is also growing rapidly. The population of Poitou-Charentes, on the other hand, is growing at slightly below the national average rate. The departments of Charente and Deux-Sèvres have declining populations, while that of Vienne is increasing. The population of Charente-Maritime is also growing, but growth is concentrated in the coastal area; inland, the department is in decline, both in population and in its economy. Poitiers (86) has a higher proportion of students among its population (32 per cent) than any town in France.

The big centres of population are Nantes (44) with 270,000 people, Saint-Nazaire (44) with 66,000, La Rochelle (17) with 80,000 – all of these on the coast – and inland, Angers (49) with 156,000, Le Mans (72) with 146,000 and Poitiers (86) with 83,000.

The population of Poitou-Charentes includes around 25,000 foreign nationals, of which 6,800 are Portuguese, 2,900 Moroccan, 1,650 Algerian and 1,150 Spanish. That of the Pays-de-la-Loire includes 56,000 foreigners, of which 9,800 are Moroccan, 9,650 Portuguese, 6,150 Algerian and 4,380 Turkish. There wer sufficient British residents in two departments for their numbers to appear in the official analysis of the 1999 census: 460 in Mayenne and 310 in Vendée.

CLIMATE

The coastal departments, Charente-Maritime, Loire-Atlantique and Vendée enjoy a maritime climate, with mild winters. With the predominating westerly winds, clouds tend only to form some distance inland. As a result, the coastal resorts have relatively high hours of sunshine per year, almost as high as on the Côte d'Azur. The other departments inland have a less pronounced maritime climate, but still with mild winters and usually temperate summers. The Loire is considered to be the dividing line between the colder regions of northern France and the warmer south, although the change is gradual. An important feature of the coastal areas is the impact of winter storms, which are sometimes severe, with winds driven at up to 150km/h (90mph). Houses and apartments with picture windows facing west, which may be delightful in summer, can be a nightmare in a winter gale, with powerful draughts letting in whistling winds and jets of rainwater.

Temperatures average around 26°C (79°F) in July and 10°C (50°F) in December and January. The table below shows the number of hours' sunshine and number of days' rainfall in selected towns in the area.

Town	Sunshine Hours	Days' Rainfall
Angoulême (16)	2,025	118
La Rochelle (17)	2,250	115
Nantes (44)	1,956	118
Angers (49)	1,944	108
Laval (53)	1,622	117
Le Mans (72)	1,825	114
Niort (79)	1,934	121
La Roche-sur-Yon (85)	1,956	113
Poitiers (86)	1,930	113

COST OF LIVING

The cost of living in the area's smaller market towns away from the coast is slightly below that in major towns. But competition is fierce between the main supermarket chains, and their prices tend to be similar throughout the area, although prices along the coast rise sharply during the summer holidays, especially those of services. Local producers often sell their produce directly via street markets, so it can be cheaper (and is often of better quality and much fresher) than supermarket produce. You must, of course, be prepared not to want strawberries or French beans in December. (On the other hand in Poitou-Charentes, you can buy oysters and mussels all year round and often find them being sold directly by the producers, who set up their stalls at weekends in many of the market squares.) If you make friends with your neighbours, you may soon find that when they have large crops of tomatoes, lettuces or apples, they will leave some outside your front door!

CRIME RATE & SECURITY

Both Poitou-Charentes, at 43 reported crimes per thousand population, and Pays-de-la-Loire, at 44, are well below the national average crime rate of 61 crimes per thousand. As in other areas of France, isolated houses left unoccupied for long periods can be prey to bogus removal men, who break in and take away the entire contents, sometimes even including items such as fitted cupboards and fireplaces. In terms of individual towns, La Rochelle has the highest crime rate of any in the area, with over 130 reported crimes per thousand inhabitants per year (the sixth highest crime rate of any major town in France). This is probably associated with an unusually high rate of drug addiction, especially among summer visitors. The crime rate in most other towns in the area is little more than half that of La Rochelle, the lowest rates being found in Cholet (49), followed by Saint-Nazaire (44), Laval (53) and Angoulême (16). (Saint-Nazaire is also one of the safest towns in France in terms of the road accident rate.) Le Mans (72), La Roche-sur-Yon (85), Nantes (44) and particularly Agen (47) have rather higher crime rates. Rates in rural areas are generally lower. For general information on crime in France, see page 52.

AMENITIES

Sports

The regions offer a variety of sports facilities, including the following:

Boating: There are many marinas on the west coast, including those at Ars-en-Ré, Boyardville, La Rochelle, Rochefort, Royan, Saint-Georges-d'Oleron, Saint-Martin-de-Ré (17), Le Croisic, Pornichet, Pornic (44), L'Epine, Jard-sur-Mer, Les Sables-d'Olonne and Saint-Gilles-Croix-de-Vie (85). France is reported to have 150,000 more yachts and motor boats that berths, and on the Atlantic coast some marinas have long waiting lists (parents are putting down the names of their sons soon after birth in the hope that they can obtain a mooring by the time they're 18!), so you shouldn't expect to be able to rent one immediately.

Many resorts have sailing schools, for both adults and children, and the larger schools organise regular regattas. For further information, contact the Fédération française de Voile (55, avenue Kléber, 75784 Paris cedex 16, ☎ 01.44.05.81.00) or, in the Pays-de-la-Loire, Y. Rousse, 44, rue Romain Rolland, BP 90312, 44103 Nantes cedex 4 (☎ 02.40.58.61.23) or in Poitou-

Charentes J-L Staub, Môle central des Minimes, avenue de la Capitainerie, 17000 La Rochelle (☎ 05.46.44.58.31).

Those who prefer to sail on dry land can try their hand at sand-yachting. At low tide, the long stretches of sand on the Charente-Maritime and Vendée coasts are ideal for this sport, which uses three-wheeled, sail-powered 'karts' reaching speeds of 120kph (75mph) – three times the speed of the wind that drives them! Training is offered by several clubs in the region, and details of clubs and sand-yacht builders are available from the Fédération française de Char à Voile (19, rue des Sables, 62600 Berck-sur-Mer, ☎ 03.21.89.99.10). For the Pays-de-la-Loire, contact the Maison des Sports, BP 167, 85000 La Roche-sur-Yon.

A more leisurely boating activity is offered in the *Marais Poitevin*, where it's possible to hire flat-bottomed boats and paddle around the maze of tiny canals.

Surfing: There's excellent surfing along the west coast, particularly in Vendée, where the best surfing beaches include those of Saint-Gilles-Croix-de-Vie, La Sauzaie, Les Dunes, Sauveterre, L'Aubraie, La Baie des Sables, Tanchet, Le Port de Bourgenay, Saint-Nicolas, Saint-Vincent-sur-Jard, Les Conches, La Terrière, La Pointe du Groin, L'Embarcadère and the unlikely sounding Bud-Bud and Le Coin à Fred.

Cycling: Much of the area is ideal for cycling, with only the gentlest of slopes to climb most of the time. There are many areas to explore, such as the *Marais Poitevin*, the Loire river banks between Angers and Nantes, and the recently restored 85km-long tow path of the Mayenne river. The tourist office in Laval (53) has a useful map of the river, which gives addresses of places to eat, sleep or camp, plus places to visit *en route*. Other guides and maps are available from departmental tourist offices (see page 125), which can also supply lists of bicycle hire companies. Further information is available from the Ligues régionales de Cyclotourisme: 11, rue du Dr A. Schweitzer, 79100 Thouars (☎ 02.41.55.06.37) for Poitou-Charentes, and 6, allée des Tilleuls, 49360 Toutlemonde (☎ 05.49.68.00.62) for the Pays-de-la-Loire.

Horse Riding: The area offers hundreds of miles of bridle paths, across the *bocage*, through woodlands and along river banks. Along some routes, overnight accommodation is available in *gîtes*. Further information is available from the Comité national de Tourisme équestre (9, boulevard MacDonald, 75019 Paris, ☎ 01.53.26.15.50), which publishes an annual brochure listing riding facilities by region and by department. Local and departmental tourist offices also have information (see page 125).

Golf: There are around 40 golf courses in the west of France, the majority in the Pays-de-la-Loire, including five near Nantes (44) and three each near Angers (49) and Sables-d'Olonne (85). The table below lists the number of courses in each department. Information (in both French and English) on how to find courses, the cost of a round (which varies between €15 and €50), etc.

is available via the Internet (🖳 www.backspin.com). Another useful website for golfers is 🖳 www.golf.com.fr.

Department	No. of Courses
Charente	1 x 9 holes, 2 x 18 holes
Charente-Maritime	2 x 9 holes, 3 x 18 holes
Loire-Atlantique	6 x 18 holes, 1 x 45 holes
Maine-et-Loire	1 x 9 holes, 4 x 18 holes
Mayenne	1 x 18 holes
Sarthe	2 x 18 holes, 1 x 27 holes
Deux-Sèvres	2 x 18 holes, 1 x 27 holes
Vendée	4 x 18 holes
Vienne	1 x 9 holes, 3 x 18 holes, 1 x 27 holes

Leisure

The following is a selection of the many leisure facilities in Poitou-Charentes and the Pays-de-la-Loire.

Walking & River Cruising: The area generally favours outdoor pursuits and is crossed by many long-distance walking routes, known as *grande randonnée* (*GR*) paths, which are numbered and signposted. (Note, however, that the approved route is not always clear, so a map is recommended.) Some departmental committees publish sets of maps. Excellent ones are available for Charente-Maritime and the Anjou area. For further information, contact the Fédération française de la Randonée pédestre (14, rue Riquet, 75019 Paris, ☎ 01.44.89.93.90) or the Comités régionaux de la Randonnée pédestre: OMS, 22, place Charles de Gaulle, 86000 Poitiers (☎ 05.49.47.86.01) for Poitou-Charentes or the Maison des Sports, 44, rue Romain-Rolland, 44103 Nantes cedex 4 (☎ 05.49.47.86.01) for the Pays-de-la-Loire. The region is also noted for its outstanding parks and gardens, most of which are open to the public.

Another pleasurable way of touring the region and its countryside well away from main roads is river cruising. The area has several navigable rivers, on which you can hire and sleep aboard a cabin cruiser for a week-end or a week. In the Pays-de-la-Loire are the Loire, Maine, Mayenne, and Sarthe rivers, and in Poitou-Charentes almost 160km (100mi) of the meandering Charente and around 100km (60mi) of the Sèvre Niortaise. The major boat-hire companies are at Jarnac (16), Saintes, Savinien-sur-Charente (17), Doan and Entrammes (53).

Festivals: As in other parts of France, there are many regional, departmental and local festivals, notably the International Folk Festival in Montguyon (17) in July. Angoulême (16) calls itself the 'City of Festivals', and among the many events that take place there is an international cartoon show in January, which attracts some 100,000 people (it's fifth largest show of any kind in France). With some 3,000 students, Angoulême also boasts the liveliest nightlife in the area.

Museums & Galleries: There are numerous museums, galleries and other places of interest in both regions, including the following: in Poitou-Charentes, the Centre national de la Bande dessinée et de l'Image and the Musée du Papier in Angoulême, the cognac museum in Cognac (16), where it's also possible to visit the major distilleries (e.g. Camus, Hennessy, Martell and Rémy Martin), the natural history and automata museums in La Rochelle, the naval museum, International Maritime Centre and a unique collection of begonias (the plant was named after a local admiral named Michel Bégon) in Rochefort, historical museums in Royan (17), Niort and Poitiers, the motorbike and bicycle museum in Châtellerault, the Maison des Marais mouillés near Coulon (86), which shows how the marshes were developed; in the Pays-de-la-Loire, the Musée des Beaux-Arts, which houses a fine collection of French paintings, and the Jules Verne Museum in Nantes, the Ecomuseum in Saint-Nazaire (44), the Apocalypse Tapestry (see page 99), modern tapestry museum, David Museum (celebrating the native sculptor Pierre Jean David), and Pinée Museum (with a rich collection of ancient art) in Angers, the Tank Museum (which claims to house the world's largest collection of armoured vehicles) in Saumur (49), the Tessé Museum of art and the motor museum in Le Mans and the unmissable Amusant Musée in Juigné-sur-Sarthe (72), which houses a collection of amusing, bizarre and above all useless gadgets!

Theme Parks: The area boasts the third and fourth most popular theme parks in France (after Disneyland Paris and Parc Astérix in Oise in Picardy) and France's leading zoo among a variety of attractions, including the following:

- Les Antilles in Jonzac (17): new, giant, covered swimming pool with a fitness centre, shops, a fake West Indies village, and a summer outdoor pool by the beach;

- Aquarium de la Rochelle (17): sea life centre featuring sharks;

- Arche de Noé in Saint-Clément-des-Baleines (17): rare parrots;

- Atlantic Toboggan in Saint-Hilaire-de-Riez (85): water park;

- Château de Barbe-Bleue in Tiffauges (85): Bluebeard's castle – museum, *château* and theme park;

- Domaine animalier de Pescheray in Le Breil-sur-Mérize (72): wildlife park surrounding a 16th–19th century *château*;

- Domaine de la Petite Couère in Chatelais (49): reconstruction of a 1900 village;

- Labyrinthus in Gémozac near Cravans (17): mazes;

- Le Futuroscope Jaunay-Clan near Poitiers (86): everything to do with the future – France's third most popular theme park, attracting over 1.5 million visitors annually;

- L'Ile aux Serpents in La Trimouille (86): snakes and other reptiles;

- Le Jardin des Oiseaux in Spay (72): 600 birds;

- Océanile in L'Epine (85): open-air water park;

- Océarium du Croisic in Le Croisic (44): Atlantic marine life;

- Papea City near Yvre-l'Evêque (72): amusement park;

- Parc d'Attractions des Naudières in Sautron (44): amusement park;

- Parc d'Attractions de Pierre Brune in Mervent (85): amusement park in the Mervent forest;

- Parc oriental in Maulevrier (49): Europe's largest Japanese garden;

- Parc zoologique in La Boissière-du-Dore (44): 500 animals;

- Planète sauvage in Port-Saint-Père (44): 'African' safari park;

- Le Puy du Fou in Les Epesses (85): spectacular displays of chariots, gladiators and marauding Vikings in a 6,000-seat Gallo-Roman amphitheatre – France's fourth most popular theme park with a million visitors per year (on Saturday evenings in summer, there's a mammoth spectacle, La Cinéscénie, which tells the story of the region, with lights, fireworks and special effects in front of 10,000 spectators – reckoned to be the greatest sound-and-light show in Europe);

- Sealand in Noirmoutier (85): sea life, including sharks and seals;

- La Vallée des Singes in Romagne (86): ape and monkey park;

- Zoo de Doué-la-Fontaine (49): 500 animals;

- Zoo de la Flèche (72): 150 animals;

- Zoo de la Palmyre in Les Mathes (17): 1,600 animals in 'natural' environment – claims to be France's leading zoo;

- Zoo des Sables-d'Olonne (85): 200 animals;

- Zoorama européen in Villiers-en-Bois (79): 600 European animals.

Casinos: There are 11 casinos on the west coast: at Châtelaillon-Plage, Fouras, La Rochelle, Royan (17), Pornic, Saint-Brévin-les-Pins (44), La Faute-sur-Mer, Les Sables-d'Olonne-la-Plage, Les-Sables-d'Olonne-les-Pins, Saint-Gilles-Croix-de-Vie and Saint-Jean-de-Monts (85). Details of all casinos and what they offer are available via the Internet (e.g. 🖳 www.journal descasinos.com – partly in English).

English-language Cinema & Theatre

There are several cinemas in the Pays-de-la-Loire which show films in their original language (*version originale/VO*) rather than dubbed into French; there are four in Nantes alone. On the other hand, Poitou-Charentes is something of a desert for English-language films, as can be seen from the list of cinemas showing *VO* films below. A useful website for finding out what films are on in a given area, which also indicates whether the films are being shown in the original language is 🖳 www.cinefil.com.

- Nantes (44) – Cinématographie (occasionally)

    Concorde (regularly)

    Katorza (regularly)
- UGC Apollo (regularly)
- Saint-Herblain (44) – UBC Ciné Atlantis (occasionally)
- Saint-Nazaire (44) – Cinéville (occasionally)
- Angers (49) – Les 400 Coups (regularly)
- Saumur (49) – Le Palace (occasionally)
- Laval (53) – Cinéville (occasionally)
- Le Mans (72) – Ciné Poche (regularly)
- Thouars (79) – Le Familia (occasionally)

Shopping Centres & Markets

Most sizeable towns have at least one supermarket, near which there are often various specialist shops. (According to a recent survey by **Que Choisir** magazine, the Intermarché in the Saint-Roch district of Angoulême (16) is one of the five cheapest supermarkets in France.) In large towns, there's often also a DIY superstore (which are useful for the handyman who doesn't know the French for 'Allen key' or 'Jubilee clip'). However, many shopping centres in small towns are dying in the face of competition from super and hypermarkets, with only chemists', newsagents and insurance brokers remaining, as well as a few *pâtisseries*, which offer better quality cakes and pastries than the supermarkets.

In compensation, traditional street markets continue to thrive, and there are weekly and daily markets throughout the area, where local people sell their own produce, which is usually very fresh. Perhaps this is because markets, particularly in rural areas, are also social occasions, when people from isolated farms meet their neighbours and exchange gossip. The table below includes the principal weekly and monthly markets in the area, as well as a few notable annual fairs, although dates and times are subject to change.

Pays-de-la-Loire

Loire-Atlantique: Châteaubriant (Wed); Le Loroux-Bottereau (Sun and an annual wine fair first Sun in March); Nantes (daily); Saint-Brevin (Thu & Sun); Saint-Nazaire (daily except Mon and an annual onion fair in mid-September); Vallet (Sun and an annual wine fair in the third week in March).

Maine-et-Loire: Angers (daily); Beaufort-en-Vallée (Wed); Chemillé (Thu); Cholet (Tue to Sat); Fontevraud-L'Abbaye (Wed & Sat); Montjean-sur-Loire (Thu and an annual hemp festival in mid-August); Saumur (Tue, Wed, Thu & Sat); Segré (Wed).

Mayenne: Lassay-les-Châteaux (Wed); Laval (Tue & Sat); Mayenne (Mon); Pré-en-Pail (Sat); Villaines-la-Juhel (Mon).

Sarthe: Bonnetable (Tue); La Ferté-Bernard (Mon); La Flèche (Wed & Sun); Fresnay-sur-Sarthe (Sat); Le Lude (Thu); Mamers (Mon); Le Mans (daily except Mon); Sablé-sur-Sarthe (Thu); La Suze-sur-Sarthe (Thu); Saint-Calais (Thu).

Vendée: Beauvoir-sur-Mer (Thu); Challans (Tue & Fri); Fontenay-le-Comte (Sat); Les Herbiers (Thu); Montaigu (Tue, Thu & Sat); Les Sablés-d'Olonne (daily); Saint-Gilles-Croix-de-Vie (Tue, Wed, Thu & Sat and an annual craft and flea market every evening in July and August); Saint-Jean-de-Monts (Wed & Sat); Saint-Michel-en-l'Herm (Thu); Talmont-St-Hilaire (Tue & Sat).

Poitou-Charentes

Charente: Barbezieux (Tue); Blanzac (third Sat in month); Chalais (Mon); Cognac (daily); Confolens (Wed & Sat); Jarnac (daily); La Rochefoucauld (daily); Ruffac (Wed & Sat).

Charente-Maritime: La Brée-les-Bains (daily); Château-d'Oléron (Tue, Wed & Thu); La Flotte (daily); Jonzac (Tue & Fri); Marennes (Tue, Fri & Sat); Mirambeau (Sat); Montendre (Thu); Pons (Wed & Sat); Rochefort (Tue, Thu & Sat); La Rochelle (daily); Saintes (daily except Sun); Sugères (Tue & Thu); Tonnay-Charente (Wed & Sat); La Tremblade (Sat).

Deux Sèvres: Bressuire (Tue); Coulonge-sur-l'Autize (Tue); Lezay (Tue); Mauléon (Fri); Melle (Fri); Niort (daily); Parthenay (Wed); Saint-Maixent-l'Ecole (Wed); Thouars (Tue & Fri and a lively late-night market on the last Saturday in July).

Vienne: Châtellerault (Tue, Thu & Sat); Chauvigny (Sat); Civray (Tue); Lusignan (Wed); Mirebeau (Wed & Sat and an annual donkey fair on the third Saturday in August); Poitiers (daily except Mon); La Roche-Posay (daily); Vivonne (Tue & Sat).

Foreign Food & Products

There are few specialist foreign product shops in the area, although most supermarkets (and particularly Carrefour) stock a few foreign items, such as American hamburger buns, British-style bread, marmalades and sauces (e.g. HP), Australian wines, and foreign spirits (e.g. Scotch and Bourbon), Dutch and Greek cheeses and Italian pasta. For general information on obtaining foreign products in France, see page 61.

Restaurants & Bars

The west coast is as well provided with restaurants and bars as any part of France and also has its share of mouth-watering regional specialities, including, in Poitou-Charentes, *mouclade* (mussels served with a white sauce flavoured with curry; the best *mouclades* are reportedly served in the old port in la Rochelle), *chaudrée* (fish soup served with garlic *croûtons*), *cagouilles* ('snails' in the local patois – usually served in their shells in bubbling melted garlic butter, but sometimes cooked in an omelette), *daube saintongeaise* (beef stew, as prepared in and around Saintes, which is the region's gastronomic capital) and *gâteau charentais* (almond cake), and, in the Pays-de-la-Loire, *rillettes du Mans* (a sort of pâté made of shredded pork), *matelote d'anguille* (pieces of eel cooked in red wine, with garlic and parsley), *fricassée de poulet à l'angevine* (chicken pieces in a creamy sauce with baby onions and mushrooms, as served in Angers since the Middle Ages) and *lièvre à la royale* (a version of jugged hare peculiar to the Vendée).

Challans in Vendée, where ducks are reared on the nearby marshes, claims to be the duck capital of France, its *poulet noir* (the meat of black-feathered hens) being particularly renowned. Also peculiar to Vendée and found on menus throughout the department is *mogette*, a small, white haricot bean simmered for hours and often served with local gammon. Other specialities of the area are Pineau des Charentes, an aperitif made from unfermented grape juice blended with cognac, and Port Salut, a cheese originally made in a Cistercian monastery near the little village of Entrammes, just south of Laval (53).

Restaurants which specialise in local cuisine include La Cité in Angloulême (16), La Ferme in Angers, Le Relais in Saumur (49), La Boîte Sel in Le Mans (72), L'Auberge de l'Ecluse in Coulon (79), La Grange au Roseaux in Lusignan and Chez Cul de Paille in Poitiers (86).

SERVICES

International & Private Schools

There are no international schools in the area; the nearest is in Bordeaux (see page 187). There are, however, a number of private schools which cater for foreign students, including the Collège privé Saint-Louis (☎ 05.46.97.00.46) in Pont-l'Abbé-d'Arnoult (17), the Lycée privé Saint Dominique (☎ 02.28. 01.72.72) in Saint-Herblain (44), the Centre international pour Enfants Château de Bellevue (☎ 02.41.61.51.42) in Le Bourg-d'Ire (49), the Lycée d'Enseignement général, Technologie et Professionnel privé Notre-Dame (☎ 02.51.69.19.33) in Fontenay-le-Compte (85) and L'Espérance (☎ 02.51. 40.24.86) in Sainte-Cécile (85).

Language Schools

Language lessons are offered by a number of public and private establishments in the area, including those listed below. Language courses are also offered by local Chambres de Commerce et d'Industrie and Centres culturels.

● Séjours internationaux linguistiques et culturels (SILC) in Angoulême (16);

● Mondes nouveaux/Horizons du Monde in La Rochefoucauld (16);

● CUFLE (Université de la Rochelle) in La Rochelle (17);

● Eurocentre in La Rochelle (17);

● Université de Poitiers in La Rochelle (17);

● Centre audiovisuel de Royan pour l'Etude des Langues (CAREL) in Royan (17);

● La Ferme in Saujon (17);

● DuFoir Cours et Graductions in le Croisic (44);

● Centre d'Enseignement du français Langue étrangère (CEFLE) at the University of Nantes (44);

● Espace linguistique (CCI de Nantes et de Saint-Nazaire) in Nantes (44);

- Centre international d'Etudes françaises at the Université catholique de l'Ouest in Angers (49);
- Ecolangues in Angers (49);
- University of Angers (49);
- Château de Bellevue in Le Bourg-d'Iré (49);
- Le Poyenval in Bazoges-en-Pareds (85);
- Centre de français Langue étrangère at the University of Poitiers (86).

Details of the above schools can be found on 🖳 www.europa-pages.com. The French Consulate in London (see **Appendix A**) publishes a booklet called *Cours de français Langue étrangère et Stages pédagogiques du français Langue étrangère en France*, which includes a comprehensive list of schools, organisations and institutes providing French language courses throughout France.

Hospitals & Clinics

Although France is reputed to have one of the world's best medical systems, it's generally recommended to attend a major hospital for any major treatment. There are teaching hospitals (*CHU*) in Angers, Poitiers and Nantes, where all services and medical procedures are available, and a main hospital in La Roche-sur-Yon (87). All four rated among the top 50 hospitals in France in a survey published in August 2002 by *Le Point* magazine (Nantes sixth, Poitiers 22nd, Angers 28th and La Roche-sur-Yon 50th).

Jonzac (17) boasts a thermal spa, where treatment is carried out under medical supervision, and seawater treatment (known as balneology or thalassotherapy) is available in Châtelaillon, the Ile d'Oléron and Ile de Ré and Royan (17), Pornic (44), Les Sables-d'Olonne and Saint-Jean-de-Monts (84).

Doctors & Dentists

The west is generally relatively poorly provided with doctors, only Charente-Maritime having above the national average proportion of general practitioners per 100,000 inhabitants and Loire-Atlantique the only department to have above the average number of specialists; Mayenne and Vendée have fewer than 143 GPs and 95 specialists per 100,000 population. Nevertheless, it's usually easy to find and register with a doctor, many of whom speak English, although the only English-speaking doctor listed with the British Consulate in Bordeaux is Dr Goolam Cassim, in Saint-Hilaire-de-Villefranche (17).

Tradesmen

The following English-speaking tradesmen and professionals are listed with the British Consulate in Bordeaux:

- Bill Buttling (builder), chez Bonnin, 16210 Chalais (☎ 05.45.98.18.56);
- Robert Goff (painter and decorator), 104 rue Grange, 16600 Ruelle-sur-Touvre (☎ 05.45.61.09.47);
- Keith Randell (builder), le Bourg, 16390 Bonnes (☎ 05.45.98.56.41);
- Mrs Catherine Broughton (estate agent), Domaine Rochebonne, 17320 Saint-Just-Luzac (☎ 05.46.85.54.23);
- Phillip Keevil (estate agent), 46 rue de Ribérou, 17600 Saujon (☎ 05.46.02.44.44);
- Mrs Susan Dixon (estate agent), ICS SARL, Les Broux 86400 Saint-Gaudent (☎ 05.49.87.45.47).

Magazines such as *French Property News* and newspapers such as *The News* (see **Appendix B**) carry advertisements by English-speaking tradesmen. French tradesmen are unlikely to speak much English but are generally reliable – and have the advantage that they often take several months to submit an invoice!

English-language Radio

There's no local radio in English, but it's possible to receive BBC Radio 4 on long wave (198) in northern parts of the area. BBC Radio 1, 2, 3, and 4 can be received on your television via the Astra satellite, and you can listen to recordings of radio programmes on Radio 1, 2, 3, 4, 5, 6 and 1Extra on your computer via the Internet (go to 🖳 www.bbc.co.uk/radio/aod/index.shtml). The World Service is on 648MW in northern parts, as well as short wave (for frequency details, go to 🖳 www.bbc.co.uk/worldservice/schedules/frequencies/eurwfreq.shtml) and via the Astra satellite in all parts of the area. Local music stations usually broadcast 60 per cent non-French language songs, most of which are in English.

English-language Press

There are no local English-language publications, but there are two English-language periodicals published in France and distributed nationally, *The News* (monthly) and *France Review* (bimonthly) – see **Appendix B**.

Consulates

The Poitou-Charentes region is covered by the British Consulate General, 353, boulevard Président Wilson, 33073 Bordeaux (☎ 05.57.22.21.00) and the United States Consulate, 10, place de la Bourse, 33000 Bordeaux (☎ 05.56.48.63.80). The Pays-de-la-Loire is covered by the British Consulate General, 18bis, rue d'Anjou, BP 111.08, 75365 Paris cedex 08 (☎ 01.44.51.31.00) and the United States Consulate, 30, quai Duguay-Trouin, 35000 Nantes (☎ 02.23.44.09.60).

Churches

There are churches in the following towns which hold regular services in English (where no church is specified, it's the only one in the village):

● Chasseneuil-sur-Bonnieure (16) – Temple Protestant;

● Cognac (16) – Chapelle Ecole de la Providence;

● Le-Grand-Madieu (16);

● Salles-de-Villfagnan (16) – services only five times a year;

● Saint-Léger-de-la-Martinière near Melle (79);

● La Merlatière (85);

● Puy-de-Serre (85);

● Magné near Gençay (86).

There are also a few churches near campsites in the area where English services are held during the summer months only, including:

● Royan (17) – Eglise les Mathes;

● Saumur (49) – Villebernier Church;

● Saint-Gilles-Croix-de-Vie (85) – La Chapelle.

Further details of English-language services in Poitou-Charentes can be obtained from Revd Michael Hepper, Porte 3, 19, avenue René Baillargeon, 86400 Civray (☎ 05.49.97.04.21). Those in northern Pays-de-la-Loire may be able to attend services in Ille-et-Vilaine or Morbihan in Brittany (see page 65), while those in the south of Poitou-Charentes may have access to services in Dordogne (see page 150) or Gironde (see page 190). The Intercontinental Church Society in the UK publishes a *Directory of English-Speaking Churches Abroad* (see **Appendix A**).

There are mosques in Angoulême, Avignon, Soyaux (16), La Rochelle (17), Nantes, Saint-Nazaire (44), Angers, Cholet (49), Laval (53), Le Mans

(72), La Roche-sur-Yon (85), Châtellerault and Poitiers (86); details can be found on 🖥 http://mosquee.free.fr. There are synagogues in La Rochelle (17), Nantes (44) and Angers (49); details can be found on 🖥 www.pagesjaunes.fr (enter 'Synagogues' in the first box and the name of the town).

Clubs

There are no recognised English-speaking clubs or associations in the area, although Anglophone contacts can be made via and the English-speaking church (see above) and through publications such as *The News* (see **Appendix B**). For French speakers, the Accueil des Villes françaises (AVF), a French organisation designed to welcome newcomers to an area, is an option (there's often at least one fluent English-speaker in each group). There are over 30 AVF groups in the Pays-de-la-Loire – in Ancenis, La Baule, Blain, Châteaubriant, Clisson, Le Croisic, Donges, Guérande, Nantes, Pontchâteau, Pornic, Pornichet, Saint-Nazaire, Sainte-Luce, Savenay, La Turballe, Vallet (44), Angers, Cholet (49), Laval, Château-Gontier (53), Château-du-Loir, La Ferté-Bernard, Le Mans, Saint-Galais, Sille-le-Guillaume (72), Fontenay-le-Comte, Les Herbiers, Montaigu, Noirmoutier, La Roche-sur-Yon and Saint-Gilles-Croix-la-Vie (85) – and 11 in Poitou-Charentes: in Angoulême (16), Jonzac, La Rochelle, Saint-Jean-d'Agely, Saintes (17), Bressuire, Niort, Parthenay, Saint-Maixent (79), Châtellerault and Poitiers (86). The website (🖥 www.avf.asso.fr) includes a directory (*annuaire*) of local groups by department as well as an online form for contacting your local AVF before you move to the area. Listings indicate whether information and services are available in English or other languages.

PROPERTY

After a relatively stagnant period at the end of the 1990s, property prices in the area have been rising by around 20 per cent per year and, where three or four years ago buyers were slow to commit themselves, they're now snapping up available homes – particularly the British, many of whom are moving away from Dordogne, for example, to the coast. House-hunters are advised to visit the area between mid-October and mid-February, when agents are less busy, but you shouldn't expect a house which you saw in November still to be available in March. On the other hand, it doesn't pay to be too hasty, and British buyers in particular should be wary of buying from other Britons, who often inflate the price of a property, knowing that prices in the UK are generally far higher. Note also that cheaper properties requiring renovation or modernisation with a reasonable plot on the outskirts of a small town or village (the foreign buyer's dream) are becoming extremely scarce in all areas.

Cholet (49), where the average property costs around €75,000, has the highest proportion of property owners (56 per cent) of any major town in France, as well as the second-highest percentage (63 per cent) of large properties (i.e. four rooms or more) and the lowest percentage (5 per cent) of vacant properties. However, the rate of new building is only average, whereas Saint-Nazaire (44) has the second-highest rate of new building (2 per cent) in France, after Bastia in Corsica.

Typical Homes

The typical, traditional house in Poitou-Charentes is a long, narrow structure, often with the main rooms facing south. In wine-producing areas there's usually an extension on the north side, used for wine making and storage, called the *chais*. Most houses have low attics, originally used for storing hay. A frustration for buyers looking for a property to renovate is that the roof structure usually has beams chest-high crossing the house from front to back, which makes conversion into bedrooms difficult. Roofs normally have traditional Roman tiles and rendered outside walls, with dressed stone around windows and doors and at external corners. Sadly, many of the larger modern houses use ready-made designs intended for Provence, which look out of place on the Atlantic coast.

In the Pays-de-la-Loire, most houses have slate roofs, a limited number using Roman tiles (most of them in the south of the region). Some older houses have exposed stone walls, but most are rendered and painted white. Most older rural houses are single storey, often with low roofs and attics which are impossible to convert into bedrooms. In the Marais Poitevin, traditional houses have thatched roofs and thick, dried-mud walls, similar to those in south-west England.

Cost of Housing

Average prices in the area are rising by around 20 per cent per year, and in some parts increases are even higher, with local agents predicting 30 per cent price rises in Vendée in 2003. Coastal areas, particularly in Charente-Maritime, are naturally more expensive than inland parts, and the area around La Rochelle and Royan has become something of a summer 'playground' for Parisians, with an inevitable effect on prices. However, there's also considerable demand for properties close to airports offering low-price flights (particularly to the UK – see page 122) and to main railway stations (see *TGV* map in **Appendix E**).

Angoulême (16) boasts the lowest average prices for older properties of any main town in the west, the average price of older properties generally being €650 per m², although this rises to between €800 and €1,200 per m² in the town centre. On the other hand, the town imposes the second-highest rates of *taxe foncière* in France (after Périgueux in Dordogne). The area's highest average property prices are to be found in La Rochelle (17). The table below gives average prices per m² for older properties in major towns in the area:

Town	Average Price per m² (€)
Angoulême (16)	650
La Rochelle (17)	1,405
Nantes (44)	1,160
Saint-Nazaire (44)	995
Angers (49)	1,025
Cholet (49)	760
Laval (53)	880
Niort (79)	780
Poitiers (86)	900

Note, however, that average property prices aren't always a reliable indication of the relative price of similar properties in different towns, as one town may have a preponderance of cheaper or more expensive properties. The prices listed in the tables below are typical but don't include the cheapest (a ruin lost in the woods, needing complete reconstruction) or the most expensive (probably with both private beach and swimming pool). A 'small' plot is reckoned to be less than 1,000m², a 'large' plot between 1,000m² and 1ha (2.5 acres).

● **Small Isolated House/Farm for Renovation**

Department	Plot	Price (€)
Charente	small	55,000
	large	60,000
Charente-Maritime	small	75,000
	large	90,000
Loire-Atlantique	small	60,000
	large	65,000
Maine-et-Loire	small	10,000
	large	40,000
Mayenne	small	20,000
	large	30,000

Sarthe	small	45,000
	large	60,000
Deux-Sèvres	small	20,000
	large	40,000
Vendée	small	45,000
	large	55,000
Vienne	small	25,000
	large	40,000

- **Renovated Village House**

Department	Bedrooms	Price (€)
Charente	2	70,000
	3–4	95,000
Charente-Maritime	2	90,000
	3–4	140,000
Loire-Atlantique	2	60,000
	3–4	165,000
Maine-et-Loire	2	60,000
	3–4	150,000
Mayenne	2	55,000
	3–4	100,000
Sarthe	2	60,000
	3–4	135,000
Deux-Sèvres	2	40,000
	3–4	105,000
Vendée	2	70,000
	3–4	105,000
Vienne	2	45,000
	3–4	125,000

- **Renovated Large House (3+ bedrooms) with Land**

Department	Location	Price (€)
Charente	country	185,000
	in/near town	280,000

Charente-Maritime	country	200,000
	in/near town	225,000
Loire-Atlantique	country	210,000
	in/near town	225,000
Maine-et-Loire	country	185,000
	in/near town	245,000
Mayenne	country	200,000
	in/near town	225,000
Sarthe	country	140,000
	in/near town	180,000
Deux-Sèvres	country	155,000
	in/near town	185,000
Vendée	country	225,000
	in/near town	265,000
Vienne	country	135,000
	in/near town	170,000

Land

There's a limited supply of sites available for building your own home. Prices vary according to whether a plot has a *certificat d'urbanisme* (*CU*), i.e. planning permission, as well as with location. Plots close to the sea or a river or which enjoy outstanding unspoilt views can be very expensive. Small rural sites of around 1,000m² start at €10,000 euros or so, rising to €40,000 euros or more for a site near a beach.

Rental Accommodation

There's a fair amount of long-term rental accommodation available in all departments: most in Loire-Atlantique and Sarthe, and least in Charente-Maritime, Laval, Deux-Sèvres and Vendée. There are few houses available in coastal areas, as their owners can earn more by offering holiday lets in the summer. Where available, unfurnished houses with two or three bedrooms are offered for rents ranging from €350 to €600 per month. Apartments are more plentiful, especially in the main towns, although there are few in La Rochelle (17) and Niort (79). Rents range from around €300 for a one-bedroom apartment to around €800 for three bedrooms.

COMMUNICATIONS

Air

There are three airports in the area (shown on the maps at the beginning of the chapter) offering direct flights from the UK as well as flights from other towns in France: La Rochelle (17), Nantes (44) and Poitiers (86). Buzz recently started a service between London Stansted and La Rochelle, which has been a great success. There's one flight per day in winter, and up to three a day in summer. (Air Lib inaugurated twice-daily services from Paris and Bordeaux to La Rochelle in July 2002, but these aren't expected to last long!) There are also two Air France flights per day to La Rochelle from Clermont-Ferrand. However, the airport facilities at La Rochelle are poor, and there's no public transport service to the town centre.

Nantes airport, which has better facilities, offers up to seven flights per day to London Gatwick (four with Air France and three with British European) and up to six flights a day to Paris Charles de Gaulle (Air France) as well as flights to Bordeaux, Clermont-Ferrand, Lille, Lyons, Marseilles, Montpellier and Nice. Buzz flies daily from London Stansted to Poitiers-Biard, a small airport with few facilities, and Air France offers daily flights from Paris.

Those in the north of the area may have access to airports in Normandy or Brittany (see page 80) or the Paris airports (see page 323), while those in the south may be within reach of Bordeaux airport (see page 202) or the airport at Périgueux (see page 156). Details of all French airports and their services can be found on 💻 www.aeroport.fr.

Sea

There are no ferry services from the UK or other countries to the west coast. The nearest ferry ports are in Normandy and Brittany (see page 81).

Public Transport

The area is well served by high-speed trains (*TGV*). Angoulême (16) and Poitiers (86) are on the main *TGV* line from Paris-Montparnasse to Bordeaux, putting them an hour and a half and just over two hours from the capital respectively. (Note that trains can only run at full speed – up to 300kph/ 185mph – as far as Tours, although new track is due to be laid as far as Bordeaux) There's also a branch line connecting Niort (79) and La Rochelle (17). Another main *TGV* line runs from Paris to Le Croisic (44) via Le Mans (72), Angers (44) and Nantes (44). There are 15 trains a day to Le Mans and Angers (taking 55 and 90 minutes respectively) and 20 a day to Nantes (taking around two hours). Laval (53) is one-and-a-half hours from Paris on the main line to Brest and Quimper in Brittany. There are also good services from Paris to La Roche-sur-Yon (3h), Cholet (2h30), Saumur (1h30), Les Sables-d'Olonne (3h30) and Saint-Nazaire (2h35). For details of the *TGV* network, see map in **Appendix E**. There are usually special prices for return tickets from London via Paris if booked well in advance. Current examples are London-Poitiers and London-Le Mans for around €100.

There are also local trains connecting main towns, and all large towns have bus services running from the centre to the suburbs. However, these services tend to finish early in the evening. There are also some bus services between towns, particularly during rush hours and to link with train arrivals and departures. In rural areas, however, bus services (apart from school buses) can be few and far between or non-existent, and a car is often essential.

Roads

Access to the region by motorway from Paris is excellent, the A10 (known as the *Aquitaine*) running to Poitiers (86), Noirt (79) and Saintes (17). Branching off it around 50km (35mi) west of Paris is the A11 (*Océane*) to Le Mans (72), Angers (49) and Nantes (44). Recently completed is the A83, which links the A10 near Niort to Nantes. There's good access to the main Channel ferry ports, particularly from the north of the area. Although not classed as a motorway, the N137 north of Nantes is virtually of motorway standard for much of the way via Rennes to Saint-Malo, from where there are sailings to Portsmouth. There's also a motorway link (A84, known as the *Autoroute des Estuaires*) from Rennes north-east to Caen, from where there's a shorter ferry route to Portsmouth. Another ferry port option is Roscoff in Finistère (around 160km/100mi west of Rennes on the N12, which is dual-carriageway almost to the port).

PLANNED DEVELOPMENTS

A number of improvements to transport networks are under way or in the pipeline, including the construction of high-speed rail track from Tours to Bordeaux (presently, the *TGV* must slow to a mere 200kph/120mph beyond Tours) and the long-promised widening of the N10 road between Angoulême and Bordeaux to make it a dual-carriageway throughout. The section of the A84 motorway north-east of Avranches is currently under construction. When finished, it will complete the Rennes-Caen motorway, creating a continuous dual-carriageway route from Nantes to Calais, via Rennes, Caen and the A29 motorway across the *Pont de Normandie* near Le Havre. A new motorway running south-west from Angers is also currently under construction. It is expected to bypass Cholet and les Herbiers and be linked to the A83 Nantes-

Niort motorway. It will probably continue in due course to La Roche-sur-Yon. In Vendée, a dual-carriageway should soon link La Roche-sur-Yon and Bournezeau (junction 6 of the A83). In the longer term, a motorway linking Fontenay-le-Comte and La Rochelle (17) is under consideration.

In Charente, a major new amusement park on the theme of 'the image' is planned for Angoulême (16) and will feature a 50m (160ft) high Tintin rocket; it will be linked with the Magelis centre (see below). Angoulême is also due for a major new sports complex, incorporating a swimming pool and ice-rink.

In Vendée, residents of Challans are protesting against the opening of a factory producing road surfacing material in the village of La Bloire, to the south of the town, and there are plans to extend the already large rubbish dump at Grand'Landes, east of Challans. Les Landes de Châtelaine, near La Bruffière in the north of the department, is the possible site of another dump, as are Les Lucs-sur-Boulogne, Saint-Philbert de Bouaine, Nieul-le-Dolent and La Garnache, while the areas around Moutiers-les-Mauxfaits and La Mothe-Achard are being considered for the siting of a nuclear waste dump. A greener form of power-generation is proposed for the Bay of Bourgneuf, north of Noirmoutier island and the Plateau des Boeufs, off Noirmoutier, as well as for Frossay on the Ile du Petit Carnet (44), all of which are prime locations for wind farms.

EMPLOYMENT PROSPECTS

Employment in the west of France is 55 per cent in the service sector, 30 per cent in industry and 15 per cent in agriculture, and the parts of the area are currently enjoying a surge in employment prospects, with a high rate of new business success, particularly in Saint-Nazaire (44), although the Poitou-Charentes region is relatively stagnant. A list of companies in each department can be obtained from the French Chamber of Commerce in London (see **Appendix A**).

Pays-de-la-Loire

The region has an active population of 1.3 million, including almost 300,000 employed in industry. The coastal region in particular attracts engineering businesses, with the workshops that make the high-speed trains (*TGV*) at La Rochelle (17), the shipyards at Saint-Nazaire (44) and the Michelin tyre factory at Cholet (49). Inland, the cognac-producing area has been badly hit by falling sales, not least due to competition from Scotch whisky, both in France and elsewhere. The region's annual gross product is €20,500 per person, which is around the average for French departments outside the Ile-de-France. The unemployment rate is currently around 10.5 per cent. Major local activities by department include the following:

Loire-Atlantique: shipbuilding, boiler-making, aircraft manufacture, wine-making.

Maine-et-Loire: slate quarrying, market gardening, vegetable and flower seed growing, poultry farming, wine-making, confectionery and tyre manufacture, food processing.

Mayenne: cereal and pig farming, cattle breeding, market gardening.

Sarthe: cattle breeding, forestry, dairy farming, cereal growing, agricultural machinery construction (in Le Mans), insurance, electronics.

Vendée: tourism, forestry, market gardening, fishing, boat-building.

Poitou-Charentes

The region has an active population of under half a million, including over 100,000 employed in industry and under 15,000 in agriculture. Gross annual product is less than €18,500 per head, amongst the lowest in France and only around half that of the Paris region. The unemployment rate is around 11.5 per cent. Except in coastal areas, the population is slowly diminishing and, as a result, employment prospects are generally poor. Exceptions are the building trade, which is particularly busy in coastal areas, where there's a continuous demand for new homes, and the tourist industry, which in 2002 has been dynamic throughout the region, although most jobs are seasonal. Note that the region boasts over 7,000 hotel beds, 1,500 beds in self-catering accommodation, over 1,000 *gîtes* and 1,000 *chambres d'hôte*, 15,000 camp-site pitches, and almost 100,000 second homes.

One of the region's major employers is the '*pôle image*' ('image centre') called Magelis on the banks of the Charente in Angoulême (16), incorporating the Centre national de la Bande dessinée et de l'Image and the Ecole supérieure de l'Image and around 30 businesses. The centre's annual international cartoon show is the fifth largest show of any kind in France.

Britons looking for work in the region should note that a small number of local factories in the region have been bought by British companies, only to close within three or four years. In some cases, the British management seems unable to acclimatise to French conditions, particularly in the field of human resources. However attractive the idea may seem to work for a British company in France, care is needed to be sure that the management really knows what it's doing and has a good track record.

FURTHER INFORMATION

Useful Addresses

● Centre régional du Tourisme de **Poitou-Charentes**, 62, rue Jean-Jaurès, BP 56, 86002 Poitiers (☎ 05.49.50.10.50)

- Maison **Poitou-Charentes**, 68, rue du Cherche-Midi, 75006 Paris (☎ 01. 42.22.83.74)

- Centre régional du Tourisme des **Pays-de-la-Loire**, 2, rue de la Loire, BP 86002, 44204 Nantes cedex 2 (☎ 02.40.48.24.20, 💻 www.paysdela loire.fr)

- Maison des **Pays-de-la-Loire**, 6, rue Cassette, 75006 Paris (☎ 01.53. 63.02.50)

- Centre départemental du Tourisme de la **Charente**, 27, place Bouillaud, 16021 Charente (☎ 05.45.69.79.09, ✉ cdtcharente@a2i-micro.fr – for *gîtes*: use the same address and phone number)

- Centre départemental du Tourisme de la **Charente-Maritime**, 85, boulevard de la République, 17076 La Rochelle (☎ 05.46.31.71.71, ✉ accueil-cdt17@wanadoo.fr – for *gîtes*: 22, rue Saint Yon, 17000 La Rochelle, ☎ 05.46.50.63.63)

- Centre départemental du Tourisme des **Deux-Sèvres**, 15, rue Thiers, BP 8150, 79025 Niort cedex 9 (☎ 05.49.77.19.70, 💻 www.tourisme-deux-sevres.com – for *gîtes*: 15, rue Thiers, BP 8524, 79025 Niort, ☎ 05.49. 24.00.42)

- Centre départemental du Tourisme de la **Loire-Atlantique**, 2, allée Baco, BP 20502, 44005 Nantes cedex 1 (☎ 02.51.72.95.30, 💻 www.cdt44.com – for *gîtes*: 1, allée Baco, BP 93218, 44032 Nantes cedex 1, ☎ 02.51. 72.95.65)

- Centre départemental du Tourisme de l'Anjou [**Maine-et-Loire**], place du Président Kennedy, BP 2147, 49021 Angers cedex 2 (☎ 02.41.23.51.51, 💻 www.anjou-tourisme.com – for *gîtes*: same address, ☎ 02.41.23.51.53)

- Centre départemental du Tourisme de la **Mayenne**, 81, avenue Robert Buron, BP 1429, 53014 Laval cedex 2 (☎ 02.43.53.18.18, 💻 www. tourisme-mayenne.co – for *gîtes*: same address and phone number)

- Centre départemental du Tourisme de la **Sarthe**, 40, rue Joinville, 72000 Le Mans (☎ 02.43.40.22.50 – for *gîtes*: 78, avenue du Général Leclerc, 72000 Le Mans, ☎ 03.43.23.84.61, 💻 www. tourisme.sarthe.com)

- Centre départemental du Tourisme de la **Vendée**, 8, place Napoléon, BP 233, 85006 La Roche-sur-Yon (☎ 02.51.47.88.32, 💻 www.vendee-tourisme.com – for *gîtes*: 124, boulevard Aristide Briand, BP 735, 85018 La Roche-sur-Yon, ☎ 02.51.62.15.19)

- Centre départemental du Tourisme de la **Vienne**, 1bis, rue Victor Hugo, BP 287, 86007 Poitiers (☎ 05.49.37.48.48, 💻 www.vienne.org – for *gîtes*: same address, ☎ 05.49.37.48.54)

● Gîtes de France, 59, rue Saint-Lazare, 75009 Paris (☎ 01.49.70.75.75,
  💻 www.gites-de-france.fr)

Useful Publications

● **The Vendée: An English Family Guide**, Angela Bird (Editions Hécate)

Useful Websites

💻 www.netcomuk.co.uk/~anjbird/index.html (information about the Vendée
compiled by Angela Bird, author of *The Vendée* – see above)

Rocamadour — The Lot Valley

The area described in this chapter is one of vast contrasts, both geographically and economically. Situated south of the centre of France, it includes the following departments: Allier (03), Cantal (15), Corrèze (19), Creuse (23), Dordogne (24), Haute-Loire (43), Lot (46), Puy-de-Dôme (63) and Haute-Vienne (87). The geography changes from west to east and from north to south. From the relatively low, rounded hills and plains in the west around Limoges (87) the terrain climbs until, in the west of the area around Clermont-Ferrand (63), the mountains reach a peak of 1,885m (6,180ft). From north to south, with a small ascent around the Plateau Millevaches (978m/3,200ft) the terrain becomes flatter and rockier until you reach the vineyards around Cahors (46) and the caves of Dordogne and Lot. The Auvergne is 25 per cent woodland, 45 per cent grassland, 20 per cent arable land and 10 per cent other uses (including urban areas). Limousin is also 25 per cent woodland, but only 30 per cent grassland and 10 per cent arable land, with 35 per cent of its land unused or built on.

Economically, the area comprises some of the richest and some of the poorest departments in France. Dordogne, with its many *châteaux* and majestic river of the same name, has become virtually self-sufficient thanks to tourism and an influx of Britons and Dutch, who have been buying houses in the area for 30 years or more. On the other hand, departments such as Creuse and Haute-Loire are suffering from the decline of agriculture and an ageing population, and parts of Lot are relatively poor, although in the area around Cahors, with its wine industry, the economy is booming.

In each section, the department of Dordogne (in the region of Aquitaine) and Lot (in Midi-Pyrénées) will be considered separately from the Auvergne and Limousin. For information about the rest of Aquitaine and the Midi-Pyrénées, see **Chapter 5**.

Dordogne

The ancient province of Périgord, Dordogne is south-west of the centre of France and is surrounded by Charente (16) and Haute-Vienne (87) to the north, Charente-Maritime (17) and Gironde (33) to the west, Corrèze (19) to the east and Lot-et-Garonne (47) and Lot (46) to the south. It's France's third-largest department, covering an area of 9,060km² (3,533mi²), and has a population of just under 400,000. Like many French departments, Dordogne is named after the main river flowing through it. It's split into four territories. In the north is 'Green Périgord', so called because of its green valleys irrigated by a multitude of streams. This territory contains the Périgord-Limousin Regional Natural Park and its main towns include Brantôme, Nontron and Riberac. In the centre is 'White Périgord', which takes its name from the limestone plateaux and contains the departmental capital, Périgueux. In the south-west corner of Dordogne is the newly identified territory of

'Purple Périgord', which includes the Bergerac area, famous for its wine grapes (hence 'purple'), and French and English fortified towns, castles and *châteaux* built during the Hundred Years War (Dordogne boasts some 10 per cent of France's 40,000 *châteaux*). In the south-east is 'Black Périgord', so called on account of the ancient oak trees covering large parts of the area and home to the valleys of the rivers Dordogne and Vézère. Perhaps the territory best known to foreigners, Black Périgord has been inhabited since prehistory and contains the famous caves at Lascaux and Les Eyzies (among others) and the picturesque towns of Saint-Cyprien and Sarlat-la-Canéda.

Dordogne has for a long time been a holiday and migration destination for Britons (the French call the area around Ribérac 'little England') and more recently Dutch and Germans. During the late 1980s, the demand was so great for ruined farms and houses that a mini-boom was created. Prices are more reasonable now and bargains can still be found, but it's still the most expensive department in this area for the simple reason that it's one of the most scenic departments in France and contains some of the country's prettiest and most dramatic towns and villages, including Brantôme, Domme, La Roque-Gageac, Sarlat-la-Canéda and Trémolat. Domme and Sarlat are the jewels of Dordogne and are so popular that they're in danger of being ruined by tourism (it's almost impossible to find a grocer's amongst the tourist shops and artist's galleries along the main road in Domme).

Most of what makes Dordogne memorable is to be found in a 15km (10mi) stretch of the river between Bergerac and Souillac (in Lot), but every village has history in its buildings, whether churches, *châteaux* or ordinary houses inhabited by the same family for generations. Dordogne is also a treasure trove of caves filled with prehistoric paintings up to 30,000 years old. Lascaux and Les Eyzies are the two major sites and perhaps the best known. The river itself provides other distractions for inhabitants and holidaymakers (see **Amenities** on page 141), although the latter can be a nuisance to the former in high season. Local cuisine includes truffles and *pâté de foie gras* (the best French *foie gras* is considered to come from Sarlat) and is noted for its duck and goose dishes.

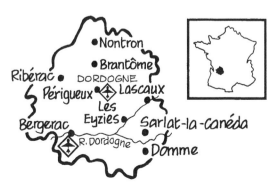

Lot

Also named after its principal river, Lot (the 't' is pronounced) is part of the Midi-Pyrénées region, which stretches from the Auvergne and Limousin in the north to the Spanish border in the south. Lot has borders with six other departments: Aveyron (12), Cantal (15), Corrèze (19), Dordogne (24), Haute-Garonne (31), Lot-et-Garonne (47) and Tarn-et-Garonne (82). It has an area of 5,200km² (3,250mi²) and a population of just over 160,000. Lot is geographically diverse, which contributes to its climatic variations (see page 139). The altitude rises from west to east as you approach the Massif Central, and the highest point in the department is 780m (2,550ft) above sea level.

Two major rivers cross the department: the Dordogne in the north and the Lot, with its many tributaries, in the south. The Dordogne basin is lush with small valleys, bubbling streams and tall cliffs (on which are perched many dramatic *châteaux*). In the southern half of the department are the *causses*, rocky plateaux and hills full of caves, and *Quercy blanc* ('White Quercy') – so called because of the white limestone used in the area's distinctive buildings. These plateaux are mainly hot and dry with little cultivation. In the extreme south, hemmed in by cliffs, are the plains of the Lot valley, covered with the vines of Cahors.

The department is rich in history and boasts many ancient and picturesque towns, including Rocamadour, a town built into the cliffs and France's second-most visited place outside Paris (after the Mont Saint-Michel in Brittany) and Souillac, 'where culture and history meet' (according to the tourist guides).

Like many of the departments described in this chapter, Lot is experiencing the decline of agriculture and ageing of the population. However, according to the last census in 1999, Lot's population has risen back to the level of 1936. This can in part be accounted for by the migration of both French and foreigners (mainly British) to the area. Tourism has contributed greatly to the economy of the department, as it has a lot to offer to both tourists and the many people who have second homes here (one in five houses is a second home). Surprisingly, a recent survey concluded that properties for sale in Lot were on average the second-most expensive in France outside Paris!

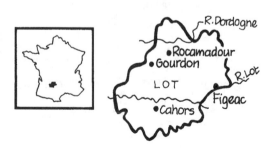

Auvergne

The Auvergne covers an area of 26,000km² (16,250mi²) at the heart of the Massif Central (the volcanic region in the centre of France) and has a population of 1.3 million. The Auvergne includes the departments of Allier (03), Cantal (15), Haute-Loire (43) and Puy-de-Dôme (63). The main towns are Ambert, Aurillac, Clermont-Ferrand, Le Puy-en-Velay, Moulins and Vichy. The region is unique in France, as Europe's largest group of volcanoes (now extinct) have created a landscape of mountains (Mont Dore reaches 1,885m/6,180ft), craters, lakes, rivers (the Dordogne springs from near Mont-Dore), springs (including Arvie, Mont-Dore, Saint-Yorre, Vichy and Volvic), spas and lava flows, all of which combine to create a huge geological park. The region contains two regional parks and two nature parks, and in February 2002 a volcano theme park opened, including volcano-related exhibits and a guided tour around the crater of an extinct volcano (see **Leisure** on page 143).

This natural heritage is complemented by a rich cultural and historical heritage: more than 500 Romanesque churches (some of which are considered France's best), almost 50 *châteaux* and ten spa towns. The Auvergne also contains ten of the 'most beautiful villages of France', four of which are in Haute-Loire. The regional capital, Clermont-Ferrand (headquarters of Michelin, the tyre manufacturer and tourist guide producer), is mainly built from dark basalt, making an impressive and unusual townscape. There are

nine ski centres, 200km (125mi) of downhill runs and more than 800km (500mi) of cross-country trails.

Water plays an important part in the economy of the region. Many lakes have formed in valleys blocked by lava streams, e.g. at Aydat and Guéry, or where volcanoes have erupted in valleys, e.g. at Chambon and Montcineyre. Many anglers and watersports enthusiasts use these lakes, along with rivers such as the Allier and the Cher. The many hot springs in the area also owe their existence to volcanic activity. Water temperature ranges from 10°C (50°F) to over 80°C (Chaudes-Aigues is the hottest spring in Europe at 82.3°C/180°F) and the springs are sought after by people who wish to 'take a cure'. Vichy, in Allier, is probably the best known spa town, having waters that are used for drinking and for balneology, and is also famous for its bottled water.

The region is predominantly agricultural with tourism slowly becoming more important. Cows are much in evidence and are used both for meat and for milk, which is made into a number of well known cheeses: Bleu d'Auvergne, Cantal, Forme d'Ambert and Saint-Nectaire. Green lentils have been cultivated in Puy-en-Velay (43) since Gallo-Roman times and are the first vegetable to be given a quality classification as for wine. Excellent wine (both red and white) is also made from the Saint-Pourçain vineyard (one of the oldest in France) stretched along the banks of the Allier.

Limousin

Limousin is the name of the old province surrounding the town of Limoges, situated between Paris and Toulouse and west of the Massif Central. It covers an area of 16,942km^2 (10,600mi^2) and has a population of less than 725,000. It's composed of three departments: Corrèze (19 – the department of President

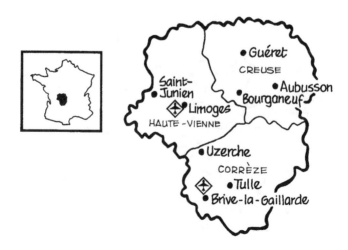

Jacques Chirac and his wife, who is a town councillor), Creuse (23) and Haute-Vienne (87). The main towns are Brive-la-Gaillarde (19), Guéret (23) and Limoges (87). The region is world-renowned for Limoges porcelain and enamels and the tapestries of Aubusson. The region has also given its name to a school of painting known as the Crozant school, after the place where Monet painted his first series, and is home to the Centre for Contemporary Art at Vassivière.

Limousin is predominantly agricultural with very little heavy industry, which makes it largely unpolluted and unspoilt by modern industrial buildings. Being in the foothills of the Massif Central, the region features rolling hills and valleys (the lowest point, around Brive-la-Gaillarde, is almost 200m/655ft above sea level and the highest is 978m/3,200ft) without the bleakness of some mountainous areas, and almost 35 per cent of the area is forested (compared with 27 per cent nationally). Its mountains and forests, coupled with the many lakes, rivers and streams that flow into either the Loire or the Garonne, make Limousin a rural holiday paradise, and it's also becoming increasingly popular with foreign homebuyers. Limousin also boasts a vast man-made lake, the Lac de Vassivière (1,100ha/2,700 acres), the largest used for water-sports in the country and featuring beaches and adjoining holiday complexes, and is noted for its chocolate and Golden Delicious apples (reputed to be the best in the world).

ADVANTAGES & DISADVANTAGES

The main advantages of this part of France are the scenic countryside, attractive towns and villages and pleasant climate. The area is steeped in history and has many natural attractions. Being south of the Loire, the regions' weather is generally better than in the north (except for the mountainous areas) and the summers aren't as hot as in the south, although summer sun and high temperatures aren't guaranteed except in Dordogne and Lot (which means that they attract many more tourists than the other areas). For many people, the Auvergne and Limousin are unexplored territory. Those that buy houses in the region are attracted by the low prices (amongst the lowest in France) and the unspoilt countryside. Dordogne and Lot, on the other hand, are in danger of being too well known and consequently expensive.

Both departments are quite 'Anglicised' with pubs, cricket clubs and English newspapers, so if you want to remain in touch with British culture they're an ideal choice. Although it's possible to avoid the Brits in Dordogne and Lot, those looking to embrace French life may do better to investigate the Auvergne and Limousin. Here, however, being able to speak French is almost essential, as there are few English shops, church services, newspapers, etc. Finding information outside the summer season, when the tourist offices are closed, can be difficult, although things have improved in recent years. Some newspapers translate the local diary of events into English, and local radio and television stations broadcast tourist information in English. It can also be surprisingly cold in Limousin in the autumn and spring, as well as in winter.

The general lack of public transport outside the main towns is another disadvantage (unless you're wedded to your car). Buses run in the largest towns but rarely venture far from the centre and in rural areas what little public transport there is stops running after 18.00. The main train lines out of Paris serve most (but not all) of the main towns and there are buses that connect the rest, but if you wish to travel from east to west or vice versa, there are fewer (and slower) trains and more stops. The road network follows a similar layout to the railways, although the A/N89 from Clermont-Ferrand to Bordeaux provides a major east-west route (see **Roads** on page 157).

Those looking to live and work in the area may be affected by the general lack of employment (see **Employment Prospects** on page 159), and those considering buying a home in Limousin should be aware that much of the area, particularly in and around the department of Haute-Vienne (87), is composed of granite, which is slightly radioactive. On the other hand, the town of Limoges (87) has more green space than almost any other major town in France, with over 100m^2 per inhabitant.

MAJOR TOWNS & PLACES OF INTEREST

These are listed below by department.

Allier (03)

Montluçon (pop. 45,000) with the attractive Saint-Pierre church and a museum of musical instruments; Moulins (22,800), the departmental capital and 'capital' of the ancient Bourbonnais region (the pasture lands of northern Auvergne, which were once an independent state belonging to the Bourbons) with an interesting cathedral; Vichy (27,700), the quintessential spa town, with *Belle Époque* glass-roofed shopping galleries; La-Loge-des-Gardes ski resort (see page 142); Hérisson (meaning 'hedgehog'!), one of France's most beautiful villages.

Cantal (15)

Aurillac (pop. 30,000), the departmental capital; Salers, one of France's most beautiful villages, with typical 15th and 16th century buildings and a cheese factory; the Parc naturel régional de Volcans d'Auvergne, the biggest natural park in France (120km/75mi from north to south and covering almost 4,000km^2/1,560mi^2); Le Lioran ski resort (see page 142).

Corrèze (19)

Brive-la-Gaillarde (pop. 51,600), the largest town in the department; Tulle (16,900), the departmental capital; Uzerche (3,500) with its grey slate roofs, turrets and bell towers; medieval Turrene and the nearby 16th century collegiate church; the villages of Collonges-la-Rouge, built from carmine sandstone, and Saint-Robert, host to an annual arts festival, considered to be among the most beautiful in France.

Creuse (23)

Guéret (pop. 15,800), the departmental capital; the Lac de Courtille, a large swimming and water activities lake; Aubusson (5,000), famous for tapestry making, with the Musée départemental de la Tapisserie and factory where tapestries are made and repaired; Bourganeuf (3,500) with its beautifully painted medieval church; Crozant with its ruined castle painted by Monet; Chambon-sur-Vouèze with its impressive church; the Gorges de Verger park, where George Sand often stayed.

Dordogne (24)

The departmental capital, Périgueux (pop. 32,000), whose Saint-Front cathedral is the largest in south-west France, with the Musée du Périgord, one of the country's most complete prehistory museums; Bergerac (28,000), famous for its wines and the Musée du Tabac; Sarlat-La-Canéda (10,500) with a concentration of medieval, renaissance and 17th century buildings and an impressive Saturday market specialising in *foie gras*, truffles and walnuts; several of France's most beautiful villages, including Beynac, Monpazier, La Roque-Gageac and Domme, a fortress town with medieval gateways perched over the Dordogne and offering spectacular views; the painted prehistoric caves at Les Eyzies and Lascaux II (an exact copy of the real thing, which is closed to the public in order to preserve the paintings).

Haute-Loire (43)

Le Puy-en-Velay (pop. 23,000), the departmental capital and a medieval Holy City known for lace making and the 'Black Madonna' in its cathedral; Brioude (7,300) with its impressive Basilique St Julien; La Chaise-Dieu with its abbey church of Saint Robert featuring carved choirs, tapestries and 'echo room'; Chapelle-Saint-Michel-d'Aiguille perched on a finger of lava rock; Arlempdes, where the remains of a medieval fortress are perched on a rock above the Loire; Les Estables ski resort (see page 142).

Lot (46)

Cahors (pop. 19,750), the departmental capital, with its 12th-century cathedral and Pont Valentré, a fortified bridge with seven pointed arches (supposedly the most photographed monument in France); Figeac (10,000), a medieval centre with 13th, 14th and 15th century buildings; Rocamadour, a spectacular medieval village built into the cliffs of the river Alzou gorge; Autoire and Saint-Cirq-Lapopie, among France's most beautiful villages; the Chapel de Notre Dame, a pilgrim destination and reportedly a place of miracles; the Gouffre de Padirac, a huge crater with a succession of 'galleries', including the Salle de Grand Dôme, bigger than the world's largest cathedral.

Puy-de-Dôme (63)

Clermont-Ferrand (pop. 140,000), the regional and departmental capital, with its Basilique Notre-Dame-du-Port – one of the most important Romanesque churches in the region – and the 12th and 13th century Cathédral de Notre Dame de l'Assomption built from dark volcanic rock with superb stained glass windows; Issoire (15,000) with its church of Saint Austremoine – one of the great Romanesque churches of the region; Thiers (15,000), a medieval town with narrow, winding streets and a knife museum; the village of Saint-Nectaire with an interesting church; Mont Dore, the highest point in central France, with its casino incorporating a children's casino(!?); six ski resorts (see page 142); the Vulcania museum near Clermont-Ferrand (see page 143).

Haute-Vienne (87)

Limoges (pop. 140,000), the regional and departmental capital, with its Musée national Adrien-Dubouché tracing the history of porcelain making; nearby Oradour-sur-Glane, a village burnt to the ground with its inhabitants by the Germans during World War II and preserved as a memorial; Saint-Junien (13,000) with its 11th century collegiate church; Saint-Leonard-de-Noblat (3,650) with its Romanesque collegiate church and railway museum; Rochechouart with its *château*; Le Dorat, an attractive village; the Lac de Vassivière (1,100ha/2,700 acres), offering many water-based activities.

POPULATION

The area covered by this chapter has one of the lowest population densities in France and few large towns; only Clermont-Ferrand and Limoges have over 52,000 inhabitants (for city and town populations, see **Major Towns & Places of Interest** above).

Dordogne has a population of almost 388,400, whereas Lot has only just over 160,000, which makes it one of the most sparsely populated departments in France, with a density of just 31 people per km² (80 per mi²) compared with the national average of around 100 people per km² (260 per mi²). The population of both departments is growing at a slightly above average rate for France, whereas the population of the Auvergne and Limousin is in decline (Champagne-Ardenne was the only other French region to decrease in population between the national censuses of 1990 and 1999 but at a much slower rate). The Auvergne has a population of 1.3 million, with 51 inhabitants per km² (132 per mi²). Vichy (03) has the fastest-ageing population of any major town in France. Limousin has 710,000 inhabitants with an average density of 42 people per km² (109 per mi²) and one of the oldest populations in France (the department of Creuse holds the record); at the last census there were 247 people over the age of 100 in the region!

Although it's generally thought that the British are the most numerous immigrants in this area, in fact the Portuguese, Moroccans, Turks and Algerians outnumber them by far. Even in Dordogne, there are over 2,300 Portuguese and almost 1,300 Moroccans. There are a further 1,380 non-EU nationals, and the British (some 80 per cent of whom are retired!) are among 4,435 resident non-French EU nationals. Lot has 1,250 Portuguese, 475 Moroccans, 380 Spanish and 150 Italians out of a total of 4,875 foreigners. In the Auvergne, of the 23,375 official non-French EU residents, 16,450 are Portuguese and the remaining 7,000 or so include all other EU nationalities as well as British, whereas there are 5,460 Moroccans, 4,625 Turks and 3,750 Algerian residents. Similarly, in Limousin, a quarter of the 20,000 or so foreign residents are Portuguese; Moroccans and Turks come next at 14 per cent each, Algerians third at 10.5 per cent and the British fourth at 5.2 per cent. All other nationalities represent less than 5 per cent of the foreign population. Haute-Vienne (87) is home to half of the foreigners living in the region, of which more than a third come from the EU. More than 75 per cent of Limousin's foreign residents live in urban areas.

LANGUAGE

Dordogne, Lot and southern parts of the Auvergne and Limousin are within the part of France where the *Langue d'Oc* or *Occitan* is spoken (see page 221), but French is also universally spoken!

CLIMATE

The climate varies considerably within the area, as described below.

Dordogne: Winters are usually wet and cold (but not too cold and not too long) and summers are hot and humid; the most pleasant seasons are spring and autumn, when the Dordogne is at its best. Périgueux enjoys as much sunshine as Toulouse, with over 2,000 hours per year.

Lot: Lot has both an Atlantic and a continental climate, which means that in places the weather is predominantly mild, while in others it's hot and dry.

Auvergne: The climate in this mountainous area is both damper and colder than that of the plains to the north and west. Winters are long and cold with often damaging late frosts, while summers are short and hot. Snow tends to fall later in the Massif Central than in the Alps and the Pyrenees, and the ski season doesn't usually start until January or even February. Clermont-Ferrand is one of the driest French towns north of Toulouse, with rain on only 90 days per year.

Limousin: Limousin's climate is oceanic and varies according to the altitude but is generally mild; summer temperatures can reach 38°C, but it can be quite cold in the autumn and spring, as well as in winter. Rainfall is generally moderate, averaging 750mm (29in) per year, although Limoges is one of France's rainiest towns, with rain on 135 days annually. Snow often falls on high ground in winter.

The table below shows the number of hours' sunshine and number of days' rainfall in selected towns in the area.

Town	Sunshine Hours	Days' Rainfall
Vichy (03)	1,880	118
Brive-la-Gaillarde (19)	1,977	120
Périgueux (24)	2,025	118
Clermont-Ferrand (63)	1,907	90
Limoges (87)	1,974	135

COST OF LIVING

The cost of living in most of the area is around average for France, although the cost of most items is inevitably higher in remote areas of the Auvergne and Limousin, where the need for a car further increases expenses. On the other hand, the higher price of property in Dordogne and Lot is a significant factor in the cost of living in these departments. Property taxes and water prices vary considerably from commune to commune (as they do throughout France) without any definable pattern, rates being set by local rather than national or regional authorities.

CRIME RATE & SECURITY

This area of France is a relatively safe place to live, and car and house insurance are among the cheapest in France. Cantal, Creuse, Dordogne,

Haute-Loire and Haute-Vienne are among the departments with the lowest (reported) crime rates in France. Périgueux (24) has seen the second-highest decrease in crime rates over the last two years of any major town in France and now enjoys the country's second-lowest crime rate. Even Allier, Corrèze and Puy-de-Dôme have only slightly higher crime rates and Montluçon (03) has the third-lowest crime rate among France's major towns. That isn't to say, of course, that crime can be ignored. In summer, in the tourist areas, there's a significant and increasing rate of pick-pocketing and theft from cars. And, as this is an area where there are many second and holiday homes which are left empty for months at a time, it's a favourite haunt of burglars. From time to time, the police remind homeowners to be on the lookout for people (generally in white vans) who 'explore' an area searching for isolated houses that are closed up; they make a number of 'passes' and, if a house is empty every time, consider it a safe target. Fortunately, this sort of crime is still fairly rare but, unfortunately, it's also on the increase. Limoges (87) in particular suffered a 30 per cent increase in crimes between 1998 and 2000. For general information on crime in France, see page 52.

AMENITIES

Sports

In an effort to combat unemployment and boost the local economy, all the departments in this area have included sport in their development strategy and, despite it not having the weather of the south or being close to the sea, the area offers a great diversity of sporting activities, including swimming, cycling (mountain, road and downhill), potholing, canoeing, hang-gliding, hiking, tennis, skiing and horse riding. From the plains around Limoges to the mountains of the Massif Central and the valleys and gorges of Lot, there's something for everyone. The information below is a selection of the facilities available; details can be obtained from regional and departmental tourist offices (see **Further Information** on page 160) and from the associations listed below.

Golf: As throughout France, golf is becoming increasingly popular in this area. The table below lists the number of courses in each department.

Department	No. of Courses
Allier	2 x 9 holes, 4 x 18 holes
Cantal	1 x 9 holes, 2 x 18 holes
Corrèze	2 x 9 holes, 1 x 18 holes, 2 x 27 holes
Creuse	1 x 18 holes

Dordogne	3 x 9 holes, 3 x 18 holes
Haute-Loire	1 x 9 holes, 1 x 12 holes, 1 x 18 holes
Haute-Vienne	2 x 18 holes, 1 x 27 holes
Puy-de-Dôme	3 x 9 holes, 1 x 18 holes

Information (in both French and English) on how to find courses, the cost of a round (which varies between €15 and €50), etc. is available via the Internet (🖳 www.backspin.com).

Canoeing & Rafting: These sports are becoming increasingly popular among both tourists and residents on the area's many rivers, particularly through the gorges of the Dordogne and Lot rivers (contact the Comité départemental de Canoë/Kayak, Bureau 218, Espace Associatif, place Bessières, 46000 Cahors, ☎ 05.65.35.91.59 and the Ligue de Canoë-Kayak d'Auvergne, Plan d'Eau, rue des Laveuses, Cournon-d'Auvergne, ☎ 04.73.84.30.06).

Skiing: Skiing is popular in the Massif Central (Auvergne), where there are nine ski centres offering 200km (125mi) of downhill runs and more than 800km (500mi) of cross-country trails:

● Cambon-des-Nieges (63), ☎ 04.73.88.62.62, 🖳 www.grandvallee.com;

● Chastreix-Sancy (63), ☎ 04.73.21.53.87, 🖳 www.sancy.com/fr/chastreix;

● Les Estables (43), ☎ 04.71.08.31.08;

● Le Lioran (15), ☎ 04.71.49.50.08, 🖳 www.lelioran.com;

● La-Loge-des-Gardes (03), ☎ 04.70.59.38.40;

● Le Mont-Dore (63), ☎ 04.73.65.20.21, 🖳 www.mont-dore.com;

● Murat-le-Quaire (63), ☎ 04.73.65.53.13, 🖳 www.murat-le-quaire.com;

● Saint-Anthème/Prabouré (63), ☎ 04.73.95.20.64;

● SuperBesse (63), ☎ 04.73.79.52.84, 🖳 www.super-besse.com.

Other Mountain Sports: In summer, the mountains are popular for **horse riding** (contact the Comité Régional FFME, ☎ 04.73.90.69.79), **mountain biking, climbing** (Montagne Auvergne, 23 place Delille, Centre Couthon, 63000 Clermont-Ferrand, ☎ 04.73.90.23.14, ✉ montagne.auvergne@wanadoo.fr and Base de la Minoterie, 19140 Uzerche, ☎ 05.55.73.02.84, 🖳 http://perso.wanadoo.fr/vezere.passion/), **caving** (Bureau de Sports Nature, Conduché, 46330 Bouziés, ☎ 05.65.24.21.07) and **hang-gliding** (Ligue d'Auvergne de Vol Libre, 4, chemin des Garennes, 63960 Veyre-Monton, ☎ 04.73.69.72.00).

Cycling: As throughout France, cycling is popular, especially in the Auvergne, where there are over 30 marked road circuits and hundreds of kilometres of marked off-road trails (contact the Ligue régional d'Auvergne de Cyclotourisme, rue Guérat, 03500 Saulcet, ☎ 04.70.45.56.87, the Comité régional Cyclisme d'Auvergne, 114, bvd Lavoisier, 63000 Clermont-Ferrand, ☎ 04.73.37.95.15, the Comité départemental de Cyclotourisme, route Angoulême, 24000 Périgueux, ☎ 05.53.35.39.58 and the Comité départemental de Cyclotourisme, Grande Rue, 46240 Labastide-Murat, ☎ 05. 65.31.08.02) and in Limousin, where there's a mountain bike centre with 400km (250mi) of trails and new downhill slopes near Guéret (contact the Comité Limousin du Cyclisme, 3, impasse Mas Neuf, 87000 Limoges, ☎ 05. 55.35.16.26 and Espace VTT-FCC des Monts de Guéret, ☎ 05.55.52.14.29). Note, however that cycling is best avoided during the peak summer season, when temperatures are high and roads, particularly in Dordogne, are full of cars and coaches. Many of the roads near the river Dordogne, for example, are extremely narrow and leave little place for two cars to pass, and cyclists risk being flattened.

Other Sports: Other popular sports include **football**, **hiking** and **tennis** (contact the Ligue Régional du Limousin, 41, rue Feytiat, 87000 Limoges, ☎ 05.55.31.81.00). **Anglers** will also find plenty of opportunity for fishing, particularly for trout and carp, in the area's many rivers and lakes. Hunting is a popular 'sport', particularly in the Auvergne and Limousin. There are hunting clubs and associations in many towns and even in some villages (see page 52).

Leisure

The area is a paradise for nature lovers with its mountains, valleys, rivers, lakes, forests and natural parks. Those interested in architecture and history will find plenty to stimulate them in the many ancient villages and *châteaux*, not to mention the caves of Lascaux and Les Eyzies, and there are also numerous vineyards (and local wines) to explore around Bergerac (24) and Cahors (46) as well as those of Saint-Pourçain in Allier. 'Taking the waters' in one of the spa towns can be combined with a (less healthy?) visit to the casino, as there are no fewer than 13 casinos in the area, all in spa towns (casinos were originally permitted only in spa towns): 12 in the Auvergne – in Bourbon-l'Archambault, Néris-les-Bains and Vichy (03), Chaudes-Aigues and Vic-sur-Cère (15), Allègre (43), La Bourboule, Chatel-Guyon, Le Mont-Dore, Royat and Saint-Nectaire (63) – and one in Limousin: in Evaux-les-Bains (23). These are open all year and offer other entertainment, such as shows and restaurants, as well as gambling. Details of all casinos and what they offer are available via the Internet (e.g. 🖳 www.journaldescasinos.com – partly in English). There are numerous fairs and festivals in the region, including the Corrèze Festival of music and drama in Limousin in August and, in the same month, a Scottish Fête in Saint-Orse (24)!

Other types of leisure facility are limited, particularly in winter, unless you live in or near a large town. There are, however, a number of zoos, animal parks, activity centres, aquariums and bird sanctuaries in the area offering (mainly in the summer months) many attractions, especially for children. The major venues are listed below.

- Hippodrome de Vichy (03): racecourse for both flat racing and trotting;
- Aquarium du Limousin in Limoges (87): 300 species and 2,500 fish;
- Aquarium du Périgord Noir in Le Bugue-sur-Vézère (24): 10,000 freshwater fish;
- L'Archipel in Cahors (46): water park;
- Bowling Club Limousin at Feytiat, near Limoges (87);
- La Cité des Insectes in Nedde (87): the name says it all;
- Corrèze Montgolfière (19): hot-air ballooning;
- La Féerie du Rail in Rocamadour (46): automatons;
- Ferme équestre la Haute Yerle in Alles-sur-Dordogne (24): horse-riding centre;
- La Forêt des Singes in Rocamadour (46): monkey park;
- Jardin d'Eyrignac in Salignac-Eyvigues (24): one of the finest gardens in France;
- Labyrinthus du Lot in Martel (46): mazes;
- Les Loups de Chabrières near Guéret (23): wolves in their natural habitat and an astronomical observatory;
- Mirabel near Riom (63): theme and animal park;
- Le Pal near Moulins (03): animal park with 500 animals from the five continents;
- Parc animalier de Gramat (46): 150 rare species of animal;
- Le Parc de la Droséra near Thiers (63): 50 models of local monuments in a 10ha (25 acre) park;
- Parc Préhistologia in Lacave (46): caves and prehistory park;
- Parc du Thot Espace Cro-Magnon in Thonac (24): prehistory park;
- Parc Zoologique du Bouy (63): zoo with 500 animals;
- Port miniature in Ambert (63): as the name suggests, a miniature port for children;
- Préhistoparc in Tursac (24): prehistory park;

- Quercyland in Souillac (46): water park;
- La Récréation in Castelnau-Montratier (46): children's activity park;
- Repriland in Martel-en-Quercy (46): 250 reptiles, including crocodiles;
- Le Village du Bournat in Le Bugue-sur-Vézère (24): reconstruction of a 19th century village;
- Vulcania near Clermont-Ferrand (63): museum dedicated to volcanoes and earth sciences.

English-language Cinema & Theatre

Some cinemas show all foreign films in the original language (*en version originale/VO*), e.g. Cinéma le Club in Brive-la-Gaillarde (19), while others do so only on certain days of the month or on demand. The cinema in Sarlat-la-Canéda (24) shows English-language films at least once a month, and English-language films can also be seen at the Cinéma Lux in Le Buisson (24). A useful website for finding out which films are on in a given area, which also indicates whether the films are being shown in the original language is 🖳 www.cinefil.com. There's also a regional film festival in Sarlat (24) during November, which shows a good selection of foreign and French films.

There are no theatres in the area that show plays in English, although you may find performances of English-language plays in French!

Shopping Centres & Markets

Most large towns have a shopping complex or a super or hypermarket with parking and several smaller shops attached. There are few multi-storey shopping centres in Dordogne and Lot, where there tend to be 'commercial zones' – i.e. a large car park surrounded by a supermarket and several other shops. There's a Nouvelles Galeries department store in the centre of Périgueux (24) and a new shopping centre called La Feuilleraie with 50 shops on the outskirts of the town (off the RN21). There's also a covered market in Domme (24). Lot has two Leclerc hypermarkets: in Pradines (with 11 shops) and Capdenac (seven shops). The two main shopping centres in the Auvergne are the Centre de Vie Saint-Jacques in Montluçon (03) and the Centre Jaude in Clermont-Ferrand (63). In Limousin, there's a multi-storey commercial centre in Limoges (87) and two large commercial zones on the outskirts of the town (Centre Beaubreuil to the north and Centre Bosseuil to the south) as well as one on the outskirts of Brive-la-Gaillarde (19) incorporating a Carrefour hypermarket.

Daily and weekly markets can be found in the largest (and some of the smallest) towns across the whole of the area. Details can be provided by local town halls and tourist offices (see **Further Information** on page 160). Some of the major regular and annual markets and fairs are listed below:

Dordogne

All year	General market (every Saturday)	Sarlat-la-Canéda (24)
	Organic market (every Tuesday)	Bergerac (24)
June to Sept	Farm market	Biron (24)
July	Evening fair	Couze-Saint-Front (24)
August	Farm market	Eyvirat (24)

Lot

All year	Traditional market	Cahors & St Martel (46)
Dec to March	Truffle market	Limogne & Lalbenque (46)
June to Sept	Evening market	Cahors & Gourdon (46)

Auvergne

June	Regional products fair	Saint-Nectaire (63)
July	Cheese and wine fair	Besse-et-Saint-Anastaise (63)
August	Cheese and cow fair	Salers (15)
	Farm market	Le Breuil (63)
	Wine fair	Saint-Pourçain-sur-Sioule (03)
	Organic fair	Charbonnières-les-Varennes (63)
October	Wine harvest and apple fair	Le Vernet (03)
	Beer fair	Vichy (03)
November	Gastronomy, apple and traditional fruit fair	Massiac (43)

Limousin

June	Red fruit fair	Châteauneuf-la-Forêt (87)
June to Sept	Regional products market	Objat (19)
August	Regional products fair	Aubusson (23)
	Organic fair	Beaulieu-sur-Dordogne (19)

September	Bread, wine and cheese fair	Evaux-les-Bains (23)
October	Mushroom festival	Brive-la-Gaillarde (19)
November	Oyster fair	Sardent (23)

Foreign Food & Products

Most of the big supermarkets and the food departments of Monoprix and Galeries Lafayette have some foreign food and products. Usually, the bigger the shop, the bigger the selection. In some areas, there are *épiceries fines* (delicatessens) that stock some foreign food. There's a stall at the Tuesday market in Le Bugue (24) selling English products, and there's a butcher in Saint-Cyprien (24) who apparently makes English sausages from spices supplied to him by Britons living in the area! The English Shop, 22, rue du Temple, 24500 Eymet (☎ 05.53.23.79.39, ✉ englishshop@aol.com) sells English groceries, gifts and books, and the Librarie Millescamps, 7, rue Saint-Front, 24000 Périgueux (☎ 05.53.09.53.25, ✉ millescamps@wanadoo.fr) sells second-hand English and Australian books. For general information on obtaining foreign products in France, see page 147.

Restaurants & Bars

As in most of France, there's a multitude of restaurants and bars in this area, especially in the tourist towns. Sadly, with the increase of globalisation, the typical French café is slowly disappearing. However, it's still possible to find bars in smaller towns and villages serving a set menu with wine at lunchtime for around €10. If you want something other than regional food and French cuisine (and pizza), e.g. Chinese or Indian restaurants, you must look in the larger towns, several of which also have a McDonald's (if you're that desperate).

Almost every village has a bar, which opens early in the morning and usually offers local papers and cigarettes as well as drinks. Some provide simple meals or sandwiches at lunchtime, but most are closed by 20.00. The Pheasant Pluckers in Château-de-Lacomte near Carlucet (46) is a British-run bar and restaurant, and the Moulin de la Geneste campsite in Condat-sur-Ganaveix (19) has an 'English' pub, while Le Chêne Vert in Rollin near Saint-Pourçain (03) boasts the Irish Corner pub. Local specialities include lentils (in the Auvergne) and locally caught fish. As in most parts of France, vegetarian food is hard to find, but it's offered at Le Café de la Rivière in Le Bourg near Beynac (24) as well as English, French and Italian dishes.

SERVICES

International & Private Schools

There are no international schools in this area and the nearest are in Toulouse and Bordeaux (see page 187). However, the University of Clermont-Ferrand (63) accepts foreign students on an exchange programme. As across the whole of France, there are private schools from kindergarten to university level, and there are two in the area which cater for English-speaking students: the Lycée privé mixte Saint Joseph (☎ 05.53.31.33.09, 💻 www.stjoseph-sarlat.fr.st) in Sarlat-la-Canéda (24) and the Lycée privé Cénevol international (☎ 04.71. 59.72.52) in Le Chambon-sur-Lignon (43).

Language Schools

Language lessons are offered by a number of public and private bodies in the area, including those listed below. Language courses are also offered by local Chambres de Commerce et d'Industrie and Centres culturels, and the YES clubs (see **Clubs** on page 151) provide English-French conversation classes.

- CAVILAM in Vichy (03);
- Greta in Guéret (23), Cahors (46), Clermont-Ferrand (63) and Limoges (87).
- AFPA in Cahors (46) and Limoges (87);
- CEL in Montluçon, Moulins and Vichy (03), Brive-la-Gaillarde (19), Guéret (23) and Clermont-Ferrand (63);
- Centre de Langues et d'Etudes françaises in Clermont-Ferrand (63);
- CNED (Long Distance Learning) in Futuroscope (86);
- Université Blaise in Clermont-Ferrand (63).

Details of the above schools can be found on 💻 www.europa-pages.com. The French Consulate in London (see **Appendix A**) publishes a booklet called *Cours de français Langue étrangère et Stages pédagogiques du français Langue étrangère en France*, which includes a comprehensive list of schools and organisations providing French language courses throughout France.

Hospitals & Clinics

Most large towns have both hospitals and clinics, either in the town centre or on the outskirts. There are teaching hospitals (*CHU*) at Clermont-Ferrand and Limoges, where all services and medical procedures can be found. Both rated among the top ten hospitals in France in a survey published in August 2002 by *Le Point* magazine (Clermont-Ferrand ninth and Limoges tenth). There are also main hospitals at Montluçon and Vichy (03), Aurillac (15), Brive-la-Gaillarde and Tulle (19), Guéret (23), Périgueux (24), Le Puy-en-Velay (43), Cahors (46), Cébazat (63) and Saint-Junien (87). No hospitals or clinics in the area have English-language services, although many doctors and consultants have some knowledge of English.

Doctors & Dentists

The proportion of doctors to inhabitants varies from department to department: Vienne has the highest number (over 184 general practitioners and 163 specialists per 100,000 inhabitants) and Puy-de-Dôme is also well provided, whereas there are relatively few specialists in Dordogne and few doctors generally in Haute-Loire (fewer than 143 GPs and 95 specialists per 100,000 people). Nevertheless, it's usually easy to find and register with a doctor. There's no recognised list of English-speaking doctors and dentists (those provided by the British and American consulates in Bordeaux – see below – cover only that city and the surrounding area). The best source of information is other English-speaking residents, as word of mouth travels faster than any printed list. However, most French doctors speak at least a little English. It's worth noting that there's a bilingual optician in Périgueux (Atol Opticiens Carrefour, ☎ 05.53.03.14.14).

Tradesmen

It's fairly easy to find English-speaking tradesmen in most areas, especially Dordogne and Lot, although they don't advertise as such in local papers and, as with doctors and dentists, the consulates in Bordeaux (see below) can supply lists of English-speaking tradesmen only in that area. The Chambre de Métiers (Chamber of Trades) can provide a list of all builders, stonemasons and other artisans, who must be registered in the *Répertoire des Métiers* (trades register). There has been a number of cases recently of unregistered builders being caught and fined. You should therefore always ask to see a tradesman's professional card and examples of his work. Magazines such as *French Property News* and newspapers such as *The News* (see **Appendix B**) carry advertisements by English-speaking tradesmen. French tradesmen are unlikely to speak much English but are generally reliable.

English-language Radio

Despite the number of Britons in the area, there's no dedicated English-language radio station (a business opportunity, perhaps?), although there's a weekly programme in English (every Saturday between 18.00 and 19.00) on Antenne d'Oc, which broadcasts on 88.1 and 89FM from Le Boulve and Cahors (46). However, BBC Radio 1, 2, 3, and 4 can be received on your television via the Astra satellite, and you can listen to recordings of radio programmes on Radio 1, 2, 3, 4, 5, 6 and 1Extra on your computer via the Internet (go to 💻 www.bbc.co.uk/radio/aod/index.shtml). The World Service is available on short wave (for frequency details, go to 💻 www.bbc.co.uk/worldservice/schedules/frequencies/eurwfreq.shtml) and via the Astra satellite. Local music stations usually broadcast 60 per cent non-French language songs, most of which are in English.

English-language Press

In larger towns it's possible to find major international newspapers such as *The International Herald Tribune*, the *Guardian* and the *European Financial Times* on the day of publication (although not normally before breakfast). There are two main English-language periodicals that are published in France and distributed nationally, *The News* (monthly) and *France Review* (bimonthly) – both of which incidentally have their offices in Dordogne (see **Further Information** on page 160 and **Appendix B**).

Consulates

The nearest British consulate for the south-west of France (i.e. covering Dordogne, Lot and Limousin) is in Bordeaux (353, boulevard du Président Wilson, BP91, 33073 Bordeaux, ☎ 05.57.22.21.10, ✉ postmaster. bordeaux@fco.gov.uk). The Auvergne is covered by the British consulate in Lyons (24, rue Childebert, 69288 Lyons cedex 1, ☎ 04.72.77.81.70, ✉ britishconsulate.mail@ordilyon.fr). There are also American Presence Posts in Bordeaux (BP 77, 33025 Bordeaux, ☎ 05.56.48.63.80) and Lyons (16, rue de la République, 69002 Lyon, ☎ 04.78.33.36.88), wheres there are consulates for most other major countries. The British consulate in Bordeaux has three telephone numbers for information on French administrative services: ☎ 05.56.11.56.56 (Dordogne), ☎ 08.36.68.16.26 (Limousin) and ☎ 05.62.15.15.15 (Lot).

Churches

Every town and almost every village has a Catholic church, although many hold services only once a month. Mass schedules for the month are posted on church doors. Not surprisingly, given its large British population, there are several churches in Dordogne where regular services are held in English, including those in Chancelade near Périgueux (Chapelle Saint-Jean de

Puy Mary, Auvergne ▶
© Dennis Kelsall

Colombage house at
Brocottes, Normandy
© Trevor Yorke (Living France)

▼ The Abbaye aux Dames, Caen, Normandy
© Trevor Yorke (Living France)

▼ Penhir Point, Brittany
© Dennis Kelsall

▼ Château de Villandry, Centre
© Dennis Kelsall

▲ *Honfleur, Normandy © Trevor Yorke (Living France)*

▼ *Beaune, Burgundy*
  © Dennis Kelsall

▲ *Gault, Provence © Dennis Kelsall*

▼ *Cathedrale Notre Dame, Caen*
  © Trevor Yorke (Living France)

▼ *Near Nice, Côte d'Azur*
  © Dennis Kelsall

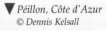
Péillon, Côte d'Azur
© Dennis Kelsall

▲ *La Trinité-Sur-Mer, Brittany © Trevor Yorke (Living France)*

▲ *St-Cirq-Lapopie, Dordogne © Dennis Kelsall*

▼ *La Rochelle, Poitou-Charentes*
© Trevor Yorke (Living France)

▲ *St-Malo, Brittany © Dennis Kelsall*

Lyons, Rhône-Alpes ▶
© *Trevor Yorke (Living France)*

▲ *Sergeac, Dordogne*
© *Dennis Kelsall*

▼ *Marseilles, Provence*
© *Trevor Yorke (Living France)*

▲ *Honfleur, Normandy*
© *Dennis Kelsall*

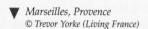

▲ *La Roque-Gageac, Dordogne*
© *Dennis Kelsall*

l'Abbaye), Chapdeuil, Limeuil (at the Eglise Sainte Cathérine) and Ribérac (Eglise Notre-Dame de la Paix). *The News* (see **Appendix B**) publishes the schedule of English-language services in Dordogne performed by the Anglican Church of Aquitaine (contact Rvd Michael Selman, 1, Lotissement de la Caussade, 33270 Floirac, ☎ 05.56.40.05.12, 💻 http://chapaq.free.fr). In Sarlat-la-Canéda, the Parish Church of Sainte Nathalène holds services in English during the summer. There are also English-language services at a number of venues in Cahors (46), for which the contact is Laurie Mort (☎ 05. 61.85.17.67). In Limousin, there's an English vicar, Michael Hepper (19, avenue René Baillargeon, 86400 Civray, ☎ 05.49.97.04.21), who travels around performing services in English.

There's a Protestant church in Clermont-Ferrand (63), Jehovah's Witnesses groups in Cusset (03), La Souterraine (19) and Saint-Aster (24), Latter Day Saints in Brive-la-Gaillarde (19) and Périgueux (24), Clermont-Ferrand (63) and Limoges (87), and Seventh Day Adventists in Notre-Dame-de-Sanilhac (24). There are mosques in Montluçon, Moulin, Vichy (03), Le Puy-en-Velay (43), Clermont-Ferrand, Thiers (63) and Limoges (87); details can be found on 💻 http://mosquee.free.fr. There's a Buddhist association (Association Dhagpo Kagyu Ling) in Dordogne and two synagogues, in Vichy (03) and Clermont-Ferrand (63), details of which can be found on 💻 www.pagesjaunes.fr (enter 'Synagogues' in the first box and the name of the town).

Clubs

English-language clubs in the area include:

- Association France/Grande Bretagne in Cahors (46) (☎ 05.65.31.61.13), Limoges (87) (5bis, rue Neuve Saint-Etienne, 87000 Limoges) and Vichy (03) (☎ 04.70.59.82.64);
- Dordogne Ladies' Club (☎ 05.53.83.82.35);
- Dordogne Organisation of Gentlemen (☎ 05.53.94.73.14);
- English Kids' Club in Beynac (24) (☎ 05.53.28.35.49);
- YES (Your English Society) in Périgueux (24) (☎ 05.53.03.46.38).

For French speakers, the Accueil des Villes françaises (AVF), a French organisation designed to welcome newcomers to an area, is an option (there's often at least one fluent English-speaker in each group). There are around 25 AVF groups in the Auvergne and Limousin – in Moulins, Monluçon and Vichy (03), Aurillac (15), Brioude, Langeac, Le Puy-en-Velay and Yssingeaux (43), Aubière, Cébazat, Chamalières, Clermont-Ferrand, Cournon, Issoire, Pont-du-Château, Riom and Thiers (63) – although curiously there's only one AVF in Lot (in Cahors) and none in Dordogne. The website (🖥 www.avf.asso.fr) includes a directory (*annuaire*) of local groups by department as well as an online form for contacting your local AVF before you move to the area. Listings indicate whether information and services are available in English or other languages. Other sources for clubs in the area are *The News* (see **Appendix B**) and the English-speaking church (see above).

PROPERTY

There are few apartments and housing estates outside the large towns, and most people moving to this area are looking for houses or farms to renovate with at least 1,000m^2 (a quarter of an acre) of land. However, in Dordogne and Lot it's difficult to find houses to renovate for the simple reason that there are very few properties left in need of renovation. It's easier to find properties that have been renovated but, of course, the price is much higher. In the Auvergne and Limousin it's also becoming difficult to find a typical stone house with a large plot. Often, when a farm or *fermette* (small farm) is sold, a local farmer will buy the land and perhaps a barn, leaving the house with either a small garden or in some cases virtually no land at all. It's worth bearing in mind that in rural areas of the Auvergne and Limousin, 10 to 15 per cent of houses have no septic tank or sanitation, and when a property is described as 'for renovation' this usually means 'requiring drainage, electricity and other basic amenities'; even when a house is lived in, it isn't necessarily habitable!

New houses are generally bought (or built) by French people and tend to be either in or near a town, although there are some new housing estates that may appeal to foreigners, especially those looking to let a property to holidaymakers. For example, near Souilllac (46) a country club has been created with swimming pools, tennis courts, a bar, a restaurant and a golf course (Souillac Country Club, ☎ 05.65.27.56.00, 🖥 wwwsouillaccoun-tryclub.com). A number of two, three and four-bedroom chalets have been built in the latest phase of its development, which are now available from €190,000. There are also plans for a 'leisure and lifestyle village' marketed by French Discoveries (UK ☎ 0121-449 1155) 35km (22mi) north-west of Limoges, where traditional-style houses in stone and wood are to be built around seven lakes in 100ha (250 acres) of woodland. Prices will range from €150,000 to over €400,000 and the complex with include a hotel, marina, health spa and shops. There are a few (*bona fide*) British estate agents in Dordogne and Lot and one in Creuse (23) – Zoë Holt (☎ 05.55.81.39.93).

Typical Properties

Houses in this area are typically built of stone, but the stone used varies from place to place – from almost black lava stone in the Massif Central to the creamy white of the Quercy plateaux. Dordogne houses are characterised by warm, yellow bricks and many have small square towers. Lot houses largely follow the same style but using whiter stone. In northern parts, houses are constructed with thick walls and small windows to keep out the heat in summer and the cold in winter; in the southern parts, windows tend to be larger. In Dordogne and Lot, older houses will typically be roofed with the Roman (or provençal) tiles favoured in the south of France, whereas in the Auvergne they're roofed predominantly with slabs of volcanic stone and in Limousin with slate. Some houses and many of the churches in Limousin are roofed with chestnut slats called *bardeaux*. The region is one of the last in France to produce *bardeaux*, and many famous buildings in other parts of the country (on the Mont Saint-Michel, for example) are roofed with Limousin *bardeaux*. Unfortunately, owing to the cost of such roofing materials, modern houses throughout the area tend to be roofed with standard red tiles.

Cost of Housing

The housing market is essentially split into two regions: Dordogne and Lot on the one hand and the Auvergne and Limousin (with slight variations between the different departments) on the other. There's a big difference, for example, between the prices of houses in Creuse and those in Dordogne for a number of reasons, including population density, demand from foreign buyers and employment opportunities. In Dordogne and Lot, many people want a house within 15km (11mi), north or south, of the river Dordogne, or within the triangle Souillac/Sarlat/Gourdon, where prices are highest, although it's possible to find reasonably priced property in other parts of the departments. In general, property prices in the area have risen around 10 to 20 per cent in the last two years and a recent survey concluded that properties for sale in Lot were on average the second-most expensive in the country after Paris. Among major towns, Montluçon (03) boasts the lowest average prices for older properties, not only in the area, but in the whole of France, while the area's highest average prices are to be found in Périgueux (24). The table below gives average prices per m^2 for older properties in major towns in the area:

Town	Average Price per m^2 (€)
Montluçon (03)	570
Vichy (03)	730
Brive-la-Gaillarde (19)	760
Périgueux (24)	1,025
Clermont-Ferrand (63)	910
Limoges (87)	860

Note, however, that average property prices aren't always a reliable indication of the relative price of similar properties in different towns, as one town may have a preponderance of cheaper or more expensive properties. The prices given below are a general guide, as values vary according to location, size, amount of land and state of repair, etc.

Small Isolated House/Farm for Renovation		**Price (€)**
Allier	small plot (less than 1,000m^2)	16,500
	large plot (up to 1ha/2.5 acres)	35,000
Cantal	small plot	26,000
	large plot	34,500
Corrèze	small plot	34,500
	large plot	36,000
Creuse	small plot	15,000
	large plot	25,000
Dordogne	small plot	40,000
	large plot	50,000
Haute-Loire	small plot	25,000
	large plot	35,000
Lot	small plot	39,000
	large plot	48,000
Puy-de-Dôme	small plot	34,000
	large plot	41,000
Haute-Vienne	small plot	33,500
	large plot	37,000

Renovated Village House		**Price (€)**
Allier	small (2 bedrooms)	20,000
	large (up to 4 bedrooms)	38,500
Cantal	small	28,000
	large	40,500
Corrèze	small	35,000
	large	40,500
Creuse	small	20,000

	large	35,000
Dordogne	small	39,000
	large	55,000
Haute-Loire	small	26,500
	large	40,000
Lot	mall	41,000
	large	55,000
Puy-de-Dôme	small	35,500
	large	50,000
Haute-Vienne	small	35,500
	large	48,000

Renovated Large House (3 Bedrooms or More) with Land		Price (€)
Allier	in country	110,000
	in or near big town	140,000
Cantal	in country	94,000
	in or near big town	150,000
Corrèze	in country	120,000
	in or near big town	135,000
Creuse	in country	76,000
	in or near big town	100,000
Dordogne	in country	160,000
	in or near big town	225,000
Haute-Loire	in country	120,000
	in or near big town	140,000
Lot	n country	130,000
	in or near big town	200,000
Puy-de-Dôme	in country	150,000
	in or near big town	170,000
Haute-Vienne	in country	130,500
	in or near big town	160,000

Land

Building land is available in all areas, although it isn't plentiful. Rather surprisingly, the largest number of plots on the market are in Dordogne, followed by Corrèze, Puy-de-Dôme and Vienne, with few in the other departments. Prices vary enormously according to location and whether main services are connected. Land in or near a small village, where there's no mains drainage, can be bought for as little as €3 per m², even in Lot, whereas land with connections to all services, including electricity and telephone, near a town can cost €100 per m² or more, even in Puy-de-Dôme, although the maximum price in the Auvergne and Limousin is usually around €50 per m². Plots range from around 400m² to several hectares, the average plot being between 1,000 and 3,000m² and costing between €10,000 and €40,000. Most local estate agents sell building plots (*terrains à bâtir* or *terrains constructibles*).

Rental Accommodation

Rented accommodation is easiest to find in the main towns. For example, in Clermont-Ferrand (63) and Limoges (87), there are apartments from studios to five-bedrooms, although smaller apartments are in demand from students, as both towns have universities. Outside the main towns, rented accommodation tends to be limited to *gîtes*, which can be expensive for a long period. It's possible to find rural houses for rent from around €380 per month for a two-bedroom property. Rents in Dordogne and Lot are higher but not excessively so. There are few agencies that deal solely in rentals, but most estate agents handle properties for rent.

COMMUNICATIONS

Air

There are several airports in the area (shown on the maps at the beginning of the chapter), although there are few direct services from other countries and in most cases it's necessary to fly via Paris. There are direct flights to Clermont-Ferrand (63) from London City airport as well as from Amsterdam, Geneva, Madrid, Milan and Turin. Buzz flies daily direct from London Stansted to Limoges (87), and British European flies from Stansted to Bergerac (24). There are flights from Paris to Brive-la-Gaillarde (19), Périgueux (24) and Clermont-Ferrand (six daily) and two flights daily from Paris to Le Puy-en-Velay (43). From the aerodrome Montluçon-Guéret (03) there are also flights to Paris on Monday mornings returning Friday evenings.

Those in the north of the area may have access to Poitiers airport (in Vienne, around 125km/80mi north-west of Limoges – see page 122) and those in the south to either Toulouse (in Haute-Garonne, around 100km/60mi south of Cahors in Lot – see page 202) or Bordeaux (in Gironde, around 100km/60mi south-west of Périgueux in Dordogne – see also page 202), Toulouse in particular providing a wider choice of flights than airports in the area. For example, Buzz offers daily flights from London Stansted to Poitiers, and British European flies from Stansted to Toulouse around seven times a week and from Birmingham to Toulouse at least once a week. British Airways flies from London Gatwick to Bordeaux and Toulouse, and Air France flies from London Heathrow to Toulouse. There are flights from Paris to Brive-la-Gaillarde (19), Périgueux (24) and Clermont-Ferrand (six daily), as well as to Bordeaux, Toulouse and Poitiers. Details of all French airports and their services can be found on 🖳 www.aeroport.fr.

Public Transport

The *TGV* from Paris runs as far as Bordeaux via Poitiers (in Vienne to the north-west of Haute-Vienne) and Angoulême (in Charente to the west of Dordogne and Haute-Vienne). For details of the *TGV* network, see map in **Appendix E**. It's possible to catch local trains from any of these towns to Périgueux (24), Souillac (46), Clermont-Ferrand (63) and Limoges (87), but services are slow and infrequent. Limoges, for example, is four-and-a-half hours from Paris, Clermont-Ferrand five hours and Souillac six. Car rental is available at most of the major stations.

A cheaper but slower alternative to the train is coach travel. For example, Eurolines offer services during the summer months from London to Limoges (direct) costing around €150 return and taking up to 12 hours, to Clermont-Ferrand (with a change at Lyons), costing €135 return and taking 16 hours, and to Bellac (87) and Souillac (both with a change at Tours).

All large towns have bus services, which run from the centre to the suburbs and, in the case of Bergerac, Clermont-Ferrand and Limoges, from the station to the airport. However, these services tend to finish early in the evening. There are also some bus services between towns, particularly during rush hours and to link with train arrivals and departures. In rural areas, however, bus services can be few and far between or non-existent, and a car is often essential.

Roads

Road access to the area is easier since the recent completion of the A20, which runs from Paris (it starts as the A10 and A71) to Toulouse via Limoges (87), Brive-la-Gaillarde (19) and Cahors (46) and is toll-free from Vierzon (around half way from Paris to Limoges) to Brive. The A20 Cahors bypass is still under construction but expected to be finished by summer 2003. The A71 continues to Clermont-Ferrand, and the A/N89 links Clermont with Tulle (19), Brive and Périgueux and continues as far as Bordeaux. (Parts of the A/N89 are motorway, including the section between Tulle and Ussel (19), and the rest is due to be motorway by 2006 – see below.) The following are approximate travelling times by motorway:

- Limoges: 4 hours from Paris and Toulouse;
- Brive-la-Gaillarde: 5 hours from Paris and 3 hours from Toulouse;
- Souillac: 6 hours from Paris and 2 hours from Toulouse;
- Cahors: 6.5 hours from Paris and 1.5 hours from Toulouse;
- Clermont-Ferrand: 4 hours from Paris and 2 hours from Lyons.

Traffic jams are almost unheard of except in the large towns and even there are usually fairly innocuous (at least by Parisian standards). Limoges and Clermont-Ferrand can become congested during rush hours, and tourist towns can be jammed in July and August. The D703, known as the *Voie de la Vallée*, along the river Dordogne from Saint-Cyprien (24) to Souillac (46) is often impassable because of the sheer volume of cars and coaches (most of them foreign). There are plans to create a diversion, but the exact route is still under discussion. The route along the river Lot between Cahors and Figeac is magnificent but also heavily used in summer and, with its many bends, can be extremely slow.

There are a number of motorways and major roads still under construction (and therefore slowed by road works), including the N145 from Montluçon (03) to Angoulême (16), which is dual-carriageway either side of Guéret (23) but otherwise only two lanes. It's a very dangerous road (it has the greatest concentration of lorry traffic of any road in France) – especially the section between Montluçon and Guéret, where there are black silhouettes of people beside the road to show how many deaths there have been! The other major road currently under construction is the A89 motorway, large parts of which have been completed. Once finished (estimates vary between 2004 and 2006) it should attract many of the lorries away from the N145, and both Brive-la-Gaillarde and Clermont-Ferrand will become important road transport hubs. (Note that Brive currently has the third-worst accident record of any major French town.) The N141/D941 from Limoges to Clermont-Ferrand is another busy road, and there have been demands for passing lanes to reduce the accident rate, although as yet nothing has been done and it looks set to remain a two-lane road for some time. For those wishing to travel south, the A75 from Clermont-Ferrand to Béziers (34) should prove a boon once it's completed, although the scheduled completion date of late 2002 may not be met.

PLANNED DEVELOPMENTS

A number of improvements to communications are planned or under way. Three new motorways – the A20, A75 and A89 – are under construction (see **Roads** on page 157), and Limoges Airport is improving its terminal to meet the demand created by daily flights to London and other destinations. By 2007, Limousin will be served by *trains pendulars* (trains that don't run on wheels but hover). Although not as fast as the *TGV*, these will be quicker than ordinary trains and will enable travellers to make the journey from Paris in two-and-a-half hours. A disadvantage is that there will be fewer stops, so that people using La Souterraine (the main station linking Creuse with Paris), for example, will have to add at least 30 minutes to their journey by travelling to Limoges or Châteauroux (36).

A project to foster agriculture and tourism in Limousin involves the development of an area of lakes and rivers in Haute-Vienne, and the Auvergne is building a new cultural, artistic, exhibition and sports centre comprising three covered halls (a total of $36,000m^2/360,000ft^2$ of floor space), an outdoor exhibition area of $6,500m^2$ ($65,000ft^2$), an 8,500-seat concert hall and theatre, and conference centres. It will be the only complex of this type between Bordeaux, Lyons, Orléans and Montpellier. In Dordogne, Sarlat-la-Canéda is due for a 'face lift', and in Lot, there's a major project to upgrade the supply of electricity to Cahors, which is likely to take a number of years.

EMPLOYMENT PROSPECTS

In both the Auvergne and Limousin, employment is 55 per cent in services, 30 per cent in industry and 15 per cent in agriculture. Although the rate of unemployment in the area is lower than the national average (the number of retired people probably distorts the figures), there are few large companies and finding employment isn't easy. Until recently, the economy was based on small (40 to 200ha/100 to 500 acre) family farms passed down through generations. However, farming is becoming less profitable, and small farms are unable to compete with the big concerns and foreign prices. Fewer people want the hard work of running a farm for little return; they prefer to look for other work, which usually means moving out of the area. The advantage of this situation is that, if you have some agricultural experience, farming is a strong option, and the French government offers substantial subsidies to farmers. Departmental Chambers of Commerce (*CCI*) can help you to set up a farming business.

In fact, a number of initiatives have been made at departmental, regional and national level to encourage companies and individuals to settle in the area, and there's financial and educational assistance for those wishing to become self-employed. Several departments offer training and grants (amounts vary from department to department) for people wanting to create a business or take over an existing company. For example, the Haute-Loire *CCI* has a monthly meeting for people wishing to create a *gîte* or a B&B to advise them on applying for assistance. The Lot *CCI* offers courses in selling, tourism and language-teaching. The Conseil régional d'Auvergne provides assistance to creators and developers of companies and can help you to obtain assistance from the national government or from the European Community. According to a recent survey by *Le Point* magazine (see **Appendix F**), Montluçon (03) is a particularly good place to start a business, as it enjoys one of the highest rates of new business success in France.

In the last few years, there has been an increase in British-owned and British-run companies. These are mostly in the service industry (e.g. tourism, estate agency) or the building trade. For example, in Lot, where agriculture was for a long time the primary economic resource, there are now more service businesses than agricultural concerns. It's possible to set up and run a tea room or a *gîte* (rural holiday cottage) or offer *chambres d'hôte* (bed and breakfast), although competition in many areas is intense. A certain number of jobs are available in the tourist industry during the summer and winter (skiing) seasons, but there's a tendency for these to go to French nationals, whatever their English-language ability, rather than to foreigners.

Note, however, that it isn't sufficient to have experience of a particular line of work; qualifications are required in order to set up a recognised business. For example, to become an estate agent you need a degree (preferably in law or accounting) or ten years' experience with an estate agency as well as a good level of French.

Long-distance working using computers is possible in some parts, but outside the main towns cable and broadband Internet connections are unheard of and not likely to be available for a few years. A list of companies in each department can be obtained from the French Chamber of Commerce in London (see **Appendix A**).

FURTHER INFORMATION

Useful Addresses

Tourist Offices

- Comité régional du Tourisme d'**Auvergne**, 44, ave des Etats-Unis, 63057 Clermont-Ferrand (☎ 04.73.29.49.49, 🖳 www.auvergne-tourisme.info)
- Comité régional du Tourisme du **Limousin**, 27, boulevard de la Corderie, 87031 Limoges (☎ 05.55.45.18.80, 🖳 www.tourismelimousin.com)

- Comité départemental du Tourisme de l'**Allier**, Pavillon des Marroniers, Parc de Bellevue, BP 65, 03402 Yzeure (☎ 04.70.46.81.50, 💻 www.destination-allier.com)

- Comité départemental du Tourisme et du Thermalisme **Cantal**iens, 11, rue Paul Doumer, BP 8, 15000 Aurillac (☎ 04.71.46.22.00, 💻 www.cdt-cantal.fr)

- Comité départemental du Tourisme de la **Corrèze**, Quai Baluze, 19000 Tulle (☎ 05.55.29.98.78, 💻 www.cg19.fr)

- Comité départemental du Tourisme de la **Creuse**, 43, place Bonnyaud, BP 243, 23005 Guéret (☎ 05.55.51.93.23, 💻 http://cg23.fr)

- Comité départemental du Tourisme de la **Dordogne**, 25, rue Wilson, BP 2063, 24002 Périgueux (☎ 05.53.35.50.24, 💻 www.perigord.tm.fr/tourisme/cdt)

- Comité départemental du Tourisme de la **Haute-Loire**, Hotel du Département, 1, place Monseigneur de Galard, 43011 Le Puy-en-Velay (☎ 04.71.07.41.54)

- Comité départemental du Tourisme du **Lot**, 107, quai Eugéne Cavaignac, 46000 Cahors (☎ 05.65.35.07.09, 💻 www.tourisme-lot.com)

- Comité départemental du Tourisme du **Puy-de-Dôme**, Place de la Bourse, 63038 Clermont-Ferrand cedex 1 (☎ 04.73.42.22.50, 💻 www.planete puydedome.com)

Estate Agents

- Agence Couloumy, La Maze, 19140 Uzerche (☎ 05.55.73.28.92, ✉ limousin.immoblier@wanadoo.fr). FNAIM registered, English-speaking.

- Bourganeuf Immoblier, 9, avenue Turgot, 23400 Bourganeuf (☎ 05.55.54.95.85, ✉ j-p.pelege@wanadoo.fr). FNAIM registered, English-speaking.

- J-N Brunet, 27, avenue de la République, 23000 Guéret (☎ 05.55.51.90.90, 💻 www.fnaim.fr/brunet). FNAIM registered.

- Tous les Immobliers Souillac, 50, boulevard Louis Jean Maluy, 46200 Souillac (☎ 05.65.37.84.41, ✉ p.t.i.s.immoblier@wanadoo.fr). FNAIM registered, English-speaking.

Useful Websites

💻 www.cg46.fr (Conseil régional de Lot. Information on the economy and population, statistics of the region and useful links)

⌨ www.correze.net (information on Corrèze, including a website address book – in French)

⌨ www.cr-limousin.fr (Conseil régional du Limousin. Information on the economy and population, statistics of the region and useful links – in French and English)

⌨ www.enlimousin.com (search engine for the Limousin region – in French)

⌨ www.quercy.net (information about the Quercy region of Dordogne and Lot – in French)

Simone Paissoni

Solicitor

Member of the Association of Franco-British Lawyers

IN FRANCE ~ FOR FRANCE

Lagrasse – Pyrénées

Jim Watson

The area of France described in this chapter includes most of the Aquitaine and Midi-Pyrénées regions, with the exception of the departments of Dordogne and Lot, which are considered in **Chapter 4**. Aquitaine is made up of the following departments: Dordogne (24), Gironde (33), Lot-et-Garonne (47), Landes (40) and Pyrénées-Atlantiques (64); the Midi-Pyrénées comprises Ariège (09), Aveyron (12), Haute-Garonne (31), Gers (32), Lot (46), Hautes-Pyrénées (65), Tarn (81) and Tarn-et-Garonne (82). Aquitaine is perhaps most famous for its wines, beaches, surfing and of course, Eleanor of Aquitaine, mother of Richard the Lionheart. The Midi-Pyrénées is renowned for skiing, spas and the pilgrimage town of Lourdes.

Until recently, and in contrast to Dordogne and Lot, the area covered in this chapter hasn't been especially popular with foreign property buyers, but with access becoming easier by air, rail and road, coupled with low increases in property prices, the south-west has seen an increase in the purchase of second and retirement homes – especially by the British and other Europeans. With a pleasant climate, plus wonderful wines and food, the area is becoming increasingly popular.

Unlike Peter Mayle's book *A Year in Provence*, which caused Britons to flood into Provence, Ruth Silvestre's book *A House in the Sunflowers* (set in Aquitaine) and Rosemary Bailey's *Life in a Postcard* (the story of buying and renovating a 13th century monastery in the Pyrenees) haven't provoked an influx of foreigners to the regions discussed here. These two books are, however, well worth a read – especially if you're think of embarking on a renovation project (see **Useful Publications** on page 206).

Aquitaine

Aquitaine owes its name to the Romans, who logically named the area Aquitania, as it had many rivers running through it (to which canals were later added). It has had a somewhat chequered history and, like Normandy, was once ruled by the kings of England (or vice versa), although it has been under French rule since 1650. The region, which covers an area of 41,310km^2 (16,135mi^2) and has a population of 2.7 million, is largely agricultural, unspoiled and sparsely populated, and it's noted for its temperate climate. Crops include corn and peppers (the hot variety), which are hung from the window ledges and beams of houses to dry. Aquitaine is one of the most varied regions of France; although predominantly flat (the majority of the region lies less than 250m/825ft above sea level), the land rises in the south at the foothills of the Pyrenees. It has over 270km (170mi) of spectacular beaches along the Atlantic coastline, known as the *Côte d'Argent* ('Silver Coast'), 30km (20mi) of which are considered to offer the best surfing in Europe (see **Sports** on page 180).

In the north of the region is the Bassin d'Arcachon, a natural inland sea with the largest beach in Europe (where incidentally 90 per cent of French oysters are grown), while the south of Aquitaine includes the so-called *Landes de Gascogne*. 'The Landes' is a flat, sandy plain (*lande* means 'moor'), roughly triangular, bounded by the sea and dunes to the west and stretching from Bordeaux (33) in the north to Dax (40) and the Golfe de Gascogne in the south and east as far as Nérac (47) and therefore covering roughly the whole of the department of Landes, as well as a good deal of Gironde and parts of Lot-et-Garonne. It was transformed during the 19th century by the planting of pine trees, which now cover virtually the entire area, creating purportedly the largest forest in Europe (the trees are now used for making paper). Part of the forest, corresponding roughly to the basin of the river Eyre, was designated a regional park (the Parc régional des Landes de Gascogne) in 1970. The

Landes is known as *'le pays de la bonne bouffe'* ('the land of good grub'), where traditional dishes include *cruchade* (a dessert), *garbure* (soup), *millas* (corn-cake) and *saupiquet* (fried ham). Gironde to the north is also generally flat (its highest point is just 165m/535ft) and much of the land is given over to vineyards.

Pyrénées-Atlantiques is part of the Basque Country (*Pays basque*), which extends from around 160km (100mi) south of Bordeaux, where the Landes give way to the foothills of the Pyrenees, across the mountains into Spain and east along the river Nive as far as Saint-Jean-Pied-de-Port. The Basque Country has its own language (see page 177), style of architecture (see page 192), sport (*pilota* – see page 182) and traditions and is itself divided into ancient 'regions', such as Labourd, Soule and Basse-Navarre. Apart from the conurbation of Bayonne, Anglet and Biarritz (known locally as the 'BAB'), where property is fairly expensive, Pyrénées-Atlantiques is sparsely populated. To the east of the Basque Country is Béarn (famous for its *sauce béarnaise*), another ancient 'region' (its capital is Orthez) surrounding the valleys of the Aspe, Barétous and Ossau in the east of Pyrénées-Atlantiques. The inland department of Lot-et-Garonne is undulating and largely rural and agricultural. It's one of the largest fruit-growing areas in France, producing apples, apricots, melons, nectarines, peaches, plums (including the mouth-watering *prunes d'agenais*) and strawberries, as well as tobacco, among other crops. (There's a famous fruit fair at Prayssas, between Agen and Villeneuve-sur-Lot.) Aquitaine as a whole is 45 per cent woodland (not surprisingly, the highest percentage in France), 30 per cent grassland, 20 per cent arable land and 25 per cent other uses, including urban areas.

Midi-Pyrénées

France's largest region (bigger than Switzerland!) borders Spain in the south, Languedoc-Roussillon to the east and Aquitaine to the west, and encompasses the French Pyrenees with Toulouse, its capital, at the centre. The Midi-Pyrénées boasts a wide variety of stunning, unspoilt scenery ranging from the majestic snow-capped peaks of the Pyrenees in the south to the pastoral tranquillity of the Aveyron, Lot and Garonne valleys in the north. The region as a whole is 25 per cent woodland, 25 per cent grassland, 35 per cent arable land and 15 per cent other uses, including urban areas.

The department of Gers is widely regarded as the heart of the ancient province of Gascony (sometimes called 'Guyenne' by the French), which is often described as France's 'Tuscany' on account of its rolling green countryside and numerous pretty villages. Neighbouring Haute-Garonne is dominated by Toulouse but reaches right down to the Pyrenees, while Hautes-Pyrénées is a largely mountainous department boasting many ski resorts (see page 180).

In the north-east of the region, Aveyron offers a variety of landscapes, including the wild, rocky area known as Les Causses, south of Millau, the town being regarded as the gateway to the Tarn Gorges – spectacular cuts through the lower Massif Central and a Mecca for hikers, canoeists, climbers and campers (the viewpoint at the top is appropriately called the Point Sublime!). The departments of Tarn and Tarn-et-Garonne in the east of the region have recently become extremely popular with foreign homebuyers, particularly the British (in many parts, you're almost certain to have British neighbours), and prices have risen accordingly.

In the south-east corner of Midi-Pyrénées, the department of Ariège has stunning scenery and is popular with a number of British and European notables, including Tony Blair, who has spent part of his summer holidays here for the past several years. (Perhaps he has been trying to strike it lucky: around 50kg (110lb) of gold is panned every year from the department's rivers!) The decline of agriculture means that there are plenty of inexpensive properties to be found, and the department has the dual advantages of being near the Pyrenees and close to Toulouse. On the Spanish border is the principality of Andorra, which offers its own ski resorts as well as tax-free shopping (if you don't mind sitting in a traffic jam waiting to cross back into France afterwards!).

The Pyrenees are popular for year-round outdoor activities, including cycling, hiking and, of course, skiing. There are more than 30 ski resorts in the area (see page 180), which are generally much less expensive than the Alpine resorts, although less challenging for advanced skiers. There are also numerous spa towns in the Midi-Pyrénées, owing to the region's many thermal springs. Lourdes, in Hautes-Pyrénées, is probably the most visited place in the region, millions of people flocking to the Roman Catholic holy shrine each year, many in search of miracle cures.

The people of the Midi-Pyrénées have long regarded themselves as a breed apart – brave and free-spirited, typified by the statue of D'Artagnan (famous as one of the 'Three Musketeers' in the novel of that name by Alexandre Dumas) in the shadow of the cathedral at Auch (32). In fact, D'Artagnan is reputed to have been modelled on Charles de Batz, Captain of the King's Musketeers and a native of Auch. Examples of the earliest forms of human art, 30,000-year old cave paintings depicting deer, bison and other animals, can be found in the grottoes of the Ariège department, and the region also retains influences of the Celts, who settled here in pre-Christian times, Romans and Moors (Arabs), who occupied the area for some 800 years. The local culture and especially the cuisine have therefore developed from both Roman and Arab roots and are celebrated in the region's many festivals

Several classic French dishes originate in this region, including *cassoulet*, made from Toulouse sausage, *magret de canard* (duck cutlet) and that most politically incorrect (but most typically French) of foods, *pâté de fois gras* (goose-liver pâté). Roquefort cheese is made here (in the town of Roquefort-sur-Soulzon in Aveyron) and another famous Gascon product is armagnac, a grape brandy similar to (but subtly different from) cognac, which is made in neighbouring Poitou-Charentes. (Many connoisseurs rate armagnac above cognac, claiming that is has a richer flavour thanks to its single distillation and oak casking.) Many armagnac producers also make a fine aperitif called Floc de Gascoigne, which is a blend of armagnac and wine, along with a number of armagnac-based liqueurs.

ADVANTAGES & DISADVANTAGES

The south-west has a range of climates to suit almost everyone. Few European countries, let alone regions, can match the south-west's ability to offer top-class skiing conditions so close to the balmy, temperate coastal plain (Provence-Alpes-Côtes d'Azur is another – see **Chapter 6**). Many regard the climate on the Atlantic coast as better than that of the Mediterranean, equally warm and sunny but with the benefit of Atlantic breezes to clear the air. Aficionados of summer outdoor pursuits should, however, always be prepared for sudden weather changes, particularly in the eastern Pyrenean mountains and in the southern reaches of the Massif Central in Tarn and Aveyron. These areas are subject to infrequent but invariably spectacular summer storms and flash floods. For that reason care should also be taken and enquiries made if you're contemplating the purchase of a riverside property. Those who favour a temperate, northern European climate will probably find the Pyrenean foothills of Haute-Garonne and Gers to their liking.

The Midi-Pyrénées is acknowledged, even by French people from other regions, to have the country's finest and healthiest cuisine. As this is one of France's prime food producing areas, local produce is abundant, varied and reasonably priced, and the red wines of Bordeaux (and the sweet white Sauternes) are regarded by many as the best in the world. The body beautiful is also catered for in many ways – health spas and thermal springs, outdoor pursuits such as walking, cycling and skiing and, on the coast, sailing, surfing and swimming, not to mention popular local sports such as golf, rugby and *pelote* (see **Sports** on page 180). For residents in search of some Mediterranean heat, Perpignan and the western Mediterranean coast is a mere couple of hours' drive from the south-easterly departments of Ariège and Haute-Garonne. And, of course, Spain is within easy reach of the southern departments.

One of the major advantages of the region (currently) is the relatively low cost of living. With the exception of the major cities, such as Toulouse and Bordeaux, and popular holiday destinations, such as Biarritz and the ski resorts, property prices are among the lowest in France. This is probably because the region isn't as accessible to the British and other northern Europeans as the Dordogne and other more northerly regions; nor are its winter sports offerings as comprehensive as those available in the Alps. The proliferation of low-cost airline services into the region may, however, cause property prices to rise in the next few years. It's also becoming increasingly popular as a holiday destination, both summer and winter, although unless you take up residence in one of the major ski resorts or seaside resorts you're unlikely to be unduly troubled by holiday crowds.

The south-west coast has 14 resorts with 'blue flag' beaches and two blue flag ports (see 🖳 www.pavillonbleu.com) but also a large number of 'black flag' beaches (considered unacceptably polluted by the Surfrider Foundation Europe – see 🖳 www.surfrider-europe.org): one in Gironde, three in Landes and no fewer than 12 in Pyrénées-Atlantiques, including two in Biarritz and two in Saint-Jean-de-Luz. Pau (64) is the 'greenest' major town in the south-west, with over 75m^2 of green space per inhabitant compared with just 17m^2 in Bordeaux (33) and 15m^2 in Tarbes (85), where there's also a lack of cycle track (Bayonne and Bordeaux are the towns for cyclists). In a survey of the 100 largest towns in France published in January 2002, *Le Point* magazine didn't rate any towns in the south-west in the country's top ten (Toulouse was highest in 12th position), but according to the criteria selected by us, Albi (81) is the seventh-best town in France to live in (see **Appendix F**).

Although the appearance of the low cost airlines has improved matters, the south-west is not as accessible from outside France as is, say, the Mediterranean coast. Although several regional airports are classed as 'international', they mainly handle scheduled flights from other French and European cities. Visitors from North America, for example, would need to travel via one of the major European hubs such as Paris or London. Internal travel from elsewhere in France has, however, greatly improved in recent years thanks to the expansion of the motorway network and the introduction of high-speed train (*TGV*) services from Paris. British visitors can now travel from the Channel ports to the south-west by car or train fairly comfortably in a day.

The people of the region have a long history of acceptance of other peoples, and are naturally friendly and outgoing. They're passionate about their food and drink and equally enthusiastic about their rugby. Display an informed interest in either and you're likely to be welcomed into the community.

Note that there are two nuclear power stations in the south-west: one at Braud-et-Saint-Louis (33), half way between Bordeaux and Royan, the other in Golfech (82) 20km (12mi) from Agen and 80km (50mi) from Toulouse. Bordeaux is also susceptible to flooding.

MAJOR TOWNS & PLACES OF INTEREST

Ariège (09)

Foix (pop. 9,100), the departmental capital (one of the smallest in France) and principal town, is steeped in history and has a mediaeval castle perched on a hill overlooking the town and the river. There's a number of *bastides* in the department, including Mazères, Le Mas-d'Azil, as well as fortified villages at Camon and Seintein. Other places of interest include the castle of Montségur, where 200 Cathars were burned at the stake for heresy by the Catholics in the Middle Ages, and the displays of prehistoric cave art and the Cathar fortress of Roquefixade. During the second world war, the Germans built a concentration camp near the village of Le Vernet, where there's now a museum dedicated to the camp's history.

Aveyron (12)

The departmental capital, Rodez (pop. 23,500), is an unpretentious town with a relatively unimposing cathedral and little to attract the tourist. The main attractions of the department lie in the spectacular countryside – the Tarn Gorge carving its way through the plateau de Larzac in the south and the rolling hills and valleys to the west. The plateau is where the Knights Templar settled in the middle of the 12th century; after the Pope suppressed the order in 1312, their possessions were transferred to the Knights Hospitallers of Saint John, who were responsible for the fortification of many of the hilltop villages; La Couvertoirade is an exceptionally well preserved example. The village of Conques, north of Rodez, with its fine half-timbered houses, is only one of nine villages in Aveyron rated among the most beautiful in France; its 11th century Abbatiale Sainte-Foy houses an exhibition of medieval gold, reckoned to be the finest in Europe. In the far south of the department near the town of Millau lies the quiet village of Roquefort-sur-Soulzon, famous for the production of the 'king of cheeses', made from ewes' milk.

Haute-Garonne (31)

Toulouse (pop. 742,000) is the fourth-largest city in France after Paris, Lyons and Lille and the country's second-largest university town, its population including some 100,000 students and academics in the Mirail suburb. The city has a Spanish feel and is often referred to as '*la cité rose*' because of the soft pink hue reflected from its red brick buildings. The medieval Les Jacobins quarter, with its narrow streets, is one of the city's main attractions, and the Place du Capitole is one of the great squares of France. With seven museums, over 50 historical monuments and a host of wonderfully decorated churches, including the Basilica Saint-Sernin, Europe's largest Romanesque church, Toulouse justifiably claims to be the cultural capital of the south-west. The southern spur of the department reaches the Pyrenees and the Spanish border and includes the spa towns of Bagnères-de-Luchon, Salies-du-Salat and Barbazan, as well as ski resorts (all above 1,400m/4,550ft) such as Superbagnères and Peyragudes (see page 180). The village of Saint-Bertrand-de-Comminges is among the most beautiful in France, and there are *bastides* at Cologne and Revel.

Gers (32)

Auch (pop. 25,000) has been the regional capital since Roman times, when it rivalled Bordeaux in importance. It boasts a lovely cathedral (with unique choir stalls). Auch and the Gers department are widely regarded as the heart of ancient Gascony, with rolling green countryside reminiscent of Tuscany in Italy. There are several fine examples of *bastides*, notably Fourcès, Plaisance and Mirande – the last now home to an annual international summer jazz festival. Although the Gers region produces Madiran wine, its most famous tipple is armagnac.

Gironde (33)

Bordeaux (pop. 735,000), France's fifth-largest city after Toulouse in Haute-Garonne, is the capital of Aquitaine and lies on the river Garonne. It attracts tourists from all round the world as the starting point for the region's famous wine trails. Saint-Emilion (2,500) is a picturesque medieval village (one of the most beautiful in France) perched above the Dordogne river 40km (25mi) east of Bordeaux. Arcachon (11,400), south-west of Bordeaux on the southern shore of the Bassin d'Arcachon, has long, sandy beaches and safe swimming which have turned it into a major seaside resort; in summer, the population swells to around 50,000. On the north side of the Bassin lies Aquitaine's answer to Saint-Tropez – Cap Ferret. The village of Blaye on the Garonne estuary north of Bordeaux is one of the most attractive in France.

Landes (40)

Mont-de-Marsan (pop. 32,000) is the capital of Landes, although the town isn't particularly inspiring – except for aficionados of sculpture, as the town is littered with nude bronze sculptures by Charles Despiau and Charles Wlerick, two local artists; the museum in the town is named after them. Mont-de-Marsan also hosts two spectacular festivals, the Fête de Flamenco and the Fête de la Madeleine during July. Dax (20,900), despite having a smaller population than the capital, is a far more vibrant place; popular with the Romans, it was the first thermal spa town in France and is also the largest. Over 100,000 visitors swell the town's population each year, half of whom come to 'take the waters'. Every March, the town plays host to the national *foie gras* fair. Bullfighting is also a tradition in Dax, as is rugby (see **Sports** on page 180). The village of Saint-Sever is regarded as one of the most attractive in France.

Lot-et-Garonne (47)

Agen (pop. 32,000), despite being the departmental capital and steeped in history, isn't a particularly interesting town, although it's a busy commercial centre and renowned for its prunes. Just outside the town is the Walibi Parc d'Attractions, a vast amusement park with water rides and other attractions (see **Leisure** on page 182). Nérac, (7,450) is a small tourist town on the river Balse with plenty of historical interest, including the 16th-century Château de Henri IV. There's a number of *bastides* (medieval towns laid out in a grid) in the department, including Montflanquin, Puymirol and Sauveterre-de-Guyenne.

Pyrénées-Atlantiques (64)

Pau (pop. 90,000) is the capital of this department with spectacular views of the Pyrenees. It has something of an Anglophone heritage, having been a favourite winter watering hole of rich and famous Britons and Americans in the 19th century, mainly because of its mild climate (see page 178). It has much English-style Victorian architecture, although the old town has retained a number of the medieval buildings. Pau has developed since the 1960s, both as a tourist resort and as a centre of industry, but retains a genteel atmosphere. Bayonne (42,000) lies on the rivers Ardour and Nive. The town's history dates back to Roman times and it's famous throughout France for its salt-cured ham (*jambon de Bayonne*), which can only be made from pigs reared on a pure cereal diet, as well as for chocolate-making. It's a vibrant town with plenty to see and do (there's even a museum dedicated to the local art of ham-making), and the Basque language (see page 177) and customs are much in evidence (Bayonne is the capital of the Basque province of Labourd). The picturesque spa town of Salles-de-Béarn nearby is the principal producer of salt for making *jambon de Bayonne* (it naturally has a salt museum!).

Biarritz (29,000) is situated on the Bay of Biscay and used to be the playground of the rich, although it has since become accessible to 'ordinary' people. Visitors come for the beaches, surfing and balneology (see **Amenities** on page 180). The town is lively all year and particularly busy in summer. Saint-Jean-de-Luz (13,000) is a popular coastal spa town (Louis XIV was married there and authorised the local fishermen to plunder foreign ships – which they're still allowed to do!). The department also boasts a number of attractive villages, including Aïnhoa (reckoned to be one of the most beautiful in France), Espelette, Labastide-Clairence, Lescar, Lescun and Mauléon-Licharre.

Hautes-Pyrénées (65)

The departmental capital, Tarbes (pop. 46,000), is a quiet place famous (at least in France) as the birthplace of Maréchal Foch and for the *haricot tarbais*, which has been described as the 'Rolls Royce of beans'! The best-known town in the department (and one of the most famous in France) is Lourdes (15,700), a Roman Catholic pilgrimage centre. Over 5 million pilgrims and tourists visit the town each year (only Paris has more hotel accommodation!), half a million of them arriving in the spring in search of a miraculous cure. The department has, however, many other attractions – ski resorts, spas, wildlife and walking. The resort of Cauterets doubles as a spa town and a ski resort. The Parc national des Pyrénées offers panoramic views across the mountains and incorporates the spectacular Cascade du Pont d'Espagne (a

440m/1,430ft high waterfall which freezes in winter) in the Cirque de Gavarnie (a natural amphitheatre amid the mountains).

Tarn (81)

Albi (pop. 64,500), the departmental capital, is situated on the river Tarn, where the light reflects off the rose-red bricks of the city. In medieval times, a blue dye was made from a plant called the *pastel* (whence our expression 'pastel blue'), a process which has been revived in the last decade. (Perhaps it was the bright blues and reds of the region that drove one of Albi's famous sons, Henri de Toulouse-Lautrec to rebel against the dull, northern greys and browns of his Parisian teachers and paint in such vivid colours.) Castres (45,500) is a historic town and the gateway to the Parc national régional du Haut-Languedoc. The nearby forest of Sidobre contains many unusual rock formations and is the world's largest granite quarrying site, where over 200 companies extract 150,000 tons of the rock each year (many of the buildings on the Champs-Elysées in Paris are made from Sidobre granite). The Sidobre region is also noted for its numerous *bastides*, such as Castelnau-de-Montmiral, Cordes-sur-Ciel, Penne-du-Tarn and Puycelci; Cordes, a fortified medieval hilltop town in the north of the department, is reckoned to be France's best preserved Gothic site.

Tarn-et-Garonne (82)

The departmental capital Montauban (pop. 53,800) is somewhat neglected in many French guidebooks, although it has much to offer, with its pink brick buildings (it's known locally as '*la ville rose*') and its reputation as the premier *bastide* in south-west France. Moissac (12,700) is renowned for fruit growing (apples, cherries, figs, kiwi-fruit, peaches, pears and plums, as well as hazelnuts and melons – a quarter of France's melons are grown here) and has an impressive abbey church and cloister, a masterpiece of Romanesque art. The *bastide* of Beaumont-de-Lomagne in the south-east of the department boasts an interesting 13th century church and holds a major garlic market in season (the Tarn valley is renowned for the production of garlic). The villages of Bruniquel and Penne are considered two of the most beautiful in France.

POPULATION

The population of the south-west of France comprises 2.9 million in Aquitaine and just over 2.5 million in the Midi-Pyrénées. The population of both regions grew faster than the national average (3.5 per cent) between 1990 and 1999: Aquitaine at 4 per cent and Midi-Pyrénées at 5 per cent. Toulouse (31) is among France's fastest-growing towns. There are around 107,000 foreign residents (including 42,500 North Africans) in Aquitaine and 100,500 (including over 33,000 North Africans) in the Midi-Pyrénées. The highest concentration of North Africans is in Gironde – primarily in and around Bordeaux. Gironde also has the highest concentration of Spanish and Portuguese with around 18,000 out of a total of 40,000 in Aquitaine. Not surprisingly, a large number (14,200) also live in Pyrénées-Atlantiques.

Other non-French EU nationals living in Aquitaine are mainly British, Dutch, German and Belgian, although they account only 0.5 per cent of the population. There are around 7,000 Britons in the region, although a major proportion of them live in Dordogne. (Of the British population in Aquitaine, around two-thirds are retired or otherwise non-working, but the proportion varies between less than 50 per cent in Gironde to around 80 per cent in Dordogne). Gironde has the next largest number of British residents. In the Midi-Pyrénées, around 13,500 Spanish and Portuguese and 8,370 other non-french EU nationals (including around 1,700 Britons) live in Haute-Garonne, mainly in and around Toulouse. The second-largest contingent of British people is to be found in Gers (over 1,000) followed by Tarn-et-Garonne (around 600). In Hautes-Pyrénées, there are almost 13,500 Spanish and Portuguese, but fewer than 800 English, Dutch, Germans and Belgians.

LANGUAGE

Practically the whole of the area covered in this chapter is within the part of France where the *Langue d'Oc* or *Occitan* is spoken (see page 221), but don't be disturbed if you hear locals conversing in a 'foreign' language; they'll also speak and understand French, although their accent will have a pronounced 'twang' (not at all like the pronunciation you learned at school), which it may take a while to get used to.

Peculiar to the extreme south-west of France is the Basque language (called *euskara, euskera* or *eskuara*), which is spoken in the western part of Pyrénées-Atlantiques in the historical provinces of Basse-Navarre, Labourd and Soule. The language's origin is a mystery, as it shows no resemblance to any other known language, although it has borrowed from Latin, French and Spanish (and our word 'bizarre' comes from Basque). Basque was passed on orally for centuries (it wasn't written until the 16th century and the first Basque book was published in 1545), and this tradition is kept alive, mainly in rural areas, by *bertsolaris*, who improvise Basque poems in various metres. There were originally eight dialects of Basque, but in the 1960s an attempt was made to unify the language and the so-called *Euskara Batua* (Unified Basque) is now the most widely used.

During the Franco regime in Spain, it was forbidden to speak Basque, but since then it has enjoyed a revival: a school network has been set up in both Spain and France for those who want their children to learn the language (there are estimated to be 50,000 school children learning Basque at any time), and over 1,000 adults enrol in Basque classes every year. *Kilometroak* is the name of a popular movement for the preservation of Basque. Basque has no official status and isn't used in local administration, although local authorities have recently begun to erect bilingual road signs and there are a few in Basque only. It's estimated that over 600,000 people speak Basque, around 530,000 of them in Spain and only 70,000 or so in France (out of a population of around 260,000 in the Basque region of France, which is called *Iparralde* in Basque); a further 25,000 people are said to understand the language. French national television broadcasts only a few minutes of Basque each day and Radio France around an hour. However, there are three local radio stations broadcasting solely in Basque, and a weekly Basque newspaper was started in 1994.

Needless to say, it isn't necessary to learn Basque (or *Occitan*) in order to be accepted by the local community in *Iparralde*, but if you can master a few words and phrases it will probably improve your chances.

CLIMATE

Because of the varied geography of the area, the south-west of France experiences a variety of weather conditions, although in general it enjoys a pleasant, temperate climate due to the influence of both the Atlantic and the Massif Central. (Gers, for example, has a more maritime climate than Aveyron.) Summer daytime temperatures can reach 38°C (100°F) during July and August with spectacular thunderstorms interrupting the sunshine, although the heat is usually alleviated by cool sea breezes. Bordeaux is the sunniest town in the area with over 2,080 hours of sunshine per year. Rainfall in the two regions is generally below the average for the country, although it varies greatly – e.g. 675mm (26in) on 101 days in Toulouse compared with Bordeaux's 850mm (33in) on 125 days. Bordeaux's wettest months are between October and January, whereas April to June are the wettest months in Toulouse. Lot-et-Garonne is generally slightly hotter and drier than neighbouring Dordogne (see page 139), while the coastal departments of Gironde and Landes have a pleasant, maritime climate. Inland, the climate changes as you approach the Pyrenees, and the Causses area of Aveyron can be windy and cold in winter but hot in summer.

In the mountains, the weather is often stormy. Annual rainfall can be as high as 1,000mm (39in) – Bayonne is one of France's wettest towns with rainfall on 143 days per year – and the area can experience severe flooding, as in November 1999, when 22 people died after almost a year's rain fell in just 24 hours, and in September 2002, when 28 deaths were reported as a result of heavy rain in the neighbouring region of Languedoc. As in the rest of Europe and indeed the world, climatic changes have produced some strange and adverse weather conditions in recent years, and the south-west of France has experienced its share of high winds and higher than average temperatures during the summer as well as the above-mentioned flooding.

In northern parts of the area, average temperatures are around 10°C during December and January. In the mountains, however, temperatures are much lower and the Pyrenees have become popular with skiers, the season lasting from December until March or April. The weather in the foothills of the Pyrenees is relatively mild all year. The table below shows the number of hours' sunshine and days' rainfall in selected towns in the area.

Town	Sunshine Hours	Days' Rainfall
Toulouse (31)	2,047	101
Bordeaux (33)	2,084	125
Agen (47)	1,984	111
Bayonne (64)	1,935	143
Pau (64)	1,849	130
Tarbes (65)	1,913	126
Castres (81)	2,077	106
Montauban (82)	2,029	105

COST OF LIVING

The cost of living is around average for France and lower in the south-west than in the south-east. This is largely because of the area's lesser popularity and the lower price of property (see page 192). As elsewhere, local and seasonal produce is good value, whereas 'exotic' products (either imported or out of season) can be expensive. Supermarket prices vary considerably according to the chain. Inevitably, the cost of most items is higher in rural areas, although the difference isn't marked. Property taxes and water prices vary considerably from commune to commune (as they do throughout France) without any definable pattern, rates being set by local rather than national or regional authorities.

CRIME RATE & SECURITY

The south-west rates fairly low in the French crime-rate stakes, probably because the majority of the area is rural. As in other regions, crime rates are higher in the major cities. Toulouse (31) has the area's highest (reported) crime rate (although not particularly high by national standards) with over 100 reported crimes per 1,000 inhabitants per year. Next come Bordeaux (33) and

Montauban (82) with around 95 crimes. 'Safest' cities are Tarbes (65) and Albi (81) with under 70 crimes per 1,000 inhabitants. However, car thefts and thefts from cars are on the increase, especially from foreign registered and rented cars.

During the summer months, forest fires are a danger, both to people and to property. Where properties are in a high-risk area for forest fires, it's often a legal requirement to ensure that firebreaks surround them. During this period the local authorities will ban bonfires and sometimes barbeques. Fines for ignoring theses bans are heavy.

Those considering living in the Basque region will no doubt be aware of the nationalist group known as *ETA*. While much publicity has been afforded to terrorist attacks carried out in Spain, France has been little affected. For general information on crime in France, see page 52.

AMENITIES

Sports

Because of its varied environment and climate, the south-west of France offers a host of sporting opportunities. Most towns have a public swimming pool and tennis courts as well as a municipal gymnasium (*salles des sports*), where there are usually facilities for a variety of sports, including basketball and volleyball. With some of the most beautiful scenery in Europe, the area offers walkers and cyclists an abundance of spectacular cycle routes and hiking trails. Bicycles can be hired in many towns for around €15 per day. For further information on cycle routes in France contact the Cyclist Touring Club (UK ☎ 01483-417217, 🖳 www.ctc.org.uk). Walkers should note that in some areas, especially in the mountainous, walks can be formidable and require appropriate clothing – particularly in winter. For further information contact the Fédération française du Pedestre (☎ 01.45.45.31.02).

Hunting is a popular 'sport' throughout France, and there are hunting clubs and associations in many towns and even in some villages (see page 52). Other popular sports in the area include:

Skiing: There are around 30 ski resorts in the French Pyrenees, most of them in Hautes-Pyrénées. Although not as famous or challenging as the Alps, the Pyrenees offer a good selection of downhill runs as well as plenty of cross-country skiing. Resorts include Ax, Guzet (09), Luchon/Superbagnères (31), Gourette, (64), Artouste-Fabrèges, Barèges, Cauterets, Gavarnie, La Mongie, La Pierre-Saint-Martin, Luz-Ardiden, Peyragudes-Balestas and Piau-Engaly (65), as well as four resorts in Pyrénées-Occidentales (see page 226) and five in Andorra (Arinsa/Pal, Arcalis/Ordino, La Rabassa, Pas-de-la-Casa/Grau Roig and Soldeu/El Tarter), which borders Ariège. Further information is available from La Maison des Pyrénées, 6, rue Vital Carles, 33000 Bordeaux (☎

05.56.44.05.65) and from 🖥 www.pyrenees.net and www.ski-andorra.com. Details of resorts and snow conditions can be found on 🖥 www.goski.com.

Surfing & Swimming: With over 14 championship surfing beaches and a further 38 surfing beaches of varying quality between Soulac in the north and Saint-Jean-de-Luz in the south, surfing is a popular sport for those living within reach of the coast. Surfing competitions are normally held in July, August and September (the Biarritz Surf Festival in July is one of the major events), although surfing is a year-round sport. There's a number of surf schools which, for around €30 to €40 per hour, will provide individual tuition. Board hire costs around €15 per day. Further information can be obtained from the Fédération française du Surf (☎ 05.58.43.55.88, 🖥 www.fedesurf. com). The sea is less suited to swimming (this is the Atlantic, not the Mediterranean), and it can be dangerous to bathe outside the prescribed beaches, although there's a number of inland seawater lakes, such as the 3,600ha (8,900 acre) Hossegor lake and the Etang de Biscarosse, where swimming is safer.

Watersports: There are other watersports facilities along the coast, principally at La Teste-de-Buch (33), Hossegor and Léon (40). Inland, the area is crossed by a number of rivers, including the Adour, Ariège, Aveyron, Baïse, Garonne, Gave d'Oloron and Gave de Pau, Gers and Tarn, as well as the Canal du Midi, which joins the Garonne at Toulouse; there's also a number of lakes, including those at Montbels (09), Blasimon, Hostens, Hourtin-Carcans, Lacanau (33), Parentis, Sanguinet, Soustons (40), Casteljaloux, Duras, Preyssas (47), Lembeye, Oloron, Thèze (64) and Gaube (65). These offer a variety of watersports – from swimming and rowing to canoeing and rafting. The river Gave d'Oloron south of Pau (64) is renowned for white-water rafting, which can be enjoyed (?) at Navarrenx and Oloron and in the Vallée d'Ossau; the rivers Gave de Pau, Adour and Neste d'Aure are also well suited to white-water sports. Details can be obtained from the Fédération française de Canoë Kayak (☎ 01.45.11.08.50, 🖥 www.ffck.org) and local tourist information offices.

Fishing: The area's lakes and rivers are also used for fishing, and the Midi-Pyrénées in particular, with some 2,500km (1,500mi) of waterways and over 2,000 lakes, is reckoned to be an angler's paradise, where fish include carp, perch, pike, shad and trout.

Horse Riding: There are many equestrian centres in the area, where mounts can be hired by the hour, half-day or day. Further information can be obtained from the Fédération française d'Equitation (☎ 01.53.26.15.50, 🖥 www.ffe.com) and the Bureau des Guides équestres transpyrénéens (☎ 05. 61.69.01.99, 🖥 www.equipyrene.com, which has information in English).

Rugby: The French are as passionate about rugby as the Welsh or New Zealanders, and in the south-west rugby has a bigger following than soccer, all the major towns having a team. Toulouse have been national champions on more than one occasion, as have Biarritz. For further information contact the Fédération française de Rugby (🖳 www.ffr.fr), which can provide a list of rugby clubs in the region.

Golf: There are over 60 golf courses in the south-west (Pau boasts France's oldest golf club, founded in 1856 – by the English, of course), many of which are considered to be the best in the country. There are more courses in the Midi-Pyrénées than Aquitaine, towns with the most courses being Bordeaux (33) and Biarritz (64) with six each and Toulouse (31) with seven. The table below lists the number of courses in each department. Information (in both French and English) on how to find courses, the cost of a round (which varies between €15 and €50), etc. is available via the Internet (🖳 www.backspin.com). Another useful website for golfers is 🖳 www.golf. com.fr. Fees vary, and Golf Pass packages are available in some areas during low season. The website 🖳 www.touradour.com/golf includes a list of all the golf courses participating in the scheme in Aquitaine.

Department	No. of Courses
Ariège	1 x 18 holes
Aveyron	2 x 9 holes, 1 x 18 holes
Cantal	1 x 9 holes
Haute-Garonne	4 x 9 holes, 4 x 18 holes, 1 x 36 holes
Gers	3 x 9 holes, 2 x 18 holes
Gironde	2 x 9 holes, 6 x 18 holes, 2 x 27 holes, 2 x 36 holes
Landes	1 x 9 holes, 3 x 18 holes, 1 x 27 holes
Lot-et-Garonne	3 x 9 holes, 3 x 18 holes
Pyrénées-Atlantiques	2 x 9 holes, 1 x 12 holes, 6 x 18 holes
Hautes-Pyrénées	1 x 9 holes, 4 x 18 holes
Tarn	1 x 9 holes, 4 x 18 holes
Tarn-et-Garonne	1 x 9 holes

Pelote: Known as *pilota* in Basque, this game is unique to the Basque region and is quite dangerous, as it's incredibly fast. It's played on an outdoor court, and pairs of teams fling a leather ball against the court walls using their hands, a wooden paddle or a scooped wicker racquet.

Leisure

The south-west boasts numerous leisure activities and attractions, many of which are available all year. There are abundant varieties of flora and fauna in the area to interest both the amateur and professional naturalist; for example, the arid plateaux of the Aveyron boast over 2,000 species, including the great tawny vulture. For the agoraphobic, there are many museums to visit, notably the Musée de l'Armagnac at Condom (32), which shows the traditional method of making armagnac and gives visitors the opportunity to taste the result, and the Musée Toulouse-Lautrec at Albi (81), which holds the largest collection of the artist's work. In addition to the many attractions listed under **Major Towns & Places of Interest** on page 174, there are numerous *châteaux*, including the 12th-century Château de Villandraut south of Bordeaux, which is a particularly fine example. (Note, however, that many places advertising themselves as *châteaux* are in fact vineyards, often not open to the public except by appointment.)

There's a good selection of plays, concerts and other musical events in major towns and cities, and even the smallest village holds events and festivals during the summer months. Bordeaux, Toulouse, and Pau all have excellent theatres, which attract quality productions and performances. Bordeaux has its own symphony orchestra, as does Toulouse, and Biarritz boasts a ballet company. There are no fewer than seven major jazz festivals, as well as numerous smaller ones, in the area. In the Basque region, traditional music can be heard in town squares, and both music and dance are performed in the streets of Bayonne (64). Details of festivals and events in the Basque region can be found on ⌨ www.guide-basque.com.

Once considered a somewhat dowdy town, Bordeaux has recently revitalised itself, particularly in the eyes of the student population, with around 40 nightclubs on the quai de Paludate, as well as jazz clubs and tapas bars. Friday night is 'roller night', when over 500 young people rollerskate around the city! Bordeaux also boasts over 60 historical monuments, an opera house, a concert hall and a new casino. Toulouse is also a lively city, with a large student population and plenty of cheap places to eat and drink. Most bars stay open until the early hours of the morning. There's also plenty to see, including a modern art gallery, the relics of Saint Thomas Aquinas (in the Les Jacobins monastery), seven museums and over 50 historical monuments.

Parks, Zoos & Theme Parks: The area boasts an abundance of parcs naturels, principally the Parc régional des Landes de Gascogne (see page 167). There are also plenty of man-made attractions (many of a historical nature), including:

- Abbaye des Automates in Clairac (47): automatons;
- African Safari in Plaisance-du-Touch (31): African and other animals in a 'natural' environment;
- Aqualand de Gujan-Mestras (33): water park in the Forêt des Landes;
- Aquarium de la Garonne et des Pyrénées in Muret (31): tropical and freshwater fish;

- Aquaval in Lautrec (81): water park;
- L'Archipel in Castres (81): water park;
- Château du Colmbier in Mondalazac (12): medieval *château* and animal park;
- Le Chaudron magique in Brugnac (47): farm animals;
- Cité de L'Espace in Toulouse (31): one of the world's best space park, museum and planetarium complexes, attracting over 300,000 visitors annually;
- La Coccinelle in Gujan-Mestras (33): a combination of traditional amusement park and zoo;
- La Colline aux Marmottes in Argeles-Gazost (65): local wild animals;
- Le Donjon des Aigles in Beaucens (65): eagles and other birds of prey;
- Ecomusée de la Grande Lande in Sabres (40): relive the traditional way of life;
- La Falaise Aux Vautours (Cliff of the Vultures) in Aste-Béon near Laruns (64): all about vultures;
- La Ferme exotique (33): 'safari' park with over 1,000 animals;
- Les Grottes de Betharram in Saint-Pé-de-Bigorre (62): 3km (2mi) of caves;
- Le Jardin des Bêtes in Gages-le-Bas (12): animal park;
- Le Jardin des Papillons (33): tropical garden with butterflies;
- Larressingle (32): medieval life;
- La Maison des Loups in Orlu (09): wolves;
- Micropolis (12): all about insects;
- Parc animalier de Pradinas (12): 250 animals;
- Musée Aquarium d'Arcachon (33): local and other fish;
- Parc aux Kangourous/Zoo d'Asson (64): 400 exotic animals and birds, including kangaroos and wallabies;
- Parc ornithologique du Teich (33): over 250 species of bird;
- Parc de Nahuques Mont de Marsan has an open-air wildlife park –. Admission is free.
- Préhistoparc in Tursac (24): prehistory park;
- La Réserve de Bisons d'Europe in Sainte-Eulalie (48): bison roaming 'free';

- Village Medieval d'Artisans d'Art in Gujan-Mestras (33): reconstruction of medieval village;

- Walibi Aquitaine in Roquefort near Agen (47): amusement park with 16 attractions, including an 18th century *château*;

- Zoo de Pessac (33): 400 animals and over 100 species.

Spas, etc: For those who want (or need) pampering there are around a dozen spas offering a variety of water cure treatments. There are three in Ariège, three in Pyrénées-Atlantiques (at Anglet, Biarritz and Cambo-les-Bains) and several in the area around Dax (40). Costs vary according to the type and number of treatments you have, but a full day's pampering will set you back between €150 and €200. Most treatments must be booked in advance. Aquitaine is also noted for its many naturist centres, of which there are at least ten.

Casinos: For those who like to have a flutter, there are over 25 casinos in the area, most also offering meals and entertainment: one in Ariège, three in Haute-Garonne, one in Gers, five in Gironde, six in Landes, six in Pyrénées-Atlantiques, four in Hautes-Pyrénées and one in Tarn. The main casinos are in Arcachon (33), where the casino is housed in the beautiful Château Deganne, Dax (40), and Saint-Jean-de-Luz (64). Details of all casinos and what they offer are available via the Internet (e.g. 🖳 www.journaldescasinos.com – partly in English).

Bullfighting: In the southern departments of the area, bullfighting (*la corrida*) is considered a noble sport and supporters ardently celebrate both the tradition and spectacle, despite the fact that bulls suffer a slow and painful death. Matadors are treated as heroes and can earn vast amounts of money. Recently, there has been a number of protests against bullfighting, both by locals and animal rights supporters. Should you have a taste for blood, the main towns that hold festivals are Vic-Fézensac (32), Dax, Mont-de-Marsan (40) and Bayonne (64).

English-language Cinema & Theatre

Bordeaux (33) has three cinemas that show films in their original language (*version originale/VO*), Toulouse (31) has two, and Biarritz and Pau (64) have one each. English-language films are also shown at Ciné 4 in Castillonnès (47). A useful website for finding out what films are on in a given area, which also indicates whether the films are being shown in the original language is 🖳 www.cinefil.com. There are two annual regional film festivals, one in Sarlat-la-Canéda (in Dordogne) during November and the other in Arcachon (33) in September. Although neither compares with the Cannes film festival, both attract a good selection of foreign and French films.

Shopping Centres & Markets

The Saint-Christoly shopping centre in Bordeaux has around 40 shops and the Galerie des Grands Hommes around 20. Toulouse has no fewer than five shopping centres, including the vast Portet-sur-Garonne incorporating a hypermarket (claimed to be the largest in France), a mall and a surrounding complex of home improvement centres, sporting and electronic goods outlets. Large IKEA and Habitat stores can also be found in Toulouse. The *centre commercial* Bosquet at Pau (64) incorporates a Champion supermarket.

Regional markets for local produce such as *foie gras* (goose liver pâté) are held weekly; the Monday market in Samatan south-east of Auch (32) attracting buyers from all over the south-west. Most towns also have weekly or daily markets, and Toulouse (31) boasts several: food on the Boulevard de Strasbourg, flowers and 'antiques' in the Place du Capitole (on Wednesdays and Sundays), proper antiques near the Saint-Sernin basilica (Thursdays to Sundays) and a huge indoor produce market specialising in fish at Place Victor Hugo. Other major weekly markets in the area are listed below:

- Bazas (33) – Saturdays
- Dax (40) – Saturdays
- Mont-de-Marsan (40) – Saturdays
- Peyrehorade (40) – Wednesdays
- Agen (47) – Saturdays
- Marmande (47) – Tuesdays to Saturdays
- Villeneuve-sur-Lot (47) – Tuesdays and Saturdays
- Mauléon-Licharre (64) – Tuesdays and Saturdays
- Nay (64) – Tuesdays
- Saint-Jean-Pied-de-Port (64) – Mondays
- Saint-Palais (64) – Fridays
- Tardets (64) – every Monday in July and August; every other Monday the rest of the year

Foreign Food & Products

With its large expatriate community, Toulouse (31) is particulary well provided with shops selling foreign products – probably better than anywhere outside Paris. Supermarkets and hypermarkets, especially Carrefour and Leclerc, stock a variety of foreign food, including such British staples as Marmite and peanut butter, and may even have aisles dedicated to non-French produce. Almost every grocery shop in the city also stocks Asian food and there are a number of Asian-run stores. Close to the Spanish border, many British products are available in smaller supermarkets (including products from Sainsbury, Tesco, Waitrose!), and in Andorra (near Ariège) the shops stock all kinds of foreign goods. There's a number of English-language bookshops in the area, including those in Bordeaux, Toulouse, and Pau, and most large towns and tourist regions have bookshops that sell books in Dutch, German and Spanish (especially near the Spanish border). For general information on obtaining foreign products in France, see page 61.

Restaurants & Bars

As in any part of France, wherever you go in the south-west you will find an abundance of bars and restaurants ranging from pavement cafés to gourmet establishments. Many offer regional specialities, such as *cassoulet* from Toulouse, *foie gras* from Périgord or Gascony, oysters from Arcachon and ham from Bayonne, and a fish stew called *ttoro*, the Basque Country's answer to *bouillabaisse*. There's also a variety of international restaurants in larger towns and cities offering Italian, Spanish, Arabic, Indian and Chinese cuisine, as well as Basque restaurants, which serve some of the spiciest dishes in France! Bordeaux boasts five Michelin-starred restaurants. As in most areas, vegetarian restaurants and menus are rare. Some restaurants (especially on the coast) are open only during the summer. Not surprisingly, prices on the coast and in cities and tourist areas tend to be a little higher that in other areas.

There are American-style fast food outlets in large towns, including Buffalo Grill, Quick and the ubiquitous McDonald's as well as self-service cafeterias such as Flunch and Casino, usually located within or near shopping complexes. Cafés and bars in villages and small towns play an important part in the local community, often serving multiple functions such as *tabac*, betting shop and *bistro*. Most open around 08.00 or 09.00, sometimes even earlier, especially on market days. Closing times often seem to depend on the volume of business and the mood of the *patron*!

SERVICES

International & Private Schools

There are two international schools in the south-west: The Bordeaux International School (53, rue de Laseppe, 33000 Bordeaux, ☎ 05.57. 87.02.11, 🖳 www.bordeaux-school.com), which takes pupils from the age of 3 to 19 and offers facilities for day students and boarders, and The International School of Toulouse (Route de Pibrac, 31770, Colomiers, ☎ 05.

62.74.26.74, 🖳 www.intst.net), which is a day school only with pupils aged between 4 and 18. Fees for these schools are several thousand euros per year. There's also a number of private schools which cater for foreign students, including the Lycée privé Institution Notre-Dame (☎ 05.34.01.36.40, 🖳 www.notre-dame-pamiers.com) in Pamiers (09), the Collège privé Sainte Marie (☎ 05.59.26.20.35) in Saint-Jean-de-Luz (64) and, for primary school pupils, the Ecole privée du Sacré-Coeur (☎ 05.59.25.46.50) in Bayonne (64).

Language Schools

Language lessons are offered by a number of public and private bodies in the area. The Alliance française has branches in Toulouse (31) and Bordeaux (33). Other public and private schools include those listed below. For private lessons expect to pay between €20 and €35 per hour. Language courses are also offered by local Chambres de Commerce et d'Industrie and Centres culturels.

- Langue Onze Sud-Ouest in Toulouse (31);
- Université de Toulouse Le Mirail in Toulouse (31);
- Cetradel in Bègles (33);
- BLS in Bordeaux (33);
- Centre d'Etude des Langues in Bordeaux (33);
- MCB Langues in Bordeaux (33);
- Centre international d'Etudes in Saint-Aubin-de-Médoc (33);
- Département d'Etudes de français in Pessac (33);
- Centre d'Etudes des Langues in Bayonne (64);
- Institut d'Etudes françaises pour Etrangers (IEFE) in Pau (64);
- Ateliers linguistiques du Tarn (ALT) in Brens (81);
- ALS Langues in Tarn (81).

Details of the above schools can be found on 🖳 www.europa-pages.com. The French Consulate in London (see **Appendix A**) publishes a booklet called *Cours de français Langue étrangère et Stages pédagogiques du français Langue étrangère en France*, which includes a comprehensive list of schools and organisations providing French language courses throughout France.

Hospitals & Clinics

There are no 'international' hospitals in the south-west, although many hospitals cater for foreign patients and there are three hospitals in Bordeaux where English is known to be spoken: the Centre Hospitalier Charles Perrens, the Fondation Jean Bergonié and the Hôpital du Groupe Pellegrin-Tripode. Hospitals in main towns, and especially teaching hospitals (*CHU*), have English-speaking staff. The teaching hospitals in Toulouse and Bordeaux were rated the second and fourth-best hospitals in France in a recent survey conducted by *Le Point* magazine (published in August 2002), although no other hospitals in the south-west featured in the top 50. Private hospitals include the Clinique Pasteur in Toulouse, which is world-renowned for its highly specialised expertise in medical and surgical cardiology and provides translators if required.

Doctors & Dentists

The south-west is generally well provided with doctors, only Lot-et-Garonne having below the national average number of general practitioners per 100,000 population and Gers and Landes having below the average number of specialists. Gironde and Haute-Garonne have the highest proportion of GPs and specialists: over 185 and 160 respectively per 100,000 inhabitants. Nevertheless, it's usually easy to find and register with a doctor, many of whom speak English. The American Consulate publishes a list of English-speaking doctors and dentists in France, which includes four dentists, two general practitioners and a number of specialist doctors in Bordeaux and one GP (!) in Toulouse. The list is available on their website as part of their Guide to Living in France (🖥 www.amb-usa.fr/consul/guideoas/guidehome.htm) and in hard copy form (☎ 01.43.12.22.22).

Tradesmen

There are plenty of skilled tradesmen in the south-west, although in remote areas it's unlikely that they will be English-speaking or foreign nationals. Magazines such as *French Property News* and newspapers such as *The News* (see **Appendix B**) carry advertisements by English-speaking tradesmen. French tradesmen are unlikely to speak much English but are generally reliable.

English-language Radio

Sud Radio on 96.1FM broadcasts a programme in English at 12.15 each weekday which can be received in most parts of the area. BBC Radio 1, 2, 3, and 4 can be received on your television via the Astra satellite, and you can listen to recordings of radio programmes on Radio 1, 2, 3, 4, 5, 6 and 1Extra on your computer via the Internet (go to 🖥 www.bbc.co.uk/radio/aod/index. shtml). The World Service is available on short wave (for frequency details, go to 💻 www.bbc.co.uk/worldservice/schedules/frequencies/eurwfreq.shtml) and via the Astra satellite. Local music stations usually broadcast 60 per cent non-French language songs, most of which are in English.

English-language Press

Only cities and large towns, towns and villages with a substantial foreign population and shops near Bordeaux and Toulouse airports tend to have English newspapers and magazines. Those that can be obtained tend to be a truncated European edition and, unless bought close to an airport, are usually the previous day's edition. There are also two English-language periodicals published in France and distributed nationally, *The News* (monthly) and *France Review* (bimonthly) (see **Appendix B**). There's no local English-language press, although in Toulouse a free publication listing events of interest to English speakers is available from Books and Mermaids bookshop, and the Bordeaux British Community and Bordeaux Women's Club (see **Clubs** below) publish English-language newsletters.

Consulates

There are over 40 consulates in Bordeaux covering countries from Algeria to Togo, including the UK and the USA. The British Consulate (353, boulevard du Président Wilson, 33073 Bordeaux (☎ 05.57.22.21.10, ✉ postmaster. bordeaux@fco.gov.uk) is open Mondays to Fridays from 09.00 to 12.00 and from 14.00 to 17.00. The American Presence Post is at 10, place de la Bourse, BP 77, 33025 Bordeaux (☎ 05.56.48.63.80, ✉ bordeauxcons@fr.psinet. com). There's also a British consulate and an American presence post in Toulouse: The British Consulate, Victoria Centre, 20, chemin Laporte, 31000 Toulouse (☎ 05.61.15.02.02); The American Presence Post, 25, allée Jean-Jaurès, 31000 Toulouse (☎ 05.34.41.36.50).

Churches

The south-west has a relatively high population of Protestants (compared with the overall 2 per cent for France), and there are a number of Anglican churches in the area with regular services in English, including:

- Toulouse (31) – Eglise Sainte Marguerite;
- Bordeaux (33) – Chapelle de l'Assomption;
- Monteton (47) – Eglise de Monteton;
- Biarritz (64) – Eglise de Saint Joseph;
- Pau (64) – Saint Andrew's.

For further details of English-language services, contact Laurie Mort (☎ 05. 61.85.17.67) for Toulouse, Michael Selman (☎ 05.56.40.05.12) for Bordeaux and Monteton, John Livingstone (☎ 05.59.24.71.18) for Biarritz or Richard Eyre (☎ 05.59.90.09.30) for Pau.

There are mosques in Bordeaux (33), Mont-de-Marsan (40), Agen, Fumel (47), Bayonne and Pau (64); details can be found on 💻 http://mosquee.free.fr. There are several synagogues in Toulouse (31) and Bordeaux (33) as well as one each in Agen (47), Bayonne and Pau (64). Details can be found on 💻 www.pagesjaunes.fr (enter 'Synagogues' in the first box and the name of the town) and 💻 www.feujcity.com (where there's also information about Kosher food shops and restaurants, Jewish associations and schools, etc.).

Clubs

There are numerous clubs and associations for the English-speaking community, which have a wealth of local knowledge and are useful points of contact for new immigrants. Both the British and American Consulates (see **Consulates** above) in Bordeaux can provide a list of clubs and associations in the Aquitaine region. Clubs and associations include:

● Anglophones in Aquitaine (☎ 05.59.83.78.74) in Pau (64);

● Bordeaux Accueil (☎ 05.56.44.62.83);

● Bordeaux British Community (☎ 05.56.08.82.46, 💻 www.bordeaux british.com) publishes a newsletter and organises monthly meetings;

● Bordeaux Women's Club (☎ 05.56.36.06.50) publishes a monthly newsletter and organises a monthly lunch and other activities.

For French speakers, the Accueil des Villes françaises (AVF), a French organisation designed to welcome newcomers to an area, is an option (there's often at least one fluent English-speaker in each group). There are around 30 AVF groups in Aquitaine and the Midi-Pyrénées – in Millau, Rodez (12), Muret, Ramonville, Revel, Saint-Jean, Saint-Orens, Toulouse (31), Auch (32), Arcachon, La Teste-de-Buch, Pessac (33), Vieux-Boucau (40), Agen, Marmande, Nérac, Villeneuve-sur-Lot (47), Biarritz, Billieère, Pau, Saint-Jean-de-Luz (64), Argeles-Gazost, Lannemezan, Tarbes, Vic-en-Bigorre (65), Albi, Aussillon, Castres, Gaillac (81) and Montauban (82). The website (💻 www.avf.asso.fr) includes a directory (*annuaire*) of local groups by department as well as an online form for contacting your local AVF before you move to the area. Listings indicate whether information and services are available in English or other languages. Other sources for clubs in the area are *The News* (see **Appendix B**) and the English-speaking church (see above).

PROPERTY

The south-west has been steadily increasing in popularity over the past 15 years or so. On the coast, Gironde is particularly popular, especially among the British, although (relative) bargains can still be found on the Garonne estuary north of Bordeaux (beyond commuting distance), including large properties with vineyards. There are fewer properties available in Landes, and these tend to be snapped up by the French. Typical *landais* houses (see below) near the coast can fetch high prices. The extreme south-west is perhaps France's best-kept secret, although prices are beginning to shoot up here too and a lot of new properties are being built in and around Pau (64).

Inland, the department of Tarn and, more recently, Tarn-et-Garonne and Lot-et-Garonne becoming particularly sought-after (and consequently expensive). Those unable to find a suitable property in Dordogne and Lot look mainly to Lot-et-Garonne, and the area between Albi, Cordes-sur-Ciel and Gaillac in Tarn has become known among estate agents as the 'Golden Triangle'. Lot-et-Garonne is now so popular with tourists that there's a shortage of almost 1,000 beds each year to accommodate them, and grants of up to 50 per cent are available to those wanting to renovate properties in order to provide tourist accommodation. Therefore, there's considerable demand for such properties and generally for habitable stone houses with plenty of land which are secluded but not isolated, and consequently there's a shortage of this type of property around Agen, Villeneuve and other main towns in the department. Properties are easier to come by in more rural areas, mainly to the north-west of Agen and north of Villeneuve.

Elsewhere, cheaper properties can be found around Rodez in Aveyron and generally on higher ground. In fact, prices tend to drop the higher you go, as areas below around 500m (1,600ft) enjoy better weather. Above this height, tiles give way to slate roofs to keep out the rain and snow (see below). There are also fewer properties generally on higher ground, where they tend to be dotted around and many are isolated.

Typical Homes

There's a number of different styles that are typical of various parts of the south-west. Typical of the major seaside resorts are elaborate brick, stone and plaster villas, the finest examples of which are to be found at Arcachon (33). Homes in the mountains of Ariège are made of granite, slate and shale, often with a facing of chalk or sand, which makes them pale or almost white. Many have a round bread oven attached to one side and opening into the kitchen. Square pigeon houses with tiled roofs sloping on all four sides, unlike the round ones found elsewhere in France, are a feature of Gers, where almost every farm has one – either free-standing or adjoining other buildings. Single-storey houses in brick or stone attached to farm buildings, often around a courtyard, are typical of Gascony, while the area around Toulouse (as far as Bram and Villefranche to the east and Montauban to the west) is characterised by yellow and red brick and Roman or provençal roof tiles (*tuiles canal*), small stones sometimes being added to the brickwork in more southern parts between Toulouse and Saint-Félix.

In the Landes, houses tend to be half-timbered, sometimes with a first floor balcony at the front of the house, under the eaves. The typical Basque Country house, found in western Pyrénées-Atlantiques, is made of white-painted stone with red timbers and shutters (or occasionally green or dark blue – the Basque flag is red and green, the sea and the sky are deep blue!). It also often has a first-floor balcony above a carved lintel, and a shallow-sloping roof of Roman tiles (the village of Aïnhoa in Pyrénées-Atlantiques is the quintessential Basque village). As you move east into Basse-Navarre, the houses become more austere, with narrow windows and chalk-coated walls decorated with grey stones. Usually single-storey, they have a more sloping roof than the Basque houses, covered partly with tiles and partly with slate and often with the name of the owner, the date of construction and sometimes a religious inscription on the lintel. Still further east, near the border between Pyrénées-Atlantiques and Hautes-Pyrénées, in the Béarn 'region', the houses are plainer still, although with doors and windows framed by Pyrenean marble. More often two-storey, their pointed, slate-covered roofs slope on all four sides.

Cost of Housing

Prices in the south-west have been rising steadily for the last 15 years and particularly sharply in the last five years or so; it's predicted that they will continue to rise in the coming years. Coastal properties in Gironde and inland houses in Tarn, Tarn-et-Garonne and Lot-et-Garonne are particularly expensive. Cheaper areas include Ariège, Aveyron, Hautes-Pyrénées and parts of Pyrénées-Atlantiques, where prices generally drop the higher you go.

Castres (81) boasts the lowest average prices for older properties in the area and the second-lowest in France (after Montluçon in Allier), while the area's highest average prices are to be found in Bayonne (64). The table below gives average prices per m^2 for older properties in major towns in the area:

Town	Average Price per m^2 (€)
Toulouse (31)	1,010
Bordeaux (33)	1,005
Agen (47)	790
Bayonne (64)	1,085

Pau (64)	850
Tarbes (65)	720
Albi (81)	805
Castres (81)	595
Montauban (82)	915

Note, however, that average property prices aren't always a reliable indication of the relative price of similar properties in different towns, as one town may have a preponderance of cheaper or more expensive properties. The tables below give an indication of price ranges for different types of properties in the 11 departments of Aquitaine and Midi-Pyrénées considered here, although it should be borne in mind that, as elsewhere, location has a significant effect on the value of property; a home with a sea-view, for example, can command a 100 per cent premium (indicated by the upper end of price ranges). Where figures are shown in brackets, this indicates that there are few properties of that type in the relevant department or area and the figures quoted are examples rather than necessarily typical; where there are no figures, there are virtually no properties of that type.

Apartments

Most apartments are of course to be found in the main cities and towns, particularly Bordeaux and Toulouse, as indicated in the table below. There are also lots of apartments available in Pyrénées-Atlantiques, whereas there are few apartments in Ariège, Aveyron, Gers, Lot-et-Garonne and Tarn.

Department/Area	Size (m²)	No. of Bedrooms	Price (€)
Ariège	25	Studio	25,000
	50	1	35,000–55,000
	70	2	40,000–65,000
	90	3	(65,000)
Aveyron			
Rodez	25	Studio	30,000–40,000
	50	1	35,000–60,000
	70	2	55,000–110,000
	90	3	70,000–125,000
Haute-Garonne			
Toulouse	25	Studio	30,000–40,000

	50	1	40,000–100,000
	70	2	60,000–140,000
	90	3	100,000–300,000
Elsewhere	25	Studio	25,000–35,000
	50	1	35,000–60,000
	70	2	40,000–100,000
	90	3	80,000–200,000
Gers	25	Studio	20,000–40,000
	50	1	(35,000)
	70	2	50,000–70,000
	90	3	(80,000)
Gironde			
Bordeaux	25	Studio	25,000–50,000
	50	1	30,000–100,000
	70	2	80,000–225,000
	90	3	150,000+
Elsewhere	50	1	50,000–100,000
	70	2	100,000–250,000
	90	3	120,00+
Landes	25	Studio	60,000–80,000
	50	1	65,000–120,000
	70	2	80,000–160,000
	90	3	100,000–225,000
Lot-et-Garonne	50	1	50,000–120,000
	70	2	60,000–140,000
	90	3	80,000–200,000
Pyrénees-Atlantiques			
Bayonne/Biarritz	25	Studio	75,000
	50	1	95,000
	70	2	130,000–250,000
	90	3	150,000–300,000

Elsewhere	25	Studio	25,000–50,000
	50	1	30,000–90,000
	70	2	50,000–110,000
	90	3	75,000–225,000
Hautes-Pyrénées	25	Studio	20,000–60,000
	50	1	25,000–70,000
	70	2	35,000–80,000
	90	3	50,000+
Tarn			
Castres	25	Studio	25,000
	50	1	25,000–50,000
	70	2	50,000–90,000
	90	3	100,000
Tarn-et-Garonne			
Montauban	25	Studio	20,000–35,000
	50	1	25,000–70,000
	70	2	60,000–175,000
	90	3	75,000–200,000

Houses

By far the greatest number of available houses is in Gironde. There are also plenty of houses for sale in Haute-Garonne, Landes, Lot-et-Garonne, Pyrénées-Atlantiques and Tarn-et-Garonne, but few in Ariège, Aveyron and Gers and very few in Hautes-Pyrénées. There are few houses for sale in Toulouse, where available properties tend to be large (and expensive). The table below shows that, in many areas, larger houses can be bought more cheaply than medium-size properties.

Department/Area	No. of Bedrooms	Price (€)
Ariège	2	(80,000)
	3	100,000–350,000
	4	100,000–550,000
Avyron	2	65,000–135,000
	3	115,000–240,000
	4	150,000–240,000

Haute-Garonne

Toulouse	2	(160,000)
	3	125,000–200,000
	4	270,000–550,000
	5	600,000+
Elsewhere	3	115,000–325,000
	4	145,000–300,000
	5	(200,000)

Gers

	2	80,000–155,000
	3	135,000–325,000
	4	140,000–400,000
	5	250,000–500,000

Gironde

Bordeaux	2	90,000–150,000
	3	140,000–250,000
	4	(200,000)
	5	(250,000+)
Elsewhere	2	75,000–170,000
	3	160,000–400,000
	4	115,000–400,000
	5	130,000–500,000

Landes

	2	60,000–170,000
	3	100,000–200,000
	4	100,000–215,000
	5	140,000–350,000

Lot-et-Garonne

	2	90,000–250,000
	3	130,000–250,000
	4	100,000–400,000
	5	140,000–450,000

Pyrénées-Atlantiques

	2	45,000–130,000
	3	135,000–350,000
	4	200,000–400,000

	5	230,000–400,000
Hautes-Pyrénées	2	40,000–160,000
	3	60,000–200,000
	4	130,000–275,000
	5	(300,000)
Tarn	3	75,000–250,000
	4	120,000–260,000
	5	(225,000)
Tarn-et-Garonne	3	85,000–225,000
	4	100,000–250,000
	5	170,000–500,000

Properties for Restoration

There are plenty of properties available for restoration in Aveyron and a number in Gers, Tarn and Tarn-et-Garonne, although bargain ruins without hidden problems (e.g. liable to flooding or the subject of lengthy inheritance battles) are hard to find. The following examples will give those looking for a house to restore an idea of the prices they can expect to pay.

Department	No. of Bedrooms	Price (€)
Aveyron	2	20,000
	3	15,000
	4	50,000
	5	70,000–85,000
Gers	2	15,000
	6	125,000
Tarn	5	45,000–100,000
Tarn-et-Garonne	4	30,000

Land

Building land is available in all areas, and there's little demand for it; it's most plentiful in Gironde, Landes and Pyrénées-Atlantiques and least plentiful in Ariège, Aveyron and Tarn. Prices vary considerably according to location and whether main services are connected. Land in or near a small village, where there's no mains drainage, can be bought for less than €5 per m², whereas land with connections to all services, including electricity and telephone, near a town can cost as much as €100 per m². The table below gives an idea of price ranges in the various departments. Plots range from around 400m² to several hectares, the average plot being between 1,000 and 3,000m². Most local estate agents sell building plots (*terrains à bâtir* or *terrains constructibles*). Note that many areas are liable to flooding and, as elsewhere in France, planning permission is becoming increasingly difficult to obtain.

Department	Price (€) per m²
Ariège	10–20
Aveyron	5–25
Haute-Garonne	5–30
Gers	5–70
Gironde	30–50
Landes	25–100
Lot-et-Garonne	5–25
Pyrénées-Atlantiques	5–60
Hautes-Pyrénées	10–35
Tarn	10–25
Tarn-et-Garonne	5–20

Rental Accommodation

Apartments: There's a fair number of apartments available for long-term rent in Gironde, Haute-Garonne and Pyrénées-Atlantiques but few or none in Ariège, Gers and Hautes-Pyrénées. Most apartments are in the main towns in each department (i.e. Agen in Lot-et-Garonne, Toulouse in Haute-Garonne, Bayonne and Pau in Pyrénées-Atlantiques, Dax and Mont-de-Marsan in Landes, Castres in Tarn, and Montauban in Tarn-et-Garonne), and few are available elsewhere. Price ranges for each department (except Hautes-Pyrénées) are shown below.

Department	No. of Bedrooms	Monthly Rental (€)
Ariège	Studio	(175)
	1	275–400
	2	400
Aveyron	Studio	125–250
	1	300

	2	375–450
	3	400–500
Haute-Garonne	Studio	275
	1	300–600
	2	425–750
	3	525–900
Gers	Studio	225–275
	1	250–375
	2	375–450
Gironde	Studio	225–375
	1	350–550
	2	600–650
	3	600–1,250
Landes	Studio	190–255
	1	370–520
	2	400–600
	3	450–575
Lot-et-Garonne	Studio	275
	1	400
	2	550
	3	750
Pyrénées-Atlantiques	Studio	200–400
	1	200–460
	2	400–650
	3	400–500
Tarn	Studio	150–250
	1	250–325
	2	300–500
Tarn-et-Garonne	Studio	200–250
	1	350
	2	425–750
	3	450–625

Houses: Rented houses are less common than apartments, and very few are to be found in most departments; Gironde and Haute-Garonne have the largest number of houses for rent. The table below gives an indication of the rental prices for houses in each department.

Department	No. of Bedrooms	Monthly Rental (€)
Ariège	4	(650)
Aveyron	2	400–550
	3	550
	4	550
Haute-Garonne	3	600–800
	4	650–1,600
	5	700–1,200
Gers	4	(1,000–3,000)
Gironde	2	400–625
	3	400–1,000
	4	1,000–2,000
	5	1,200+
Landes	2	375–650
	3	400–700
	4	600–1,000
	5	800+
Lot-et-Garonne	2	400
	3	550–650
	4	400–700
	5	850
Pyrénées-Atlantiques	3	800–950
	4	750–800
Tarn	2	400–450
	3	425–550
	4	650–1,000
Tarn-et-Garonne	2	550
	3	550–650

4	650–700
5	900

COMMUNICATIONS

Air

The recent spread of low-cost scheduled services to regional airports in the south-west has made the area more accessible, particularly from the UK. The Irish low-cost airline Ryanair operates two daily scheduled flights from London Stansted to Biarritz (64). Buzz also operates out of Stansted with daily flights to Toulouse (31) and twice daily to Bordeaux (33). Flybe (formerly British European) flies from Birmingham, Glasgow, Edinburgh and Belfast to Toulouse. Among the traditional carriers, which have had to respond to the competition from the low-cost airlines by curring their prices, British Airways fly from London Gatwick to both Bordeaux and Toulouse. Those with property in eastern parts of Midi-Pyrénées may be able to take advantage of flights to Carcassonne in Aude (see page 244).

Although some other airports in the south-west purport to be 'international', most handle only flights from within the EU and from North Africa. Travellers from other parts of the world must change at Paris, London, Amsterdam or Brussels. Air France is the leading carrier to regional airports and has connections to all regional airports from both Paris airports: Roissy-Charles de Gaulle and Orly. Another airline that flies from Orly is Air Liberté Express, a low-cost division of Air Lib, which offers flights to Toulouse and Lourdes. Major airports in the area are shown on the maps at the beginning of the chapter. Details of all French airports and their services can be found on 🖥 www.aeroport.fr.

Sea

British people buying a home in the south-western part of the area may wish to take advantage of ferry services between the UK and northern Spain. P&O Portsmouth Ferries (UK ☎ 0870-242 4999, 🖥 www.poportsmouth.com) operates a twice-weekly service between Portsmouth and Bilbao. The outward ferry departs Portsmouth at 20.00 on Tuesdays and Saturdays and takes 36 hours, with two nights on board; the return ferry leaves Bilbao at 12.30 on Thursdays and Mondays, taking 28 hours. The typical off-peak (February) cost of a return trip for two adults with a medium-sized car and sharing a two-berth cabin is around £600, rising to over £700 if two children and a four-berth cabin are included. As always, there's a variety of special deals, and costs can compare favourably with a Channel crossing and a return drive from north to south, incurring toll charges and possibly with overnight stays in hotels *en route*. Note that travellers must book a cabin and that pets aren't allowed. The drive from Bilbao to Biarritz is less than 160km (100mi).

Alternatively, Brittany Ferries (☎ 0870-536 0360, 🖳 www.brittanyferries. com) operates from mid-March to mid-November, sailing on average twice weekly between Plymouth and Santander – Mondays/Wednesdays from Plymouth and Tuesdays/Thursdays from Santander. Prices are broadly comparable with those of P&O Ferries to Bilbao, although the euro-conscious traveller can save money by opting for a couchette rather than a cabin (not an option with P&O). However, Santander is approximately 100km (60km) further than Bilbao from the French border.

Public Transport

Rail: The *TGV* runs from Paris (Montparnasse) to Bordeaux, although it must slow to a mere 200kph (120mph) from Tours (see map in **Appendix E**). South-west France has a comprehensive internal rail network, the Midi-Pyrénées region alone boasting over 100 stations, and from Bordeaux there are ordinary rail links to Toulouse and beyond via Agen (47) and to Lourdes and Tarbes (65) via Dax (40) and Pau (64). There are also spurs leading to Arcachon (33) and (from Dax) to Bayonne and Hendaye (64). (There's also a spectacular train journey from Foix (09) across the Pyrenees into Spain.)

Motorail (car sleeper) services are available at all times of year from Boulogne, Calais, Dieppe and Paris to all parts of south-west France, although the cost is quite high and there are height restrictions (most 4x4s and 'people carriers' cannot be accommodated). Note that you're unable to access your vehicle during the journey, and there have been UK newspaper and TV reports of vehicles being damaged in transit.

Bus, Coach, Métro & Tram: Eurolines and National Express offer coach services from London (Victoria) to Bordeaux. Within the area, urban public transport is excellent in all areas, with comprehensive bus services in all major towns and cities. In addition, Toulouse has a recently extended underground (*métro*) system linking Basso-Cambo in the west with Joliment in the east, and Bordeaux has started construction of a tramway, scheduled for inauguration at the end of 2003 but not expected to be completed until 2006 (in the meantime, residents of the city are entitled to the free loan of bicycles!). As in other parts of France, services between towns and in rural areas are infrequent or non-existent.

Roads

The south-west is generally well served by both motorways and trunk roads. Most motorways are toll roads and are very well maintained. The main motorways from the north to the south-west are the A10 Paris to Bordeaux and the A20, which branches off the A10 at Orléans and runs as far as Toulouse. The A62 links Bordeaux and Toulouse, and the A64 runs from Toulouse to Pau and beyond, linking with a short stretch of the A63 from near Dax to Spain. Another short stretch of the A63 runs south from Bordeaux to Arcachon and towards Dax; the intervening distance is covered by the N10, which is due to be upgraded to motorway.

Bordeaux can be reached in around seven to eight hours from the Channel ports or three to four hours from the Spanish ports (see above), and Toulouse in eight to nine hours from the Channel ports or four to five hours from the Spanish ports. Bordeaux is experiencing acute traffic congestion at rush hours during the construction of its new tramway (see above), which has caused the closure of one of the bridges across the Garonne.

Driving standards in the south-west are generally below average for France (i.e. terrible), and Gers has the highest road death rate of any department in the country, with over 270 deaths per million inhabitants. You have been warned!

PLANNED DEVELOPMENTS

A number of transport improvements are in the pipeline, including Bordeaux's new tramway, which promises to put an end to the city's traffic problems (?) but may not be completed until 2006, an electric bus service in Arcachon and extensions to the Toulouse *métro*. Toulouse is also to be the site of a new *médiathèque* (library and media centre). One of the largest developments in the area is the new Aéroconstellation site near Blagnac (31) – see below – which will spawn two new towns to accommodate workers: Andromède with 2,400 homes and Monges-Croix-du-Sud with 650 homes, expected to be habitable by 2005.

EMPLOYMENT PROSPECTS

Services account for 60 per cent of the population in the south-west, industry 25 per cent and agriculture 15 per cent. The main industry sectors are aerospace, chemicals, electronics, energy, oil (Elf), paper, pharmaceuticals and wine making. Blagnac (31) is the site of a vast new industrial park called Aéroconstellation, where the new 550-seat Airbus A380s will be built, directly and indirectly employing some 9,000 people. Major service sectors include call centres, logistics and tourism. According to a recent survey by *Le Point* magazine (see **Appendix F**), Albi (81) is a particularly good place to start a business, as it enjoys one of the highest rates of new business success in France. A number of companies advertise in both French and English on their websites. There's a variety of seasonal work in the area, for which no particular skills or qualifications are required, ranging from fruit and grape picking in the summer/autumn to bar and other ski resort work in the winter, but you must apply several months in advance to secure a position.

FURTHER INFORMATION

Useful Addresses

- Comité régional de Tourisme d'**Aquitaine**, Cité mondiale, 23, Parvis des Chartrons, 33074 Bordeaux (☎ 05.56.01.70.00, 💻 www.crt.cr aquitaine.fr)

- Comité régional du Tourisme de **Midi-Pyrénées**, 54, boulevard de l'Embouchure, BP 2166, 31022 Toulouse cedex 2 (☎ 05.61.13.55.55, 💻 www.tourisme-midi-pyrenees.com)

- Comité départemental du Tourisme de l'**Ariège-Pyrénées**, 31bis, avenue du Général de Gaulle, BP 143, 09004 Foix (☎ 05.6102.30.70, 💻 http:// ariege pyrenees.com.)

- Comité départemental du Tourisme de l'**Aveyron**, 17, rue Aristide Briand, BP 831, 12008 Rodez (☎ 05.65.75.55.70, ✉ aveyron-tourismecdt@ wanadoo.fr)

- Comité départemental du Tourisme de la **Haute-Garonne**, 14, rue Bayard, BP 845, 31015 Toulouse cedex 6 (☎ 05.61.99.44.00, 💻 www.cdt-haute-garonne.fr)

- Comité départemental du Tourisme du **Gers** en Gascogne, 3, boulevard Roquelaure, BP 106, 32002 Auch (☎ 05.62.05.95.95, ✉ cdtdugers@ wanadoo.fr)

- Comité départemental du Tourisme de la **Gironde**, 21, cours de l'Intendance, 33000 Bordeaux (☎ 05.56.52.61.40, 💻 www.tourisme-gironde.cg33.fr)

- Comité départemental du Tourisme des **Landes**, 4, avenue Aristide-Briand, BP 407, 40012 Mont-de-Marsan (☎ 05.58.06.89.89, ✉ cdt. landes@ wanadoo.fr)

- Comité départemental du Tourisme de **Lot-et-Garonne**, Maison du Tourisme, 4, rue André Chénier, BP 32147, 47005 Agen (☎ 05.53. 66.14.14, ✉ cdt47@ wandadoo.fr)

- Mission touristique des **Pyrénées-Atlantiques**, 22ter, rue Jean-Jacques de Monaix, 64000 Pau (☎ 05.59.30.07.28)

- Agence du Tourisme du **Pays Basque**, 4, allée des Platanes, BP 811, 64108 Bayonne (☎ 05.59.46.52.52, ✉ cdt@cg64.fr)

- Agence du Tourisme du **Béarn**, 22ter, rue Jean-Jacques de Monaix, 64000 Pau (☎ 05.59.30.01.30)

- **Hautes-Pyrénées** Tourisme Environnement, 6, rue Eugène Ténot, BP 450, 65004 Tarbes (☎ 05.62.56.70.65, ✉ tourisme.hautes-pyrenees@ wanadoo.fr)

- Comité départemental du Tourisme du **Tarn**, 41, rue Porta, BP 225, 81006 Albi (☎ 05.63.77.32.10, ✉ cdt-du-tarn@wanadoo.fr)

- Comité départemental du Tourisme de **Tarn-et-Garonne**, 2, boulevard Midi-Pyrénées, BP 534, 82005 Montauban (☎ 05.63.21.79.09, ✉ tourismedutarnetgaronne@lemel.fr)

Useful Publications

- **A Harvest of Sunflowers**, Ruth Silvestre (Allison & Busby) – sequel to **A House in the Sunflowers** (see below)

- **A House in the Sunflowers**, Ruth Silvestre (Allison & Busby)

- **Life in a Postcard: Escape to the French Pyrenees**, Rosemary Bailey (Bantam Books)

Useful Websites

- 💻 www.123voyage.com – includes a guide to south-west France

- 💻 www.guide-basque.com (details of festivals and events in the Basque region)

- 💻 www.bordeauxbritish.com (Bordeaux British Community)

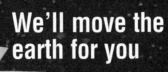

Menton – The Mediterranean Coast

Jim Watson

The Mediterranean coastal area described in this chapter comprises the whole of the administrative region of Languedoc-Roussillon and most of that of Provence-Alpes-Côte d'Azur, including the departments of Alpes-de-Haute-Provence (4), Alpes-Maritimes (6), Aude (11), Bouches-du-Rhône (13), Gard (30), Hérault (34), Lozère (48), Pyrénées-Orientales (66), Var (83) and Vaucluse (84). The only other department in Provence-Alpes-Côte d'Azur, Hautes-Alpes (05), is described in **Chapter 7**.

The magazine *Le Point* has more than once elected Aix-en-Provence (13), the 'capital' of Provence, the best French town to live in (see **Appendix F**), and *The Riviera Times* recently wrote with reference to the Côte d'Azur: "Sun, blue skies, warm sea, delicious food and tasty wines, idyllic villages and an allure of luxury. Surely that's the life we are all looking for?" Provence-Alpes-Côte d'Azur is the most popular region in France for holiday and retirement homes and has a large foreign community, the British, Germans and Italians being among the largest buyers of second homes. In 2001 there were around 8,000 official British residents (Peter Mayle's televised book, *A Year in Provence*, caused countless Brits to pack up and head south). Popularity, of course, has its price, notably in respect of property costs, which have risen beyond the reach of many, who may look instead towards Languedoc-Roussillon, which currently has only half as many British residents as Provence-Alpes-Côte d'Azur.

Languedoc-Roussillon

Languedoc-Roussillon, often referred to simply as 'the Languedoc' (after one of the two ancient languages of France, the *langue d'Oc*, the Roussillon part corresponding approximately to the Pyrénées-Orientales department) or by the French, confusingly, as *le Midi*, has an area of 27,376km² (17,010mi²) and a population of 2.3 million. It contains the coastal departments (from east to west) of Gard, Hérault, Aude and Pyrénées-Orientales, as well as Lozère, which is inland. The region resembles a hammock stretched between Mount Lozère 1,700m (5,580ft) in the north and Mount Canigou 2,784m (9,135ft) in the south. Lozère has the highest average altitude in France of 1,000m (3,280ft). Bordered by the Pyrenees, Andorra and Spain in the south, Languedoc-Roussillon extends north as far as the Massif Central (where Lozère is France's most sparsely populated department). It has a long Mediterranean coastline of virtually uninterrupted sandy beaches, stretching some 180km (110mi) from the Petite Camargue nature reserve in Gard, through Hérault, Aude and Pyrénées-Orientales, with its beautiful beaches and cliff inlets (*calanques*) of pink rock, to the Spanish border. Overall, the region is 30 per cent woodland, 15 per cent grassland, 10 per cent arable land and 45 per cent other uses (including urban areas – the second-highest proportion in France).

Few French regions are more steeped in history than Languedoc (home of the heretical Cathars), which also offers an abundance of excellent (but under-rated) wines such as Corbières, Minervois and Côtes du Roussillon. It encompasses the largest wine production area in Europe (Béziers claims to be France's wine capital!). The region has a vast range of scenery and landscape, including the beautiful Cévennes national park and Tarn valley areas (famously written about by Robert Louis Stevenson in his ***Travels with a Donkey***), the tranquil Canal du Midi, the gentle rolling hills of the Pyrenees, home to a handful of protected bears living in the wild, and the dramatic beauty (not always appreciated by the Tour de France cyclists) of the high Pyrenees peaks.

Languedoc is noted for its relaxed pace of life and is a popular hideaway for those seeking peace and tranquillity. It has its own ancient language (*Occitan*) and many towns close to the Spanish border have a Catalan feel (Catalan is also spoken here). See **Language** on page 221.

A number of purpose-built resorts have been created on the *Côte vermeille* (Vermillion Coast) in the last few decades, including Argelès-sur-Mer,

Gruissan, St Cyprien, Port Bacarès, Port Leucate and Cap d'Agde, where apartment blocks are mostly unattractive if you're looking for a home with character. Collioure, on the other hand, known as the 'jewel of the Vermillion Coast', is a most attractive (and expensive) port. Overall, Languedoc-Roussillon is popular with second homeowners, property being much cheaper here than in the Provence-Alpes-Côte d'Azur region, its adjacent 'competitor' on the Mediterranean coast.

Provence-Alpes-Côte d'Azur

Provence-Alpes-Côte d'Azur, abbreviated to PACA by officials and residents, contains the coastal departments, running west to east to the Italian border, of the Bouches-du-Rhône, Var and Alpes-Maritimes, and the inland departments of Alpes-de-Haute-Provence and Vaucluse. The inland department of Hautes-Alpes (in the Rhône-Alpes region) is also included in this section, as it 'belongs' more to the Mediterranean coast than to the Alps, which are considered in **Chapter 7**. Slightly larger than its Mediterranean neighbour, Languedoc-Roussillon, the PACA region occupies an area of 31,400km^2 (19,510mi^2) and has a population approaching 4.6 million. Economically, it's the second most important region in France after the Ile-de-France. Overall, the region is 40 per cent woodland (the second-highest proportion in France), 15 per cent grassland, 10 per cent arable land and 35 per cent other uses (including urban areas).

The Provence area comprises the Alpes-de-Haute-Provence, Bouches-du-Rhône and Vaucluse departments and part of the Var, although opinions differ as to exactly where Provence ends and the Côte d'Azur (Azure Coast) begins. The Côte d'Azur was 'discovered' by the British, who dubbed it the 'French Riviera' and helped to create the world's first coastal playground for the rich and famous. At the end of the 19th century, Queen Victoria was influential in developing the area's popularity through her visits to Hyères (just east of Toulon), which was then considered the western extremity of the Côte d'Azur. Today, many people regard Saint-Tropez, 45km (28mi) further east along the coast, as the limit of Provence and the start of the Côte d'Azur (known locally as *la Côte*). Another school of thought (whose members understandably include many local estate agents) believes that the Côte d'Azur lies between Hyères and the conurbation of Fréjus-Saint-Raphaël (east of Saint-Tropez). There are also those who consider the French Riviera as the stretch of coastline from Menton, close to the Italian border, to just beyond Cannes, the Côte d'Azur encompassing the French Riviera and extending to Saint-Tropez. (Note that Monaco, although geographically part of the Riviera/Côte d'Azur, is a separate principality and not part of France.)

Wherever it exactly begins and ends, Provence is a fascinating land of romance, history (it has its own ancient language, Provençal, now spoken only in Italy) and great beauty and is celebrated for its excellent climate, attractive scenery, fine beaches, superb cuisine and fashionable resorts. It's one of the most exclusive areas of France, and few places in Europe can compete with its ambience and allure, glamorous resorts and beautiful people. However, it's also a region of stark contrasts, with a huge variety of landscape and scenery encompassing extensive woodlands, rugged mountains, rolling hills, spectacular gorges (the Grand Canyon du Verdon is the deepest cleft in the surface of Europe), dramatic rock formations, lush and fertile valleys carpeted with lavender, extensive vineyards (which stretch to the foot of the rugged Alpilles mountains in Vaucluse), and a ravishing coastline dotted with quaint fishing villages and fine beaches.

A journey through Provence is an indulgence of the senses, and its diverse vegetation includes cypresses, gnarled olive trees, almond groves, umbrella pines, lavender, wild rosemary and thyme, all of which add to its unique and seductive sights and smells. Provence produces a number of excellent wines and includes the prestigious vineyards of Châteauneuf-du-Pape, Gigondas (mostly red) and Lilac (red, white and *rosé*) plus popular and drinkable wines such as Côtes du Lubéron and Côtes de Provence.

The region contains many beautiful areas, notably the Lubéron National Park (Parc naturel régional du Lubéron), the heart of the provençal countryside and still a fashionable area for holiday homes and visitors, in spite of or perhaps because of Peter Mayle. The Camargue, between Arles and the sea (from which it was reclaimed), is one of the most spectacular nature reserves in France and famous for its wild horses. Provence also contains a wealth of beautiful historic Roman towns and dramatically sited medieval villages (see **Major Towns and Places of Interest** on page 216), and both Marseilles and Nice provide sea links (see **Communications** on page 244) to Corsica and North Africa, where the holiday resorts of Morocco and Tunisia are popular with the French (being former protectorates where French is still widely spoken).

Although the Alpes-Maritimes and Bouches-du-Rhône departments have very little coastline which isn't built-up, Var has perhaps the most attractive, unspoilt coastline in the PACA region, between Hyères and Fréjus-Staint-Raphaël.

ADVANTAGES & DISADVANTAGES

For many people the climate on the Mediterranean coast is one of its principal attractions, although you may find bright sun most of the year round boring and the stifling summers unbearable. Northern Europeans may miss the lack of marked changes of season on the coast, although the *Tramontane* mountain wind, affecting the coastal area from Perpignan to Narbonne, can be extremely nippy and parts of Languedoc-Roussillon suffer heavy rain at times. The department of Alpes-Maritimes is officially an earthquake risk area, although the likelihood of a serious earthquake is minimal.

Partly because of the climate, the Mediterranean coast is considered to be one of the healthiest areas to live in France, and the mortality rate (from all causes) is lower here than almost anywhere else in the country (despite worse than average driving standards!). There's no shortage of general practitioners and specialists in the Languedoc-Roussillon and PACA areas, particularly on the coast; in fact, you're almost spoilt for choice. Although the Aquitaine and Midi-Pyrénées regions in the south-west (see **Chapter 5**) are recognised by several official organisations as offering the healthiest foods in France, the Languedoc-Roussillon region is considered by many gourmets (or perhaps gourmands?) to be a second 'south-west', offering an extremely varied cuisine, with Italian and Arab influences and also a Spanish influence from the Spanish colony in Toulouse.

Another advantage of buying a property on the Mediterranean coast is that most parts of the area are easily accessible from most parts of the world, and the increase in budget flights within France and from other European countries (notably the UK) as well as recent improvements in the French high-speed train network – see **Communications** on page 244) enable you not only to travel to your property frequently and cheaply but also to escape the summer heat if you wish. Spain and Italy are quickly reached from the western and eastern ends of the coast respectively (Barcelona, for example, is just a few hours from Perpignan by road, while Florence, Venice and the

Italian lakes are within striking distance of Alpes-Maritimes and parts of Alpes-de-Haute-Provence). Residents can also take advantage of the continued expansion of the Mediterranean cruise business (see page 245), which offers a leisurely way to enjoy the European and North African Mediterranean coasts and the Mediterranean islands.

On the debit side are the high rates of crime (see page 224) and unemployement (see page 248), but perhaps the major disadvantage of the area is the cost of living there. The PACA region is the second most expensive in France (after Paris), although Languedoc-Roussillon has an appreciably lower cost of living (see page 224). Property prices follow this pattern (see page 240) and you can pay two or three times as much for a property on the Mediterranean coast as for a similar home in a less popular area of France.

The popularity of the area causes another of its major disadvantages. Around 25 million tourists visit the PACA region every year, and Languedoc-Roussillon region is in the top five French tourist areas. The entire coastline in both regions (with the exception of Marseilles and, to a lesser extent, Toulon) is a tourist area in high season (June to September), when visitors from inland areas as well as other parts of France and the world triple or quadruple the population. The coast is dotted with campsites as well as hotels and self-catering accommodation, all of which are filled to overflowing. So, if you buy a property near a main resort and close to the beach, apart from paying a premium and probably having a small amount of land, you should expect traffic congestion and general noise and bustle in the high season. You can still, however, enjoy the beach and Mediterranean swims just before or after the high season (especially if you're used to English Channel temperatures) on a coast that regains its charm. The high season is of course good news if you've bought a seaside property with letting for part of the year in mind, when the Côte d'Azur is a better investment than Languedoc-Roussillon even allowing for the higher property prices.

Major inland towns and tourist attractions (see below) have similar high season inconveniences. These may also extend to certain festival periods, not necessarily in the summer. There are, however, numerous inland locations, particularly in the Languedoc area, where peace and quiet, relaxation and seclusion can be found all year round. Extreme seclusion, if you're seeking a hermit's lifestyle, can be found in the Lozère department, which has de-populated by some 50 per cent over the last 150 years.

Of all France's major towns, Nice (06) is the worst affected by flooding (it has been flooded 19 times in the last 30 years), closely followed by Marseilles (13) and Antibes (06) with 17 and 16 floods respectively since 1982. Nice also suffers a lack of green space (a mere 1m^2 per inhabitant) and a shortage of cycle track, as do Aix-en-Provence, Béziers, Cannes, Marseilles and Toulon. Carcassonne (11) has more green space than almost any other town in France (over 136m^2 per inhabitant), and keen cyclists should favour Avignon, where there's more cycle track per inhabitant than anywhere else in the area. Marseilles has also been the scene of occasional attacks by Corsican terrorists. Entressen (13) is the site of Europe's largest open refuse tip, which was due to close in 2002 but may remain in use until 2007.

On the plus side, the Mediterranean coast boasts the largest number of 'blue flag' beaches and ports of any of the areas considered in this book (34 resorts with 'blue flag' beaches and 37 blue flag ports) – the majority in Pyrénées-Orientales, Hérault and Var (see 🖥 www.pavillonbleu.com), although there's also a number of 'black flag' beaches (considered unacceptably polluted by the Surfrider Foundation Europe – see 🖥 www.surf rider-europe.org): one in Antibes (06), three in Cassis and one each in Marseilles and Martigues (13), and two in Palavas-les-Flots (34). Even if you aren't up to surfing, the generally stable weather allows you to step out of the door and go for a long walk or cycle at a moment's notice. Golf, on the other hand, requires a not inconsiderable annual budget even if you play (or want to play) once a month on a public course. Membership of a private club costs at least €2,000 per year. Sea swimming is possible for five or six months a year (depending on your tolerance of the cold), and there are plenty of public swimming pools which, however, have a tendency to overheat the water.

As far as integration is concerned, the PACA region in particular has become such a mixture of non-Mediterranean French people, French colonials (*pieds-noirs*) from Algeria, other Mediterranean nationalities and Northern Europeans that newcomers to the area will almost certainly detect a certain apprehension, reserve and perhaps mistrust on the part of the original locals, natives of the region. Probably accounting for less than half the population, France's 'Mediterranean Man' may be difficult to really fathom and get to know, especially if you don't make the effort to show that you have a long-term contribution to make towards community or village life; persist and you should be rewarded.

MAJOR TOWNS & PLACES OF INTEREST

Cities, towns and villages of interest to foreign homebuyers are listed below by department (in alphabetical order), with approximate population figures for each town or city, as well as the major tourist attractions in each department.

Alpes-de-Haute-Provence (04)

Digne-les-Bains (pop. 16,000), the unpretentious departmental capital, with its healthy mountain air at 600m (1,900ft) altitude and curative (?) baths, the town surrounded by some of the most beautiful countryside in France; Manosque (19,000) with motorway link to cosmopolitan Aix-en-Provence enabling a rapid transition from the relaxed lifestyle in the southern French Alps to the animated Bouches-du-Rhône; Entrevaux, one of France's most beautiful villages; a number of good ski resorts, offering a range of altitudes and difficulties, e.g. Barcelonnette 1,135m (3,725ft), Val d'Allos 1,800 to 2,600m (5,900 to 8,530ft) and, for more experienced skiers, La Foux d'Allos, also around 1,800 to 2,600m (out of season, they're sturdy tests for walkers); the Parc National du Mercantour, the largest conservation area in the two Mediterranean regions, some 75km (45mi) from west to east, visited by over half a million people each year – there are chamois on the upper slopes, eagles and a variety of Alpine plants. No dogs are allowed and there are no residential properties.

Alpes-Maritimes (06)

Nice (pop. 350,000), the departmental capital and unofficial capital of the Côte d'Azur, the quintessential Riviera town with its strong Italian architectural style; nearby Sophia Antipolis, France's 'Silicon Valley' with its concentration of high-tech businesses; Cannes (67,000), created by the English and rated the most 'pleasant' town in France by *Le Point* magazine, with its famous Film Festival, the ultimate in sophistication (and prices!) and the wealthiest French town outside the Ile-de-France; Grasse, 30km (19mi) inland, France's perfume capital (45,000); Cagnes-sur-Mer (44,000), between Cannes and Nice, famous for its horse racing (the only course in the department); Antibes (73,000), a yachting centre, particularly for the rich and famous; Menton (67,000, including suburbs up to Monaco), sedate, laid-back and aristocratic with a colourful annual lemon festival; Isola 2000, a purpose-built ski resort (the sunniest in France) two hours' drive from Nice; two of France's most beautiful villages, Eze-Village and Peillon.

If your budget enables you to purchase a superb villa with landscaped gardens and deluxe swimming pool with all the trimmings and a clear panoramic view of the nearby sea, try to avoid Saint-Tropez, the entrance to Antibes and the Corniche coastal roads near Monte Carlo, because the high season road traffic is horrendous. (A helicopter would be a good investment if you absolutely have to be in one of these localities!) In the low season, however, they're glorious.

Aude (11)

Carcassonne (pop. 45,000), the regional capital (known as 'Cork-assonne' by the Irish and British now flocking to the area), one of France's major tourist attractions (reckoned to be the second-most visited town after Paris) with the largest and best preserved medieval walled fortress in Europe; Narbonne (47,000), just off the coast, the ancient regional Roman capital; Limoux

(10,200), known for its white wine (Blanquette de Limoux) and a lively town with a well known winter carnival and the only piano museum (Le Musée du Piano) in France; Lagrasses, one of France's most beautiful villages; the Canal du Midi, a man-made canal 240km (148mi) long, running from Toulouse (Midi-Pyrénées) and crossing the Aude and Hérault departments to the Mediterranean near Cap d'Agde – the Midi's 'equivalent' of the UK's Norfolk Broads.

Bouches-du-Rhône (13)

Marseilles, spelled *Marseille* by the French (pop. city centre 800,000), capital of Bouches-du-Rhône and the PACA region and France's oldest city (over 2,500 years), has a poor reputation and a rather faded grandeur, but much restoration work is in progress and the old docks have been transformed into an up-market area with luxury waterfront apartments and classy restaurants; it isn't a tourist city (the local people are true Mediterraneans) but has plenty to offer historically and sociologically, particularly in the old port and Canebière main street areas, and since the 1998 World Cup (when several matches were played in the city) has become a fashionable place for foreigners to live and is particularly popular with the Dutch.

Other major towns and places of interest are Aix-en-Provence (pop. including suburbs 130,000), the pre-French Revolution capital of Provence, 15 minutes north of Marseilles and in sharp contrast, with sophisticated boutiques and people; Arles (50,000) with its well preserved Roman arena (*les Arènes*) where bullfights are 'staged' and international exhibition centre; the Camargue conservation area, which spills over into the Gard department, inhabited by semi-wild bulls and horses, an unrivalled variety of birds including pink flamingos, small and larger mammals, such as red foxes, coypus and wild boar; Les-Saintes-Maries-de-la-Mer, on the south-west tip of the Camargue, the gypsies' Mecca around 25th May every year, when they celebrate their patron saint Sarah; Martigues, a modern 'Venetian' development with houses built along canals; Les Baux-de-Provence, one of France's most beautiful villages.

Gard (30)

Nîmes (pop. 135,000), the departmental capital, renowned as the best example of a Roman town outside Italy but with a curious admixture of avant-garde buildings and to be avoided at Whitsun and at grape-harvesting time (September), unless you're a bull-fighting/running aficionado and enjoy huge *ferias*; Alès (40,000), at the foot of the Cévennes slopes, once an important industrial and mining town but now turning increasingly to tourism; the Pont du Gard, a two thousand-year-old Roman bridge, one of the most visited historical sites in France; La Roque-sur-Cèze, one of the most beautiful villages in France.

Hérault (34)

Montpellier (pop. 230,000), one of the world's oldest university seats, the capital of Hérault and the Languedoc-Roussillon region and its economic driving force with high-tech industrial zones such as Agropolis and Euromédecine – one of the most cosmopolitan, dynamic and progressive towns in France (and recently rated among the ten best French towns to live in – see **Appendix F**); Béziers (70,000), with its ancient bridge (le Pont Vieux), an easy-going town and the unofficial capital of the largest wine-producing region in France; Sète, the most important fishing port on the French Mediterranean coast – in contrast to Montpellier, insular and 'authentic' and, like Marseilles, inhabited largely by native French Mediterraneans; the Cap d'Agde, the largest purpose-built bathing resort in Europe with sleeping accommodation for 100,000 and incorporating a huge naturist centre; Saint-Guilhem-le-Désert, one of France's most beautiful villages.

Lozère (48)

Mende (pop. 11,800), the capital, situated in the very centre of the department; Châteauneuf-de-Randon, a completely unspoilt (no souvenir shops), authentic village with a commanding view of the Margeride plateau in the north of the department; the Cévennes, scene of Robert Louis Stevenson's *Travels with a Donkey* (his journey actually started in the adjacent Haute-Loire department and ended, 220km/136mi later, in Gard).

Pyrénées-Orientales (66)

Perpignan (pop. 107,000), the departmental capital, with its strong Catalan influence (it's only 30km/19mi from the Spanish border); Collioure, small, pretty port crowded with tourists in summer; Villefranche-de-Conflent, one of the country's most beautiful villages; mount Canigou, 2,784m (9,135ft), which on a clear day can be seen from Marseilles.

Var (83)

Toulon (pop. 160,000), with the largest harbour in continental Europe (France's Mediterranean naval base), offering prestigious properties in the hills above the town with panoramic sea views; Hyères (49,000) with its palm trees and medieval old town, combining the attractions of Provence and the

Côte d'Azur; Saint-Tropez (known as 'Saint-Trop' – *trop* meaning 'too much'!), crowded, colourful, glamorous, outrageous, and architecturally quite pretty (pop. 6,000 in the low season; overrun in the summer); the seaside resorts of Fréjus-Saint-Raphaël (41,000), with their beautiful, sandy beaches and Roman arena; Port-Grimaud, a modern 'Venetian' development with houses built along canals; Bargème, one of France's most beautiful villages; Mont Saint-Victoire, painted by Cézanne; the Grand Canyon du Verdon (also called the Gorges du Verdon, but the locals prefer to compare it with the American Grand Canyon), Europe's deepest canyon.

Vaucluse (84)

Avignon (pop. 87,000), City of the Popes with the Popes' Palace and, of course, the nursery-rhyme bridge (only half remains) – home to important metallurgy and textile industries and a major drama festival in July; Carpentras (25,000), which boasts France's oldest synagogue, and nearby Mont Ventoux – at 1,912m (6,270ft) the highest mountain in Provence; three of France's most beautiful villages, Bonnieux, Gordes and Roussillon; Fontaine-de-Vaucluse, a village in a natural beauty spot where a mysterious 'fountain' springs from 308m (1,010ft) below ground (Vaucluse, meaning 'enclosed valley', gave its name to the village before the department); the Lubéron, a mountainous conservation area extending some 50km (30mi) from the southern French Alps almost to the Mediterranean.

POPULATION

The population of the two regions is around 6.9 million, Provence-Alpes-Côte d'Azur having twice as many inhabitants as Languedoc-Roussillon, although the latter's population has almost doubled in the last 40 years. Languedoc-Roussillon has the fastest-growing population of any region in France (an increase of 8.5 per cent between 1990 and 1999) and PACA is the country's third-fastest growing region (5.8 per cent in the same period), the department of Var and the town of Montpellier (34) being among the fastest growing in France. However, these increases have been largely due to migration rather than a high birth rate, and population ageing is a significant factor in many towns, especially Cannes. A slow-down in property price rises in 2002 may spark a new influx of foreign homebuyers. The student population of the major towns in the area varies considerably: from over 30 per cent in Aix-en-Provence (13) – the second-highest proportion of any town in France – and to 5 per cent in Marseilles (13), 3 per cent in Toulon (83), 2 per cent in Carcassonne (11) and Béziers (34), and a mere 1 per cent in Antibes, Cannes (06), Arles (13) and Sète (34).

The approximate populations, including official foreign resident numbers, of each department are given below; for the populations of major towns, see **Major Towns & Places of Interest** on page 216.

Alpes-de-Haute-Provence (04): Population 140,000, of which 1,000 are Algerians, 1,000 Moroccans, 850 Italians, 650 Portuguese and 130 Britons.

Alpes-Maritimes (06): Population 1 million, of which 19,000 are Tunisians, 17,000 Italians, 9,500 Algerians, 8,500 Moroccans, 6,000 Portuguese and 4,300 Britons.

Aude (11): Population 320,000, of which 3,600 are Moroccans, 2,900 Spaniards, 1,200 Algerians, 1,100 Portuguese, 700 Armenian Turks, 700 Britons and 600 Italians.

Bouches-du-Rhône (13): Population 1.9 million, of which 47,000 are Algerians, 14,500 Moroccans, 13,000 Tunisians, 7,600 Italians, 6,000 Spaniards and 1,400 Britons.

Gard (30): Population 630,000, of which 15,500 are Moroccans, 5,000 Algerians, 3,900 Spaniards, 2,400 Portuguese, 1,600 Italians, 900 Tunisians, 650 Britons and 500 Armenian Turks.

Hérault (34): Population 900,000, of which 21,000 are Moroccans, 8,200 Spaniards, 4,900 Algerians, 2,100 Portuguese, 1,800 Britons, 1,700 Italians, 1,100 Armenian Turks and 800 Tunisians.

Lozère (48): Population 73,000, of which 1,250 are Portuguese, 500 Moroccans, 250 Armenian Turks and a sprinkling of Britons, Italians and Spaniards.

Pyrénées-Orientales (66): Population 400,000, of which 9,000 are Spaniards, 2,500 Portuguese, 4,000 Moroccans, 3,500 Algerians, 700 Britons, 500 Armenian Turks, 500 Italians and 250 Tunisians.

Var (83): Population 900,000, of which 10,000 are Moroccans, 9,000 Tunisians, 7,600 Algerians, 5,000 Italians and 1,500 Britons.

Vaucluse (84): Population 500,000, of which 16,000 are Moroccans, 4,500 Spaniards, 4,000 Algerians, 2,100 Italians, 1,800 Tunisians and 600 Britons.

LANGUAGE

Languedoc-Roussillon is the homeland of France's second language, the *langue d'Oc* (also known as *Occitan*), which was once spoken throughout southern France, while those in the north spoke the *langue d'Oïl* (*oc* and *oïl* are the two medieval words for 'yes' in the respective areas). (The language is sometimes called Provençal, but in fact this was just one of the dialects of *Occitan* and is now spoken only in Italy.) Although the *langue d'Oïl* has become the national *lingua franca*, *Occitan* was the everyday language of most of the rural population of the south until well into the 20th century and still survives in most of southern France (as many as 31 departments, according to some surveys), where it's estimated that there are around 3 million speakers of *Occitan* (around a third of whom use the language daily) and a further 1.5 million who can read or understand it. (It's also spoken in parts of Spain and Italy.)

Although most speakers are older people, there has recently been an attempt to revive the language, for example through *Occitan*-language pre-schools (*calandretas*), where there are around 1,500 pupils at any time, and it's taught as an optional subject in some state schools. The language has no official status, although around 40 minutes of *Occitan* programmes are broadcast every week by France 3 and there's a number of local radio programmes in the language, as well as articles in local newspapers and a number of *Occitan* magazines.

Related to *Occitan* (and to French) is Catalan (also known as Castillian), which is spoken by around 6 million people, mostly in Spain but also in Andorra (where it's the official language) and parts of Pyrénées-Orientales in France (as well as in a single village in Sardinia!) – a region known as Catalonia.

Although it isn't necessary to learn *Occitan* or Catalan in order to be accepted by the local community, if you can master a few words and phrases it will probably improve your chances. Note also, however, that French is spoken with a pronounced 'twang' in southern France (not at all like the pronunciation you learned at school), which it may take a while to get used to.

CLIMATE

The Mediterranean coast proves that you cannot generalise about French weather. The climate is, of course, Mediterranean (hot, dry and sunny except for the habitual heavy rain in early spring) as opposed to continental (inland) or maritime (oceanic) climates, but the high mountains not too far from the coast and the Mediterranean sea can have a sudden influence. Mountainous areas inland may also have heavy rain after the middle of August. Beneficial micro-climates also exist in certain localities, e.g. Hyères (83), which has a number of rest homes (so Queen Victoria obviously knew a thing or two when she elected to visit there).

The Cévennes area in Languedoc is the wettest in France with some 2,000mm (80in) of rain annually, as cold and hot air streams collide over the mountains (known as the *effet Cénévol*). In 2002, flash floods killed 23 people in parts of Gard, Hérault and Vaucluse; in the town of Sommières near Nîmes (30), six months of rain fell in just a few hours. The Languedoc-Roussillon region has typically hot, dry summers and much colder winters than the Côte d'Azur, where Nice probably has the smallest variation in temperatures throughout the year (never a sustained heat-wave and mild in the winter months), although it's the French city worst affected by flooding (see page

The Mediterranean Coast 223

215). The high land in the Lubéron area of Vaucluse also experiences much colder temperatures in winter than the Var coast and the Riviera. Monthly rainfall on the coast varies between around 20mm in July and 170mm in November.

In recent years there has been no pattern to the arrival and departure of snow on the ski slopes and other medium to high-altitude areas. In 1999 there was heavy snow at the beginning of November on land around 400m (1,300ft) in the Bouches-du-Rhône and Var departments, and in May 2002 there were heavy snowfalls (after the winter snow had melted) in some areas above 800m (2,600ft) in Languedoc-Roussillon. Nevertheless, these areas are inevitably colder in winter and milder in summer than lower-lying parts.

The Mediterranean coast also experiences the strong *Tramontane* and *Mistral* winds, and the PACA region is occasionally visited (usually overnight) by the warm and gentler sand-bearing *Scirocco* wind from the Sahara. The frequency of the *Mistral* is variable; it's particularly strong in February, March and April and less so in July and August. The Nice area, in summer, is often a few degrees cooler than the rest of the coast on account of a partially clouded sky: there's no *Mistral* here to chase the clouds away.

Average daytime temperatures in summer vary little between the towns along the Mediterranean coast. In June they're around 26°C (79°F), in July and August, around 28°C (82°F), and in September around 25°C (77°F), although slightly cooler around Nice and hotter inland, away from sea breezes. In the winter, from January to March, average temperatures are noticeably lower in the Montpellier area, just off the coast, than in the areas around Nice, Perpignan and Toulon. Toulon is France's sunniest city and one of the sunniest spots on the Mediterranean coast, with an average of around 2,900 hours' sunshine per year. The table below shows the number of hours' sunshine and number of days' rainfall in selected towns in the area.

Town	Sunshine Hours	Days' Rainfall
Antibes (06)	2,694	63
Cannes (06)	2,694	64
Nice (06)	2,694	63
Carcassonne (11)	2,506	94
Aix-en-Provence (13)	2,836	60
Arles (13)	2,836	57
Marseilles (13)	2,836	57
Nîmes (30)	2,669	67
Béziers (34)	2,687	57
Montpellier (34)	2,687	59

Sète (34)	2,687	57
Perpignan (66)	2,506	56
Toulon (83)	2,899	60
Avignon (84)	2,595	68

Average summer sea temperatures in Centigrade (and Fahrenheit in brackets) for the eastern and western coasts are shown below:

	May	June	July	Aug	Sep	Oct
Montpellier to Toulon	15 (59)	19 (66)	19 (66)	20 (68)	20 (68)	17 (62)
Hyères to Menton	17 (62)	19 (66)	20 (68)	22 (72)	22 (72)	19 (66)

COST OF LIVING

The PACA region is the second most expensive in France (after Paris) and the Alpes-Maritimes department is the most expensive area in the region. Property prices follow this pattern (see page 240). Languedoc-Roussillon has an appreciably lower cost of living. Shopping around (if time permits) for food can save an adult couple at least €150 per month, as there's plenty of choice.

CRIME RATE & SECURITY

The PACA and Languedoc-Roussillon regions are numbers two and three respectively (after the Ile-de-France) in the crime-rate charts and include all but 5 of the 13 towns with the highest (reported) crime rates in the country: Avignon (84), which has the highest crime rate of any town in France with over 170 crimes per 1,000 inhabitants (in the year 2000 after a 27 per cent increase in crime since 1998), Carcassonne (11), Cannes (06), Nîmes (30), Montpellier (34), Béziers (34), Nice (06), where crime increased by over 20 per cent between 1998 and 2000, and Aix-en-Provence (13). Also in the national bottom 20 towns are Perpignan (66) and Antibes (06), although the number of reported crimes in Antibes fell by almost 20 per cent between 1998 and 2000. On the other hand, Lozère in Languedoc-Roussillon is the French department with the lowest crime rate, due no doubt to its predominantly rural nature.

Here, as in France generally, drug-associated crimes, including physical attacks, have increased markedly over the last ten years while (detected) financial skulduggery, despite publicity suggesting the contrary, has diminished. Marseilles retains a (largely undeserved) unsavoury international reputation (its crime rate is only the 23rd-highest of the 100 major towns in

France), and the city centre doesn't attract tourists or foreign homebuyers. Its most dangerous neighbourhoods are the 13th, 14th and 15th *arrondissements* to the north of the centre and the 4th in the city centre, where violent crime and the burning of parked vehicles aren't uncommon. There has also recently been an increasing number of crimes on trains between Marseilles and Nice, but by far the most common crime is burglary, which is rife in resort towns such as Cannes (where people have been burgled while having dinner on the terrace!). To a lesser extent, Nice and Toulon have earned unfavourable reputations through political (financial) scandals since the 1990s.

Car thefts are frequent throughout the area (as reflected in car insurance premiums), and driving standards are poor – even for France (see page 247). Forest fires are another hazard and are prevalent in the dry summer months, and you should ensure that the grass and vegetation surrounding your house surrounding your house are trimmed back at least to the statutory minimum distance of 50m (165ft) from the building (local regulations can increase this to 100m). It should also be noted that there are no fewer than six high-risk factories in and around Sète (34).

Despite all this, the Mediterranean coastal area remains a fairly safe (and extremely healthy) place to live, provided you exercise care and take the usual precautions – don't let the sun 'go to your head'! For general information on crime in France, see page 52.

AMENITIES

Sports

Both PACA and Languedoc-Roussillon are popular with sportspeople. It goes without saying that the whole of the Mediterranean coast is a paradise for watersports lovers, and there's also a wealth of other sporting facilities in resort and main town areas, although facilities are lacking in some rural areas. Traditional community sports centres, housing several activities together where you walk in, pay and play, are rare. Public swimming pools (usually overheated) and well maintained tennis courts are, on the other hand, quite common. They're usually good value and you can often purchase a coupon of tickets (*carnet*) reducing the unit entrance price. *Complexes sportives* or *halles/palais/salles des sports* are municipal gymnasiums providing a court for the local basketball, handball or volleyball team. Local town halls (*mairies* or *hôtels de ville*) should be able to provide you with a list of sports clubs and associations in their area, and the local Office des Clubs sportifs publishes an annual directory.

Golf: Despite the high cost of playing golf regularly, due partly perhaps to the water bills incurred in maintaining the lush greens and fairways, golf is one of the fastest growing sports in the area. The PACA region has around 45

18-hole courses and 25 schools with nine-hole and practice courses. The greatest concentration of courses is to be found around Cannes (06), where there are six. For more information contact the Ligue Golf PACA, domaine Riquetti, chemin départemental 9, 13290 Les Milles (☎ 04. 42.39.86.83). The Languedoc-Roussillon region also has several first-class courses, near to the main towns, several of which offer both 9 and 18-hole rounds. The Comité régional de Tourisme (CRT) issues a five-round ticket for €138 valid for 21 consecutive days for golf courses in the region. For more information contact the CRT, 20, rue de la République, 34000 Montpellier (☎ 04.67.22.81.00, 🖳 contact.crtlr@sunfrance.com). The table below lists the number of courses in each department (there's also an 18-hole course in Monaco).

Department	No. of Courses
Alpes-de-Haute-Provence	3 x 18 holes
Alpes-Maritimes	2 x 9 holes, 9 x 18 holes, 1 x 27 holes
Aude	1 x 18 holes
Bouches-du-Rhône	3 x 9 holes, 5 x 18 holes
Gard	1 x 9 holes, 2 x 18 holes
Hérault	1 x 9 holes, 5 x 18 holes, 1 x 36 holes
Lozère	3 x 9 holes
Pyrénées-Orientales	2 x 9 holes, 1 x 18 holes, 1 x 27 holes
Var	1 x 9 holes, 11 x 18 holes
Vaucluse	1 x 9 holes, 4 x 18 holes

Information (in both French and English) on how to find courses, the cost of a round (which varies between €15 and €50), etc. is available via the Internet (🖳 www.backspin.com). Another useful website for golfers is 🖳 www.golf.com.fr.

In property advertisements in French, watch out for the word 'golfe', which means bay or gulf, as opposed to 'golf', which means golf. (Watch out for the prices as well!)

Skiing: The departments of Alpes-Maritimes and Alpes-de-Hautes-Provence are within a short drive of the Alps and their incomparable ski resorts (see page 262), while Pyrénées-Occidentales has its own resorts, at Font-Romeu, Les Angles, Porté-Puymorens and Pyrénées 2000, and is close to those of Ariège and Andorra (see page 180). Although not as famous or challenging as the Alps, the Pyrenees offer a good selection of downhill runs as well as plenty of cross-country skiing.

Other Sports: Languedoc-Roussillon is a stronghold of French rugby, whereas soccer fans have two first-class professional teams to idolise in

PACA – those of Marseilles and Monaco. In high season, the lakes of Castillon, Esparron-Gréoux and Quinson near the Grand Canyon du Verdon in Var have first-class aquatic facilities (such as white-water rafting and canoeing) with qualified staff.

Leisure

Few areas of France can match the Mediterranean coast for the excellence and variety of its attractions, many of which are available all year round. Apart from the simple pleasures of beaches for sun-worshippers, beautiful and spectacular countryside for nature lovers, and mountains and seas for sports enthusiasts, the natural light and contrasting colours of the sea and landscapes are ideal for would-be artists. (The area was home to Cézanne, Picasso and Van Gogh.) Contact the cultural services department of your town hall for details of workshops or associations. The *Officiel des Arts* (🖳 www.od-arts.com) publishes a weekly list of major art exhibitions taking place throughout France. English-language newspapers (see **English-language Press** on page 235) should also be consulted.

Festivals: The area is renowned for its festivities, which include carnivals in Nice (06) for three weeks in February and in Limoux (11) every weekend from mid-January to the end of March, and the famous Cannes (06) Film Festival in May, to gain admission to which, however, you must be able to show a 'professional interest' in the cinema (see below). The department of Var is known for its summer jazz festivals, including those at Brignolles, Ramatuelle and Tourves. One of the oldest festivals in the area is the annual sausage fair in Le Val (83), which has been taking place every August/September for over 370 years and attracts gourmands from all over France; among the oddest is the Fête de l'Ours (Bear Festival) in the pretty Catalan village of Prats-de-Mollo-la-Preste (66), where every February villagers don bear suits and paint their faces in celebration of the once-feared creature.

Museums & Culture: If you're a culture vulture, the area is rich in historical (particularly naval) museums. For example, on Mount Faron, near Toulon, there's a museum commemorating the liberation of Provence in 1944, and there's a museum of prehistory just over the departmental border from the Grand Canyon du Verdon, at Quinson (04) in Alpes-de-Haute-Provence (☎ 04.92.74.09.59, 🖳 www.museeprehistoire.com). Nice (06) boasts 12 museums (the largest number in any French town other than Paris) and Marseilles ten; Aix-en-Provence (13) has over 60 historical monuments. Many local French newspapers publish weekly magazines or supplements containing a detailed programme of local events and entertainment. The CityVox website (🖳 www.cityvox.com) has lively information in English on what's going on in Aix-en-Provence, Avignon, Marseilles, Montpellier and Nice and in French for Nîmes and Perpignan.

Casinos: Not surprisingly, there are more casinos in this area than in almost any other part of France – over 35 in the two regions, including one in Alpes-de-Provence (04), ten in Alpes-Maritimes (06), two in Aude (11), four in Bouches-du-Rhône (13), one in Gard (30), seven in Hérault (34), one in Mende (48), seven in Pyrénées-Orientales (66) and five in Var (83). Details of all casinos and what they offer are available via the Internet (e.g. 🖥 www. journaldescasinos.com – partly in English).

Theme Parks: There's a number of theme parks in the area (mostly open between the middle of June and early September, weather permitting), including:

- Aqualand in Port-Leucate (11), Cap-d'Agde (34) and Saint-Cyprien (66): water parks;

- Aquatic park at Saint-Cyprien (66);

- Aquarium de Bagnuls-sur-Mer (66): Mediterranean sea life;

- Aquarium de Cannet in Cannet-en-Roussillon (66): tropical fish;

- Aquarium du Cap-d'Agde (34): sea life;

- Aquatica in Fréjus (83): water park;

- Atlantide Parc in Saint-Jean-du-Gard (30): sea life;

- La Bambouseraie in Anduze (30): tropical gardens;

- Le Catalan in Casteil (66): wildlife park;

- El Dorado City in Ensuès-la-Redonne (13): Wild West theme park;

- Géospace in Montpellier (34): observatory and botanical institute;

- L'Ile des Embiez in Six-Fours-les-Pins (83): sea life;

- Kiddy Parc in Port d'Hyères (83): farm animals;

- Les Loups du Gévaudan near Marvejols (48): wolves in a 'natural' environment;

- Marineland at Biot near Antibes (06): featuring killer whale and dolphin acts – one of France's leading aquariums, attracting over a million visitors per year;

- Musée océanographique de Monaco: marine and maritime museum;

- OK-Corral in Cuges-les-Pin (13): Wild West park – the largest theme park in southern France, attracting half a million visitors per year;

- Parc animalier des Angles (66): Pyrenean wildlife in 'natural' environment;

- Parc ornithologique de Pont-de-Gau in Les Saintes-Maries-de-la-Mer (13): bird park;

- Réserve de Sigean (11): 'African' game park;

- Seaquarium in Le Grau-du-Roi (30): fish and aquatic mammals;

- Le Village des Tortues in Gonfaron (83): 2,500 turtles and tortoises;

- Zoo de la Barven (13);

- Zoo du Cap-Ferrat (06): 300 animals;

- Zoo et Jardin exotique in Sanary-sur-Mer (83): zoo and garden.

English-language Cinema & Theatre

All major towns with a large university student population, such as Aix-en-Provence (13) (Cinémas Renoir), Avignon (84), Montpellier (34), Nice (06) and Toulon (83) (Cinéma le Royal), have at least one cinema dedicated to showing foreign films (mainly American and British) in their original language version (*version originale/VO*). Programmes and further information are available from local newspapers and tourist offices. A useful website for finding out what films are on in a given area, which also indicates whether the films are being shown in the original language is 🖳 www.cinefil.com. Don't expect always to see the latest commercial blockbuster; *VO* films may be avant-garde or offbeat. Also, although cinemas are being modernised, they don't generally offer grandiose comfort and large screens with stunning sound systems. Municipal cultural centres (*maisons de la culture*) may also show films in *VO* at a subsidised price of around €5. All films are shown in *VO* at the annual Film Festival Cannes (whose citizens visit the cinema more frequently than those of any other major town in France), but unless you're involved in the film industry you're unlikely to be able to obtain tickets. (Incidentally, La Ciotat, in Bouches-du-Rhône (13) is recognised as the birthplace of motion pictures.)

Quality theatre and opera performances are staged in all major cities and towns, and the performances in Marseilles and Avignon are particularly renowned in the area. Opera tickets range from around €35 to €50 compared with theatre tickets, which can be had for as little as €20 at local *maison de la culture* performances. The Red Pear Theatre Company, Villa la Timonerie, avenue Malespine, 06600 Antibes (Alpes-Maritimes ☎ 04.93.61.01.71) presents plays in English.

Shopping Centres & Markets

On the outskirts of large towns (and also in the centres of Marseilles, Nice and Toulon) there are huge shopping centres (*centres commerciaux*) with hypermarkets and accompanying open-air or underground parking, attractive boutique shopping galleries (*galeries marchandes*), DIY stores, furniture stores, garden centres and sports equipment and sportswear stores. The main hypermarket chains are Auchan, Carrefour and Géant Casino, with an exception at the out-of-town Nice site of Cap 3000, where there's a Lafayette Gourmet (part of the Groupe Galeries Lafayette) hypermarket. The Grand Littoral and Grand Var regional centres, to the west of Marseilles and the east of Toulon respectively, are particularly large. The Auchan hypermarket at Le Pontet (next to Avignon) is the largest hypermarket in the whole.

While buying food in shopping centres is more a necessity than a pleasure, markets – whether for fresh meat, fruit, vegetables, fish, cheese and bread or flowers, artisans' products or bric-a-brac – are colourful, entertaining and an experience not to be missed. Food is generally more expensive than in hyper and supermarkets, but additional quality is there and it's best to buy what's local and in season, e.g. Cavaillon cantaloupe melons from May to September, and wild strawberries (*fraises des bois*) in the spring. Good bargains are to be had for clothes and shoes, particularly if you become a regular customer with the same stall-holder. Montpellier has a renowned *marché paysan* on Sunday mornings selling only local products (*produits du terroir*) and the Marché du Plan Cabanes, a bazaar with a distinctive African and Arabic flavour. The Cours Lafayette in Toulon has a daily provençal market offering almost everything under the sun (and normally under the sun). The fish market on the old port (le Vieux Port) at Marseilles and the flower market near the old part of Nice are also recommended. Active participation in the truffle market in Aups (83) between mid-December and mid-March, on the other hand, isn't wise unless you have money to burn, with prices between €300 and €600 per kilogram!

Foreign Food & Products

Supermarkets sell few foreign foods with the exception of biscuits, cereals (including Weetabix), confectionery, preserves, smoked salmon, Chinese and Vietnamese foods, delicatessen foods and some cheeses. However, there are a few specialist shops in PACA where foreign 'delicacies' can be found, e.g. the Comptoir Irlandais in Toulon (83), which sells British and Irish food, including cheddar, chutney, Marmite and smoked salmon.

There are specialist English and Chinese furniture shops in most cities, including Habitat stores, which can be found in Montpellier, Marseilles, Toulon, Nice and Vallauris (06). IKEA furniture stores are located at Vitrolles (13) near Marseilles-Provence airport and at Toulon. If you live near Carcassonne, a trip to Toulouse, where there's an IKEA and a Habitat, is worth considering.

There are English-language book shops in Nice, Cannes, Marseilles and Aix-en-Provence, and from around May to October paperback display units with English, German and Dutch bestsellers appear in book shops, newsagents and supermarkets along the Mediterranean coast and inland as far as Avignon (84). You will also find, all year round, pictorial guides and souvenir books with English text which describe particular areas, and possibly books by local-interest authors such as Peter Mayle. For general information on obtaining foreign products in France, see page 61.

Restaurants & Bars

There's an almost infinite variety of restaurants offering authentic languedocien and provençal regional dishes (fish and *produits du terroir*), gastronomic French cuisine, international hotel cuisine, Arab stews (*couscous*), Greek salads, Italian pasta, Spanish paella and Chinese and Vietnamese specialities. Establishments vary from seasonal beach shacks and attractive terrace and pedestrian-area town and village brasseries and bistros to Michelin-starred gourmet restaurants, of which there are no fewer than five in Avignon (84). The two regions offer beautiful country and sea views, which contribute to the enjoyment of the meal and, of course, influence the price. If you're dining out, the best value and quality cuisine is more readily found in the hinterland of Provence and not on the coast.

On a day-to-day basis, self-service cafeterias such as Flunch and Casino offer a variety of hot and cold dishes enabling you to have a quality three-course meal for around €8. If you have a young family, McDonald's and Quick (the French fast-food chain) offer the usual hamburger menus, complemented by regional salad dishes, and if you're really in a hurry all large towns have pavement kiosks selling substantial hot and cold half-baguette sandwiches.

Regional specialities include sea fish and molluscs, e.g. octopus salad (*salade de poulpe*), freshwater fish, especially in the Tarn valley streams, and anchovies (*anchois*) from the Mediterranean, hams and cheeses from Cévennes area, herbs and red vegetables from Languedoc, lamb from the mountains, notably around Sisteron in Alpes-de-Hautes-Provence, and locally reared ostrich, which provides an alternative to a traditional roast. Italy is the overriding foreign influence on the regional dishes in PACA, particularly along the Côte d'Azur, including salads, fish and meat dishes plus pastas – a somewhat lighter diet than that of Languedoc-Roussillon, which is nevertheless regarded as 'healthier'. Local speciality dishes include Carcassonne *cassoulet* of white beans, mutton and sausage, *salade niçoise* (Nice salad), *bouillabaisse* (also a Nice speciality) and wild boar (*sanglier*) stew. Blanquette de Limoux is a sparkling white wine produced using champagne methods, but don't expect the taste to compare with that of a quality champagne. Local sweet white wines (*vins doux naturels*) are often drunk as an *apéritif*, which is an acquired taste for northern palates.

A wide selection of coffees, ranging from light *arabica* to stronger *robusta* flavours, can be enjoyed in coffee shops, usually found in *galeries marchandes* (see **Shopping Centres & Markets** on page 229). You should pay from €1 to €1.50 for a small cup, according to the category and location of the establishment.

SERVICES

International & Private Schools

International schools in the PACA and Languedoc-Roussillon regions are concentrated in the Riviera area, although the International School at Toulouse (see page 187), which is under two hours' drive from Carcassonne (11), is a possibility if you're planning to live in that area. Details of the principal schools in the area (including Monaco) are given below.

- Centre international privé pour l'Education et la Culture (☎ 04.42. 60.84.25) in Luynes (06);

- The International Bilingual School of Provence (☎ 04.42.24.03.40) in Aix-en-Provence (13);

- The International School of Monaco (☎ 0377-9325 6820, 🖳 www.is monaco.org);

- The International School of Nice (☎ 04.93.21.04.00);

- The International School of Sophia Antipolis (ASEICA, ☎ 04.92. 96.52.24, 🖳 http://64.177.205.70/home.html);

- Mougins School (☎ 04.93.90.15.47, 🖳 http://mougins-school.com) in Sophia Antipolis (06).

There are many private schools (*écoles privées*), mostly Roman Catholic but also Jewish and Protestant (the Nîmes area is a Protestant stronghold), from primary (*écoles primaires*) to secondary (*collèges* and *lycées*) level, providing study courses up to the French *baccalauréat* examination with all its options. There are also two private primary schools catering specifically for English-speaking students:

- Ecole privée active bilingue 'Le Pain de Sucre' (☎ 04.93.73.70.41, 🖳 www.ecoledupaindesucre.com) in Cagnes-sur-Mer (06);

- Ecole privée internationale 'Le Pain d'Epice' (☎ 04.93.44.75.44, 🖳 www. ecoledupaindesucre.com) in Nice (06);

Language Schools

The Côte d'Azur area has the greatest concentration of language schools in France outside Paris; Nice (06) and Montpellier (34) between them offer over 40 schools, including the Alliance française, which also has a branch in Marseilles. There are other schools in Manosque and Moustiers-Sainte-Marie (04), two in Antibes, three in Cannes, one each in Cap d'Ail, La Napoule, Le Rouret, Menton, Sophia-Antipolis, Villefranche-sur-Mer and Villeneuve-Loubet (06), two in Aix-en-Provence and one each in Istres and Noves (13), one each in Saint-Bonnet-du-Gard, Saint-Geniès-de-Comolas (30), Béziers and Loupian (34), two in Sète (34), two in Perpignan (66), one each in Hyères, La Seyne-sur-Mer and Toulon (83), and three in Avignon and one each in Castellet and Morières-les-Avignons (84), as well as two schools in Monaco. Details of the above schools can be found on ⌨ www.europa-pages.com. The French Consulate in London (see **Appendix A**) publishes a booklet called *Cours de français Langue étrangère et Stages pédagogiques du français Langue étrangère en France*, which includes a comprehensive list of schools, organisations and institutes providing French language courses throughout France. Language courses are also offered by local Chambres de Commerce et d'Industrie and Centres culturels.

Hospitals & Clinics

The majority of towns have at least one public hospital, and cities such as Marseilles, Montpellier, Nice and Toulon have several that are particularly well equipped. Marseilles, Montpellier and Nice have teaching hospitals (*CHU*) and many of their graduate specialists remain on the Mediterranean coast as hospital consultants. In fact, the *CHU* in Montpellier was rated France's best hospital in a survey published in August 2002 by *Le Point* magazine, and five other hospitals in the area were rated in the top 45 (the *CHU* in Nice 20th, the Hôpital Saint-Joseph 32nd, the Hôpital d'Adultes la Timone 37th and the Hôpitaux sud 40th (all three in Marseilles) and the *Centre hospitalier* in Avignon 44th. Insomniacs should note that the Montpellier *CHU* has a specialist unit devoted to (lack of) sleep and sleep-related problems.

As well as *cliniques chirurgicales*, there are also *cliniques-polycliniques*, the equivalent of private general hospitals, in the large towns in the two regions. *Cliniques chirurgicales* should not be confused with *cliniques chirurgicales esthétiques* (cosmetic surgery clinics), which aren't lacking along the Riviera! In coastal towns, you should find at least one doctor in each hospital service that speaks good enough English to understand and converse with you.

If you're planning to live in a remote village in the mountains, e.g. in Alpes-de-Haute-Provence (04), take into account that the nearest hospital and maternity unit may be up to an hour's drive away on a winding road, which for part of the winter may be snowbound.

Doctors & Dentists

The Mediterranean coast generally has a high proportion of doctors and dentists to inhabitants, particularly along the coast and in large inland towns, where there are usually over 184 general practitioners and 163 specialists per 100,000 population). Only Lozère has relatively few doctors (around 150 GPs and fewer than 95 specialists per 100,000 inhabitants). Nevertheless, it's usually easy to find and register with a doctor, many of whom speak English. The British Consulate in Marseilles (see **Consulates** on page 235), which is responsible for the Languedoc-Roussillon and PACA regions, has a list of English-speaking doctors and dentists. Accueil des Villes françaises (AVF) information centres for new arrivals, which are found in large towns and are listed in the yellow pages, may also be useful (see **Clubs** on page 237).

Tradesmen

There's no list of English-speaking and other foreign tradesmen in the area, although there are a number in the major resorts and towns. Consult the advertisements in English-language newspapers and magazines and English magazines covering French property (see **English-language Press** on page 235, **Useful Publications** on page 250 and **Appendix B**). The British Consulate in Marseilles (☎ 04.91.15.72.10) may be able to fax or send you a list of officially registered builders (whose work is automatically guaranteed by insurance cover) in your area, although this will include French and foreign tradesmen, who may speak little English.

English-language Radio

Riviera Radio (FM 106.5), based at Monte Carlo, can be received from the Italian border to Saint-Tropez and in summer (for some climatic reason) as far as Toulon, but not, for example, on the Var coast around Le Lavandou. Radio International (FM 100.5, 110.7, 100.9 and 101.90), also based in Monaco, can be received in an even smaller area. It's possible to receive BBC Radio 1, 2, 3, and 4 on your television via the Astra satellite, and you can listen to recordings of radio programmes on Radio 1, 2, 3, 4, 5, 6 and 1Extra on your computer via the Internet (go to 🖳 www.bbc.co.uk/radio/aod/index.shtml). The World Service can be received on short wave (for frequency details, go to 🖳 www.bbc.co.uk/worldservice/schedules/frequencies/eurwfreq.shtml)

and via the Astra satellite. Local music stations usually broadcast 60 per cent non-French language songs, most of which are in English.

English-language Press

The *International Herald Tribune* is widely available on the day of publication, and the *Guardian* and the *European Financial Times*, printed in Frankfurt, are available in some areas the same day. Cosmopolitan cities such as Nice, Aix-en-Provence and Montpellier have other English-language daily newspapers available the day after publication; although they may also be sold in some other towns and coastal villages throughout the low season, they're more extensively available in the high season. The *Guardian Weekly* and the *Weekly Telegraph* are available all year round, in certain areas, and are a good way to keep abreast (almost) with British news. Alternatively, they can be airmailed to you directly at reduced rates on subscription. Certain Maisons de la Presse and shopping centre newsagents sell English-language magazines, ranging from *Women's Day* to the *National Geographic Magazine*. *The Riviera Reporter*, a monthly magazine, and *The Riviera Times* (incorporating *The Monaco Times*), a monthly newspaper, are published in Alpes-Maritimes (see **Useful Publications** on page 250). Another monthly newspaper is *The News*, which covers the whole of France (see **Appendix B**).

Consulates

The list below includes the American and British Consulates General and Honorary Consulates in the area. For Austria, Finland, Germany, Italy, the Netherlands, Norway and Sweden, the Consulates General are in Marseilles, for Canada in Nice, and for Ireland in Antibes (see the yellow pages under 'Ambassades, consulats et autres représentations diplomatiques'). The Danish Honorary Consul in Marseilles (☎ 04.91. 13.13.80) is available on Thursday mornings only. For details of embassies and consulates for other nations, consult the yellow pages for Marseilles, Nice or Paris.

● British Consulate General, 24, avenue du Prado, 13006 Marseilles (☎ 04.91.15.72.10);

● Honorary British Consul, 26, avenue Notre Dame, 06000 Nice (☎ 04.93.62.13.56);

● Honorary British Consul, 33, boulevard Princesse Charlotte, BP 205, MC 98005 Monaco (☎ 0377-9350 9966);

● Mr N. Paget, 271 Le Capitole, bâtiment A, 64, rue Alcyone, 34000 Montpellier (☎ 04.67.15.52.07);

- United States Consulate General, 12, boulevard Paul Peytral, 13286 Marseille cedex 6 (☎ 04.91.54.92.00);

- United States Consulate, 7, avenue Gustav V, 06000 Nice (☎ 04.93. 88.89.55).

Churches

Evangelical, Orthodox, Protestant and other churches and Jewish synagogues, offering regular services, are well represented throughout the area, and the Gard (30) department is a stronghold of the French Reformed (Protestant) Church (*Eglise réformée*). There are churches in the following towns which hold regular services in English:

- Aix-en-Provence (13);

- Beaulieu-sur-Mer (06) – Saint Michael;

- Cannes (06) – Holy Trinity;

- Grasse (06) – Saint John the Evangelist;

- Marseilles (13) – All Saints;

- Menton (06) – Saint John;

- Montauroux (83) – The Community of the Glorious Ascension;

- Nice (06) – Holy Trinity & International Baptist Church;

- Saint-Paul-de-Vence (06) – International Baptist Church;

- Saint-Raphaël (83) – Saint John the Evangelist;

- Toulon (83) – Babptist Church and Eglise Evangélique;

- Vence (06) – Saint Hugh.

Monaco also has an Anglican church. Contact the Holy Trinity (Church of England) in Nice (☎ 04.93.87.19.83) for information regarding Anglican services in English. For further information on finding churches and English-language services in France, see page 65.

There are numerous mosques in the area: Cagnes-sur-Mer, Cannes, Menton, Nice (06), Carcassonne (11), Arles, Marseilles (13), Beaucaire, Nîmes (30), Béziers, Lunel (34), Perpignan (66), Fréjus, Toulon (83), Sorgues and Valreas (84); details can be found on 🖳 http://mosquee.free.fr. There are also several synagogues in Marseilles and three in Montpellier (34), details of which can be found on 🖳 www.feujcity.com (where there's also information about Kosher food shops and restaurants, Jewish clubs, associations and schools, etc.) as well as one each in Narbonne (11), Fréjus, Toulon (83), Avignon and Carpentras (84), details of which can be found on

🖥 www.pagesjaunes.fr (enter 'Synagogues' in the first box and the name of the town).

Clubs

The generally fine weather throughout the two regions means that there's a wealth of clubs for outdoor activities. These include hunting (*chasse*), *boules*, which is marginally safer, and sailing (*clubs nautiques*), in addition to the usual indoor and outdoor games, sports and activities. Town halls have details, and the France Télécom directory website (🖥 www.pagesjaunes.fr) is a rapid means of finding clubs in a particular area.

International clubs and associations such as Lions also exist, with branches in major towns. If you want to join an expatriate club, Alpes-Maritimes (06), Bouches-du-Rhône (13), Hérault (34) and Var (83) are the places to be, and your consulate (see **Consulates** on page 235) will have details. For example, there's an American Association in Marseilles at 3, avenue Parc Borely, 13008 Marseilles (▤ 04.91.77.18.83). See also the local press and articles in English-language newspapers and magazines such as *The News*, *The Riviera Times* and *The Riviera Reporter* (see **Useful Publications** on page 250).

For French speakers, the Accueil des Villes Françaises (AVF), a French organisation designed to welcome newcomers to an area, is an option (there's often at least one fluent English-speaker in each group). There are 15 AVF groups in Languedoc-Roussillon – in Carcassonne, Castelnaudary, Limoux (11), Alès, Bagnols-sur-Cèze, Beaucaire, Nîmes, Uzès, Villeneuve-lèz-Angles (30), Béziers, Clermont-l'Hérault, Lunel, Montpellier (34), Mende (48), and Perpignan (66) – and 35 in PACA: in Digne, Forcalquier, Manosque, Sisteron (04), Antibes/Juan-les-Pins, Cagnes-sur-Mer, Cannes, Le Cannet, Grasse, Mandelieu, Nice, Sophia Antipolis, Vence (06), Aix-en-Provence, Carry-le-Rouet, Châteaurenard, La Ciotat, Eguilles, Martigues, Salon-de-Provence, Tarascon, Le Tholonet, Vitrolles (13), Cavalaire, Draguignan, Hyères, Le Luc, Saint-Cyr-sur-Mer, Saint-Raphaël, Sainte-Maxime, Toulon (83), Avignon, Carpentras, Cavaillon and Le Pontet (84). The website (🖥 www.avf.asso.fr) includes a directory (*annuaire*) of local groups by department as well as an online form for contacting your local AVF before you move to the area. Listings indicate whether information and services are available in English or other languages. Other sources for clubs in the area are *The News* (see **Appendix B**) and the English-speaking church (see above).

PROPERTY

Most properties in the Mediterranean coastal area are purchased by French people (around 25 per cent of French executives have a second home), and permanent foreign residents account for only 6 to 7 per cent of the total population, although in some parts (e.g. Cannes) British buyers make up a significant proportion of homebuyers. Following a long period of stagnation, and at times regression, in the early and middle 1990s, property prices on the Mediterranean coast escalated towards the end of the decade. There was a slow-down at the beginning of the new century, but since then prices have begun to rise again.

In Languedoc-Roussillon, Montpellier and the Hérault department account for approximately 50 per cent of all property sales and developments. There have been steep price rises in one or two parts of the region, notably in and around Nîmes (30), where prices rose by up to 30 per cent in the year following the arrival of the *TGV*, and in Uzès (30), where 100 per cent increases have been recorded between 2001 and 2002, thanks largely to an influx of British buyers taking advantage of new low-cost flights. Marseilles is also enjoying something of a property boom, with luxury, two or three-bedroom waterfront apartments selling for over €200,000 and any good quality properties being snapped up within a day or two of coming on the market. Cheaper properties are to be found in Gard.

If you're physically prospecting the departments, you will find no shortage of estate agents (over 350 in Cannes, 300 in Nice and 270 in Cap d'Antibes, for example). The free magazines *Logic-Immo* and *Mag Immo*, published fortnightly, are full of property advertisements, with colour photographs and are widely available from stands outside bakers and estate agents. The English-language *French Property News* (see **Appendix B**) also has some advertisements. Recently built or off-plan luxury apartments and villas are available from property development companies such as Kaufman Broad (🖳 www.KetB.com), FDI Promotion in Montpellier (✉ fdi-promotion@fdi-promotion.fr), George V Provence Languedoc (☎ 04.95.09.33.83), Meunier Méditerranée in Nice (☎ 04.92.29.25.30, 🖳 www.meunier-habitat.fr), Bouygues Immobilier (🖳 www.bouygues-immobilier.com) and Marignan Immobilier (🖳 www.marignan-immobilier. com), but prices are well above the averages given below. Coast & Country is an English estate agent based in Nice (25, boulevard Carnot, 06300 Nice, ☎ 04.92.04.99.99, 🖳 http://coast-country.com) with an office in Mougins (La Palombière, 71, avenue de Tournamy, 06250 Mougins, ☎ 04.92.92.47.50).

Typical Homes

In both the PACA and Languedoc-Roussillon regions, newer houses (i.e. those up to around 25 years old) normally follow a set regional style as regards facades (and their stucco colouring) and roofs. If you're seeking a property with distinctive character and, for example, open stone-work, you should visit older properties, which have usually been built in the traditional way (*construction traditionnelle*) with solid interior brick, (i.e. not partition) walls. (Estate agents' descriptions specify *construction traditionnelle* when it features in a newer property, as it's a selling point.) Houses in all categories often have small north-facing windows and larger, but not enormous, south-facing windows. A basement (*sous-sol*) running under the entire ground floor is often a feature of new properties.

In **Languedoc-Roussillon**, apart from the blocks of unattractive apartments and properties that were constructed around 20 years ago in the purpose-built coastal resorts, there's perhaps a greater variety of property types than in PACA. The new and recent 'Mediterranean' style house, which is similiar to the provençal style (see below) is prevalent, as are solidly built terraced *maisons de village* in village centres. Mountain areas have heavier built properties than those on the coast and stone is a much favoured building material.

In Montpellier and the Hérault department, there's the usual mix of luxury apartment developments and new and recent villas, many of which are built on one level, bungalow style. You may still find genuine fishermen's cottages (*maisons de pêcheur/cabanons*) in the Camargues conservation area – long, single-storey buildings (*longères*) similar to those found in Normandy and Brittany. Exposed stone-work Catalan properties are sought after on the *Côte Rocheuse* (Rocky Coast) near the Spanish border. There are many vineyard properties in this region with pink or ochre walls and slate tiled roofs (*toits de lauzes*), features shared by their smaller *mazet* 'cousins' – rectangular, stone built one-room lodges. In the sheep-rearing areas there are traditional stone or wooden converted sheep shelters (*bergeries*), built to resist the strong winds.

Along the coast of **PACA**, the major resort towns have relatively few large properties: just 24 per cent of homes in Cannes and Nice (06) consist of four rooms or more, and 28 per cent in Antibes (06). There's a concentration of modern provençal houses and villas, with red or ochre stucco facades and terracotta roof tiles. There are also Italianate villas, which feature pyramid-shaped roofs. New blocks of apartments, often having a 'Florentine' flavour, are more visually attractive than their heavier-looking predecessors, built around 20 years ago. Deluxe apartment blocks often feature magnificently landscaped gardens, with a private swimming pool and tennis courts. You may find an old fisherman's cottage for sale from time to time.

The town centres of Aix-en-Provence, Marseilles and Nice feature bourgeois town houses (*hotel particulier/maison de maître*), usually converted into elegant, self-contained apartments. All villages have solidly built old houses, often terraced, which may have substantial accommodation on two or three floors. Rural specialities in the old property category are small farmhouses (*mas*), large houses (*bastides*), converted oil mills, Camargue reed-matted *cabanes* and (in the southern Alps) houses with long sloping roofs. If you want a property with a large plot, look inland and don't even consider the coastline of Alpes-Maritimes.

Cost of Housing

The PACA region is the second most expensive for property in France, marginally behind the Ile-de-France, with average property prices for *all* categories combined (i.e. new, recent and old properties, apartments and houses) around €1,700 per m^2 (€170 per ft^2). However, away from the coastal strip, prices fall dramatically, although there are other expensive pockets, such as the area around the Grand Canyon du Verdon. Prices in Languedoc-Roussillon are around average for France and comparable with those in neighbouring Midi-Pyrénées (see page 193) and in Brittany and Upper Normandy (see page 68). Average property prices for all categories of property combined in Languedoc-Roussillon are around €1,100 per m^2 (€110 per ft^2), although prices in Montpellier (34) are generally well above the region's average.

Béziers (34) boasts the lowest average prices for older properties in the area (and the third-lowest in France), while the area's highest average prices are to be found in Cannes and Antibes (06), where the average home is more expensive than anywhere else in the country outside the Ile-de-France and where prices for waterfront properties have doubled in the last two or three years. The table below gives average prices per m^2 for older properties in major towns in the area:

Town	Average Price per m^2 (€)
Antibes (06)	2,540
Cannes (06)	2,345
Nice (06)	1,525
Carcassonne (11)	685
Aix-en-Provence (13)	1,565
Arles (13)	760
Marseilles (13)	1,090
Nîmes (30)	795
Béziers (34)	625
Montpellier (34)	980
Sète (34)	1,035
Perpignan (66)	695
Toulon (83)	965
Avignon (84)	830

Comparative average property prices are given below for coastal and inland areas of the Languedoc-Roussillon and PACA regions. The number of rooms excludes the kitchen, bathroom, WC and other utility rooms. 'New' normally means under five years old, and 'old' more than five years old. Note that prices for apartments don't include private parking spaces or garages, which are often offered for sale separately. Prices for single private parking spaces start around €4,000 in Languedoc-Rousillon and around €5,000 in PACA; garages cost twice as much!

● **Languedoc-Roussillon (Coast)**

New two/three-room apartment of 50–70m^2: €75,000 in Béziers (34), €85,000 in Perpignan (11) and €95,000 in Montpellier (34) ;

Old two/three-room apartment of 50–70m^2: €40,000 in Narbonne (66) and Perpignan, €50,000 in Béziers and €58,000 in Montpellier;

New four/five-room house with a 500m^2 plot: €90,000 in Béziers, €100,000 in Perpignan, €110,000 in Narbonne and €135,000 in the Montpellier area.

● **Languedoc-Roussillon (Inland)**

New two/three-room apartment of 50–70m^2: €85,000 in the Nîmes (30) area and in Carcassonne (66);

Old two/three-room apartment of 50–70m^2: €40,000 in Carcassonne and €50,000 in Nîmes and the Mende (48) area;

New four/five-room house with a 1,000m^2 plot: €90,000 in Carcassonne and €110,000 in the Nîmes area;

Old four/five-room house with a 1,000m^2 plot: €70,000 in the Mende area, €90,000 in Carcassonne and €116,000 in the Nîmes area.

● **PACA (Coast)**

New two/three-room apartment of 50–70m^2: €100,000 in Toulon (83) and €150,000 in Cannes (06);

Old two/three-room apartment of 50–70m^2: €65,000 in Toulon and €95,000 in Cannes;

New four/five-room house with a 500m^2 plot: €150,000 in Toulon (not the town centre) and from €250,000 in the Cannes area. You may find old properties with considerably more land, e.g. 2,000m^2, for around €275,000, e.g. in the Aix-en-Provence (13) area.

● **PACA (Inland)**

New three/four-room apartment of 80m^2: €110,000;

Old two-room apartment of 50m²: €40,000 (€75,000 in Avignon (84); ·

New four/five-room house on a 500m² plot: €90,000 (€120,000 in Avignon);

Old four/five-room house with up to 3,500m² plot: €100,000 (€110,000 in Avignon with a 1,000m² plot).

Land

In **Languedoc-Roussillon**, the coastal area of Pyrénés-Orientales around Canet Plage, Saint-Cyprien and Argelès has been heavily developed over the last 25 years, resulting in a scarcity of available building land. Permission to build near Collioure is difficult to obtain. Little private building land is available in Nîmes either, partly because of archaeological excavation work and partly because of municipal development. In Montpellier and its suburbs, most private building land is in the area around Port Marianne. The municipality has its own property company, which controls around 60 per cent of this land. There's virtually no land available to the north of the city.

In **PACA**, it's becoming increasingly difficult to find building land for houses in the narrow strip between the coast and the mountains in Alpes-Maritimes, partly because of coastal construction regulations (*la loi littoral*) and partly because of the topography of the terrain. Apartment block developers tend to snap up what is available. Urbanisation in Var is causing concern (even among local *notaires*!), as an increasing amount of agricultural land is being built on. There are plenty of plots available in towns throughout the region, although most of them are too small for a reasonable-size house and certainly wouldn't accommodate a swimming pool.

A plot of around 600m² (6,000ft²) is a good size, although if you're planning to build a large swimming pool with paved surrounding area, up to 1,000m² (10,000ft²) may be a more sensible size. Care should be taken not to buy or build a property in a riverside area which is liable to flooding; local authorities have issued building permits and may still do so for plots in suspect areas. Bear in mind also the *Tramontane* and *Mistral* wind factors (see page 222). For example, an exposed situation on level ground with a beautiful view of the western Pyrenees means you receive the brunt of the *Tramontane*.

Average prices (in €) for building land are shown below:

	up to 600m²	600–1,000m²	1,000–2,500m²
Languedoc-Roussillon (Coast)			
Perpignan (66) area	32,000	52,000	54,000
Narbonne (11) area	28,000	39,000	28,000*
Béziers (34) town	28, 000	45,000	33,000*
Montpellier (34) area	60,000	69,000	88,000

Languedoc-Roussillon (Coast)

Mende (48) area	23,000	22,000	22,000
Carcassonne (11) area	21,000	23,000	24,000
Nîmes (30) area	34,000	39,000	38,000*

PACA (Coast)

Aix (13) town	72,000	95,000	109,000
Aix (13) area	44,000	59,000	69,000
Marseilles (13) area	64,000	84,000	80,000*
Toulon (83) town	54,000	86,000	89,000
Hyères (83) town	72,000	97,000	152,000
Nice (06) town	45,000	118,000	112,000*

PACA (Coast)

Avignon (84) area	34,000	40,000	40,000*
Dignes (04) area	15,000	25,000	22,000*

* Note: prices reflect the availability and relative unpopularity of large plots.

Rental Accommodation

There's a shortage of properties for rent in the Mediterranean coastal area generally, where it's almost impossible to find a furnished (*meublé*) apartment or house. Rental properties are particularly scarce in the Pyrénées-Orientales (66) and Aude (11) departments of Languedoc-Roussillon. Although you may find a property through French property magazines, such as *Les Annonces Immobilières*, published monthly, or via the Internet (e.g. 🖳 www.123immo.com), it's best to deal with a reputable local estate agent that specialises in rental properties (check the agent's window to see if it features *biens à louer* or *locations habitations*). Contact the National Federation of Estate Agents (FNAIM, 12, rue Faubourg St Honoré, 75008 Paris, ☎ 01.44.20.77.00, 🖳 www.fnaim.com) for a list of members in your department.

The rates listed below are approximate average monthly rates, exclusive of maintenance and standing charges, for long-term lets. You may find quite respectable properties below these figures and there are certainly luxury properties far above them. Holiday or short-term lets, for one to four-week periods, particularly at the peak of high season, i.e. July to mid-August, can cost three or four times these rates or even more in the purpose-built coastal resorts of Argelès-sur-Mer, Gruissan, Saint-Cyprien, Port-Bacarès, Port-

Leucate and Cap-d'Agde in Languedoc-Roussillon, as well as in Saint-Tropez and other exclusive spots on the Riviera. An apartment in Cannes, for example, can cost up to €3,000 per week (more during the Film Festival), which means of course that, if you own a property there, you can let it for that amount.

The number of rooms in a property (expressed in advertisements by F or T, followed by a number) includes living rooms and bedrooms, but excludes the kitchen, bathroom, WC and any other utility rooms.

	One-bed Apartment	Three-bed House
Avignon (84)	€400	€900
Aix-en-Provence (13)	€450	€1,000
Cannes (06)	€450	€1,200
Carcassonne (66)	€350	€700
Hyères (83)	€450	€900
Marseilles (13)	€450	€900
Montpellier (34)	€450	€770
Nice (06)	€450	€1,100
Nîmes (30)	€350	€700
Perpignan (11)	€325	€700
Toulon (83)	€400	€900

If you're renting a substantial house (*villa*) with garden, it normally has a swimming pool. If it doesn't, you should check whether you will have the use of one.

COMMUNICATIONS

Air

The Mediterranean coastal area is easily accessible by air from most countries. The main international airports are Marseilles-Provence at Marignane, 25km (16mi) from the coast at Marseilles, and Nice-Côte d'Azur (France's second busiest airport) to the west of Nice. There are also good air connections for Languedoc-Roussillon (particularly if you're living or staying in the Aude or Pyrénées-Orientales departments) via Toulouse international airport, which is in the adjacent region of Midi-Pyrénées (see page 202). Flying times from London airports are around 90 minutes. Transatlantic flights operate mainly to and from Nice. The area has several other airports which boast international flights: Carcassonne, Montpellier, Nîmes, Perpignan and Toulon/Saint-Tropez (formerly Toulon/Hyères).

Since the end of the 1990s, the Mediterranean coast has become a low-price destination for travellers from the UK, Ireland, Holland and Sweden with the emergence of budget airlines, such as Virgin Express, Buzz, EasyJet, Airlib Express, Goodjet, Go (now owned by EasyJet), Ryanair, Transavia and most recently British Midlands's BMIbaby. Ryanair, for example, offers low-cost flights to Carcassonne and Perpignan from London Stansted and is to inaugurate flights from Brussels, Dublin, Salzburg, Stockholm and Venice to either Montpellier or Nîmes airport in 2003 or 2004. BMIbaby operates between East Midlands and Nice. Return tickets to Mediterranean airports, e.g. Marseilles-Marignane, Nice and Toulon/Saint-Tropez, from the London area airports of Luton and Stansted cost around €100. It's worthwhile checking the low-cost airlines' summer and winter schedules and frequencies, as they may differ considerably. Other UK carriers include British Airways, who have regular flights to Montpellier (from Gatwick) as well as to Marseilles and Nice in addition to regular flights to Toulouse, and Aer Lingus, with flights from Dublin to Nice three times a week.

Among French airlines, Air France offers a direct London-Perpignan flight. If you need to change in Paris, Air France flies several times a day to Montpellier airport from Paris Orly and Roissy-Charles de Gaulle, and Air Lib (formerly AOM and Air Liberté) flies four times a day to Perpignan from Orly. Air Littoral flies to Nîmes four times a day and to Béziers three times a day from Orly. French airline companies' tariff structures are complex, but there are some attractive prices if you're a regular traveller or if you book sufficiently in advance. Airports are shown on the maps at the beginning of the chapter. Details of all French airports and their services can be found on 🖳 www.aeroport.fr.

Sea

Apart from numerous yachting and motorboat marinas along the coast and companies offering deep-sea fishing and pleasure boat trips, there are regular ferry boat services for passengers and their cars. Between them, the Société nationale maritime Corse-Méditerranée (SNCM) and Corsica Sardinia Ferries offer sailings from Marseilles, Toulon and Nice to Corsica, Sardinia, Algeria and Tunisia. There are also ferries from Sète (34) to Tangiers, Morocco. There's a plan to introduce a ferry service from the small fishing port of Port-Vendres (near Collioure in Pyrénées-Orientales) to Barcelona in Spain. Mediterranean cruise ships have ports of call (depending on the route) at Sète, Marseilles, Toulon and Nice. Sète, Marseilles and Nice are major cargo ports, and Toulon is the French navy's Mediterranean base.

Public Transport

High-speed trains (*TGV*) now take just three hours from Paris to Marseilles and under five hours to Perpignan. Other towns in the area served by *TGV* include Nîmes and Montpellier. (These services have proved so popular that Air France has cut the cost of its flights to Montpellier and pulled out of Nîmes altogether.) Marseilles is only one hour from Lyons by *TGV*. In addition, there's a summer service, between late July and early September, direct from London to Avignon. (For details of the *TGV* network, see map in **Appendix E**.) The state run rail network (SNCF), which provides services to all sizeable towns in the two regions, has first-class safety and punctuality records. Train fares are extremely reasonable, and inexpensive season tickets are available to salaried employees living in 'dormitory' towns and commuting, for example, to major towns such as Montpellier, Marseilles and Nice. Local trains (*omnibus*) stop at most stations but don't have timetables! If you work late, you must commute by car. If you want to savour the blue sea and the sandy beaches, take a semi-fast train between the main towns along the coast or the The Nice to Digne narrow gauge railway (*chemin de fer de Provence/train de pignes*), which offers a picturesque winding journey of 153km (95mi) taking around three hours.

All major towns and cities have at least one local bus company providing a frequent and usually punctual service, at reasonable prices, up to around 22.00 throughout the week. From major towns to smaller nearby towns, there's usually a half-hourly service from Mondays to Saturdays (hourly on Sundays), terminating around 20.00. So, if you're spending an evening out in a major town but live outside the town, a car or taxi is essential. Taxi fares are reasonable and strictly regulated, but not all taxi drivers speak English. Buses to rural villages and outlying areas may run only once a day, or less frequently. There are school bus services in rural areas.

Public transport (usually privately operated) in some of the major towns in the two regions is as follows:

Carcassonne (11): There's a free shuttle service, every 15 minutes in high season, to the fortified old town.

Marseilles (13): There are single-decker buses and also, in central areas, trolley buses and trams, as well as an underground (métro) service – the only one in the Mediterranean area in France – with two lines, from the town centre to the suburbs; a tourist train runs around the old port (Vieux Port) area, and you can cross the old port with a frequent ferry service.

Montpellier (34): A tram system runs north-west to south-east; the TAM bus company operates throughout the town and suburbs; the Petibus minibus service runs in the pedestrian area of the old town (cars are banned from almost the whole town centre), as does a sightseeing train; open four-wheeled carriages ply the tourist trade along the esplanade and in the Place de la Comédie.

Toulon (83): A frequent passenger ferry service from the adjacent town of La Seyne, ideal for people working in the centre of Toulon, takes around 10 minutes; there's also a tourist train in the pleasure port and old town area.

Roads

If you're driving down from Paris to the PACA region, it's difficult to avoid the notorious bottleneck at Lyons, particularly in holiday periods, but the 'Wily Bison' website (💻 www.bison-fute.equipement.gouv.fr) provides invaluable forecasts and up-to-the-minute reports. If, on the other hand, you're driving from Paris to the Roussillon area, you can pick up the A20, 80km (50mi) south of Orléans, for Toulouse and at Toulouse take the A61 for Carcassonne and Narbonne. Michelin suggests a route from Paris to Perpignan of around 900km (550mi) with motorway toll charges of around €35, and another route, from Paris to Nice, of a similar distance with toll charges of around €60. In the Languedoc-Roussillon region, the motorway south from Clermont-Ferrand (in the Auvergne region) to the Hérault department is subject to long-term widening work in the area around Lodève, so reduced speed is inevitable.

All towns along the Mediterranean coast, from Perpignan to Nice, are linked by the A9, A54, A50, A52 and A8 motorways. If you're driving directly from Perpignan to Nice and wish to avoid the conurbations of Marseilles and Toulon, Michelin's useful website (💻 www.quelleroute.com) proposes a motorway route, via Nîmes and Aix-en-Provence, of 470km (290mi) taking just four hours (if you're very lucky!) and costing around €30 in tolls. If you wish to drive from Nice to Dignes-les-Bains (04) reasonably quickly, take the motorway route via Aix-en-Provence.

Needless to say, roads along the Côte d'Azur become hopelessly clogged in the summer months, when it can take three hours to drive from Cannes to Saint-Tropez (or vice versa) – a distance of around 75km (45mi).

Main roads and motorways are, almost without exception, in excellent condition. Departmental roads are also well maintained, while smaller local roads (*chemins vicinaux*) vary in quality according to the state of the local community's coffers. The condition of mountain roads often depends on the severity of the previous winter or last period of heavy rain. For private country roads leading to isolated properties, you may need a four-wheel drive vehicle.

Road users should note that drivers on the Mediterranean coast are among France's worst (which is saying something!): Antibes (06) has the dubious distinction of being France's most dangerous town in terms of your likelihood of being killed or injured on the roads, with over nine deaths or serious injuries per 1,000 inhabitants in the year 2000 – over ten times as many as in Béziers (34), one of France's safest driving towns – and Cannes, Nice (06), Nîmes (30) and Avignon (84) aren't far behind.

PLANNED DEVELOPMENTS

A number of developments are either in prospect or under way in the Mediterranean coastal area. The *TGV* network is being extended and improved, both for services to the coast and for those along the coast. By 2005 Spain will be accessible from Paris, with *TGV*s running to Barcelona via Perpignan in five-and-a-half hours; Perpignan to Barcelona will take just 50 minutes. An Institut national de la Statistique et des Etudes économiques (INSEE) survey indicates that some half a million people plan to set up home in the region between 2002 and 2015.

Aix-en-Provence: Attracted by the sunshine and the rapid communications with Lyons and Paris (as well as the nearby Marseilles-Marignane airport), multi-national, national and smaller high-tech companies are moving to the ever expanding industrial estate of Aix-les-Milles.

Marseilles: The principal development here is the Euro-Méditerranée project, initiated in 1995 and due to be completed in 2010. Its aim is to revitalise and renovate the centre of Marseilles and the Port Autonome (the third-largest cargo port in Europe), where old warehouses are being transformed into modern office blocks, to make Marseilles the commercial hub of southern Europe.

Montpellier: The city's urban development continues southwards – one day it will reach the sea – and a new town hall, Gaumont cinema complex and *TGV* station are taking shape.

Nice: A tramway will be built in the centre of Nice, and there's a project to link the city by tram to nearby Sophia Antipolis (France's answer to Silicon Valley) as well as to a second technology park (called the Nice-Méridia Technopark), scheduled to open March 2003, although the link may not be in service until 2006.

Toulon: After over ten years and one major technical hiccup (the tunnel caved in), a road tunnel crossing the town finally open in summer 2002, although only to east-west traffic; the reciprocal tunnel should be open by the end of 2006.

EMPLOYMENT PROSPECTS

PACA has a high proportion of service businesses (75 per cent), with only 20 per cent of employment in industry and 5 per cent in agriculture. Employment in Languedoc-Roussillon is split 65 per cent services, 25 per cent industry and

10 per cent agriculture. Languedoc-Roussillon holds the record for unemployment in France at around 4 per cent above the national average, and the PACA region also has an above average unemployment rate. Particularly badly affected are Marseilles (13), Béziers, Montpellier and Sète (34), and Perpignan (66), where there are large numbers of long-term unemployed. Sète suffers the country's highest rate of unemployment at over 25 per cent, although it also enjoys a high rate of new business success. The area also has some of the lowest average annual salaries in France, at below €17,000.

Salaried: The best executive appointment prospects are in the important growth areas of Aix-en-Provence (13) and Montpellier (24). For executive level appointments in a national company you must have excellent written and spoken French and be able to show that your educational qualifications are at least the equivalent of the French *diplôme* (an international Masters degree is impressive). If you have specialised technical or technological knowledge and experience (e.g. in computers, boat building and design or boat maintenance and repair, or the maritime or shipping business), English may be sufficient with some basic French.

There are expected to be thousands of job opportunities for R&D, biotechnology, multimedia and educational high-flyers when Nice's new Technopark (see above) opens in March 2003. At the other end of the employment spectrum, unskilled, semi-skilled and skilled workers are always in demand in industrial production, which includes food, clothes, cabinet making and car mechanics. Bouches-du-Rhône has the greatest number of jobs offered in this category. (Alpes-Maritimes, with a population of around 1 million, has a similar number of job opportunities in this category as Hérault and Var together, each of which has a population of around 900,000.) Specialist opportunities include wool weaving in Lodève (34) and silk working in the Cévennes area.

Casual, high season jobs in the tourist trade will always exist (you should apply in good time), but note that the peak of the high season is short – July and August – when, for example, 50 per cent of the annual visitors to PACA are there. *The English Yellow Pages* is a directory of English-speaking businesses in the south of France, covering mainly the Mediterranean coast between Monaco and Saint-Tropez; although aimed at customers, it may be helpful to those looking for employment. Copies are available from English Yellow Pages, 1, avenue Saint-Roch, 06600 Antibes (☎ 04.92.90.49.34, 🖥 www.englishyellowpages.fr). A list of companies in each department can be obtained from the French Chamber of Commerce in London (see **Appendix A**). See also **Appendix C** for a list of useful Internet sites for jobseekers.

Self-employment: Once you've digested all the paperwork and high social security payments that self-employment involves, building work (if you're qualified and experienced), tourist services (preferably not seasonal, e.g. all year round B&B), and estate agency work (gain experience with an estate agent or follow an intensive course) are some of the possibilities. If you opt for estate agency, consider specialising in certain types of property as a bilingual agent, as French estate agents in these regions are particularly thick on the ground. Buying a going concern is easier, although more costly, than creating a new business and more likely to be successful in the long term. Those considering setting up a business in Marseilles should investigate a recent scheme called Capital Local Marseille, which helped over 120 new business ventures in the two years following its introduction in 2000.

FURTHER INFORMATION

Useful Addresses

Tourist Offices

- Comité régional du Tourisme du **Languedoc-Roussillon**, 20, rue de la République, 34000 Montpellier (☎ 04.67.22.81.00, 🖳 www.crlangue-docroussillon.fr/tourisme)
- Comité régional du Tourisme (**PACA**), 10, place de la Joliette, 13002 Marseille (☎ 04.91.56.47.00, 🖳 www.crt-paca.fr)
- Comité départemental du Tourisme des **Alpes-Maritimes**, 55, promenade des Anglais, 06000 Nice (☎ 04.93. 37.78.78)
- Comité départemental du Tourisme des **Alpes-de-Haute-Provence**, 19, rue Docteur Honnorat, 04000 Dignes (☎ 04.92.31.57.29)
- Comité départemental du Tourisme de l'**Aude**, rue Moulin-de-la-Seigne, 11000 Carcassonne (☎ 04.68.11.66.00, 🖳 www.audetourisme.com)
- Comité départemental du Tourisme des **Bouches-du-Rhône**, Le Montesquieu, 13, rue Roux de Brignoles, 13006 Marseilles (☎ 04.91. 13.84.13 and 04.91.33.01.82)
- Comité départemental du Tourisme du **Gard**, 3, place des Arènes, BP 122, 30010 Nîmes (☎ 04.66.36.96.30, 🖳 www.cdt-gard.fr)
- Comité départemental du Tourisme de l'**Hérault**, avenue des Moulins, 34184 Montpellier Cedex 4 (☎ 04.67.22.81.00)
- Comité départemental du Tourisme du **Lozère**, 14, boulevard Nenri-Bourillon, BP 4, 48002 Mende (☎ 04.66.65.60.00)
- Comité départemental du Tourisme des **Pyrénées-Orientales**, 16, avenue des Palmiers, 66000 Perpignan (No office for visitors; write or phone: ☎ 04.68.51.52.53)

- Comité départemental du Tourisme du **Var**, 1, boulevard Foch, BP99, 83300 Draguignan (☎ 04.94.50.55.50)
- Comité départemental du Tourisme du **Vaucluse**, 12, rue Collège da la Croix, 84000 Avignon (☎ 04.90.80.47.00)

Useful Publications

- **The Riviera Reporter**, 56, chemin de Provence, 06250 Mougins (☎ 04.93.45.77.19, 🖳 www.Riviera-reporter.com)
- **The Riviera Times**, 8, avenue Jean Moulin, 06340 Drap (☎ 04.93. 27.60.00, 🖳 www.rivieratimes.com)
- **Spirit of Place PROVENCE**, Russell Ash and Bernard Higton (Pavilion Books)

Useful Websites

🖳 www.provenceweb.fr (tourist information about Provence)

🖳 www.camargue.fr (information about the Camargue)

Aiguille du Midi
cable car – The Alps

7.

THE ALPS

The area covered by this chapter runs from Lac Léman ('Lake Geneva'), the largest lake in western Europe, southwards towards the Mediterranean and is bounded by the Italian border to the east and the Rhône to the west. It includes part of the regions of Rhône-Alpes and Provence-Alpes-Côte d'Azur and part or all of the following departments: Hautes-Alpes (05), Drôme (26), Isère (38), Savoie (73) and Haute-Savoie (74). (The former province of Dauphiné corresponds approximately to the north-eastern part of Drôme and the Isère and Hautes-Alpes departments.) It's the most mountainous area of France, the Alps being Europe's biggest mountain range, 'shared' between France, Italy and Switzerland. The average altitude of the mountains in the Alps is 1,150m (3,772ft); the eastern area of the Alps has the highest peaks and forms a natural barrier with Italy. The most mountainous department is Isère, followed by Hautes-Alpes, Savoie, Haute-Savoie and Drôme. Mont Blanc, altitude 4,807m (15,767ft) in Haute-Savoie is the highest peak in Europe (excluding the mountains of Georgia). The Mont Blanc road tunnel and the Tunnel du Fréjus road and rail tunnel cut through the Alps, from Haute-Savoie and Savoie respectively, linking France to Italy (see **Planned Developments** on page 277).

The Alps area is of course noted for its majestic mountain scenery, which is unrivalled at most times of the year, and it's probably France's most picturesque region with its dense forests, lush pasture land, fast-flowing rivers, huge lakes and deep gorges. It's a paradise for sports fans and nature lovers with superb summer sports, such as rock-climbing and canyoning (abseiling and water-chute descents), hiking and walking, all-terrain cycling, hang-gliding and paragliding, and white-water sports, while winter sports and ski resorts offer some of the best facilities in Europe for downhill (Alpine) and cross-country (Nordic) skiing and snowboarding (see **Sports** on page 261). Albertville (73), Chamonix (74) and Grenoble (38) have all been venues for the Winter Olympic Games. Top ski resorts include Chamonix, France's mountaineering capital, Courchevel, Megève, Méribel and Val d'Isère (see page 142). The Alps therefore have two high seasons: the usual summer period, and the winter skiing season (December to April), the two peaks within the latter being the school holidays at Christmas and Easter (see **Sports** on page 261).

The Alps is the third most popular tourist area in France, after Paris and the Côte-d'Azur, and Annecy is one of the most popular tourist towns in France after Paris, but property prices are well below those of Paris and prestigious towns on the Riviera. Lower property prices than neighbouring Switzerland attract many Swiss who live in the area and commute to work in Geneva and other Swiss cities.

ADVANTAGES & DISADVANTAGES

One of the principal attractions of the Alps is the breathtaking, picture post-card scenery: in summer, lush green mountain slopes, with the highest mountain peaks permanently snow-capped, overlooking beautiful lakes; and, in winter, Christmassy snow-covered landscapes on high land everywhere. Healthy, sleep-inducing mountain air is in pleasant contrast to increasingly congested and polluted large cities in France, such as Marseilles and Strasbourg. On the other hand, the higher you live, the colder it gets – and it can get **very** cold.

The Alps is possibly the leading area in France for the variety and quality of outdoor activities available (see **Sports** on page 261 and **Leisure** on page 263). With over 1,200km^2 (465mi^2) of ski slopes, the French Alps have more skiing than either Switzerland (840km^2/326mi^2) or Austria (790km^2/306mi^2). A disadvantage is that the ski slopes are often crowded, especially during school holidays. Around 15 per cent of French families take regular skiing holidays and 80 per cent of French skiers go to the Alps every winter (the other 20 per cent choose the Jura, Massif Central, Pyrenees and Vosges – and the same percentages apply to foreigners taking skiing holidays in France).

Low-cost international flights (see **Air** on page 275) to Geneva and Grenoble make the northern Alps (Isère and the Savoy departments) readily accessible. If you're considering the southern Alps for residence or holidays, however, bear in mind that there's no major airport in or near the Hautes-Alpes department. Marseilles-Marignane airport can be two hours' drive from Gap (05), and there's no motorway link from Grenoble (38) to Briançon (05) and Gap. The *TGV* runs from Paris to Lyons (Rhône) and to Valence (26), from where Chambéry (73), Grenoble (38), and Annecy (74) are readily accessible (see **Public Transport** on page 276), although getting to a small town or village high in the Alps by public transport may not be so easy.

Property prices in the Alps are above the national average, with especially high prices in and around top tourist areas such as Annecy. Nevertheless, even here prices are well below those of Paris and major resorts on the Côte d'Azur, and properties in or near ski resorts are generally considered to be an excellent investment. Establishing social contacts and making friends with French people native to the area is easier, for example, than with the French Mediterraneans, who are more reserved (despite outward appearances). All this is good news if you're considering a property purchase, whether as an investment or as a permanent or holiday home, or for letting.

The following points may help you to decide whether to choose an area in the northern Alps (departments 26, 38, 73 and 74) or the southern Alps (05) – note that Drôme (26) is considered part of the northern Alps, although it's west of Hautes-Alpes (05):

- The northern Alps area is national, even international, in feeling, the four university sites at Grenoble attracting the largest number of foreign students in France outside Paris. The Geneva urban area spills into France here. Lyons is just one hour from Grenoble and Valence, and Grenoble itself is an important, dynamic city.

- The southern Alps is quieter, rural and more laid-back, with smaller, local businesses. (You might consider working and living in the northern Alps, and retiring to the southern Alps?)

- It's drier, sunnier and warmer in the southern Alps.

- Good road and rail links between the northern Alps departments provide the opportunity of sampling the numerous ski resorts, whereas communications are more limited in the southern Alps, where there are also fewer ski resorts.

- Property prices are generally lower in the southern Alps (see **Cost of Housing** on page 271).

Those in search of a town with plenty of green space should favour Gap (05) and Annecy (74), the former having more green space per inhabitant (over

156m²) than any other major town in France except Besançon (although curiously Gap makes little provision for cyclists, with no cycle track at all). Note also that there are nuclear power stations in Saint-Paul-Trois-Châteaux south of Drôme (26), and in Saint-Alban-du-Rhône/Saint-Maurice-l'Exil around 50km (30mi) south of Lyons in Isère, as well as one in neighbouring Ardèche near Montélimar, Privas, Le Teil and Valence.

MAJOR TOWNS & PLACES OF INTEREST

The major towns and other places of interest, including ski resorts, are listed below by department. The altitude given for each of the main ski resorts is the lowest at which skiing is normally possible. Note that there are sometimes considerable altitude differences between the highest and lowest slopes, so the highest slopes in each department are also indicated.

There are two national conservation areas in the Alps, each with around 800,000 visitors annually: the Parc national de la Vanoise, extending approximately between Méribel, Les Arcs and Val d'Isère (73) and covering some 2,000km² (780mi²) with over 100 mountain peaks exceeding 3,000m (9,840ft), and the Parc national des Ecrins, extending approximately between Les Deux-Alpes (38) and the northern part of Hautes-Alpes, an area of 2,700km² (1,040mi²). The parks are divided into 'inner zones', where there are strict regulations to protect all wildlife, and 'outer zones', where skiing and walking are permitted.

There are also four regional conservation areas (*parcs naturels régionaux*): Queyras, in the eastern part of Hautes-Alpes, covering 1,600km² (615mi²); Vercros, in the area approximately between Die (26) and Grenoble, covering 1,780km² (685mi²); le Massif des Bauges, forming a triangle approximately between Chambéry, Annecy and Albertville and covering 8,100km² (3,125mi²); and Chartreuse, approximately between Chambéry, Grenoble and the valley of the Isère river, covering 6,900km² (2,655mi²). Building regulations and permits in these areas are strictly controlled. If you really want to get away from it all, you should consider the Parc naturel régional du Queyras in Hautes-Alpes, whose human population is only around 3,000.

Drôme (26)

The departmental capital, Valence (pop. 65,000), which marks the start of Provence, is around one hour's drive from both Lyons and Grenoble. There are five ski resorts in the department, the main one being Col de Rousset at 1,367m (4,484ft) in the Parc naturel de Vercors in the *Préalpes* (lower Alpine slopes) in the north-east of the department. The upper slopes at Valdrôme are the highest in the department, at 1,300m (4,264ft). Névache and Saint-Véran are reckoned to be among France's most beautiful villages.

Hautes-Alpes (05)

Gap (pop. 37,000), at 735m (2,411ft), is the highest departmental capital in France, but Briançon (pop. 11,000), in the centre of the department, is more interesting historically, with its fortified medieval upper town area. At an altitude of 1,310m (4,300ft) it rivals Davros (Switzerland) as the highest town in Europe. There are around 25 ski resorts, of which approximately half are classed Nordic (for cross country skiing). The main resorts are Serre-Chevalier at 1,350m (4,428ft) and Montgenèvre at 1,829m (6,000ft), both just a few miles from Briançon. The upper slopes at La Grave-La-Meije are the highest, at 3,550m (11,644ft).

Isère (38)

Grenoble, the administrative capital of the Alps region, is a progressive city (pop. 160,000) with four university campuses attracting many foreign students. The capital of the former Dauphiné province, it's spectacularly situated amid surrounding mountains and is around 100km (60mi) from both Annecy (74) and Gap (04). Isère has no fewer than 40 ski resorts, principally Alpe d'Huez at 1,860m (6,100ft) and Les Deux-Alpes at 1,650m (5,412ft). The upper slopes at Les Deux-Alpes are the highest, at 3,600m (11,808ft).

Savoie (73)

Chambéry (pop. 56,000) is the department's capital and a university town, with an interesting *château*, the residence of the former Dukes of Savoy. Aix-les-Bains (26,000), 20km (13m) north of Chambéry on the Lac du Bourget, is the Alps' spa town par excellence. Bonneval-sur-Arc is reckoned to be one of France's most beautiful villages. Albertville (18,000), to the east of the Parc régional du massif des Bauges conservation area, was the venue for the 1992 Winter Olympic Games. Savoie has around 20 ski resorts, including several of the best known in France: Courchevel at 1,850m (6,068ft), Méribel at 1,450m (4,756ft), one of the most beautiful Alpine ski resorts, and Pralognan la Vanoise at 1,410m (4,625ft), which together comprise the so-called Trois Vallées, Les Arcs at 1,600m (5,248ft), Les Menuires at 1,850m (6,068ft), Val d'Isère at 1,850m (6,068ft), Tignes at 2,100m (6,888ft) and Val Thorens at 2,300m (7,544ft) – one of the highest Savoie stations. The upper slopes at Val Thorens are the highest, at 3,300m (10,725ft).

Haute-Savoie (74)

The capital Annecy (pop. 51,000), on the northern tip of the Lac d'Annecy, is one of France's most visited towns and has a delightful historic town centre built along canals (Annecy is known as the 'Venice of the Alps'), although it's usually crowded with tourists (the area around Annecy and the Lac d'Annecy is to be avoided at weekends and in the peak of the summer season). On the French (south) side of Lac Léman are Thonon-les-Bains, rich in Italian architecture, and Evian-les-Bains (almost adjacent – the combined population is 29,000), famous for its mineral water. There are around 25 ski resorts in the department, the largest, oldest and one of the most exclusive being Chamonix-Mont Blanc (pop. 10,000) at 1,050m (3,444ft), the starting point for the thousands of walkers every year who climb Mont Blanc. (If you've set your heart on this, you must be fit and suitably equipped; there are around 150 rescues every year and several fatalities, and some people experience mountain 'sickness' at over 3,000m (9,840ft). Information about guides can be obtained from the tourist office, 85, place du Triangle de l'Amitié, BP 25, 74400 Chamonix, ☎ 04.50.53.00.24, 💻 www.chamonix.com.) Other ski resorts include Avoriaz at 1,280m (4,200ft) and Megève at 1,113m (3,650ft). The upper slopes at Chamonix are the highest, at 3,842m (12,600ft).

POPULATION

With a total population of around 2.7 million, the departments of Drôme, Hautes-Alpes, Isère, Savoie and Haute-Savoie have a population slightly in excess of Languedoc-Roussillon (see **Chapter 6**), which covers a similar area. The population has increased by around 6 per cent over the last ten years, compared with the national average of 4 per cent. Isère is one of the most densely populated departments in France, while Hautes-Alpes, with under eight people per km^2 (20 people per mi^2), is one of the least. The proportion of students among the population of the major towns is generally low; Grenoble (38) has the highest proportion of students (12 per cent). The total and official foreign populations of each department are given below.

Drôme (26): Total population 440,000, of which 6,000 are Moroccans, 5,000 Algerians, 2,700 Portuguese, 2,500 Tunisians and around 275 Britons.

Hautes-Alpes (05): Total population 122,000, of which 800 are Italians, 700 Algerians, 350 Moroccans and just over 100 Britons.

Isère (38): Total population 1.1 million, of which 15,500 are Algerians, 12,000 Italians and 12,000 Portuguese, 5,500 Turks and 1,500 Britons.

Savoie (73): Total population 373,000 of which 6,000 are Algerians, 6,000 Italians, 4,500 Portuguese, 3,300 Moroccans and 650 Britons.

Haute-Savoie (74): Total population 632,000, of which 7,500 are Algerians and 7,500 Italians, 6,500 Portuguese, 6,000 Turks and 1,100 Britons.

For the populations of main towns, see **Major Towns & Places of Interest** above.

LANGUAGE

Occitan or the *Langue d'Oc* is spoken in southern parts of the area (see page 221), although it isn't necessary to learn it, as French is also universally spoken.

CLIMATE

The Alps is noted for its extremes of temperature, with heavy snow (on high ground) throughout the winter months and hot sunshine in summer, although cool summer evenings are usual high in the Alps. The climate is most pleasant in spring and autumn. The higher and further north you go, the colder and more humid it becomes. The southern Alps (Hautes-Alpes) have more sun and less rain – a generally milder climate than the northern Alps. However, the natural barrier of the Alps disrupts normal weather patterns and there are often significant local climatic variations. For example, while the average annual rainfall in the mountains is over 800mm (30in) it sometimes exceeds 2,000mm (80in) in the Grande Chartreuse area, Isère. Annual rainfall at Embun (05) and Bourg-Saint-Maurice (73), both of which are at around 870m (2,850ft), is 716mm (28.5in) and 971mm (38in) respectively.

In Grenoble, rainfall is spread more or less evenly throughout the year, with between 50mm (2in) and 100mm (4in) per month and an annual total of around 980mm (38.5in). In summer, daytime temperatures throughout the Alps are generally between 20°C (67°F) and 30°C (86°F), although Grenoble can be like a cauldron with temperatures frequently exceeding 30°C. Grenoble enjoys around 2,030 hours of sunshine per year, compared with 2,505 hours in Embrun and 2,025 hours in Bourg-Saint-Maurice. The table below shows the number of hours' sunshine and number of days' rainfall in selected towns in the area.

Town	Sunshine Hours	Days' Rainfall
Gap (05)	2,506	83
Valence (26)	2,026	81
Grenoble (38)	2,031	110
Chambéry (73)	2,027	110
Annecy (74)	2,027	110

COST OF LIVING

The area is generally cheaper than Paris and the Ile-de-France or the Mediterranean coast. However, Isère (38) and the Savoy departments (73 and

74) are more expensive than Drôme (26) and Hautes-Alpes (05). The cost of living is also higher in main towns such as Grenoble (38) and Annecy (74) and in the major ski resorts, where shops have high prices all year round and not just during the skiing season.

CRIME RATE & SECURITY

The Rhône-Alpes region is fourth in the French crime league table (a respectable distance behind the Ile-de-France, Provence-Alpes-Côte-d'Azur and Languedoc-Roussillon), although it should be noted that the region includes the city of Lyons, where the crime rate is relatively high, as well as the Alps, where (particularly in rural areas) crime is uncommon. In fact, the town of Gap (05) enjoys the lowest (reported) crime rate of any major town in France. Chambéry (73), on the other hand, is among the 20 towns with the highest crime rates (and suffered an increase of over 20 per cent in crimes between 1998 and 2000); Valence (26), Grenoble (38) and Annecy (74) also have higher than average crime rates. On average in the area, there are around 62 reported crimes annually per 1,000 inhabitants. If you're seeking a property to let, note that agents which are members of FNAIM (the national association of estate agents) are required to insure against damage caused by lessees. If you're absent from a property for a prolonged period, advise the local police, who may keep an eye on it for you. For general information on crime in France, see page 52.

AMENITIES

Sports

Multi-sports complexes are rare in the Alps, as they are throughout most of France. The municipal *salle des sports* usually houses a gym and perhaps a separate room for table tennis and is home to the local basketball, handball and volleyball teams. Municipal tennis courts (normally well maintained) and municipal swimming pools (usually overheated) are reasonably priced. Swimming pools often operate a *carnet* system, reducing the unit entrance price. Private sports clubs may include swimming, rowing, cycling, rugby, sailing, skiing, gymnastics, volleyball and judo. You can also swim in mountain lakes in the summer (check with a local guide beforehand) and in designated beach areas alongside lakes such as the Lac d'Annecy (74) and Lac de Serre Ponçon (05). The water temperature is around 20°C (68°F) in July and August. Avoid the areas at the eastern ends of both these lakes, Le Bout du Lac (73) and Embrun (05), unless you like crowds or want to chug about in a motor boat or paddle a pedalo.

Skiing: Skiing is, of course, the sport the region is best known for, and it includes many of the world's top resorts (see **Major Towns & Places of Interest** on page 257). Their international popularity, however, means that resorts are often crowded, particularly during school holidays at Christmas and Easter. French state schools are divided between three 'zones', each of which has a different holiday period, in order to minimise crowding on the ski slopes, but there are still traffic jams around Lyons at peak times. Grenoble, for example, is in Zone A, Marseilles in Zone B and Paris in Zone C. Holiday dates can be checked with your town hall or a French diary. Information to help you choose the most suitable ski resort can be obtained from Ski-France (61, boulevard Haussmann, 75008 Paris, ☎ 01.47.42.23.32, 💻 www.ski france.fr), who will provide details of access, ski slopes, accommodation and après-ski activities, as well as advice as to the best destinations for family skiing, the latest snowboard activities, Nordic skiing, club stations (those providing a range of après-ski entertainments and local amenities) and traditional style Alpine ski villages. Altitudes are given, the state of the snow and the number of skiing slopes by grade of difficulty (from green, the easiest, through blue and red to black, the most difficult). Around 45 of the Alpine ski resorts adhere to the '*Les p'tits Montagnards d'Hiver*' club for young children. This guarantees a kindergarten for children from 18 months old, ski schools (with sleigh areas and separate ski slopes) for three to four year olds with qualified instructors, initiation to the latest snow sports for the oldest children in the next age group, and free ski lifts for the under fours, with reductions for those aged 5 to 12.

Snowboarding has been practised since the early 1980s and the French association became the Fédération française de Snowboard in 1994. Snowboarding facilities are available in many ski resorts, and Avoriaz (74) and Chamonix (74) have especially well adapted sites. Half-pipe snowboarding (like dry land skateboarding on 180° concave slopes) is well catered for at Chamrousse (38), Val d'Isère (73), Avoriaz, Chamonix and Flaine (74). Another advanced form of skiing is acrobatic mogul skiing (*ski sur bosses*), for which Val d'Isère (73) is particularly well suited. Risoul, at 1,850m (6,068ft), near Vars and the Italian border in Hautes-Alpes, now attracts almost 50 percent of its clientele from snowboard enthusiasts.

A useful website for winter sports enthusiasts is that of the Fédération française des Sports de Glace (💻 www.ffsg.org), which offers information on all sports practised on ice, e.g. skating, bobsleighing, sledging, skeleton (sledging face down!), ice-hockey and curling.

White-water Sports: Various white-water sports are available near Thonon-les-Bains (74) in the Dranse canyon, in the torrents around Chamonix (74), on the Durance river (05) and along the Isère river (several departments) and can be great fun, provided you like waves and fresh (i.e. cold!) water. If you're really brave, you can even try white-water swimming!

Hiking: Walking is popular in the area's national and regional parks, e.g. the Vanoise national park and the Queyras regional park (see **Major Towns & Places of Interest** on page 257). There's a tremendous variety of Alpine flowers, and animal wildlife includes marmots, chamois and ibex goats. Details are available from the Fédération française de Randonnée pédestre, 14, rue Riquet, 75019 Paris (☎ 01.44.89.93.93).

Fishing: Fishing is another popular sport in the area; salmon and pike are found in the rivers of Isère (38) and trout and turbot in Savoy's lakes.

Golf: There are nine 18-hole golf courses in Haute-Savoie: extremely prestigious courses at Chamonix and Evian-les-Bains, three in Savoie, three in Isère in the area around Grenoble, and one in Hautes-Alpes (in Gap). There are also several 'compact' courses, i.e. those with nine holes or under. Not all golf courses are open all year round. Contact the Ligue Rhône-Alpes de Golf, 7, quai Général Sarrail, 69006 Lyons (☎ 04.78.24.76.61) for details. Information (in both French and English) on how to find courses, the cost of a round (which varies between €15 and €50), etc. is available via the Internet (🖳 www.backspin.com). Another useful website for golfers is 🖳 www.golf. com.fr.

Spectator Sports: As far as spectator sports are concerned, there are no major professional football teams in the Alps, but there's a fine athletics stadium at Annecy, with beautiful views of surrounding mountains, where international meetings are held. The recently built (1992) Olympic rink at Albertville has ice hockey and ice-skating events. See also **Planned Developments** on page 277.

Leisure

The Alps is a particularly rich area for culture. There are many historical museums relating to the Franco-Italian history of the Alps, a museum devoted to the novelist Stendhal, who was born in Grenoble, and a fine-arts museum in the same city. The Abbey of Hautecombe, burial places of the princes of Savoy and the remains of Roman baths at Aix-les-Bains are of particular historical interest, as are the ramparts by Vauban in the old fortified town of Briançon, the Château de Menthon-Saint-Bernard, near the Lac d'Annecy and the secluded monastery of the Grande Chartreuse near Cambéry.

Major towns have theatres, occasionally staging opera. Both Albertville and Grenoble have large indoor stadiums/entertainment centres which stage international shows such as Holiday on Ice and the Lord of the Dance (for information see 🖳 www.albertville.com and 🖳 www.ville-grenoble.fr). The CityVox website (🖳 www.cityvox.com) also has regularly updated information, in French only at present, on current and future events in Annecy, Chambéry, Gap, Grenoble and Valence. Information is also provided by regional newspapers, including *L'Essor savoyard*, *La Maurienne* (every

Friday) and *Le Dauphiné libéré* (🖳 www.ledauphine.com), which has local editions.

Spas & Casinos: The region boasts a number of spa towns, each with a casino (casinos were originally permitted only in spa towns), including Allevard, Urage-les-Bains, Villard-de-Lens (38), Aix-les-Bains (two), Brides-les-Bains, Challes-les-Eaux (73), Annecy, Annemasse, Chamonix-Mont-Blanc, Evian and Saint-Gervais-les-Bains (74). Details of all casinos and what they offer are available via the Internet (e.g. 🖳 www.journaldescasinos.com – partly in English).

Theme Parks: There are a number of theme parks and attractions in the region, including:

- Aquarium d'Aix-les-Bains (73): fish and bird park;

- Aquarium tropical du Val-de-Drôme in Allex (26): sea life;

- Aventure Parcs in Autrans and Les Deux-Alpes (38) and Les Gets (74): activity parks;

- Ferme aux Crocodiles in Pierrelatte (26): 500 crocodiles;

- Forêt aux Champignons et Insectes géants in Saint-Antoine-l'Abbaye (38): giant insects and mushrooms;

- Le Jardin des Découvertes in Die (26): butterflies;

- Parc Animalier de Merlet in Les Houches (74): wildlife park;

- Vivarium d'Yvoire (74): reptile park;

- Walibi Rhône-Alpes at Les Avenières near Grenoble (38): amusement park which attracts over 400,000 visitors annually.

In the adjoining departments of Rhône are a bird park in Villars-les-Dombes (01), 'Aero City' in Aubenas and a safari park in Peaugres (07), a zoo at Saint-Martin-de-la-Plaine (42) and a wolf and bird park in Courzieu (69).

Other interesting places to visit include the Evian water-bottling plant (by appointment between mid-June and mid-September only) and the Caves et Distillerie de la Chartreuse in Voiron (38), where the famous liqueur has been distilled by the monks since 1605.

English-language Cinema & Theatre

The university towns of Chambéry and Grenoble each have one cinema dedicated to showing foreign films (mainly American and British) in their original languages (*version originale/VO*). In Chambéry, it's the Curial (☎ 04.79.33.42.47) and in Grenoble, the Club (☎ 04.76.42.41.41). Prices are around €5 per film. Films tend to be avant-garde or offbeat – not commercial block-busters. Don't expect deluxe seats, a panoramic screen and popcorn! Some municipal cultural centres (*maisons de la culture*) regularly show *VO* films at a subsidised price, also around €5. A useful website for finding out what films are on in a given area, which also indicates whether the films are being shown in the original language is 💻 www.cinefil.com. There are no regular English-language theatre performances in the area.

Shopping Centres & Markets

The principal regional shopping centre (*centre commercial*) is the Grande Place in Grenoble, with a Carrefour hypermarket, shopping mall (*galerie marchande*) and major DIY, garden centre, furniture and sportswear stores offering overall more than 8ha (almost 20 acres) of sales area. There are area shopping centres throughout the Alps, some with hypermarkets, including Albertville, Annecy, Bourg-de-Péage (26), Briançon and Valence. The major hyper and supermarket companies are Auchan, Carrefour, Casino, Géant Casino and Leclerc.

Local specialities include a variety of dry and smoked hams (from Savoy departments), sausages and sausage meat, dried and salted goats' legs (*cuisses de bouc*), cow and goat cheese, including the strong-tasting *reblochon*, *fondue savoyarde* and Montélimar nougat. The area around Nyons in southern Drôme (strictly speaking in Provence) is renowned for its olive oil, and Grenoble is famous for its walnuts and walnut products. Although the Alps isn't known for its wines, Savoy's white wines are agreeable. Local craftsmen's products, such as woodcarvings, can be found in boutiques throughout the region.

Most towns and villages have daily or weekly markets. The major markets in the area are in Annecy, which specialises in handicraft products, Rumilly and Saint-Gervais-les-Bains (all in 74). General markets offer local dairy produce, fruit and vegetables. Especially appetising are local cheeses and fruit such as bilberries, raspberries and strawberries (particularly in the Chambéry area).

Foreign Food & Products

Hyper and supermarkets sell few foreign foods, with the exception of biscuits, cereals, preserves, Norwegian and Scottish smoked salmon, Chinese and Vietnamese foods, Italian pasta, delicatessen foods and some cheeses. From time to time Guinness and British beers are stocked (Kronenbourg, a French brewer, brews an English-style beer; packs are marked '*tradition anglaise*').

Specialist English and Chinese furniture shops are found in most large towns and cities. IKEA, the Swedish furniture manufacturer, whose good quality pine furniture is ideal for holiday chalets, have a large store in Lyons (Rhône), around one hour's drive from Grenoble or Valence. Gift shops sell pictorial guides and souvenir books with English text describing local and regional beauty spots, and in the high seasons some book shops stock a selection of English-language paperbacks. For general information on obtaining foreign products in France, see page 61.

Restaurants & Bars

There's a tremendous variety of restaurants offering international cuisine and regional dishes. They're generally good value, especially in low season. You may find a comfortable restaurant, or *brasserie*, with a fine mountain view, offering a three-course lunch, without wine, for around €15. (At the opposite end of the scale is the three-Michelin-star Auberge de l'Eridan in Annecy, where the 11-course (!) menu will set you back almost €200 per head.) Local specialities include *fondue* and *raclette* (melted cheese – *you* melt the cheese – with boiled potatoes and cold meats), *gratin Dauphinois* (potatoes, cheese and cream) and *tartiflette* (a diced-bacon flan). In bars, large coffees with milk or cream (*café crème*) are popular at breakfast time. Expect to pay at least €2. If you want a beer like brown ale, try Pelforth *brune* bottled beer: around €3. If you're on a full day's shopping binge in a shopping centre, self-service cafeterias such as Casino's offer good quality three-course meals at reasonable prices.

SERVICES

International & Private Schools

There are no international schools in this area, but the Collège privé international Sainte-Croix des Neiges (☎ 04.50.73.01.20, 🖥 www.ste-croix-des-neiges.com) in Abondance (74) caters specifically for English-speaking students.

Language Schools

Language lessons are offered by a number of public and private bodies in the area, including those listed below. Language courses are also offered by local Chambres de Commerce et d'Industrie and Centres culturels.

● Université d'Etudes et de Loisirs des Alpes du Sud in Gap (05);

● Logos in Gières (38);

● Centre Universitaire d'Etudes françaises in Grenoble (38);

● Centre international de Formation et d'Echanges linguistiques in Albertville (73);

- IFALPES Chambéry in Chambéry (73);

- Institut Savoisien d'Etudes françaises in Chambéry (73);

- Alp'lingua – Institut Alpins des Langues in Hauteluce (73);

- IFALPES d'Annecy in Annecy (74);

- CILFA in Annecy-le-Vieux (74);

- Altiplano in Chamonix (74);

- INSTEAD – Institute of Foreign Education in Chamonix (74).

Details of the above schools can be found on 🖳 www.europa-pages.com. The French Consulate in London (see **Appendix A**) publishes a booklet called *Cours de français Langue étrangère et Stages pédagogiques du français Langue étrangère en France*, which includes a comprehensive list of schools and organisations providing French language courses throughout France.

Hospitals & Clinics

All cities, large towns and major ski resorts (such as Chamonix) have at least one public hospital. Grenoble, with 2,500 medical students, has a teaching hospital (*CHU*) with the widest range of equipment and specialists. It was rated the 14th best hospital in France in a survey published in August 2002 by *Le Point* magazine. No other hospitals in the area were rated in the top 50, although there were three in nearby Lyons: the Hôpital Edouard-Herriot (23rd), the Centre hospitalier Lyon-Sud (38th) and the Hôpital de la Croix-Rousse (43rd). In large hospitals you should find at least one doctor in each department that speaks English, although the only general hospitals included in the US Embassy's list of hospitals where English is spoken are the Debrousse (for children), du Parc, Eugène André, la Sauvegarde, Protestant, Sainte-Anne Lumière and Saint-Louis hospitals in Lyons. If you're buying property in a rural, mountainous area, take into account access time and difficulty to the nearest hospital, especially in the event of an emergency in winter when there's heavy snow. If you have an accident on the ski slopes, the mountain ambulance (helicopter) service is extremely well organised.

Balneology centres (consult the yellow pages under 'Cures' or 'Thermalisme') with saunas and thermal baths are concentrated in the two Savoy departments and also near Briançon in Hautes-Alpes. Establishments cater for those merely seeking relaxation as well as for the infirm.

Doctors & Dentists

The Alps area generally has above the national average proportion of doctors and dentists to inhabitants; Hautes-Alpes is particularly well provided with doctors, having over 184 general practitioners and 163 specialists per 100,000 population. It's usually easy to find and register with a doctor, many of whom speak English. If you require a list of doctors and dentists who speak English, and the British Consulate in Lyons (see **Consulates** on page 269) doesn't have a list for your area, your local chemist (*pharmacie*) may be useful.

Tradesmen

It may be difficult to find English-speaking tradesmen in the area. Magazines such as *French Property News* and newspapers such as *The News* (see **Appendix B**) carry advertisements by English-speaking tradesmen. The British Consulate in Lyons (☎ 04.72.77.81.70) may be able to fax or send you a list of officially registered builders (whose work is automatically guaranteed by insurance cover) in the area, although this will include French and foreign tradesmen, who may speak little English.

English-language Radio

There's no local radio in English, but it's possible to receive BBC Radio 1, 2, 3, and 4 on your television via the Astra satellite, and you can listen to recordings of radio programmes on Radio 1, 2, 3, 4, 5, 6 and 1Extra on your computer via the Internet (go to 🖳 www.bbc.co.uk/radio/aod/index.shtml). The World Service can be received on on short wave (for frequency details, go to 🖳 www.bbc.co.uk/worldservice/schedules/frequencies/eurwfreq.shtml) and via the Astra satellite. Note, however, that positioning a satellite dish correctly in a mountainous area may be tricky, or perhaps impossible, for proper reception. Local music stations usually broadcast 60 per cent non-French language songs, most of which are in English.

English-language Press

The *International Herald Tribune*, published in Paris, is widely available on the day of publication, and the *Guardian* and *European Financial Times*, printed in Frankfurt, are available, also on the day of publication in some areas. Large towns and cities, such as Annecy and Grenoble, have other English-language daily newspapers available the day after publication, and other towns and mountain resorts have these in the high seasons. The *Guardian Weekly* and *Weekly Telegraph* are available all year round in certain areas or can be ordered on subscription. The *International Herald Tribune* is available on subscription but is often delivered the day after publication. Certain Maisons de la Presse newsagents sell English-language magazines, ranging from popular women's household magazines to *The Economist* and *Time Magazine*. *The News* is an English-language monthly newspaper covering the whole of France with a regular section on happenings in Rhône-Alpes (see **Appendix B**).

Consulates

There are no foreign embassies or consulates in the Alps area, except two Italian Honorary Consuls in Chambéry and Grenoble. Austria, Belgium, Canada, Denmark, Finland, Greece, Ireland, Italy, Luxemburg, the Netherlands, Portugal, Sweden, the UK and USA have consulates in Lyons (69), Norway in Francheville (69) and Spain and Switzerland in Villeurbanne (69). The British Consulate General is at 24, rue Childebert, 69288 Lyon cedex 1 (☎ 04.72. 77.81.70), the United States Consulate General at 16, rue de la République, 69002 Lyon cedex 02 (☎ 04.78.38.36.88 and 04.78.38.33.03). For contact details of other consulates refer to the local yellow pages under 'Ambassades, consulats et autres représentations diplomatiques'. For details of consulates and embassies of other nations consult the yellow pages for Lyons or Paris.

Churches

Regular services in English are held in the following towns:

- Annecy (74) – Notre-Dame de Liesse;
- Evian (74) – Notre-Dame;
- Grenoble (38) – Centre Oecuménique Saint-Marc.

There's also an Anglican church with services in English in Lyons (at Le Foyer l'Escale Lyonnaise) in the department of Rhône.

There are mosques in Briançon (05), Valence (26), Grenoble (38), Albertville (73) and Bonneville (74); details can be found on ▣ http://mosquee.free.fr. There are also four synagogues in Grenoble (for details, go to ▣ www.feujcity.com, where there's also information about Kosher food shops and restaurants, Jewish clubs, associations and schools, etc.) and one in Valence (as well as five in Lyons), details of which can be found on ▣ www.pagesjaunes.fr (enter 'Synagogues' in the first box and the name of the town).

Clubs

There are clubs for numerous indoor and outdoor activities, ranging from archery (*tir à l'arc*), bridge, board games (*jeux de société*) including chess (*échecs*), and computing (*informatique*), to paint-ball, paragliding and parachuting. If you're a keen skier or walker, joining a skiing or walking club, particularly if you live all year round in the Alps, is strongly recommended. You benefit from the experience of others, visit other areas and possibly enjoy group reductions on lifts as well as making a new circle of friends. Consult the yellow pages under 'Clubs, associations de loisirs', local and departmental tourist offices and the Office des Clubs sportifs at your town hall.

The International Rotary Club has several branches in Annecy, Chambéry and Grenoble and also branches in Aix-les-Bains, Albertville, Chamonix and Valence. Consult the website (🖳 www.rotary-francophone.org) and click on 1780 for the full list.

For French speakers, the Accueil des Villes françaises (AVF), a French organisation designed to welcome newcomers to an area, is an option (there's often at least one fluent English-speaker in each group). There are around 20 AVF groups in the Alps – in Crest, Montélimar, Romans, Valence (26), Bourgoin-Jallieu, Claix, Grenoble, Meylan-Grésivaudan, Vienne, Voiron (38), Aix-les-Bains, Chamonix-Mont-Blanc, Chambéry, Saint-Jean-de-Maurienne (73), Annecy, Annemasse, Bonneville and Saint-Julien-en-Genevois (74). The website (🖳 www.avf.asso.fr) includes a directory (*annuaire*) of local groups by department as well as an online form for contacting your local AVF before you move to the area. Listings indicate whether information and services are available in English or other languages. Other sources for clubs in the area are *The News* (see **Appendix B**) and the English-speaking church (see above).

PROPERTY

Property prices are above the national average in the Alps with especially high prices in and around tourist towns such as Annecy (74), although even here prices are well below those of Paris and top resorts on the Riviera. Typical village houses (see below) are much sought after and are rarely for sale in or near ski resorts. Properties in or near ski resorts are usually an excellent investment and there are currently tax advantages to be gained from buying new property and letting it out. Demand for new property is particularly strong in Isère and the two Savoy departments.

Valence (26) boasts the lowest average prices for older propertiesin the Alps, while the area's highest average prices are to be found in Annecy (74). The table below gives average prices per m² for older properties in major towns in the area:

Town	Average Price per m² (€)
Valence (26)	750
Gap (05)	1,020
Grenoble (38)	1,145
Annecy (74)	1,835

If you're a UK resident and you're starting your search from home, there are property search companies such as Alpine Apartments Agency, Zigi Davenport, Hinton Manor, Eardisland, Herefordshire HR6 9BG (☎ 01544-388234, 💻 www.alpineapartmentsagency.com) specialising in Alps and lakeside properties. Consult also the articles and advertisements in *French Property News* and *Focus on France* (see **Appendix B**). The French property magazine, *Logic-Immo*, published every three weeks, is full of advertisements, many in colour (💻 www.logic-immo.com). There are editions for Drôme, Savoie and Haute-Savoie. You will find these in stands in front of estate agents' offices (look for the FNAIM member sign: a yellow diamond) and bakers (*boulangeries*).

Typical Homes

These include elegant traditional farmhouses (*mas*) in their own grounds in Isère, detached Swiss-style lakeside and mountain chalets, stone village houses (rarely on the market), even rarer barn-type sloping-roof Alpine valley houses, probably requiring renovation or conversion, and modern provençal houses (see **Typical Homes** on page 238) in and around Valence. *Construction traditionnelle*, which means with solid (brick) interior walls, is a strong selling point for new and recent houses, and estate agents' descriptions, normally scanty on details, emphasise this. Note that small chalets or apartments which are large enough for holidays may be cramped, even if there are only two of you, as a main residence. A room or rooms with an attractive, sunny outlook should be a priority.

Cost of Housing

Generally, the higher you live, the higher the prices. Haute-Savoie is the most expensive department for older property (houses and flats), but *slightly* cheaper than Savoie for new apartments. New houses in Savoie are considerably more expensive than in Haute-Savoie, particularly in the Albertville area. Drôme is the cheapest department. Luxury properties, with two to five rooms (i.e. one to three or four bedrooms), cost from €1,500 to €2,000 per m².

Below is a table giving average sale prices of properties sold in some of the main towns, cities and lakeside resorts in 2001. 'New' means under five years old, and 'old' applies to all other properties. The number of rooms excludes the kitchen, bathroom, WC and other utility rooms. The average price per room (for houses) and per m² (for apartments) is useful for checking if a property is correctly priced. Note that 'old' houses often have much larger plots than 'new' houses, which sometimes accounts for the disparity between relative prices.

	Price (€)	Room Price (€)	Plot Size (m²)
New Houses (5–6 rooms)			
Valence/local area	110,000	25,000	1,700
Grenoble (town)	170,000	35,000	700
Albertville/local area	565,000	90,000	585
Thonon-les-Bains/local area	165,000	33,000	600
Old Houses (4–6 rooms)			
Valence/local area	105,000	20,000	2,000
Grenoble (town)	150,000	30,000	1,500
Albertville/local area	150,000	30,000	2,100
Aix-les-Bains (town)	150,000	30,000	840
Chambéry (town)	150,000	30,000	670
Annecy (town)	280,000	60,000	850
Thonon-les-Bains/local area	170,000	35,000	1,200
Gap (town)	170,000	35,000	1,600

	Price (€)	Price per m² (€)
New Apartments (3 rooms)		
Valence/local area	90,000	1,200
Grenoble	95,000	1,300
Albertville/local area	155,000	2,500
Aix-les-Bains (town)	140,000	1,900
Chambéry (town)	90,000	1,200
Annecy (town)	150,000	2,100
Thonon-les-Bains/local area	120,000	1,700
Gap (town)	105,000	1,400
Old Apartments (2–3 rooms)		
Valence/local area	50,000	750
Grenoble (town)	75,000	1,200
Albertville/local area	100,000	1,700
Aix-les-Bains (town)	55,000	900
Chambéry (town)	70,000	1,050

Annecy (town)	125,000	1,900
Thonon-les-Bains/local area	75,000	1,200
Gap (town)	70,000	1,050

Ski resorts: Not surprisingly, ski resorts generally command higher property prices, and prices vary according to the prestige of the resort, situation within the resort, construction quality and finish, floor area (for apartments), aspect and outlook, balcony size, etc. Most of the top resorts are in the Tarentaise valley in Savoie, where Méribel is particularly popular with the British (there are around 75 chalets owned by Britons). Courchevel and Val d'Isère, which have more 'cachet' than Méribel and are correspondingly more expensive (and have fewer available properties), are the next most popular. In fact, Courchevel is one of the most expensive resorts anywhere in the Alps; every barn and cowshed is eagerly eyed by property developers and you need to be quick, in the know or plain lucky (as well as rich!) to secure a property. Méribel-les-Allues, the 'real' village below the ski resort, is somewhat cheaper but has poorer access to the slopes; two-bedroom apartments can be had for as 'little' as €200,000.

Occasionally, land does become available and a new development appears (e.g. Méribel Village, comprising 250 apartments, all of which were bought for between €100,000 and €750,000 in 1998). A major development is planned for Les Arcs (which is to be linked in 2003/04 with La Plagne to create one of the largest ski areas in the Alps), where an American-style resort with 800 reasonably luxurious apartments is to be built just below Arc 2000 (it's to be called Arc 1950, with reference to its altitude). Prices are expected to be start at around €200,000 for a 40m^2 apartment.

Average prices (per m^2) for new and recent properties on or near ski slopes are given below:

● **Mont Blanc area (74)**
 – Chamonix   €3,500
 – Megève   €4,000

● **La Tarentaise area (73)**
 – Les Arcs   €3,000
 – Courchevel   €6,000
 – Méribel   €4,000
 – Tignes   €3,500
 – Val d'Isère   €5,000
 – Val Thorens   €3,000

- **Le Bourg d'Oisans area (38)**
  - Alpe d'Huez   €2,500
  - Les Deux-Alpes   €2,500

If you're looking to buy a three or four-bedroom chalet to turn into accommodation for holidaymakers, you can expect to pay around €1.5 million. (In fact, such properties rarely even appear on the market!) A number of property development companies specialise in deluxe flats near ski slopes, including Monceau Gestion Privée (☎ 01.46.38.65.12, ✉ monceaugp@ aol.com) and Christophe Bauvey, 35, avenue Général de Gaulle, 69300 Caluire (☎ 04.72.27.04.92).

Land

Not surprisingly, there's very little land left to build on in the popular resorts. The table below gives average purchase prices for plots up to 600m², between 600m² and 1,000m², and between 1,000m² and 2,500m² (over half an acre) in major towns, cities and lakeside resorts. (If you plan to build a swimming pool, work out where you're going to position it: a 600m² plot may not be sufficient.)

	Up to 600m²	**600–1,000m²**	**1,000–2,500m²**
Valence/local area	€23,000	€30,000	€27,000*
Grenoble (town)	€28,000	€65,000	€60,000*
Albertville/local area	€20,000	€30,000	€38,000
Aix-les-Bains (town)	€45,000	€52,000	€58,000
Chambéry (town)	€42,000	€50,000	€13,000*
Thonon-les-Bains/ local area	€10,000*	€50,000	€60,000
Gap (town)	€30,000	€45,000	€57,000

*   Note that the average purchase prices for Thonon-les-Bains up to 600m² and Valence, Grenoble and Chambéry 1,000–2,500m² are distorted by the fact that the relevant size of plot is difficult to find in those areas.

Rental Accommodation

Unfurnished property for rent is difficult to find, although you may find something through the French property magazines such as *Le Journal des Particuliers* (🖥 www.journaldesparticuliers.com) and *Les Annonces Immobilières* (🖥 www.entreparticuliers.com); go to the section 'Locations'.

You can also try the website 🖳 www.123immo.com. The FONCIA group are the leading property rental specialists in France. They have over ten offices throughout the Alps, including Annecy, Bourg-Saint-Maurice, Grenoble, Thonon-les-Bains and Valence. Consult their website (🖳 www.foncia.fr) for full details. The National Federation of Estate Agents (FNAIM), 12, rue du Faubourg Saint Honoré, 75008 Paris (☎ 01.44.20.77.00, 🖳 www. fnaim.com) can also provide a list of its members specialising in property rentals. Check to see if '*Locations*' is displayed in the windows of these agents.

The table below is an indication of average monthly rents for four-room properties (excluding kitchen, bathroom, WC and any other utility rooms).

	Studio Apt	4-room Property
Annecy	€400	€1,000
Chambéry	€350	€700
Grenoble	€350	€750
Valence	€300	€500

Holiday apartments and flatlets are usually let on a weekly basis. The two weeks just before, during and after Christmas are the most expensive, with another peak in February. For example, a 30m^2 apartment in Chamonix (not the cheapest of ski resorts) sleeping up to four people costs between €300 and €400 per week in the summer months, between €300 and €500 per week in the period January to March, and around €700 a week over Christmas. INTERHOME, 15, avenue Jean Aicard, 75011 Paris (☎ 01.53.36.60.00, 🖳 www.interhome.fr) is one of the chalet apartment specialists. Their website has an English option and you can quickly access the resort that interests you, the type of accommodation, current availability and weekly rental price.

COMMUNICATIONS

Air

The two main airports in the area are Grenoble Saint-Geoirs (☎ 04.76. 65.48.48), served by Air France from Paris Orly and by Buzz's low-cost flights from London Stansted, and Annecy-Haute-Savoie (☎ 04.50. 27.30.06), which handles four flights a day from Paris (flying time around 75 minutes) but receives no international flights.

The nearest major airports are Geneva (☎ +41 4122-717 7111, 🖳 www. gva.ch), on the Swiss-French border, and Lyon-Saint-Exupéry (☎ 04.72. 22.72.21, 🖳 www.lyon.aeroport.fr) in Rhône, both of which handle flights from many European countries, including several airports in the UK and, of course, flights from Paris. (Lyons has a second airport, Lyon-Bron, which handles mainly business flights within France.) For example, Air France flies direct to Lyons and Geneva from Paris' Orly and Roissy-Charles de Gaulle airports, and British Airways flies to Lyons from London Heathrow, Birmingham, Edinburgh and Manchester and to Geneva from Heathrow, London Gatwick and Manchester. Geneva is also served by Maersk Airlines (a subsidiary of British Airways) from Birmingham and by flights from London City Airport, and there are low-cost flights from Gatwick and Amsterdam with EasyJet.

Other nearby airports are Chambéry/Aix-les-Bains, served by twice daily Hex Air flights from Paris (flying time around 55 minutes), and Marseilles-Marignane (see page 244) in Bouches-du-Rhône (13), which is some two hours' drive from Hautes-Alpes. The website 🖥 www.aeroport.fr gives all flight schedules to and from French airports, details of airports and their proximity to main towns, and on-going transport links. Airports in the area are shown on the map on page 254.

Public Transport

The *TGV* calls at the main towns and cities in the northern Alps and at Gap, but not Briançon, in the southern Alps. Lyons (Rhône) is just two hours from Paris, and Valence (26) can be reached in 2 hours 25 minutes. The *TGV* continues (on normal track, at present) to Chambéry (3h), Grenoble (3h 10m), and Annecy (3h 45m) and there's even a direct service to Moutiers (from London Waterloo!) near the Trois Vallées. For details of the *TGV* network, see map in **Appendix E**. There's also an excellent rail service between cities and main towns, and weekly season tickets are excellent value for commuters, although mid-evening timetables for suburban commuters tend not to exist! If you work late or irregular hours, or live outside a main town, you need to travel by car.

The major towns and cities have frequent, and usually punctual, bus services, reasonably priced, running up to around 22.00 during the week. The service from major towns to smaller nearby towns is less frequent and tends to terminate around 20.00, with perhaps a bus every hour on Sundays. If you live in a semi-rural area, a car is essential. School bus services exist in semi-rural and rural areas.

There's a number of other local public transport services that are mainly for tourists, including a cable car from the centre of Grenoble to the Fort de la Bastille, offering a superb view over the city, four-wheeled open carriages running around the Lac d'Annecy, *le petit train de Chambéry*, offering a 40-minute tour of the pedestrian streets (one of the largest pedestrian town centres in France), and the *train de Montenvers*, the highest cog railway in France at 2,400m (7,870ft), which will take you (and around 900,000 other visitors annually) from Chamonix to the largest glacier in France (40km²/16mi²). There are also pleasure boats on the four largest lakes in the Alps, Lac de Serre Ponçon (05), Lac du Bourget (73), the largest natural lake in France, Lac d'Annecy (74) and Lac Léman/Lake Geneva (74). (Some lakes have restaurant boats on which you can enjoy gastronomic dining at night with superb views of the lake and surrounding mountains.)

Roads

The Alps region has a denser motorway network than any other part of France, so communications by road are generally excellent, at least between major towns. For example, Grenoble can be reached (at the legal speed limit) in just over five hours from Paris via Lyons, only 8km (5mi) of the journey not being on motorways (the motorway toll cost is around €35 for a car). If your destination is Haute-Savoie, you can avoid Lyons by leaving the A6 at Mâcon and taking the A40.

Within the Alps, Isère, Savoie and Haute-Savoie are well linked by motorways (*autoroutes*) and major dual-carriageways. For example, Grenoble is linked to Chambéry (55km/34mi) by motorway, Chambéry to Annecy (45km/28mi) is mostly motorway, and Annecy to Chamonix is also mostly motorway, with dual-carriageway terminating just before the Mont Blanc tunnel. Chambéry to Albertville (around 45km/28mi) is mostly motorway, but there are only main roads (*routes nationales*) between Albertville and Annecy, (around 50km/31mi). To reach Briançon in the southern Alps from Grenoble can take over two hours, with just 25km (15mi) of motorway out of a total distance of 160km (100mi).

Local mountain roads vary in condition. If they're access roads to ski resorts, they will be well maintained and kept open throughout the winter. Other mountain passes may be closed during periods of heavy snow. If you drive in winter, make sure you have snow tyres (*pneus-neige*).

PLANNED DEVELOPMENTS

The major long-term project, confirmed in January 2001, is the Lyons to Turin *TGV* link (to be completed by 2015), involving the construction of a 52km (33mi) tunnel through the Alps from Saint-Jean-de-Maurienne(73) to the Suse valley in Italy. Turin will then be under three hours from Lyons and just over four from Paris. The plan also is to develop a roll-on, roll-off heavy goods vehicle train service taking up to 7,000 lorries a day into Italy, reversing the present concentration of 80 per cent of goods transported by road. Hundreds of thousands of lorries will be taken off the Alpine roads, considerably reducing air pollution as well waiting times at the Mont Blanc and Fréjus road tunnels. (Switzerland has been doing this for the last 25 years).

Another major project is a six-year plan (2000 to 2006) to improve the road system around the Lac du Bourget in Savoie, to further improve the quality of the lake's water and to develop the local economy while preserving the historical heritage and natural landscape. Around 200,000 people, half the population of Savoie, live on or near the lake. The plan involves Brussels (i.e. the European Community), the French state, regional and local governments, and local conservation and cultural associations.

At more local levels, Albertville continues to enjoy prestige following the 1992 Winter Olympic Games and is restoring its Conflans medieval area, while Briançon, influenced by its huge Italian neighbour, Turin (venue for the 2006 Winter Olympic Games), is bringing its ice-rink up to international standards, with a further plan to make it part of a new multi-sports complex housing an athletics and football stadium.

EMPLOYMENT PROSPECTS

Job prospects are considerably better in the northern Alps, where the rate of unemployment is around 10 per cent, than in the southern Alps, where the rate is around 14 per cent. Additionally, Valence and Grenoble are, with the *TGV* and motorway links, within commuting distance of Lyons. Grenoble is an important industrial town and is classed among the top five towns in France for scientific research. The Isère department is the seventh-biggest exporting department in France. Geneva, which is the headquarters of several international companies and institutions, has dormitory areas spilling over into Haute-Savoie. Some of the major industries and companies in the principal towns in the Alps are:

Gap (05): craftwork, printing and textiles;

Valence (26): electronics, mechanical engineering and textiles;

Grenoble (38): computers, electrical engineering, electronics and mechanical goods; chemical and metallurgical works; also a nuclear research centre;

La Tour-du-Pin (38): shoe manufacturing and textiles;

Chambéry (73): dressmaking, chemicals, glass and metallurgical works;

Annecy (74): Alcatel (telephone equipment), Salomon (golf and ski equipment) and Sopra (computers).

There's a market for bilingual (French and English) and trilingual (with German, Italian or Spanish) management secretaries with international companies such as Galderma at Annecy, part of the Nestlé-Oréal Group, as well as with smaller companies concentrating on export. Engineering positions with large companies in electronics and computing often specify proficiency in English, although you must of course have excellent verbal and written skills in French and preferably an engineering degree or *diplôme* recognised in France. There may also be management opportunities which require English for transport, order management and despatch specialists with international companies. Salaries for engineering and management positions range between €25,000 and €40,000 per year, according to experience. APEC, the executive appointments division of the national employment organisation (Agence nationale pour l'Emploi/ANPE) publishes a weekly review, *Courrier Cadres*, with a nationwide job advertisements section and articles about the employment market (🖳 www.apec.fr). See **Further Information** on page 250 for APEC offices in Rhône-Alpes and useful websites. A list of companies in each department can be obtained from the French Chamber of Commerce in London (see **Appendix A**).

There are always jobs available for unskilled, semi-skilled and skilled blue collar workers in industrial production (see 🖳 www.anpe.fr), provided you have basic French. There are slightly fewer jobs available in this category in the two Savoy departments, taken together, than in Isère, although the Isère department and Savoy departments' populations are approximately the same. Although its population is larger than that of Savoy, Drôme has even fewer production jobs available.

There are also summer and winter seasonal jobs in the hotel and restaurant trades. If you're seeking employment as a ski instructor you must, of course, demonstrate your proficiency in speaking French (and English), and you normally require a French certificate of skiing competence (*brevet* or *diplôme d'état*). Local knowledge of the various slopes and their intricacies is also required. Remember also that, even with the latest snow-producing equipment, the length of the season cannot be guaranteed.

Self-employment: If you're prepared for the cumbersome regulations, heavy paperwork and high social security contributions (the French government, including the right wing one elected in June, 2002, always promises to make things easier, self-employment is an option, although setting up in business is no easier in the Alps than anywhere else in France (or the world). The tourist trade, estate agency and building renovation work (if you're sufficiently experienced) are possibilities. It's easier and less risky to buy a going concern.

FURTHER INFORMATION

Useful Addresses

- APEC, the executive appointments division of the national Job Centre organisation (Agence nationale pour l'Emploi/ANPE) has offices in several towns in the region:

- APEC, Gare des Brotteaux, 14, place Jules Ferry, 69458 Lyon Cedex 06 (☎ 04.72.83.88.88)
- APEC, Europole, Immeuble WTC, 5, place Robert Schuman, BP 1529, 38025 Grenoble (☎ 04.76.84.47.77)
- APEC, 57, avenue de Lautagne, BP 117, 26904 Valence cedex 9 (☎ 04.75.75.91.96)
- APEC, 57, avenue Bertholet, 74000 Annecy (☎ 04.50.10.10.30)

● Comité régional du Tourisme **Rhône-Alpes**, 104, route de Paris, 69260 Charbonniéres les Bains (☎ 04.72.59.21.59)

● Comité départemental du Tourisme des **Hautes-Alpes**, 8 bis, rue Capitaine de Bresson, 05000 Gap (☎ 04.92.53.62.00)

● Comité départemental du Tourisme de la **Drôme**, 26140 Saint-Rambert d'Albon (☎ 04.75.31.01.00)

● Comité départemental du Tourisme d'**Isèr**e, 14, rue de la République, 38000 Grenoble (☎ 04.76.54.34.36)

● Agence touristique départementale de **Savoie**, 24, boulevard Colonne, 73000 Chambéry (☎ 04.79.85.12.45)

● Comité départemental du Tourisme de **Haute-Savoie**, 56, rue Sommeiller, 74000 Annecy (☎ 04.50.51.32.31)

Graham Platt

Specialist English Solicitor – French Avocat

Residential & Commercial Property
Probate

*For a unique service by a senior Solicitor admitted to
practice in both France and England with
satisfied clients in both jurisdictions*

Bank House
150 Roundhay Road
Leeds LS8 5LD

Tel: 0113 249 6496
Fax: 0113 248 0466
E-mail: grahamplatt@foxhayes.co.uk

The Sacré-Coeur ~ Paris

The region of Ile-de-France, in northern central France, comprises eight departments. The city of Paris, a department unto itself (75), is the heart and soul of the Ile-de-France, which is sometimes referred to as the *région Parisienne*. The three departments immediately adjacent to Paris, which make up the so-called *petit couronne* ('small crown' or 'small wreath') are Hauts-de-Seine (92), Seine-Saint-Denis (93) and Val-de-Marne (94). The outer circle of departments is called the *grand couronne* ('large crown' or 'large wreath') and consists of Seine-et-Marne (77), Yvelines (78), Essonne (91) and Val-d'Oise (95). Ile-de France means 'island of France' and, although the region isn't literally an island, it's more or less surrounded by rivers and was therefore considered an island through much of French history.

The Ile-de-France covers 12,070km^2 (around 4,700mi^2), a little over 2 per cent of France's land mass, but houses over 15 per cent of France's population. (Those who live in the Ile-de-France are called *Franciliens* or *Franciliennes*.) As these figures indicate, the Ile-de-France is the most densely populated region in France, with an average of around 900 inhabitants per km^2 overall. Paris is Europe's most crowded capital, with over 20,000 people per km^2 (over 50,000 per mi^2), almost five times the population density of London, compared with a mere 200 inhabitants per km^2 (around 500 per mi^2) in relatively rural Seine-et-Marne. Overall (and obviously there are wide variations), the region is 20 per cent woodland, 20 per cent grassland, 50 per cent arable land and 30 per cent other uses (including urban areas).

The Ile-de-France is also, not surprisingly, the wealthiest region in the country in terms of the number of people with high incomes. Of the 100 main cities and towns in France, the Ile-de-France contains six of the seven wealthiest – Saint-Germain-en-Laye and Versailles (78), Boulogne-Billancourt, Neuilly-sur-Seine and Rueil-Malamison (92) and Paris itself (the other is Cannes in Alpes-Maritimes). Together, these are home to almost 37 per cent of the country's richest people (almost 17 per cent of French people liable to wealth tax live in Neuilly!).

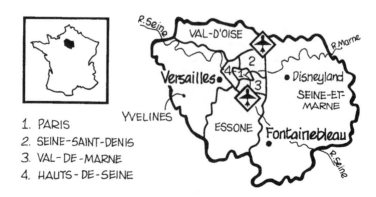

1. PARIS
2. SEINE-SAINT-DENIS
3. VAL-DE-MARNE
4. HAUTS-DE-SEINE

◀ *Ailefroi, Rhône-Alpes* © *Dennis Kelsall*

▲ *St-Chély, Gorges de Tarn*
© *Dennis Kelsall*

▲ *Gimel-les-Cascades, Massif Central*
© *Trevor Yorke (Living France)*

▲ *Nice, Côte d'Azur*
© *Trevor Yorke (Living France)*

◀ *Eyrignac, Dordogne* © *Dennis Kelsall*

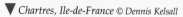
Chartres, Ile-de-France © Dennis Kelsall

▲ *St-Nazaire-en-Royans, Le Vercors © Dennis Kelsall*

◄ *Mont-St-Michel, Normandy © Trevor Yorke (Living France)*

▼ *Near St-Ome Nord © Trevor Yorke (Living France*

▲ *Kayserberg, Alsace © Dennis Kelsall*

▲ Maroilles,
Nord-Pas-de-Calais
© Trevor Yorke
(Living France)

▲ Pont-en-Royans, Le Vercors
© Dennis Kelsall

◀

Gargilesse-Dampier, Dordogne
© Dennis Kelsall

▼ La Suisse normande,
Normandy
© Dennis Kelsall

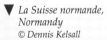

▲ Vannes, Brittany © Trevor Yorke (Living France)

▲ Gordes, Provence © Dennis Kelsall

▲ Le Barroux,
Provence
© Dennis Kelsall

◄
Baie des Anges,
Nice, Provence
© Trevor Yorke (Living France)

▼ Rennes, Brittany
© Trevor Yorke
(Living France)

▲ Near Sergeac, Dordogne
© Dennis Kelsall

The Ile-de-France region offers a wide range of living environments and types of accommodation, as do the various districts (*arrondissements*) and neighbourhoods of the city of Paris. Each department and each district has a general character and reputation, although there are exceptions and 'atypical' towns and districts in each area.

Paris

The 'City of Light' is the most popular tourist destination in the world. Named after the Parisii tribe, which settled on the Ile de la Cité in the third century BC, it's also the capital of France and the political centre of a highly centralised (most would add highly bureaucratic) system of government. One in three French companies with 100 or more employees make Paris their headquarters, as do two-thirds of all companies in France with over 500 employees, and Paris is Europe's third-largest financial market (after London and Frankfurt). Paris is also well known as a cultural capital, with many of the world's great museums and galleries, as well as world renowned restaurants, cafés and *bistrots*, and enjoys a deserved reputation for fashion, romance and passion. The city is divided into 20 *arrondissements*, each of which is a distinct political unit with its own town hall (*mairie*), mayor (*maire*) and police headquarters (*préfecture*) handling day-to-day administrative matters for local residents, including marriages, birth records, death certificates and voting. (The Mairie de Paris is an administrative centre for the 20 district governments and not normally open to the public.)

The numbering system for the *arrondissements* starts at the Palais du Louvre, formerly the French king's primary residence located roughly at the centre of the city, and proceeds in a clockwise spiral out to the city limits (see map below). Almost all addresses and directions in Paris include the relevant *arrondissement* number (as well as the nearest underground station). For example, the post code 75016 indicates the 16th *arrondissement*.

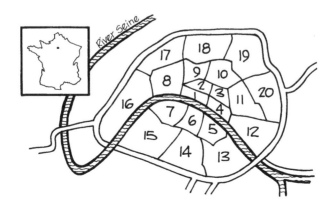

In an effort to lessen dependence on Paris, the government established five of satellite towns in the mid-1960s, with the intention of making these 'new towns' (*villes nouvelles*) self-sufficient in terms of employment, local commerce and public services. The *villes nouvelles* are Cergy-Pontoise in Val-d'Oise to the north, Saint-Quentin-en-Yvelines to the west, Evry in Essonne to the south, and Marne-la-Vallée and Sénart in Seine-et-Marne to the east. Although the experiment wasn't entirely successful, the *villes nouvelles* have managed to dilute the concentration of jobs, people and services in the capital to a certain extent and offer a less frenetic alternative to the urban intensity of Paris itself (see page 291).

West

To the west of Paris lie the departments of Hauts-de-Seine and Yvelines, a favourite residential area for corporate executives, including a large number of expatriates. Their popularity is due mainly to the easy access to the cluster of corporate offices at La Défense, a modern, high-rise development on the western edge of Paris. Hauts-de-Seine is home to 1.4 million residents, while the much larger Yvelines has 1.35 million inhabitants. The western suburbs have the reputation of being rather well-to-do, expensive and *chic*, although there are also pockets of council housing. The *ville nouvelle* of Saint-Quentin-en-Yvelines, just to the south of Versailles, houses the *préfecture* for the department.

North

The departments to the north of Paris are Seine-Saint-Denis and Val-d'Oise, home to 1.4 and 1.1 million residents respectively. Both departments are highly industrialised, many commercial enterprises taking advantage of their proximity to Paris' major airport, Roissy-Charles de Gaulle, which straddles the border between Val-d'Oise and Seine-et-Marne. They're also the location of the largest and most troubled of the *banlieues* (the French for 'suburb', which has in recent years acquired a connotation of 'socially undesirable'), with a concentration of immigrants (particularly from North Africa) and high unemployment. However, there are also many charming areas and small towns with excellent public services and direct access into Paris. Val-d'Oise is home to the *ville nouvelle* of Cergy-Pontoise, situated along a northward bend in the river Seine. Some people (mainly estate agents) include the neighbouring department of Oise (60), or at least its southern sector, in the Ile-de-France, as more and more people now choose to live there (in a rural setting) and commute into Paris.

East

To the east of Paris are the departments of Val-de-Marne and Seine-et-Marne. This area has long been rather ignored by trendy (some might say 'snooty') Parisians, in much the same way as the east end of Paris itself (like that of London) is considered '*déclassé*', but this is starting to change. Thanks to the location of the new Bibliothèque de France (the so-called 'Mitterand Library') on the east side of the city and a general push towards redevelopment around the Gare de l'Est, Gare de Lyon and Bastille, there has been a resurgence of interest in the eastern suburbs. As in many other urban areas of the world, young professionals are starting to take advantage of lower property prices and contributing to an overall 'gentrification' of formerly run-down neighbourhoods. Seine-et-Marne is a largely rural department that curls around to the south of Paris as far as Fontainebleau and Nemours. It's home to two of the *villes nouvelles*, Marne-la-Vallée (best known as the site of Disneyland Paris – see page 300) and Sénart to the south near Melun. The eastern and southern edges of Seine-et-Marne have a distinctly rural character, which is no surprise given the fact that the neighbouring regions are Champagne and Burgundy, with their vineyards and villages.

South

Between Seine-et-Marne and Yvelines, the department of Essonne stretches from the southern edge of Orly airport (part of which is in Val-de-Marne) past Etampes. The northern part of Essonne is heavily built-up, the *ville nouvelle* of Evry housing its *préfecture*. Evry is the site of the newest cathedral in France, completed in 1995 (in fact France's only 20th century cathedral) – a stark modern building with large stained glass panels and a rooftop garden, complete with trees. Further south, the department rapidly becomes more rural as it approaches the large agricultural region of Centre-Val-de-Loire (see page 340). Essonne is also home to the scientific research centre at Saclay, which attracts students and research personnel from around the world (see page 292).

ADVANTAGES & DISADVANTAGES

Most of the advantages of living in the Ile-de-France come from being near Paris, which is the focus for all aspects of French life, including government, education, culture, entertainment and transport, and it isn't far from the country's geographical centre. You're most likely to be able to find a job in the Paris region, irrespective of your profession, particularly if you're interested in working for a large international company. Wages are the highest in France (although so are taxes, property prices and the cost of living).

Paris and its environs are home to the largest number of English-speaking foreigners in France, and there are many expatriate resources available, from clubs and associations to schools, language classes, English-speaking professionals and services and Anglophone publications and publishers. There are well established British and American communities, which enjoy a rapport with their embassy and consular officials. Officials often work with expatriate groups to plan and host receptions, meetings and events for the respective community members. While the embassies concentrate on serving the business and diplomatic communities, the consulates make services available to individuals, such as renewing passports and other documents and providing lists of local clubs, events and English-speaking professionals in the Paris area.

The large foreign population means that there's the widest selection of 'exotic' (i.e. imported) products in France. It isn't usually difficult to find a source of food and goods you miss from 'back home', whether you're from the UK, the USA, Australia or any other part of the world. There are shops and restaurants offering food and other products from China, Thailand, Africa, the Caribbean, Mexico, Algeria, Morocco and a host of other foreign goods that can be difficult or impossible to find in other regions of France. The specialities and delicacies of almost all the French regions are also on offer at restaurants and shops throughout the Ile-de-France.

Even if you aren't a 'city person', the Ile-de-France offers a variety of non-urban living environments, including the wide open spaces of southern Essonne and the lush forests surrounding Fontainebleau and Rambouillet. There are many small towns in the region, and even the larger towns tend to be divided into communes and neighbourhoods with distinctive characteristics and a sense of community. Not surprisingly, Paris and the surrounding towns are largely built-up and have relatively little green space. Most spacious is Sarcelles (95) with over 35m^2 of green space per inhabitant, followed closely by Rueil-Malmaison (92); at the other end of the scale are Neuilly-sur-Seine (92) and Corbeil-Essonnes (91), the latter with a mere 0.2m^2 of green space per inhabitant. (Even Paris itself has 14m^2 per inhabitant.) Nevertheless, the Ile-de-France is a relatively healthy place to live, the mortality rate (from all causes) being lower than the national average (Neuilly-sur-Seine is apparently the healthiest place in all of France, with a mortality rate less than half that of Valenciennes in Nord, although it may have something to do with the average wealth of the inhabitants!).

Of course, life in the Ile-de-France also has its disadvantages. Paris, and much of the urbanised area immediately surrounding the city, can be crowded, noisy, dirty, and maddeningly bureaucratic. Everyone who has visited Paris seems to want to live there, and many are sorely disappointed to discover that taking up residence can be very different from living as a tourist. Like many city dwellers, Parisians tend to be busy people in a hurry, and it can be difficult to develop friendships in the local community, particularly if your French isn't fluent.

If you're planning to live in the suburbs, you should check the air corridors for Paris' two airports. Recent changes to the air traffic control corridors approaching both airports have angered local residents, who claim that the new *couloirs aériens* create far more noise over residential areas than the old routing system. Although local protest groups contend that 2,300 communes in the Paris area are being adversely affected by the changes (landing and take-off patterns change from day to day, according to weather conditions and the runways being used), most of the dissent comes from the department of Essonne (91), particularly the towns and communes in the densely populated area around Orly. Protest groups have also sprung up around the airport at Roissy, mostly in opposition to the construction of a new runway, which they expect will add further noise and pollution, although it's highly unlikely the airport authority (Aéroports de Paris/ADP) will back down on any of its plans.

The region as a whole is the most expensive in France, although costs are lower the further you are from the centre of Paris. Competition for well paid, desirable jobs is intense, thanks to the perceived 'glamour' of working in or near Paris. For those without job qualifications, particularly those who don't speak fluent French, there simply are no jobs, unless you're willing to work illegally, which is risky. Bosses in Paris (as in much of France) are expected to be authoritarian taskmasters whose prime directive is to get the most work possible out of employees during their 35-hour working week. That is starting to change, particularly in international companies headquartered in Paris, but employees still tend to be suspicious of bosses who show more than a modicum of interest in members of staff and may be quick to complain of any violation of the numerous and sometimes petty labour laws.

Outside the city, access to jobs, transport and resources may be limited. Not all parts of the Ile-de-France are equally well served by the regional transport network. In some areas, owning a car (or two, in the case of a family) is a necessity when shops, schools and public transport aren't within walking distance or where rural roads have turned pedestrians into an endangered species. Rush hour traffic can be a nightmare when entering and leaving Paris. The same is true at the start and end of school holiday periods, when everyone in Paris seems determined to leave or return on the same day. Strikes, demonstrations and other 'man made' disturbances often wreak further havoc on traffic and public transport, although most locals have managed to develop a philosophical attitude towards the situation.

In the large, semi-rural areas of Essonne and Seine-et-Marne, it can be impossible to find local doctors, dentists or any professional person willing to admit to speaking or understanding English or even to explain procedures clearly in French, which can be frightening in an emergency situation. Another (unexpected) drawback to living in or near Paris is that long-lost friends and family members have a tendency to 'drop by' and will of course gratefully accept your offer to show them around the city. Although this can be fun for a while, some expatriates quickly tire of acting as tour guides and having their spare bedrooms constantly occupied by visitors.

Nevertheless, Paris is a city like no other in the world, and the vast majority of its inhabitants and those of the surrounding region feel that the advantages of living there greatly outweigh the disadvantages.

MAJOR TOWNS & PLACES OF INTEREST

Paris

Paris is of course the Ile-de-France's major place of interest and it's possible to set yourself up in Paris and never need or want to leave the city limits. Paris is a big city, however, and some districts (*arrondissements*) are of greater interest to foreign buyers than others. Like London, it's divided by the river, and there's much debate as to whether it's preferable to live to the north (known as the *rive droite* or 'right bank') or to the south (*rive gauche*) of the Seine. Generally, the lower numbered *arrondissements* are considered the most desirable by Parisians, although in typical French fashion there are exceptions and you may well find that your criteria for evaluation are rather different from those of the natives.

North of the river, the 1st to 4th *arrondissements* (usually referred to simply as 'the first' 'the second' etc.) make up what many regard as the heart of the city, not to mention its historic centre. The 1st contains the royal residences of the Palais du Louvre and the Palais Royal, as well as the former marketplace of Les Halles, now converted into an enormous underground shopping centre. The 2nd *arrondissement* includes the historic Bourse (stock market), the garment district and many banks and insurance offices, while the 3rd and 4th include the Marais ('marsh') district, the centre of Paris' Jewish community and a trendy residential area complete with alternative lifestyle bars, discos and late night hang-outs.

Across the Seine is the 5th *arrondissement*, the Latin Quarter (so called because its student population once conversed in Latin), which is home to the Sorbonne and a plethora of student (as well as tourist) shops and restaurants. The 6th is something of a transition zone between the Latin Quarter and the considerably more upmarket 7th and includes the Luxembourg Garden and Palace, now home to the French National Senate. The 7th, referred to as the Saint-Germain-des-Prés district, is dominated by the Eiffel Tower and the Champs de Mars, the Ecole militaire, the Hôtel des Invalides (not a hotel but a former hospital and now a military museum) and numerous government buildings (including the Assemblée nationale in the Palais Bourbon) and embassies. It's a highly sought-after (and therefore expensive) *arrondissement*, although some Parisians find it too austere and cold for their liking (a case of sour grapes perhaps?).

Back on the north side (*rive droite*) of the Seine is the 8th *arrondissement*, Paris' most expensive, which includes the Champs-Elysées, some of Paris' top hotels (including the Georges V), the Elysée Palace (the President's home), and the designer shops on and near the Avenue Montaigne. The 9th is known as a 'lively' *arrondissement*, in both the positive and the negative senses. Many of the large Paris department stores are here, as well as the Opéra Garnier and a host of theatres, cinemas and restaurants, which means that it tends to be crowded and noisy until late into the evening.

The 10th is best known for its railway stations (the Gare de l'Est and the Gare du Nord) and hospitals, while the 11th and 12th are part of the long-neglected eastern side of Paris that's starting to come into its own, thanks to a number of urban renewal projects. The old Bastille district, which spans the two *arrondissements*, is beginning to attract artists, musicians and other creative people.

Back on the left bank, the 13th, 14th and 15th are largely residential areas, with many small neighbourhoods and shops and a proliferation of parks, as well as the Tour Montparnasse, Paris' second-highest building. The 16th, on the right bank and with the Bois de Boulogne as its western border, is alleged to be the preferred *arrondissement* for Paris' 'new money' crowd (as opposed to the 'old money' residing in the 7th). It's a popular area for diplomats and their families, as a number of embassies are located there, as well as the multinational Organisation for Economic Cooperation and Development (OECD).

The 17th is largely residential, although not as fashionable (or expensive) as the 16th. The 18th is Paris' 'hilly' district, and includes the Sacré Coeur church perched on Montmartre and overlooking the rest of Paris – a beautiful spot but hopelessly crowded with tourists almost year round. The 18th generally has the reputation of being rather run-down, and the Montmartre, Barbès and Pigalle areas, which comprise Paris' red-light district, are considered seedy, if not dangerous, by most Parisians (see **Crime Rate & Security** on page 295).

The 19th and 20th are working-class districts, traditionally looked down upon by most Parisians, but there has been considerable renovation and redevelopment in recent years. The Parc de la Villette, with its museums and exhibition and concert halls is located in the 19th, while the famous Père Lachaise cemetery (see **Leisure** on page 299) is in the 20th.

Villes Nouvelles

The so-called *villes nouvelles* (see page 286) were established in the mid-1960s in an attempt to draw some of the congestion away from Paris and into the relatively sparsely populated countryside (and unofficially to move a large amount of council housing out of central Paris). Since then, local government officials have generally made great strides in developing local industry, shopping and other resources. Although the term *ville nouvelle* is often used by the French as a pejorative to indicate the proliferation of ugly high-rise buildings and the artificiality of government attempts to create new communities, each of these 'agglomerations' of towns and communes has developed its own character, aided by public investment in local schools, attractions, activities and events. For those who prefer modern living (e.g. lifts that can take more than two people at a time) and clean, simple lines to the ornate style of Parisian apartments, the *villes nouvelles* offer new construction and many of the advantages of planned urban development.

Saclay & Fontainebleau

More recently, the French government has devoted much time and money to the development of a scientific research centre at Saclay, a town in Yvelines just off the N118 trunk road (*route nationale*) south-west of Paris. The research centre and nearby university department attract large numbers of visiting scientists from around the world, and the area around Saclay has developed clusters of both employment and residential areas, including Massy, Palaiseau, Orsay, Les Ulis and Gif-sur-Yvette. The area is well served by public transport into Paris and offers a range of housing and shopping comfortably outside the city limits.

Another major centre of learning is at Fontainebleau, to the south of the city in Seine-et-Marne. Fontainebleau is the site of INSEAD, Europe's most prestigious graduate business school. Like Versailles, Fontainebleau was once a royal holiday retreat and the surrounding area is lush and dense with trees, thanks to the national forest that used to form part of the royal hunting grounds. INSEAD lends the town a distinctly international flavour, attracting a constant flow of teachers and students from around the world. Most residents find Paris a bit too far to commute daily, although there are frequent trains and direct access via the A6 motorway for those who want the best of both worlds.

Western Suburbs

The area stretching from the city limits to the town of Versailles has long been regarded as Paris' most desirable suburban area (the prevailing westerly winds blew the smoke and other pollution from the city centre towards the east, where the poorer folk lived!) and is extremely popular with English-speaking expatriates and corporate executives on secondment. For English-speakers there are obvious advantages to the west side, from the availability of resources (international and private schools, English-speaking doctors, dentists and hospitals, etc.) to the proximity of other Anglophones. Particularly popular, on account of their proximity to Paris and pleasant ambiance, are the towns of Neuilly, Boulogne-Billancourt, Saint-Cloud and Saint-Germain-en-Laye, but there are numerous smaller towns throughout the area with large concentrations of English-speaking expatriates.

POPULATION

According to the latest census (taken in 1999), the population of the Ile-de-France is almost exactly 11 million, over a sixth of the population of France, including almost 40 per cent of all foreigners living in France. In all, there are around 1.3 million foreigners, accounting for almost 12 per cent of the region's population, more than double the overall average for France (5.6 per cent), although there has been a gradual decline in the number of foreigners over the last decade, due both to the naturalisation of older immigrants and to migration away from the Paris area into other regions of France.

Traditionally, Paris and the Ile-de-France region have been a magnet for young French people, drawing population from the countryside. This is still true in some towns surrounding Paris, particularly Rueil-Malmaison (92) and Evry (91), the latter also boasting the lowest population ageing rate of any major town in France. In recent years, however, this trend seems to have reversed, thanks largely to government-sponsored development of industry and employment in the regions. More and more *Franciliens* are moving elsewhere to escape crowded living conditions, traffic congestion, pollution and the high cost of living in and around Paris. Saint-Germain-en-Laye and Versailles (78), Corbeil-Essonnes (91), Saint-Denis (93) and Paris itself are all decreasing in population. Although the latest census figures showed a slight increase in overall population since the previous count (in 1990), the Ile-de-France is growing much more slowly than most other parts of France. Even foreigners coming to France to join family members now have a greater tendency to settle in other regions. The populations of Créteil (94) and Evry (91) comprise a high proportion of studens (around 20 per cent), compared with 3 per cent in Neuilly-sur-Seine (92) and a mere 1 per cent in Corbeil-Essonnes (91), Rueil-Malmaison (92) and Sarcelles (95).

By far the most numerous foreign nationals in the Ile-de-France are the Portuguese, with over 270,000 official residents. Algerians and Moroccans number 190,000 and 145,000 respectively. Completing the top ten foreign nationalities are (in order): Tunisians, Turks, Spanish, Italians, Malians, Yugoslavians and Congolese, accounting in total for a further 285,000 people. Contrary to the fears of those on the political far right, the 1999 census showed that percentage increases in the foreign population were virtually identical to those in the native population, although there have been some shifts in the immigrants' countries of origin over the past decade (notably increases in immigrants from the former Yugoslavia and other conflict-torn regions of the world).

The greatest concentration of foreigners is in Seine-Saint-Denis, where there are many immigrants of Algerian, North African and sub-Saharan African origin. *Immigrés* make up almost 20 per cent of the population in this department, often living in high-rise *HLM* (council flats or subsidised housing blocks). Yvelines and Hauts-de-Seine to the west contain concentrations of Moroccans, particularly in the towns of Mantes-la-Jolie, Canteloup-les-Vignes and Les Mureaux (in Yvelines) and Gennevilliers, Clichy and Villeneuve-la-Garenne in Hauts-de-Seine. Val-de-Marne is home to many Portuguese immigrants and is increasingly popular with Asians seeking to move out of Paris. The departments of the *grand couronne* generally have much lower proportions of foreigners, except for Val-d'Oise, whose foreign population of around 11 per cent includes many Turkish immigrants. Within Paris, the proportion of foreigners is around 15 per cent, with distinct communities of Asians in the 1st, 2nd and 10th *arrondissements* and a concentration of African immigrants in the 18th and 19th.

There are relatively few Britons and Americans living in the Ile-de-France, and their numbers tend to rise and fall according to the needs of the multinational corporations headquartered in the Paris area. It's estimated that there are between 5,000 and 10,000 Britons and 5,000 to 8,000 Americans living in and around Paris (the French statistical institute, INSEE, doesn't publish these figures). Paris is hardly a popular retirement destination, and many English-speaking expatriates in the area are 'transient' executive families making a two to five-year tour of duty with an international company or students enjoying a 'Paris experience' as part of their studies. The few permanent residents of British or American background include those married to French nationals.

CLIMATE

The climate in Paris, as in much of the north of France, is temperate, with cool winters and warm summers. Average temperatures in January range from just above freezing to 5 or 6°C. Winters tend to be damp and gloomy, as in much of northern Europe, although the temperature only rarely dips below freezing and heavy snow and severe frosts are extremely rare. In July, average temperatures range from night time lows of 15°C (62°F) to daytime highs of around 25°C (77°F). Summer temperatures over 30°C (85°F) are rare events and normally last only for a few days. The region enjoys an average of around 1,800 hours' sunshine per year and average rainfall is between 600 and 700mm per year (similar to that of London) on around 112 days per year. Winter is slightly wetter than summer (although there are occasionally impressive thunderstorms during July and August), but otherwise rainfall varies little across the seasons. Thick fog is a common phenomenon in spring and autumn in the open fields and woodlands of the *grand couronne*.

The greater Paris area tends to create its own micro-climate, due to the concentration of industry, vehicles and people (the French government in particular generates a lot of hot air, or so some residents contend). This means that temperatures in Paris are generally a degree or two warmer at all times of the year than in the region overall. In summer, a layer of cool air and cloud sometimes traps the warmer air in the river basin (a phenomenon known as temperature inversion), and the whole city becomes smoggy, hot and unpleasant until a thunderstorm breaks or the high cloud layer dissipates or is blown away to the east. (This is one reason Parisians are more than happy to leave the city to the tourists in July and August, when temperature inversions are most likely to occur.) Various anti-smog procedures are then put into effect, including the reduction of speed limits and the banning of certain vehicles from the *boulevard périphérique*, the city's ring road.

COST OF LIVING

Not surprisingly, the cost of living in the Ile-de-France, and in Paris in particular, is the highest in France. Average supermarket prices, for example, are 5 to 10 per cent higher in Paris than the national average, although in the outer departments of the Ile-de-France the difference is no more than 3 or 4 per cent and supermarkets can be found selling goods at below average prices.

CRIME RATE & SECURITY

Like any big city, Paris has a higher level of crime than the country as a whole, including pick pocketing and bag snatching (particularly on the underground), burglary (especially when flats and houses are obviously vacant for weeks at a time during the summer holidays), and more serious forms of urban crime (not to mention allegations of corruption and misuse of public funds by local politicians!).

There has been a steady increase in the number of violent crimes recorded in the last few years, although this may be partly due to a change in reporting style among the French media, which used to more or less ignore local crime stories. Violent crime occurs mainly in the 18th, 19th and 20th *arrondissements* and in the suburban areas of Essonne and Seine-Saint-Denis. Most gang activity takes place in the latter region, and the town of Saint-Denis, where the number of reported crimes increased by almost 45 per cent (the highest rate in France) between 1998 and 2000, has the second-highest crime rate in France. Paris itself has the fifth-highest crime rate among France's major towns, but the only other town in the Il-de-France with a particularly high crime rate is Créteil (94), where the number of reported crimes increased by over 20 per cent between 1998 and 2000. For details of crime rates and safety in major towns in France, see **Appendix F**.

On the other hand, Saint-Germain-en-Laye and Versailles (78), and Neuilly-sur-Seine and Rueil-Malmaison (92) enjoy some of the country's lowest crime rates. Note also that most violent crimes (e.g. armed robbery) are directed at 'anonymous' targets – banks, jewellers' and armoured cars – rather than against individuals and you're far less likely to be a victim of violent crime than to be injured crossing the street.

There are a few areas of Paris that most people advise avoiding, at least late at night – primarily the Pigalle 'red light' district and Barbès in the Montmartre district, which has a reputation for more serious crimes against unwitting tourists. The Bois de Boulogne and, to a lesser extent, the Bois de Vincennes also have a reputation for late night crimes involving drug dealers and prostitutes, although during the day these are popular public parks, considered safe for all. Commercial Area 13 of the Défense business district is also a favourite haunt of thieves.

Terrorism has been a threat in Paris in the past, mostly in the form of bombings of public areas, including the underground. However, the government's programme of raising public awareness and encouraging people to report suspicious packages left unattended seems to have been successful. Large department stores may hire security guards to check bags and packages when you enter, which can be annoying, although most residents find it reassuring and it seems to be effective. At times of 'high alert', it isn't unusual to see heavily armed police, *gendarmes* and even the *CNS* (national security service) on the streets of Paris, particularly in the underground and around national monuments, embassies and consulates. For general information on crime in France, see page 52.

AMENITIES

Sports

Thanks to the 1998 football World Cup, Paris now has an 80,000-seat sports stadium, the Stade de France, located in La-Plaine-Saint-Denis, just north of the city. The stadium was built with public funds in order for France to have an appropriate venue for international sporting events, such as the World Cup, the Olympic Games (Paris lost its bid for 2008 to Beijing, but is expected to try again), and various European and world athletic championships. After the 1998 World Cup, management of the Stade de France was turned over to a concession of private companies, although the facility is still under the direction of the Ministry for Sports and Youth, which has promised to find a resident first division football team for the stadium in order to assure a minimum of 20 games per year. Currently the Stade de France is used for a variety of sporting events, concerts, performances and trade shows, although these take up only a handful of dates each year. Information about the stadium and scheduled events there can be found on the Stade de France website (🖳 www.stadefrance.fr).

Outside Paris, most communes have a variety of sporting facilities and sports clubs, which often hold exercise and fitness classes open to local residents and their families. Many towns have a small stadium for matches and events and some towns offer tennis clubs, swimming pools and other sports facilities at nominal prices to local residents. Non-residents may be able to use the facilities by paying a higher fee.

Football: For football fans, the 'home team' for all of the Ile-de-France is Paris Saint-Germain. PSG, as it's known, plays its home matches at the Stade Parc des Princes, which is part of the sports complex at the southern end of the Bois de Boulogne. The stadium holds around 48,000 spectators and houses the administrative offices of the team, as well as a shop selling team regalia. Tickets for matches can be purchased online at the PSG website (🖳 www.psg.fr) or at various ticket outlets throughout the Ile-de-France. PSG is a first division team, normally ranked in the top 20 to 25 in Europe.

Tennis: Tennis is the other major sporting passion in the Paris region, with considerable attention devoted each June to the international tournament held at Roland Garros. (You may have heard this referred to as the 'French Open', but the locals speak only of 'Roland Garros,' the French tennis champion after whom the tennis facility in the Bois de Boulogne sports complex is named.) Tickets to any of the matches are highly prized and obtainable only from the Fédération française de Tennis (FFT), which gives priority to its own members.

For those who want to play rather than watch, there are tennis clubs throughout the Ile-de-France region, most of which are affiliated to the FFT. Membership of a local FFT tennis club not only entitles you to advance Roland Garros tickets, but also offers other benefits (e.g. reduced court fees, insurance and reciprocal privileges at other FFT tennis clubs throughout France). The cost of family membership of a tennis club varies from around €100 to €500 per year, depending on the size of your family and whether or not the annual fee includes court time, lessons or other benefits. Nearly all tennis clubs in the Ile-de-France include FFT membership in their annual fees. Generally speaking, the most expensive clubs are those in the city of Paris or in the inner western suburbs. Clubs on the fringes of the Ile-de-France may charge as little as €70 per year for membership, with fewer additional charges or even free use of the courts on a first-come-first-served basis.

Fitness Clubs: American-style gyms have opened in the city of Paris and in the more fashionable suburbs. Many are operated as franchises, often within larger hotels. These include Vit'Halles, Gymnase Club, Forest Hill (part of the hotel chain of the same name) and others, all offering a dizzying assortment of fitness programmes – everything from weight training and standard fitness machines to nutritional counselling, squash and racquetball, billiards, dance exercise and even (at the Forest Hill chain) 'aqua-sports' parks with wave machines and hydrotherapy. Many hotels now offer health club facilities, which may be open to the public on a membership or per-visit basis.

It's difficult to compare prices for fitness facilities, as the services offered vary greatly and most clubs have trial offers and off-peak or long-term membership discounts. If you're working for a French company with a *comité d'entreprise* (a sort of employees' activity organisation), check whether there's a group membership you can take advantage of – usually for a fitness centre near your place of work. It's normally possible to negotiate a one or two-month trial membership for as little as €10 to €20, although you may be restricted to odd hours or certain facilities or have to pay an additional fee per visit. For €8,000 to €9,000 per year, you may be entitled to all the services and features of a well equipped club, including a personal fitness evaluation and nutritional counselling or time with a personal trainer. However, most memberships are negotiable if you're prepared to bargain for the services you want or need.

Golf: Golf has become very popular in France in recent years, and there are over 65 golf courses in the Ile-de-France region, mostly in the outer departments: one each in Seine-Saint-Denis and Val-de-Marne, five in Hauts-de-Seine, nine in Val-d'Oise, 13 in Essonne, 16 in Seine-et-Marne and no fewer than 24 in Yvelines, including five 36-hole and two 45-hole courses (the latter among five courses near Versailles). Parisian residents tend to favour the courses in the western suburbs, although there are also several popular courses near Disneyland Paris (in Marne-la-Vallée) to the east. One of the best resources for information regarding the location, fees and terms of golf courses in the Ile-de-France is the *Pariscope* website (🖳 www. pariscope.fr), better known for cinema and theatre reviews (see below). Under the 'Sport' section, golf clubs are listed by department, complete with directions, maps, number of holes (i.e. 9 or 18) and green fees. Information (in both French and English) on how to find courses, the cost of a round, etc. is also available from 🖳 www.backspin.com. Another useful website for golfers is 🖳 www.golf.com.fr.

Most golf courses are open to the public year round, although the more 'exclusive' clubs (e.g. in Versailles and Fontainebleau) may restrict non-members to the low season or certain days of the week or may require the invitation of a club member. Some clubs require a qualifying handicap. Green fees for most courses are around €25 to €50 during the week, and €35 to €80 at weekends.

Horse Racing & Riding: The French, particularly the Parisians, are well known as fans of horse racing, and there's a number of racecourses (*hippodromes*) in the Ile-de-France, including the Hippodrome d'Auteuil in the Bois de Boulogne on the western edge of Paris. Off-track betting is popular in the many PMU shops and bars throughout the area (identifiable by the green PMU signs in the windows) where bets can be made and races followed on television. Horse riding as a participant sport is also popular, and there are many stables (*écuries*) and riding schools (*écoles d'équitation*) throughout the region.

Cycling: Cycling is another popular sport in France, for both spectators and participants. The *Tour de France* takes place every year in July, and the final stage on the last Sunday of the month winds its way along the back roads of the Ile-de-France, usually through Essonne or Seine-et-Marne, before culminating in a sprint up the Champs-Elysées. (The centenary 2003 race will also start in Paris.) There are numerous cycling clubs in the area, whose members can be seen most Sundays (when the weather permits and sometimes even when it doesn't!) in their brightly coloured club outfits. The French Cycling Federation (Fédération française de Cyclisme) is the main cycling organisation in France and its website (🖳 www.ffc.fr) contains information about local clubs and all kinds of cycling, from off-road to indoor racing and stunt riding. Alternatively, contact either your *mairie* (many cycling clubs are sponsored by the town officials) or ask at a local bicycle shop.

Other Sports: There are, of course, numerous other sporting facilities and clubs in the Ile-de-France, including a few English-speaking sports clubs (see **Clubs** on page 315).

Leisure

There's no shortage of leisure opportunities in the Ile-de-France region, whether cultural, physical or purely fun.

Museums & Monuments: Not surprisingly, Paris has more museums and monuments than any other city or town in France; there are over 400 historical monuments and almost 70 national museums within the city, from the Louvre, spectacularly housed in the former royal palace, to specialist galleries such as the Musée Picasso, the Musée Rodin and the Musée Grévin, Paris' answer to Madame Tussaud's. If you aren't an art lover, there are plenty of other kinds of museum, from the historic (e.g. the Musée Carnavalet, dedicated to the history of the city of Paris, and the Musée de l'Histoire de France, located in the Hôtel de Soubise complex where the National Archives are also housed) to the scientific (e.g. the Palais de la Découverte, just off the Champs-Elysées, and the Cité des Sciences et de l'Industrie at the Porte de la Villette). There are also museums dedicated to textiles, natural history, coins and medals, music and musical instruments and even individual performers (e.g. Edith Piaf and Georges Brassens). Most museums and monuments in Paris are owned and operated by the national government, and tourist offices throughout the city carry information about these and other attractions.

As well as Paris' most famous buildings, the Eiffel Tower and Arc de Triomphe, Notre Dame and the Sacré-Coeur, there are numerous less well known places to visit, including the Pompidou Centre, *Les Invalides* and Napoleon's tomb, and the Montparnasse and Père Lachaise cemeteries. These are both surprisingly popular tourist attractions, as many famous people are buried there. Père Lachaise is the final resting place of Chopin, Molière, Oscar Wilde, Edith Piaf, Jim Morrison (whose grave is often littered with hashish offerings from devoted fans) among numerous others, while in Montparnasse lie the remains of Jean-Paul Sartre, Samuel Beckett, Man Ray and Jean Seberg.

Parks & Gardens: Although one of the world's most densely populated cities, Paris has a wealth of attractive parks and gardens, including the Jardin du Luxembourg, the Jardin des Tuileries, the Parc Monceau (all of which offer playgrounds for children and entertainment including puppet shows and concerts during the summer months) and the Parc de la Villette in the 19th, which incorporates an open-air cinema and number of 'futuristic' attractions. On the outskirts of the city are the Bois de Vincennes and the Bois de Boulogne, which despite its popular image as a trawling ground for prostitutes of the most outlandish varieties also offers camping grounds, sports fields, hiking trails and picnic and restaurant facilities. Further information can be obtained from guidebooks and from the Paris *Office de Tourisme* on the Champs-Elysées or one of its branch offices in the main railway stations or at the base of the Eiffel Tower. The *Office de Tourisme* is also available online (🖥 www.paris.org). Many expatriate clubs and organisations organise outings to local museums and monuments or sights that may not be open to the general public, e.g. the Hôtel de Ville, the main city hall of Paris, which is open only to group tours.

Theme Parks: The Ile-de-France is home to the biggest (and, for many French people, the most controversial) of all French theme parks, **Disneyland Paris**. Originally opened as Euro-Disney, the park has been blamed for everything from contributing to the destruction of European culture to gross violation of workers' rights (e.g. by requiring female employees to shave their legs and underarms and banning all facial hair on male workers). While still considered something of a threat to local culture, Disneyland Paris is now more or less accepted as a feature of the landscape (and is more popular with the locals than many would care to admit). Located just outside Marne-la-Vallée, Disneyland includes not only the theme park itself but also Walt Disney Studios Park (an attraction dedicated to the art of film making, a topic near and dear to the hearts of the French), Disney Village (containing shops, restaurants, bars, discos and a Wild West show), Disney Hotels, and Golf Disneyland. The hotels and golf courses do a booming business in seminars and meetings, particularly for large corporations, and it isn't uncommon for a business meeting at one of the nearby hotels to include an afternoon or evening admission to Disneyland. There's a direct *RER* line (A) from Paris, the station being located in the centre of the Disney complex. For those travelling by car, the park is well sign-posted from the A4 motorway.

A single admission to the parks for one day costs €38 for an adult, €29 for a child. Various combination tickets are available for multiple days, admission with parking or in conjunction with other services (golf or hotel accommodation, transit passes, etc.). Tickets are available in Disney stores throughout Europe, in many Paris underground stations, ticket outlets and travel agencies and from the Disney website (🖳 www.disneyland paris.com). There's even a variety of discounted season tickets for Ile-de-France residents who can't get enough of the place (you must present proof of residence in one of the eight departments of the Ile-de-France region). Some season tickets are restricted to non-peak times or dates, but many cost no more than two or three days' worth of single admissions. See the website for details.

Those who prefer a more 'traditional' French theme park (or who find Disneyland too expensive or too crowded) head for **Parc Astérix**, at Plailly (60) just outside the Ile-de-France region on the A1 motorway towards Lille. Parc Astérix is France's second-most popular theme park, where rides, shows and the general décor are themed on the plucky little Gaul and his friends, made famous by the comic book series. Unlike Disneyland Paris, Parc Astérix is only open during the summer season, roughly from Easter until the end of September, and only at weekends during school terms. Single admissions are €30 for adults, €22 for children for the day, and there's a season pass available for €65 (adults) or €45 (children). Tickets for Parc Astérix are available online at their website (🖳 www.parcasterix.com) and at most *RER* and SNCF (railway) stations and travel agencies in the Ile-de-France region, often packaged with train tickets and/or hotel accommodation.

Other theme parks and attractions of note in and around Paris include:

- Aquaboulevard (15th *arrondissement*): Europe's largest aquatic park;
- Le Château et Parc de Thoiry (78): wildlife park where visitors are caged and the animals roam 'free';
- Famiparc in Nonville (77): amusement park;
- France miniature in Elancourt (78): as the name suggests, scale models of famous places in France;
- Le Jardin des Plantes (5th): botanical gardens;
- Le Parc aux Etoiles in Triel-sur-Seine (78): space theme park;
- Parc de l'Emprunt in Souppes-sur-Long (77): animal and amusement park;
- Zoo de Vincennes (12th): 1,200 animals.

There are also leisure parks at Jablines-Annet (77), Saint-Quentin-en-Yvelines, Trappes, Verneuil-sur-Seine, Villennes-sur-Mer (78) and Draveil (91). Just north of the Ile-de-France region is La Mer de Sable ('The Sea of Sand') in Ermenonville near Senlis in the department of Oise, which celebrates the American Wild West, with spectacular horse riding displays.

Châteaux: Outside the city limits, there are many attractions and activities to occupy your leisure time. For example, there are literally hundreds of *châteaux* in the area, from the world famous Versailles to lesser known royal estates such as Vaux-le-Vicomte (near Melun south of Paris), Sceaux (just outside Paris to the south), Saint Jean de Beauregard (near Les Ulis in Essonne) and Chantilly (just north of the Ile-de-France in the department of Oise). Many towns have their own *châteaux* open to the public, which can be located by following the brown and white road signs on main roads. There are also the forests (*forêts*) of Rambouillet, Vincennes, Fontainebleau, Saint-Germain and Montmorency.

Festivals: During the spring and summer months, Paris hosts a variety of street festivals, fairs and special events, the best known of which is probably the Fête de la Musique on 21st June. Designed as a midsummer's night party, this features open air concerts and performances in all the *arrondissements,* including appearances by famous popular musicians and groups, all free of charge. Paris's Parc Floral is the site of the Festival Classique au Vert, an *al fresco* classical music festival that takes place every weekend during August and September. In August 2002, the banks of the Seine were closed to traffic and transformed (at vast expense) into 'Paris Plage', complete with sand, palm trees and deck chairs; it remains to be seen whether this will become an annual event.

Other Attractions: Many of the *villes nouvelles* have concert venues which attract popular local performers, singers and comedians, and most sports arenas and stadiums host short-run concerts and shows from time to time. Many communities organise local fairs and festivals, street dances (common on or around 14th July), and 'music and light' shows (*son et lumière*) celebrating historical events. Strangely, however, there are no casinos in Paris or anywhere else in the Ile-de-France. Each of the departments has its own tourist office, providing information about local leisure opportunities, and almost all the departments publish monthly or quarterly guides to local events.

As Paris is the transport hub of France, it's possible to get to almost every other part of France and to many other parts of Europe within a few hours, whether by car, train or plane. For example, the region is within comfortable day-trip distance of Giverny (Monet's house and garden) in Eure (see page 35) and Chartres (with its magnificent cathedral) in Eure-et-Loire. Thanks to the newest *TGV* line, even Marseilles is a mere three hours away by high-speed train.

English-language Cinema & Theatre

The multi-screen cinemas along the Champs-Elysées and the Boulevard Montparnasse show all the latest films, with foreign films in both their original language with French subtitles (*version originale/VO*) and dubbed into French (*version française/VF*). *VO* films are also shown at many other cinemas throughout Paris and in the inner suburbs, particularly to the west of the city, although the suburbs generally suffer from a dearth of cinemas and most residents travel into the capital to watch the latest films. In the outer suburbs, the availability of *VO* films varies. In Seine-Saint-Denis, for example, you're likely to find Indian, Tunisian and Iranian films in *VO*. In Seine-et-Marne, where many Asians have settled, Japanese films (including Manga cartoon films, popular with young people) are often shown in *VO*. Fontainebleau cinemas offer a wide selection of films in *VO*, thanks to the large international population. In Essonne, where the foreign population is small and scattered, English-language films in *VO* may be shown only in the larger towns close to Paris (i.e. Massy, Chilly Mazarin and Bretigny-sur-Orge) and in a few small community cinemas that specialise in 'art' films (e.g. the community centres in Orsay and Dourdan).

Cinema listings are published in local newspapers and magazines, as well as in a number of Paris-based activity magazines, such as **Pariscope**. There are a number of online cinema listings for the Ile-de-France (e.g. *Pariscope* 🖥 www.pariscope.fr and *Allociné* 🖥 www.allocine.fr), where you can search by department and even book tickets online. *Allociné* is also available on television, if you have digital cable or satellite service, offering previews and reviews of current films, behind the scenes reporting and show business news, although, like **Pariscope**, it's mainly in French. A useful website for finding out which films are on in a given area, which also indicates whether the films are being shown in the original language is 🖥 www.cinefil.com.

Plays are seldom performed in English in the professional theatres in Paris, which often present plays by Shakespeare and other English-language writers in French translation. However, Les Amis du Jardin Shakespeare du Pré Catelan (in the 16th) present a Shakespeare play in English at least once a year and the Dear Conjunction Theatre Company performs plays in English as well as in French at various venues.

There's a number of amateur English-language theatre groups in the inner western suburbs, notably The International Players in Saint-Germain-en-Laye (78). Performances are generally advertised in expatriate newsletters or on lampposts and in local shop windows. Several of the towns sponsor French amateur theatre clubs, which may occasionally perform in public but almost always in French (participating in one of these productions is an enjoyable way to improve your language skills). The local *mairie* may organise evening outings to attend plays, operas or concerts in Paris or elsewhere, including transport by coach.

Shopping Centres & Markets

The boulevard Haussmann, at the southern end of the 9th *arrondissement*, is often considered the shopping 'centre' of Paris, thanks mainly to the two large and well known department stores (*grand magasins*), Galeries Lafayette and Au Printemps, but also to a concentration of shops and boutiques of all kinds. Many of the stores in this area attract tourists at all times of the year, and the area is generally crowded. Both Galeries Lafayette and Au Printemps carry a wide selection of clothing, household goods, electronics and furnishings for the home, and you can enjoy a snack, meal or simply a drink in their many cafés and restaurants. The same is true of the other *grands magasins* in Paris: Samaritaine in the 1st, the Bazar de l'Hôtel de Ville (BHV) in the 4th and Bon Marché in the 7th, although each has its own character and specialities. All the *grands magasins* offer their own credit cards, which entitle you to rebates, credits and discounts throughout the year.

Other major shopping areas in Paris include the Montparnasse Shopping Centre at the Tour Montparnasse (in the 14th) and the adjacent neighbourhood, particularly the Rue de Rennes, the Forum des Halles and surrounding neighbourhood, and the Champs-Elysées and the area along the Rue Montaigne with its chic designer shops. Virtually every residential neighbourhood, however, has its own shops, at least for food.

Outside Paris, most towns have a cluster of smaller shops, including at least one bakery (*boulangerie/pâtisserie*), butcher's (*boucherie*) and shops selling sausages and processed meats (*charcuterie*) and prepared foods (*traiteur*). In smaller towns, the bakery or butcher's generally carries a small assortment of tinned vegetables, packaged items (rice or noodles), drinks, including alcohol, and other essential foostuffs. Shops are normally open from 10.00 to 19.00, Mondays to Saturdays, smaller shops (particularly those outside Paris) closing for an hour or two at lunchtime. In some areas, smaller shops are closed all day on Mondays or, in a few cases, on Monday mornings. Those food shops (bakers', butchers', cheese shops and *traiteurs*) that are open Sunday mornings are, in most cases, closed all day on Mondays. Many small shops close for a month's holiday during the summer, but in the case of bakers' and butchers', they must display an advance notice of their closing dates, indicating what provision has been made for supplying bread and meat to their loyal customers, either at a nearby shop or with the help of a van making the rounds at a specified time each day.

Most towns (and many neighbourhoods in Paris) also have open-air street markets, usually at least once a week, and in a few places daily. In the towns, there are often signs prohibiting parking in the town centre or main square on market days. Most open-air markets are open from early morning (07.00 or 07.30) to around 12.30 or 13.00, although a few markets stay open until 16.00 or even 17.00. For staple items or between market days, there are grocery shops (*supermarchés* or *superettes*), most of which are open six days a week until the early evening (although most local shops still close for an hour or two at lunchtimes).

For 'mass' shopping, there are shopping centres with a supermarket or hypermarket (over $2,500m^2/27,000ft^2$) and a variety of other stores (for garden supplies, hardware, clothing and shoes) on the outskirts of larger towns in *Zones d'Industries* or *Zones d'Activités* (*Z.I.* or *Z.A.* on most street signs). The major hypermarkets in the Ile-de-France are Auchan, Carrefour and Cora. In some areas you'll also find Champion, Intermarché, Leclerc and Shoppi as well as other chain stores, although generally these are smaller and concentrate on food and household products. The shopping centres and *zones* in and around Paris often include large, international stores, such as IKEA, Office Depot, Pier Import and Toys 'R' Us, as well as French DIY and garden chains such as Bricorama, Mr. Bricolage and Truffaut. Shopping centres are usually named after the nearby town, with the designation II ('two'), e.g. *Parly II*, *Les Ulis II*, *Velizy II*. The *Parinor* centre is on the way to Roissy-Charles de Gaulle airport, and the *Belle Epine* centre is near Orly. Some of these centres are permitted to stay open on Sundays, as they're considered part of the 'tourist trade' and thus eligible for exemption from normal retailing regulations. Centres offer large, usually free, car parks, but these can be full to overflowing on Saturday afternoons, especially in the weeks before Christmas. Most larger shops and chain stores are open continuously throughout the day (i.e. without closing at lunchtimes).

Foreign Food & Products

In the city of Paris, and increasingly in the western suburbs, there's a number of shops that specialise in imported foods, both British and American as well as from many other countries. These shops advertise in English-language publications as well as in expatriate club newsletters and frequently online. Marks & Spencer used to be the best purveyor of British goods and foods in the Paris area; its main store in boulevard Haussmann has been bought by Galeries Lafayette, which now features a British Food Hall in the recently renovated building. The Grande Epicerie de Paris is an international grocery store, owned by Le Bon Marché (which is in turn owned by Harrods) offering foods from Britain, the USA and other countries around the world. There's also a number of small British shops throughout Paris, often owned and run by expatriates. Among the American community in Paris, Thanksgiving (in the 4th *arrondissement*) and The Real McCoy (in the 7th) are probably the best known specialist food shops, featuring many popular brands and items not normally obtainable in France.

Although the French are notoriously reluctant to import anything, many supermarkets and hypermarkets have recently established 'exotic' (i.e. foreign) food sections that offer items from Britain and the USA, as well as many Italian, North African, Chinese, Spanish and Portuguese foods. Nevertheless, the selection of items is usually small and sometimes provides a startling (or amusing) insight into the French view of 'typical' foreign fare. For example, British food shelves often contain little more than marmalade, Heinz soups, biscuits and tea, while American 'delicacies' usually consist of microwave popcorn, cake and muffin mixes and barbecue sauce. A few imported items are also starting to appear on the shelves of some grocery shops in the Paris area, notably muffins and crumpets, American-style hamburger buns and some Australian wines and beers. For general information on obtaining foreign products in France, see page 61.

Restaurants & Bars

It goes without saying that Paris is chock full of restaurants (including over 70 Michelin-starred restaurants), bars, cafés, *bistrots* and every other sort of eating and drinking establishment. Restaurants are generally open only during meal times, i.e. from around 12.00 to 14.00 and from 19.00 until 23.00 or midnight. Cafés, *bistrots*, *brasseries*, bars and *salons de thé* are generally open all day and offer simpler fare (salads, sandwiches and grilled dishes) at any time. It's still true that in most cafés and *bistrots* you can 'occupy' a table all day for the price of a cup of coffee or a drink while you read your newspaper, sort through your mail or chat with friends. (Tipping generously helps.) Most restaurants accept major credit cards, although a few of the fancier Parisian establishments still refuse to accept credit cards or cheques.

The Paris area hasn't produced any distinctive local cuisine, but it does benefit by attracting excellent bakers and chefs from all the other regions of France. The *Michelin Red* guide and the *Gault Millau* are still considered the authorities on rating (and sometimes berating) the restaurants of Paris. Dining at Michelin favourites such as the Tour d'Argent, Lasserre and Taillevent can require booking up to three months in advance (not to mention having a small fortune to burn!). But you don't need to push the boat out to dine well in Paris, and most neighbourhoods have several restaurants, often tiny establishments that may seat only a handful of people. Thanks to the immigrants and the tourists, there's a growing number of 'ethnic' restaurants in and around Paris, including a wide range of Asian restaurants (Chinese, Japanese, Thai, Cambodian, Indian and Vietnamese), Algerian and Moroccan restaurants and a small but growing selection of Mexican, South American and Caribbean establishments. In the 18th and 19th *arrondissements*, you can find

Senegalese, Cameroon and other sub-Saharan African specialities. Couscous (an assortment of meats and vegetables cooked as a sort of spicy stew and served over steamed semolina) has practically become a French national dish and is very popular as a 'fast food' option for lunch.

Outside the city, almost every small town has at least one bar or restaurant, usually within walking distance of the church. The menu may vary from *sandwichs* and *steak frites* to various local and regional dishes, like *cassoulet* or *pot au feu* or the ever-popular *moules* (steamed mussels). The variety of ethnic foods may depend on the local foreign population, but most towns, even in the farthest reaches of the region, can claim at least a pizza restaurant and possibly a Chinese restaurant or take-away. Chinese *traiteurs* are becoming increasingly common in shopping centres, usually with seating available for consuming your purchases on site. There are also some surprisingly good classic French restaurants tucked away in the outer suburbs, usually with prices that are a fraction of those charged in the centre of Paris. Unfortunately, these establishments tend to close or change ownership with amazing frequency, so it isn't wise to base your choice of area on the presence of a particular restaurant! Nevertheless, sharing, comparing and debating the relative merits of newly discovered restaurants is a good (not to mention enjoyable) way to assimilate yourself into French life.

Despite their philosophical objection to *le fast food* (dubbed *le néfaste food* meaning 'unhealthy food') in general and McDonald's (*McDo's* in local parlance) in particular, the French have developed some chain restaurants of their own. *La Crée* is a chain of seafood restaurants offering reasonably priced fish and seafood (*fruits de mer*), including oysters, in a pleasant although functional setting. *La Courte Paille* ('the short straw'), whose restaurants are easily recognisable by their round, thatched roofs, offers dishes grilled over an open flame in the dining room and is popular with families, no doubt because of its basic, simply prepared meats, served with salad and *frites*, and reasonable prices. Buffalo Grill is a steak house *à la française*, complete with 'cowboys' and 'cowgirls' as waiters and waitresses. Most chain restaurants are located in or near shopping centres or industrial estates or just off busy motorway exits.

SERVICES

International & Private Schools

For families with children, the availability of suitable schools plays a crucial role in determining the choice of area in which to live. Although many schools provide transport, this may be along specific routes only, and it may not be practical for children to travel from the outer reaches of Seine-et-Marne or Essonne, where there are few, if any, international schools or private schools with international programmes. Most international schools with English-language curricula are located in the city of Paris or in nearby towns to the west. Private schools include the American School of Paris (in Hauts-de-Seine at 41, rue Pasteur, BP 82, 92216 Saint-Cloud, ☎ 01.41.12.82.82, 💻 www. asparis.org), The British School in Paris (in Yvelines at 38, quai de l'Ecluse, 78290 Croissy-sur-Seine, ☎ 01.34.80.45.90, 💻 www.rmplc.co.uk/eduweb/ sites/paris), Marymount International (an independent Catholic school in Hauts-de-Seine at 72, boulevard de la Saussaye, 92200 Neuilly-sur-Seine, ☎ 01.46.24.10.51, 💻 www.ecole-marymount.fr) and the International School of Paris (in the 16th *arrondissement* at 6, rue Beethoven, 75016 Paris, ☎ 01. 45.27.15.93, 💻 www.isparis.edu).

There's also a number of private bilingual or trilingual schools, such as the Ecole active bilingue (70, rue du Théâtre, 75015 Paris, ☎ 01.44.37.00.80, 💻 www.eabjm.com) with three locations in Paris (in the 7th and 15th), according to age group) and Eurécole (in the 16th at 5, rue de Lübeck, 75116 Paris, ☎ 01.40.70.12.81, 💻 www.eurecole.com), which teaches sports in English, art in German and other subjects in French for primary students (up to around age ten). Other schools in the region which cater for English-speaking students are the Ecole nouvelle privée Emilie-Brandt (☎ 01.47.58.53.40, 💻 www.ecolemiliebrandt.asso.fr) in Levallois-Perret and the Lycée (☎ 01. 46.26.60.10) in Sèvre (both in 92). Both the British and American Embassies maintain lists of international and bilingual schools on their websites, and every other year the Association of American Wives of Europeans (AAWE, 34, avenue de New York, 75116 Paris, 💻 www. aaweparis.org) holds an 'open house' where local private schools promote their services to prospective students and their parents.

Admission to international, private and multi-lingual schools is usually on a competitive basis, involving entrance exams and interviews with the prospective student and family members. Private schools can be expensive (costing €2,000 to €5,000 or more per term), and many have an ever-changing student population, as they cater for the itinerant expatriate executive community.

A few French state schools offer international programmes, bilingual tracks or special language sections, which can be ideal for children (as well as for their parents, who don't have to pay tuition fees!). Being a native speaker of English doesn't guarantee a student a place in the English section of a state-sponsored international programme, although it certainly helps. The French school system favours students who demonstrate particular aptitudes in maths and the sciences and will look favourably upon English-speaking students who excel in these areas.

At kindergarten and nursery school level, there are many English-language and bilingual programmes available throughout Paris, including Montessori schools, which are particularly popular with the French. Many expatriate clubs run or arrange play-groups and informal day activities in English for pre-school children.

As far as post-secondary education or further education for adults is concerned, there are university level programmes conducted in English in and around Paris, e.g. at the American University in Paris, New York University in France, Schiller International University and at several business schools offering joint French/American programmes. Britain's Open University maintains an office in Neuilly-sur-Seine (92), where you can obtain information about its distance learning courses and degree programmes and attend tutoring sessions for the courses once you're enrolled. Details can be found on the OU website (⌨ www.open.ac.uk).

Language Schools

There's a wide variety of classes, courses and language learning programmes available in the Paris area, and your choice will depend largely on how much time and money you have or want to spend. The world-famous and highly regarded Sorbonne Language and Culture programme offers all levels and intensities of French lessons for prices ranging from €2,500 for a beginner's summer course to nearly €20,000 for a year's intensive instruction in both the language and culture of France. The Alliance française (AF) is popular with many expatriates, as they can start language training in their home countries and continue the same programme on arrival in France. The AF in Paris offers 16 to 18-day courses ranging from €250 to €550, depending on the number of hours' tuition per day. Individual private tuition at the AF can be arranged for €47 per hour. The AF school is on the boulevard Raspail in the 6th *arrondissement*.

Both the Alliance française and the Sorbonne are part of the French government's *francophonie* mission to promote and encourage the study and use of the French language throughout the world. Teaching methods used draw heavily upon the standard teaching of foreign languages in French schools and tend to focus on grammar, translation and written language skills. While both programmes have excellent reputations for teaching French, students who are primarily interested in conversational fluency may prefer other types of programme.

There are around 30 private language schools in Paris, each specialising in a particular approach to language learning. Berlitz offers three-hour per day intensive sessions with no more than three students per class for around €550 per week and puts more emphasis on conversational skills than the Sorbonne or AF programmes. Other private schools offer four-week courses for between €200 and €500, depending on how many hours per week you can stand – usually 10 to 20. Class sizes can vary from 6 to 20 and the programme may also offer tours or lectures on French culture and history. The most popular of the private language schools include the Institut Parisien (operated by the Nouvelles Frontières travel group), Ecole Eiffel and Ecole des Roches, but there are many others. Language schools advertise heavily in expatriate newsletters and often in the travel sections of British and American newspapers. Most language schools offer 'degressive' fee scales, meaning that the hourly rates go down if you're willing to commit to a longer course, in some cases dropping as low as €3 to €4 per hour.

Language classes are also offered by the Collège franco-britannique, the British Council and the British Institute in Paris, the Open University (based in Neuilly-sur-Seine in Hauts-de-Seine) and the British School of Paris (see **International & Private Schools** above). The Anglophone Parents' Association in Chantilly in the department of Oise just north of the Ile-de-France region organises classes for the children of English-speaking families.

Outside Paris, Berlitz and Inlingua have offices and classrooms throughout the Ile-de-France and there are also the following private schools in Yvelines and Hauts-de-Seine:

● Institut international de Rambouillet in Rambouillet (78);

● Ecole Yvelines Langues in Saint-Germain-en-Laye (78);

● Ecole de la Tournelle in Septeuil (78);

● Metropolitan Languages in Boulogne (92);

● Citylangues in La Défense (92);

● France Campus in La Défense (92);

● Linguarama in Puteaux (92);

● Centre international d'Etudes in Sèvres (92).

Details of the language schools can be found on ⌨ www.europa-pages.com. The French Consulate in London (see **Appendix A**) publishes a booklet called *Cours de français Langue étrangère et Stages pédagogiques du français Langue étrangère en France*, which includes a comprehensive list of schools, organisations and institutes providing French language courses throughout France.

There are advertisements for private tutors in most expatriate publications and newsletters, ranging from offers to swap French tuition for English practice (i.e. basically free) up to around €50 or €60 per hour for a qualified teacher. There are also a number of conversation groups, where you can practise your French under the guidance of native speakers or trained instructors. Some groups charge €8 or €10 per session (usually an hour or two), while some expatriate organisations make conversation groups or other French practice sessions a benefit of membership. It's often possible to find a local student or public school teacher who's willing to give French lessons in exchange for help with their English if you post a small card or sign in the window of your local bakery or butcher's shop.

Language training may be offered by your employer (who can count its cost towards the annual 'continuing education' levy each employer must pay).

Hospitals & Clinics

Paris is the centre of the health care and hospital industry in France and boasts the most prestigious and best-equipped hospitals in the country, although there are acknowledged shortages of some advanced technical equipment, such as CAT scanners and MRI machines. There are over 100 hospitals and clinics serving Paris and the surrounding area. Specialist facilities include maternity centres, eye and ear facilities and the world-renowned Neckar Hospital for Sick Children. Outside the *petit couronne*, there's usually a choice of at least two hospitals within a radius of 25km (15mi), wherever you live.

No fewer than 13 hospitals in the Ile-de-France were rated among the top 50 hospitals in the country in a survey published in August 2002 by *Le Point* magazine: in Paris itself, the Hôpital Cochin (rated third), Hôpital Pitié-Salpêtrière (seventh), Hôpital Necker (13th – see above), Institut mutualiste Montsouris (15th), Hôpital Saint-Louis (25th), the Hôpital Bichat (26th), Hôpital Tenon (39th) and the Hôpital Lariboisière (45th); in Hauts-de-Seine (92), the Hôpital Ambroise-Paré in Boulogne-Billancourt and the Hôpital Foch in Suresnes (joint 34th); and in Val-de-Marne (94), the Hôpital Henri-Mondor (30th) and the Centre hospitalier intercommunal (47th) in Créteil and the Hôpital Bicêtre in Le Kremlin-Bicêtre (41st).

In Paris you can find English-speaking staff at many of the larger hospitals, but that isn't always the case outside the city, especially in the *grand couronne*. There are two private English-speaking hospitals in the Paris region: The Hertford British Hospital (also known as the Hôpital Franco-Britannique) in Levallois-Perret (92), and the American Hospital of Paris, which is actually in Neuilly (92). Both hospitals offer English-speaking staff and British and American-trained doctors. Fees and charges at both hospitals can usually be reclaimed through the French social security system and most complementary insurance providers (*mutuelles*). For those with private expatriate insurance, some forms of treatment or extended stay may require pre-approval. The American Hospital also serves as something of a social centre for the English-speaking community in Paris and the western suburbs, hosting lectures and discussions on a variety of health care topics.

Doctors & Dentists

The Ile-de-France generally has above the national average proportion of doctors to inhabitants, and Hauts-de-Seine and Val-de-Marne are particularly well provided, with over 184 general practitioners and 163 specialists per 100,000 population, although Val-d'Oise has relatively few doctors (fewer than 143 GPs and around 125 specialists per 100,000 inhabitants). Nevertheless, it's usually easy to find and register with a doctor in all departments. As in the case of hospitals (see above), you're far more likely to be able to find English-speaking doctors and dentists in the city of Paris or in the inner western suburban areas, where English-speaking foreigners tend to live. The American Consulate publishes a list of English-speaking doctors and dentists, which is available on their website as part of their Guide to Living in France (💻 www.amb-usa.fr/consul/guideoas/guidehome.htm) or on request (☎ 01.43.12.22.22) in hard copy form. Most of the practitioners on this list are located in Paris or at one of the two English-speaking hospitals (see above).

Outside Paris and particularly in the *grand couronne*, it can be difficult to find an English-speaking doctor (or at least one who's willing to use English with a patient). Most medical personnel understand at least some English, particularly medical terms, but you need to be prepared to speak French or bring along a fluent friend or family member to help translate.

Tradesmen

The main source for English-speaking workers and tradesmen is *France-USA Contacts* (*FUSAC*), a free bi-weekly magazine consisting of small advertisements (see **English-language Press** below). You can also locate handymen, computer repair technicians, satellite installers, etc. through the various expatriate clubs (see **Clubs** on page 315), as this sort of work is popular with expatriates whose residence status is still 'undetermined'. Note, however, that it's strictly illegal in France to hire undocumented or unlicensed workers, although cases against individuals aren't often prosecuted. Magazines such as *French Property News* and newspapers such as *The News* (see **Appendix B**) carry advertisements by English-speaking tradesmen. French tradesmen are unlikely to speak much English but are generally reliable – and have the advantage that they often take several months to submit an invoice!

English-language Radio

Radio France internationale (RFI) broadcasts in English for three-and-a-half hours every day in the Paris region on 738MW: a one-hour news and magazine programme at 07.00, including a French lesson; a one-hour news programme at 14.00 (replaced on Sundays by a report on cultural events in France); and a one-and-a-half hour news and magazine programme at 16.30.

It's also possible to listen to recordings of programmes on your computer via the Internet (go to 🖳 www.rfi.fr/fichiers/Langues/rfi_anglais_main.asp).

You may be able to receive BBC Radio 4 on long wave (198) in some parts of the region. BBC Radio 1, 2, 3, and 4 can be received on your television via the Astra satellite, and you can listen to recordings of radio programmes on Radio 1, 2, 3, 4, 5, 6 and 1Extra on your computer via the Internet (go to 🖳 www.bbc.co.uk/radio/aod/index.shtml). The World Service can be received on 648MW in some parts, as well as on short wave in all areas (for frequency details, go to 🖳 www.bbc.co.uk/worldservice/schedules/frequencies/eurwfreq.shtml) and via the Astra satellite. Local music stations usually broadcast 60 per cent non-French language songs, most of which are in English.

English-language Press

English language newspapers are generally available at many of the larger newsstands and kiosks in Paris and much of the surrounding area. The *International Herald Tribune* is published in Paris and is considered by many to be the leading journal for the expatriate community. *The Financial Times* and *USA Today* are also available throughout the region on a same-day basis. In the city, it's often possible to find same-day copies of the London *Times* or the *Guardian* at 'international' newsstands. In addition, many newsstands carry the *Economist* and the international editions of American news weeklies such as *Time* and *Newsweek*. Home delivery of newspapers, including English-language dailies, is sometimes available, but outside Paris receipt on the day of publication isn't always guaranteed.

In the Paris region, there are a number of locally published English-language magazines and guides, including *Paris Voice*, *France-USA Contacts* (*FUSAC*), and *Irish Eyes*. These are available on subscription or free at pick-up points around the city, including shops, schools, most English-language clubs and many 'ethnic' restaurants with a large English-speaking clientele. (Mexican restaurants seem to be a particularly popular distribution point.) *FUSAC* is a collection of advertisements, including ads for jobs, apartments, dating services, classes, and even personal ads. *Paris Voice* and *Irish Eyes* are general interest magazines, geared towards the American and Irish communities respectively.

Paris has several English-language bookshops, including WH Smith for British books and Brentano's for American publications. There are several shops specialising in buying and selling used books in English, such as Tea and Tattered Pages, which also boasts its own café. Outside Paris, it can be difficult to find English-language titles in local shops, although in the western suburbs boot and rummage sales organised by international schools and expatriate organisations are a popular way of picking up (and disposing of) used books. Some expatriate clubs also maintain 'swapping libraries' to share titles among their members. For general information on obtaining foreign products in France, see page 61.

Embassies & Consulates

Being the national capital, Paris is home to the embassies and consulates of every country that has diplomatic relations with France. Addresses and phone numbers can be found in telephone directories under 'Ambassades'. Both Britain and the USA have separate embassies and consulates (see **Useful Addresses** on page 329), although they aren't far apart. Generally speaking, for matters relating to individuals living in France, you'll need to contact the consulate; embassies tend to deal with political and business matters. Both the British and American embassies maintain websites (⌨www.amb-grandebretagne.fr and 🖥 www.amb-usa.fr) containing a considerable amount of information for their expatriates living in France. Be sure to check your embassy or consulate's opening hours before making a trip into Paris, as many (including both the British and American embassies) have very limited public office hours. Strict security measures at all diplomatic missions mean that foreign nationals living in or around Paris are encouraged to conduct most business (including registration and passport renewal) by post.

Churches

There are places of worship for most religions in Paris, including many offering English-language services. For example, there's a number of Anglican churches, including Saint Michael's (in the 8th *arrondissement* opposite the British Embassy) and Saint George's in the 16th, Saint Joseph's Roman Catholic Church in the 8th, a Church of Scotland (Presbyterian), whose new church in the 8th opened in March 2002, an American Church (7th) and the American Cathedral (8th). Several of the English-speaking churches in Paris also serve as community centres, offering meeting rooms and social programmes for the Anglophone community.

Outside Paris, there are churches in the following towns which hold regular services in English:

- Fontainebleau (77) – Chapelle du Lycée Saint-Aspais;
- Versailles (78) – Saint Mark's;
- Gif-sur-Yvette near Chevry (91) – Eglise Saint-Paul;
- Maisons-Lafitte (78) – Holy Trinity Church;
- Rueil-Malmaison (92) – Emmanuel Baptist Church.

Saint Peter's Anglican church in Chantilly (in Oise, just outside the Ile-de-France) also holds English-language services.

There are also English services for Jews, Buddhists, Jehovah's Witnesses and Latter Day Saints (Mormons), although some may be held in the church hall of another denomination or in rented premises. There are mosques in every *arrondissement* of Paris as well as at least a dozen in each of the other departments of the Ile-de-France (over 30 in Seine-Saint-Denis); details can be found on ⌨ http://mosquee.free.fr. There are also numerous synagogues in Paris (for details, go to ⌨ www.feujcity.com, where there's also information about Kosher food shops and restaurants, Jewish clubs, associations and schools, etc.), one in Yvelines, two each in Seine-et-Marne and Essonne, four in Val-d'Oise, five in Seine-Saint-Denis, six in Hauts-de-Seine and eight in Val-de-Marne, details of which can be found on ⌨ www.pagesjaunes.fr (enter 'Synagogues' in the first box and the name of the department or town).

Clubs

The Paris area is home to a large number of clubs and societies founded and run by groups of expatriates, including national groups (e.g. the Association franco-écossaise, The Clan MacLeod society of France, The Caledonian Society of France, The Paris Welsh Society and The Royal Society of Saint George), university-based groups (e.g. The Alumnae Club of Paris, the Alumni of the University of Edinburgh in France, The Cambridge Society of Paris and The Oxford University Club), professional associations (e.g. The Association of British Accountants in France, The Chartered Management Institute, The Institute of Directors, The Institution of Civil Engineers and The Institution of Electrical Engineers), women's clubs (e.g. American Women's Group of Paris, The British and Commonwealth Women's Association, the International Women's Club and MESSAGE – the Mother Support Group) and others (e.g. the Association France Grande-Bretagne, The British Freemasons in France, the French branches of British Guides in Foreign Countries and of the Scouts, The English-speaking Union France, The Royal British Legion for ex-servicemen, The Salvation Army and the TOC H Association for elderly people). In fact, the choice can be literally overwhelming (one of the biggest problems for many expatriate clubs is scheduling their events so as not to conflict with each other!).

There's also a number of English-speaking sports clubs in the region, including the British Rugby Club of Paris in Saint-Cyr-l'Ecole (78), the Standard Athletic Club in Meudon-la-Forêt (92) and the Thoiry Cricket Club in Château-de-Thoiry (78), and several arts groups, including The English Cathedral Choir of Paris, The International Players (an amateur drama group), the Paris Decorative and Fine Arts Society and The Royal Scottish Country Dance Society. There's also an English Language Library for the blind in the

17th *arrondissement*. A list of the most popular organisations is available from the American Consulate (see page 329) or through the British Consulate's British Community Committee (⌨ www.britishinfrance.com). Both lists are included in the consulates' websites and are updated regularly. The British Consulate also publishes a free *Digest of British and Franco-British Clubs, Societies and Institutions*, most of which are in the Ile-de-France.

During October, many organisations hold 'open houses' or other events to welcome new expatriates, and the popular 'Bloom Where You Are Planted' programme, organised by and at the American Church in Paris, invites representatives from the various clubs and expatriate associations in Paris to speak at its orientation sessions. Participants in the 'Bloom' programme receive a copy of the guidebook published for use in the sessions. If you can't attend in person, copies of the programme handbook are on sale at WH Smith and other English-language bookshops in Paris. Most clubs and associations in Paris shut during July and August, when many members join the Parisian exodus to the countryside or head home, so if you arrive in the summer don't be discouraged at the lack of activity; by October, there will be more than you can handle.

On the fringes of the Ile-de-France, there may not be many groups accessible to non-French speakers unless you're in an area with a concentration of foreigners, such as Fontainebleau or Versailles. Private and international schools (see page 307) generally have an active parents' association and often need volunteers to help organise and run after-school activities for students.

For French speakers, the Accueil des Villes françaises (AVF), a French organisation designed to welcome newcomers to an area, is an option (there's often at least one fluent English-speaker in each group). There are over 65 AVF groups in the Ile-de-France region, including 19 in Hauts-de-Seine and 24 in Yvelines, although there are only two in Paris itself. The website (⌨ www.avf.asso.fr) includes a directory (*annuaire*) of local groups by department as well as an online form for contacting your local AVF before you move to the area. Listings indicate whether information and services are available in English or other languages. Other sources for clubs in the area are *The News* (see **Appendix B**) and the English-speaking church (see above).

PROPERTY

Although Paris itself is the world's most visited city, the residents of the Ile-de-France don't spend their holidays there, abandoning it almost totally to foreign tourists in July and August. Therefore, there's little in the way of holiday homes, timeshares or tourist communities, such as can be found in mountain or coastal resort areas of France. Residential property in the Ile-de-France is automatically considered to be a 'primary residence' (*résidence principale*). You're also far less likely than in almost any other area of France to find a tumble-down farm or *château* going for a song that you can 'fix up' as a second home. Even virtual ruins can command top prices, in accordance with the property value mantra: 'location, location, location'.

Not surprisingly, the rate of new building in Paris and the major surrounding towns is low or – in the case of Evry (91), Rueil-Malmaison (92) and Sarcelles (95) – virtually non-existent. However, many areas on the edges of the Ile-de-France are undergoing something of a construction boom, as land previously held for agriculture is gradually being converted to housing estates. Along the *routes nationales* of Seine-et-Marne, Essonne, Yvelines, and at the outer limits of Val-d'Oise, you're likely to see signs directing you to housing estates in the process of construction, with countdowns of the number of homes or plots left to sell.

There are at least half a dozen weekly publications, costing between €2 and €5 and available at newsstands throughout the region, which are dedicated to property advertisements, both for rent and for sale. *De Particulier à Particulier*, one such journal that carries only direct ads (i.e. where sellers are trying to avoid an estate agent's hefty commission), devotes almost half of its 300 to 400 pages each week to properties in the Ile-de-France region. Other property advertising journals concentrate on new properties or focus on 'luxury' properties. There are also many estate agents throughout the region, including the American franchise, Century 21, which handles both purchases and rentals as well as land, commercial property and property management, although most estate agents cover limited areas of the city and it can be worthwhile using a foreign-based buying agent, who will deal with several local agencies to find suitable properties for you to view. Many estate agencies and property publications have websites, with search functions to help you narrow your choice by specifying a price range, size, location or other criteria (see also **Appendix C**).

Typical Homes

Homes in and around Paris tend to be small by British and (particularly) American standards, whether apartments or houses. In fact, they're small even by French standards: the average Parisian home consists of 3.18 rooms compared with the national average of 3.86, and only just over 20 per cent of Parisian homes have four rooms or more (the lowest percentage of any major town in France). In the centre of Paris, it's possible to find single room lodgings as small as 9m^2 (90ft^2) where you share toilet and shower facilities with your neighbours. A house or apartment of 85 to 100m^2 is considered standard for a small family, i.e. with up to two children. Any residence over 100m^2 is considered large – even luxurious – and may be priced accordingly.

Most residential buildings are made of stone or concrete block and are sturdily built. Older buildings in the centre of Paris and the surrounding towns are highly sought-after, even though their architecture may limit the modern conveniences that can be installed. Many Parisians, in particular, prefer 'authenticity' to sleek, modern architecture and the latest gadgets. Many older buildings of six or seven floors have no passenger lift simply because there isn't enough space in which to install one. Even apartment blocks that boast of an *ascenseur* may have only a one or two-passenger cage-style lift tucked into a corner of the spiral staircase, sometimes only available to upper floor residents by means of a key or code.

Not surprisingly, Paris has the highest proportion of old properties of any major town in France: over 65 per cent of buildings date from before 1950 (compared with less than 20 per cent in Montpellier, for example), and in certain areas (e.g. the 2nd *arrondissement*), over 90 per cent of properties were built before the first world war. Paris also has the highest proportion of homes without a bath or shower and a high percentage (10 per cent) of vacant properties. Saint-Denis (93) has the lowest percentage of property owners (22 per cent) of any major town in France.

Apartment buildings, whether new or old, tend to have rather plain, boxy exteriors, architectural niceties being saved for the interiors. It's possible to find some spectacular apartments – featuring ornately carved mouldings, high ceilings and wooden flooring that creaks when you walk on it – concealed in apparently unremarkable buildings. *Franciliens* tend to create their own privacy zone within and around their homes. Windows are usually small, particularly those looking onto the street, and most homes have shutters (*volets*) to exclude the outside world when appropriate, both at night and when the family is away. Larger windows and balconies or terraces are reserved for the side of the home that faces away from the street, whether into a communal courtyard or a private garden. Most houses are protected by walls, tall fences or hedgerows, with high gates (often locked) at the entrances to the front door and drive or garage.

In older buildings, many apartments have long, narrow, airless corridors, with small rooms leading off on both sides. Floor plans are often haphazard, as large single residences have been split into individual flats and space has had to be made for electrical wiring, plumbing and telephone services not in existence when the buildings were first constructed. Tiny toilets are often sandwiched between rooms wherever plumbing connections are convenient, and traditional French 'bathrooms' (sometimes referred to as *salles d'eau*) normally contain only a basin and bathtub or shower – no toilet. Kitchens tend to be small and may come fully equipped or with just basic appliances (sink, cooker and maybe a refrigerator). In some cases, you must install your own cupboards or shelving. The water heater and gas or electricity meters may be simply hung on the wall or contained in a utility box, usually in the kitchen.

Apartments in newer buildings are more likely to boast a '*cuisine américaine*', which means that the kitchen is open to the adjoining room (usually the lounge or dining room) or separated only by a counter. Newer apartment blocks are more likely to have spacious lifts and may even have a garage, usually directly underneath the building. Houses, both detached and semi-detached, still exist in a few areas of Paris, although they don't come onto the market very often.

Apartments can also be found outside the centres of Paris and other large towns. These may be above shops or in newly constructed apartment blocks, complete with parking facilities and nearby shops. However, the ideal for many *Franciliens* is to have their own house with a (sometimes very small) piece of land, and in most cases detached houses are the norm. Older houses are solidly built and often meticulously fitted out and decorated inside. However, there are also many older properties that are falling into disrepair. New homes are mostly built to standard designs and may or may not include kitchen appliances and other fittings. *Franciliens* tend to be traditional in their decorating tastes, and it's rare to find a house decked out with state-of-the-art appliances or with a highly unusual layout or styling. Most interior walls are built in cement block, so modifications are difficult or impossible to make, particularly if they involve knocking through a supporting wall.

Houses in estates or in the centre of even the smallest town must usually conform to a particular style, and there are numerous restrictions as to how a house must be designed: distance from property lines, location of windows (so as not to disturb the neighbours' privacy), maximum height, etc. Houses located near restricted land (agricultural or forest) may be subject to special land use regulations. If you buy an existing house, you may not be permitted to cut down trees, add additional rooms or even build a terrace or garage unless your plans can be justified to the local and regional officials, irrespective of much of the surrounding land you own.

Cost of Housing

Not surprisingly, property prices in the Ile-de-France are the highest in France and form the basis of comparison for prices in the rest of the country. The five French towns and cities with the highest average property prices are all in the Ile-de-France, the average home in Neuilly-sur-Seine (92) costing on average almost ten times as much as in Montluçon in the Auvergne, five times as much as in Toulouse, twice as much than in Cannes and Antibes and over 60 per cent more even than in Paris. (Small consolation is that property taxes in Neuilly are the lowest in France!) The Ile-de-France's lowest average property prices are to be found in Sarcelles (95), where property taxes are also relatively low. The table below gives average prices per m² of older properties in major towns in the Ile-de-France.

Town	Average Price per m² (€)
Paris (75)	2,975
Saint-Germain-en-Laye (78)	3,355
Versailles (78)	3,355
Corbeil-Essonnes (91)	1,100
Evry (91)	1,100
Boulogne-Billancourt (92)	2,440
Neuilly-sur-Seine (92)	5,030
Rueil-Malmaison (92)	3,050
Saint-Denis (93)	1,370
Créteil (94)	1,675
Sarcelles (95)	990

Note, however, that average property prices aren't always a reliable indication of the relative price of similar properties in different towns, as one town may have a preponderance of cheaper or more expensive properties. In the city of Paris you can expect to pay up to €100,000 for a tiny studio. The smallest 'studettes' (estate agent terminology for a studio of 20m² or less) start at around €50,000 and can cost €80,000 to €90,000 in a desirable area or if they include special features (e.g. a lift!). Standard one-bedroom apartments range from 25 to 40m² and cost between €100,000 and €200,000, depending on the location. A standard three-room (i.e. two-bedroom) flat can cost from €200,000 to €300,000. A penthouse near the Place Charles de Gaulle (Etoile) will set you back at least €1 million.

Features and factors that increase prices include proximity to shops and restaurants, nearby access to public transport, a 'quiet' neighbourhood or nearby parks, availability of parking, a terrace, balcony or courtyard, a lift, and location in a building of 'grand standing' (which can mean either a luxury building or one of established reputation).

Most apartments are part of a 'community property' (co-propriété) arrangement, where residents share common costs (e.g. lighting in hallways, maintenance of lifts, gardien's salary, etc.) and building maintenance charges. When it's time to paint or sandblast the exterior of the building, mend the roof or substitute a digi-code system for the gardien who's retiring, you'll be summoned to a meeting to vote on the work, and then be assessed your share of the costs. Co-propriété meetings can become very heated and 'political', and of course the proceedings are governed by an entire body of rules and regulations decreed by the state.

If a Parisian house comes onto the market, you should expect to pay €250,000 to €300,000 for a mere 60 or 70m² in an outer *arrondissement* (e.g. the 18th and 19th). In more desirable districts (e.g. the 12th, 13th and 17th), a house priced under €500,000 is liable to need 'some work' (i.e. be virtually uninhabitable without major renovation).

Outside Paris there's a wide range of apartments and houses on offer, with prices in the €100,000 to €250,000 range depending on factors such as location and ease of access to Paris (by motorway or public transport) as well as size and amount of land, restrictions on building or renovation, and general condition of the property. Prices for properties just outside the city limits are often virtually identical to those in Paris itself, particularly in upmarket parts of Neuilly-sur-Seine, Boulogne-Billancourt and Issy-les-Moulineaux. Generally speaking, the farther away from Paris, the lower the prices, except for homes in and around Versailles, a highly desirable residential area having large homes with spacious grounds. To a lesser extent, residential property in or very close to a town centre with shops and access to public transport and other services is more expensive than property in the countryside, some distance from town services and conveniences.

If you have money to burn, you can always splash out on a *château*, *manoir*, or other *propriété de caractère*, complete with extensive grounds, woods, equestrian facilities or other special features, starting at around €500,000. This sort of property is generally to be found in the outer reaches of the region, although now and then a spectacular *maison de ville* or other unusual residence comes up for sale in the *petit couronne*. There are entire publications dedicated to larger and more elegant residences, such as **Demeures de Charme**, produced by the publishers of **De Particulier à Particulier** (see **Appendix B**).

Land

Close to Paris, not surprisingly, most building land is already built upon. However, many areas on the edges of the Ile-de-France are undergoing something of a construction boom, as land previously held for agriculture is gradually being converted to housing estates. Where large tracts of land have been reclassified for residential use, plots are normally sold to builders, who then package them with a house built to one of their standard designs. The advantage of this arrangement is that the builder has already secured the necessary permits, although you won't obtain an individually designed home. Within a housing estate, there may be several builders offering similar land-plus-building options, all designed to result in final costs around €200,000.

In the western suburbs of Paris, a plot ready to build on (not part of a housing estate) and with access to all mains services costs between €150 and €300 per m². As with housing costs, the further out you go, the lower the costs. In the outer reaches of Essonne or Seine-et-Marne, for example, land prices are between €50 and €100 per m².

If you're considering building your own home, note that houses in the suburbs must conform closely to local standards, which are carefully monitored by town officials. There are strict rules regarding the placement of a house on a plot, as well as restrictions on the positioning of windows, so as not to invade the privacy of neighbours. It's unlikely that you will be able to obtain building permission for a radically styled house that clashes with the general ambiance of your town or village. In fact, in most towns, you're limited to a prescribed choice of colours if you choose to paint the exterior.

If you hire an architect and independent construction company to design and build a house on your own piece of land, expect to pay at least €150,000 over and above the cost of the land. 'Mass-market' construction companies normally offer a range of standard house plans that can be built for around €70,000 or more, depending on the size and the extent of customisation you want. This type of standardised home will meet most communes' requirements (see below), although it may not be the last word in originality.

Rental Accommodation

In Paris itself, monthly rents start at around €500 for a studio apartment (which can be as small as 20m²/200ft²), to which you normally need to add 10 to 20 per cent for charges such as water, rubbish collection and communal costs (e.g. maintenance of common areas or the services of a *gardien*). Even smaller flats (called *studettes* in the adverts) can be found for as 'little' as €350 per month, fully furnished (how much furniture can you fit in a 10m² room?). These tiny units, often converted maid's quarters in older buildings and sometimes with shared bathrooms or toilets, are highly sought-after by students and others on a limited budget.

Three-room apartments (i.e. two bedrooms and a living room) are the standard rental accommodation, prices ranging from around €900 per month to €1,500 or more, depending on the size of the apartment, equipment included and, of course, location. Charges are sometimes included in the quoted price, but you should usually allow an additional €50 to €150 per month if they aren't part of the basic rent. Apartments in older buildings (sometimes centuries old) are highly sought-after and rents can be sky high (as much as €8,000 per month) in buildings of 'character' in desirable districts, such as along the Champs-Elysées (where there are still a few private apartments), in certain neighbourhoods in the 16th and nestled among the designer shops in parts of the 8th.

Outside Paris, you can find both apartments and houses for rent, costs generally declining as you move away from the city. It's possible to rent a three-room apartment with 75m² of living space for less than €1,000 per month in many areas of the *grand couronne*. There's a premium to be paid, of course, for flats that include parking space and those located close to shopping, public transport and other amenities. Monthly rents for detached houses start at around €1,000 for a house of around 70 to 85m² with a small garden (e.g. 300 to 500m²), prices varying according to similar factors as for an apartment (see above).

For an overview of rents throughout the Ile-de-France region, consult the publication *De Particulier à Particulier* (see **Appendix B**), which is also available online in searchable form and in English (🖳 www. pap.fr).

COMMUNICATIONS

Air

Both of France's major international airports are located in the Ile-de-France. Charles de Gaulle (CDG), also known as Roissy-Charles de Gaulle or simply Roissy, after the town in which the airport is located, is 27km (17mi) north of the city, just off the A1 motorway, while Orly, in the town of Antony, is 16km (10mi) south of the city, just off the N186. Between them, they handle flights from almost every part of the world. Around 25 million passengers use Orly every year, and twice as many pass through CDG. Most long-haul flights arrive and depart from CDG, while Orly handles many inter-European flights and all flights of a few smaller airlines not accorded gate space at CDG.

Both airports offer taxi, private coach and public transport connections to Paris, and there's a *TGV* station at CDG, which is handy for those making connections to the farthest corners of France. The B line of the *RER* (see below) runs out to CDG, where there are two stations, one for each of the main terminals. At the southern end of the same line, a special rail connection, called the *Orlyval*, takes you from the Antony stop directly to the airport terminals at Orly. There are frequent shuttle buses between the two airports for those making connections (or for those who live closer to the 'wrong' airport for their travel needs). Most local taxis outside Paris have special rates for passengers going to either of the two airports, and you can often arrange with your local taxi service to pick you up at the airport on your return. For those who drive to the airport, there are long-term car parks at both CDG and Orly, which charge a flat fee per day (currently €10) irrespective of how long you leave your car. Even for short periods, this can be cheaper than taking a taxi from your home to the airport and saves you the inconvenience of having to carry heavy luggage on buses or trains.

Details of all French airports and their services can be found on 🖳 www. aeroport.fr.

Public Transport

Paris is easily accessible *TGV* from Brussels and London. The Eurostar from London Waterloo takes around three hours (the journey time should be reduced with the completion of the high-speed track from London to the tunnel terminal in 2003). Those wishing to escape Paris can reach the furthest parts of France within a few hours (Marseilles is just three hours away). For details of the *TGV* network, see map in **Appendix E**.

Travellers within the Paris area are blessed with one of the best public transport systems in the world. Fares (which are heavily subsidised by the government) are very reasonable, the network is extensive and services are frequent and generally reliable. Those who need to commute into and out of Paris from other parts of the Ile-de-France are particularly well served. Within the city and in much of the surrounding area, there's usually a choice of modes of transport, including the underground (*métro*), the *RER* (*réseau express régional* – an express commuter railway, which runs underground through the centre of Paris), traditional suburban commuter trains, buses and, in a few areas, trams.

Two-zone tickets (covering the city of Paris and all *métro* lines) cost €1.30 each or €9.60 for a book (*carnet*) of ten. There's a variety of reduced fares offered on both single tickets and *carnets* to students, children and senior citizens. There are also day passes covering all travel within certain zones (e.g. the *Mobicarte*), multi-day passes designed for tourists (incorporating discounts for museum and other site admission fees) and weekly and monthly passes for commuters. Employers in the Ile-de-France are required to pay half of the cost of a monthly commuter pass (*carte orange*) for all employees who choose to travel to work by public transport, and the passes allow you unlimited travel within the specified zones even when you aren't commuting. Monthly *cartes oranges* range from €46 for the Paris two-zone area to €128 for an eight-zone pass that will take you beyond the Ile-de-France borders.

The popularity of the Paris area public transport system has its down side, however. Transport workers (*cheminots*) are prone to strike for a day or for a few hours, on one or more lines or routes, whenever the government proposes any change to their cushy pay and benefits packages. (In 1995, the month-long general strike in Paris was a major factor in unseating the Prime Minister, Alain Juppé.) Oddly enough (at least to most foreigners) the *Franciliens* tend to sympathise with the strikers and their cause, despite the massive inconvenience transport strikes cause. Morning news broadcasts include the extent of any strikes called for that day, and traffic reports mention routes to avoid where demonstrations (*manifestations*) are planned.

Public transport between suburbs can be much less efficient, as local bus routes are often designed primarily to feed commuters to the major railway stations or employment centres, mostly at morning and evening rush hour periods. Bus services are sometimes available during the day to nearby shopping centres or between larger cities and towns, but schedules and routes change frequently according to demand. Outside the *petit couronne*, most residents agree that a car is almost a necessity unless you live in the centre of a substantial town or within walking distance of a regional rail or bus route.

Roads

In France, and particularly in the Ile-de-France region, almost all roads lead to Paris (in fact much of the French road system is based on a 'hub and spoke' pattern with roads radiating from major cities and towns). Most of the major motorways in the area fan out from the *boulevard périphérique*, the main ring road that defines the city's perimeter and connects its various 'gateways' (*portes*). Major motorways include the A1 to the north, the A13 to the west, the A4 to the east and the A6 and A10 heading south-east and south-west respectively. All of these are wide, well maintained highways, which become toll roads once you leave the metropolitan region (i.e. roughly at the outer edges of the Ile-de-France) and are the main thoroughfares used by office workers and executives commuting into and out of Paris. Many residents of the outer reaches of the Ile-de-France leave for work as early as 5.30 or 6.30 each morning to beat the rush, as a journey that takes 30 or 45 minutes in light traffic can easily stretch to two hours in 'normal' rush hour congestion (make that three hours if there's a strike on the underground or railways, a serious accident or heavy rain or snow!). In bad weather, at the start and end of a holiday period, and whenever there has been an accident, traffic can soon come to a standstill, with queues stretching for several kilometres.

Perhaps surprisingly, Paris doesn't have the worst road accident record among French towns, although there's a fatal accident every day on average on the *périphérique*. In fact, your chance of being killed or injured on the roads in the capital is no greater than it would be in a provincial town such as Annecy, Bayonne, Bordeaux or Clermont-Ferrand and far less than in many towns on the Mediterranean coast (see page 247). Outside Paris, Neuilly-sur-Seine (92) and Sarcelles (95) are among France's safest driving towns and Hauts-de-Seine has the lowest accident record of any department in France, with a 'mere' 31 deaths per million inhabitants per year. Nevertheless, driving in Paris isn't for the faint-hearted and resembles a continuous ride on the 'dodgems' at the funfair, particularly around the Place de la Concorde and the infamous Etoile! Parking is another problem in the city, where it's considered acceptable to shove other cars out of the way in order to create a space for your own (many residents leave their handbrakes off to minimise damage). To Parisians, a car is a tool rather than an ornament and is treated accordingly!

A number of 'peripheral' roads have been built to link the *villes nouvelles*. The N104 (known as the *Francilienne*) runs east-west across Essonne from near Les Ulis to Evry, where it turns northward to join the A1 close to Roissy-Charles de Gaulle airport. The N186 connects the west side of Paris to the research centre at Saclay and continues to the south of Palaiseau where it turns east, running past Orly airport. The A86 is a ring road that starts north of Paris, running out to Versailles and then forming an east-west corridor connecting Versailles with Créteil to the south. These newer ring roads offer alternative routes to the main *autoroutes* in and out of Paris, although often they can be as congested as the *périphérique*.

By contrast, roads connecting the various suburbs, particularly between departments (road construction is a departmental matter), are generally smaller, not always well maintained and often lined with trees. When departmental roads pass through small towns or villages, they often narrow to one lane in each direction or even less, thanks to the placement of historic buildings and the careless parking habits of local citizens. The French love of fast driving makes town officials keen to place speed bumps and other obstacles (large cement planters are popular) on roads running through residential areas or past schools. Speed traps are fairly common in some areas, although 'helpful' French drivers generally warn oncoming traffic by flashing their headlights!

The French tradition of taking holidays for the whole of July or August means that traffic jams on the first and last weekend of these two months are nothing short of horrendous, with the very worst traffic on the weekend that marks the return of the July vacationers and the departure of those with August holidays. Jams are almost as bad during the school holidays in February or March, when many Parisian families head for the mountain regions of the Alps, the Jura, the Massif Central or the Pyrenees to take advantage of state-sponsored ski schools. Friday weather reports on radio and television generally include traffic forecasts from an agency known as *Bison futé* ('Wily Bison'), which gives predicted levels of traffic congestion using a series of colour codes: green for moderate traffic, yellow for congestion, red for severe congestion and every now and then black for 'you'd be better off walking'.

PLANNED DEVELOPMENTS

Plans to construct a third 'Paris' airport to the north of the city in the town of Soissons, well outside the Ile-de-France region (actually some 120km/75mi from the centre of Paris!) have raised considerable controversy, over both the location and the question of whether a third airport is actually needed in the light of expansion plans for Roissy-Charles de Gaulle. In mid-2002, the newly elected government rejected the plan, which in any case would take at least ten years to realise.

Within Paris, the DeLaNoe administration has announced its intention to improve the city's environment. One of its first moves was to pass a 'pooper scooper' law, aimed at forcing Parisians to pick up after their pampered poodles, who have traditionally left the city's pavements dotted with *crotte*. The success of this scheme (although not total) has prompted the city government to move on to bigger and more ambitious environmental projects, including the closure of some city streets to petrol-powered traffic on Sundays. During the summer of 2002, some 3km (2mi) of the road along the south bank of the Seine was closed to traffic and turned into 'Paris Plage' – complete with deck chairs, sand and (potted) palm trees! These projects have been extremely popular with many Parisians, and it's expected that similar plans will be unveiled, possibly including the mayor's avowed determination to establish permanent pedestrian zones within the city.

Outside the city, in Boulogne-Billancourt (92), permission has recently been granted for the redevelopment of around half of the old Renault works on the Ile Seguin, abandoned by the car company in 1992, where more than 5,000 homes are to be built, half for sale and half for rent at low rates. The development will incorporate schools, nurseries and open spaces, a modern arts centre and a scientific research complex and will be served by its own tramway.

EMPLOYMENT PROSPECTS

With Paris at its heart, the Ile-de-France region is very much the centre of French economic, cultural, and political life. Paris is also the third-largest financial market in Europe, behind London and Frankfurt. Most international companies with a presence in France have their national or regional headquarters in or near Paris. In fact, the Paris region provides over 20 per cent of all employment in France and thus is usually the first destination for most newcomers seeking employment. The office complex at La Défense, on the western edge of Paris, provides employment for 140,000 people and houses the headquarters of many of the largest international companies doing business in France. There are also a number of sites near the *villes nouvelles* outside Paris where large office parks have been or are being developed. Not surprisingly, service businesses account for around 75 per cent of employment in the Ile-de-France region, and industry most of the remaining 25 per cent, with little agriculture.

Paris has the highest percentage of workers among its inhabitants of any major town in France (53 per cent), although its employment profile is atypical, with 24 per cent *cadres* (executives and managers) – almost double the national average. Towns such as Saint-Germain-en-Laye and Versailles (78), Boulogne-Billancourt, Neuilly-sur-Seine and Rueil-Malmaison (92) have the country's highest average earnings and lowest unemployment rate, although they're little more than dormitory towns, as a high proportion of inhabitants work in Paris. On the other hand, Corbeil-Essonnes (91), Saint-

Denis (93) and Sarcelles (95) have some of the country's highest new business failure rates.

Paris is a popular location for expatriate executives, and in many companies transfers or secondments to Paris are eagerly sought-after and generally reserved for upper level managers deserving of 'rewards'. However, French companies are reluctant to take on foreign employees, managers in particular, for a number of reasons, including language problems and culture clashes. Most employers in the Ile-de-France expect job candidates to speak and understand French well enough to function on a day-to-day basis with colleagues, even in offices or companies where English is commonly used. While some executive-level employees in international companies can function with minimal French, it can be almost impossible to find work in the area if you cannot carry on a conversation (or employment interview) in French. Many large employers provide language training as part of their required 'continuing education' – both English lessons for French staff and French lessons for foreign staff.

There's a shortage of experienced high-tech workers in many fields (notably computer-related areas) to the extent that the government has created a special exemption in the work permit process, although the exemption doesn't automatically apply to anyone with computer experience. It helps greatly if you're a qualified engineer (*ingénieur*), as the French have great respect for technical and scientific qualifications.

For English-speakers, jobs are usually limited to bilingual secretaries and administrative or personal assistants. English-language teachers are also in considerable demand, although the best jobs in this field usually require a qualification such as a TEFL or TESOL certificate. In the business world, bookkeepers and accountants are often required to have knowledge or experience of what the French call 'Anglo-Saxon' accounting (*la comptabilité anglo-saxonne*), although you'll also need to have a basic understanding of the peculiarities of the French system. A list of companies in each department can be obtained from the French Chamber of Commerce in London (see **Appendix A**).

Non-EU citizens generally need to have a special skill or experience to justify an employer selecting them in preference to a French or other EU national. (The process for an employer to obtain a work permit for a non-EU foreigner is long and arduous, so most will opt for a local or EU candidate if they can.)

The Paris area offers greater potential than other parts of France for those willing to work 'under the table' in unskilled and unregistered jobs, although competition for the available 'jobs' can be fierce because of the large number of illegal foreigners (*les sans papiers*). Be aware, however, that controls are also more frequent in and around Paris than in other regions and the penalties are severe if you're caught.

FURTHER INFORMATION

Useful Addresses

- American Citizen Services (US Consulate), 2, rue Saint-Florentin, 75001 Paris (☎ 01.43.12.22.22)
- British Consulate, 18bis, rue d'Anjou, 75008 Paris (☎ 01.44.51.31.00)
- British Community Committee, 68, quai Lois Blériot, 75016 Paris (☎ 01.45.25.28.34)
- The British Council, 9, rue Constantine, 75007 Paris (☎ 01.49.55.73.00)
- British Embassy, 35 rue du Faubourg St. Honoré, 75383 Paris cedex 08 (☎ 01.44.51.31.00)
- US Embassy, 2, avenue Gabriel, Paris 75008 (☎ 01.43.12.22.22, 💻 www. amb-usa.fr)

Useful Publications

- **At Home in Paris** (Junior Service League of Paris)
- **Bloom Where You Are Planted** (Women of the American Church) – the handbook accompanying the annual programme at the American Church in Paris (see page 316)
- **FUSAC** (France-USA Connections) – a free fortnightly publication containing advertisements published for and by the Anglophone community in Paris
- **Paris Voice** – a free monthly journal published in English

Useful Websites

Websites for departmental *Conseils généraux* are normally the best starting point for basic information on each department in the region and usually include links to many other services and features in the area. However, there's little or no information available in English:

Conseils Généraux

- 💻 www.essonne.fr (Essonne – due to re-open at the end of 2002)
- 💻 www.hauts-de-seine.net (Hauts-de-Seine – this site is actually a portal linking the *Conseil général* site and many other official sites within the department)
- 💻 www.cg77.net (Seine-et-Marne)

🖥 www.cg93.fr (Seine-Saint-Denis – under construction in mid-2002)

🖥 www.cg94.net (Val-de-Marne)

🖥 www.cg95.fr (Val-d'Oise)

🖥 www.cg78.fr (Yvelines)

Miscellaneous

🖥 www.aaweparis.org (Association of American Wives of Europeans) – a source for *Guide to Education*, *Vital Issues* and other publications

🖥 www.adp.fr (ADP, the Paris airport authority) – includes an English-language section

🖥 www.amb-grandbretagne.fr (British Embassy and Consulate)

🖥 www.amb-usa.fr (US Embassy and Consulate)

🖥 www.britishinfrance.com (British Community Committee)

🖥 www.fusac.fr (FUSAC)

🖥 www.iledefrance.fr (Région Ile-de-France) – includes an English-language section, although not all information is available in English

🖥 www.paris-france.org (City of Paris) – official Paris website, with many links to city government offices and useful addresses and phone numbers; English-language version available

🖥 www.parisvoice.com (Paris Voice journal)

Simone Paissoni

Solicitor

Member of the Association of Franco-British Lawyers

IN FRANCE ~ FOR FRANCE

Tri-lingual English solicitor established in Nice for over seven years provides expert advice and assistance on all aspects of property purchase and ownership in France, with emphasis on inheritance law and taxation. I ensure that you not only feel entirely comfortable and involved in your transaction, but also that your interests are being fully represented and complied with.

Tel: +33 4 93 62 94 95   Fax: +33 4 93 62 95 96
Email: spaissoni@magic.fr
22 avenue Notre Dame, Nice 06000, France

Autlin ~ Burgundy

9.

OTHER AREAS

The preceding chapters have examined the most popular regions of France with foreign homebuyers. The remaining mainland regions, in the centre, east and north-east of the country are summarised below (roughly anti-clockwise), along with Corsica. Although these are less popular with foreign buyers, all have their attractions.

Nord-Pas-de-Calais

The Nord-Pas-de-Calais region in the far north of France contains the departments of Nord (59) and Pas-de Calais (62). It's one of France's smallest regions and shares a border with Belgium, from where it derives its Flemish influence and beer-producing traditions. The region was (along with Picardy – see below) the birthplace of 19th century manufacturing in France and contains the country's only major conurbation outside Paris. Although derided as industrialised, over-populated and one of France's least attractive regions, it has many beautiful areas and is noted for its clean beaches, undulating countryside, secluded woods, scenic river valleys (particularly the Canche and Authie), colourful market gardens, fine golf courses and many pretty, peaceful villages.

The region's main towns include Amiens, Arras, Calais, Cambrai, Dunkerque, Lille (the regional capital), Montreuil, Roubaix, Saint-Omer, Tourcoing and Valenciennes (see **Major Towns & Places of Interest** on page 347). The region's coastline, known as the *Côte opale* ('Opal Coast'), has a number of pleasant resorts, including Berck, Boulogne, Etaples, Hardelot, Le Touquet (the most fashionable) and Wimereux. There wasn't the expected surge in property prices after the opening of the Channel Tunnel, although prices are now rising quite quickly, particularly at the lower end of the market

and there are few small farmhouses left for renovation. Nevertheless, homes in the region remain relatively inexpensive, although coastal areas are naturally more expensive than the interior. As well as frequent ferry services to the UK via Calais and the Channel Tunnel (*Tunnel sous la Manche*), the area has excellent road connections with Paris and the rest of France via the A26 and A25 motorways, and with Belgium and northern Europe, and is also linked with Brussels, London, Paris and the rest of France by *TGV* and Eurostar trains (see map in **Appendix E**).

Picardy (Picardie)

The region of Picardy contains the departments of Aisne (02), Oise (60) and Somme (80) and is one of the least known regions of France. It's mainly famous for its battlegrounds from the first and second world wars, particularly the Somme, although the region is rich in earlier history and architecture. Picardy has a generally flat and uninteresting agricultural landscape, with just a 37km (23mi) coastal strip around the mouth of the river Somme near Abbeville, although this is one of a number of attractive areas, including the valleys of the Aisne, Oise and Somme rivers. The region's main towns include the regional capital Amiens (80), Beauvais, Compiègne, Chantilly, Saint-Omer and Saint-Quentin. Picardy has some of the lowest property prices in France, although it isn't popular with foreign buyers. The Oise department is the most expensive of the three on account of its proximity to Paris. Picardy is crossed by the *TGV* line from Paris to Lille (see map in **Appendix E**) as well as by the A1, A16, A28 and A29 motorways and is within easy reach of England, via the Channel Tunnel or Calais ferries.

Champagne-Ardenne

The Champagne-Ardenne region (often called simply Champagne) contains the departments of Ardennes (08), Aube (10), Marne (51) and Haute-Marne (52). The region is celebrated for the sparkling wine after which it's named, and the production of champagne dominates most aspects of life in the region. Its main towns include Charleville-Mézières, Épernay, Reims, and Troyes (10), the regional capital. Reims is home to the *Grandes Marques* of champagne, such as Veuve Cliquot and Charles Heidsieck, although Épernay is the centre of champagne production. Reims cathedral is one of the most beautiful in France as well as historically the most important, being where the country's kings were crowned.

The region is highly cultivated and, although not one of France's most attractive areas, it's noted for its rolling landscape, immense forests (Verzy forest contains beech trees that are over 1,000 years old), deep gorges and vast rivers. Champagne-Ardenne also contains one of Europe's largest artificial lakes, the Lac du Der-Chantecoq near Saint-Dizier. Ardennes (which shares a border with Belgium) is the region's most picturesque department and its rolling, wooded landscape is dotted with ramparts, fortified castles and farmhouses. The Champagne-Ardenne region isn't popular with foreign

homebuyers, despite property being relatively inexpensive, particularly in Ardennes. However, it becomes more expensive the nearer you get to Brussels in the north and Paris in the west (the western Aube is the most expensive area). The area has good road connections and is served by the A4 and A26 motorways.

Lorraine

Lorraine (or Lorraine-Vosges as it's also called) is situated in the north-eastern corner of France bordering Germany, Belgium and Luxembourg, and contains the departments of Meuse (55), Meurthe-et-Moselle (54), Moselle (57) and Vosges (88). Like Alsace (see below), Lorraine has been fought over for centuries by France and Germany, between whom it has frequently swapped ownership (the region retains a strong Germanic influence). Although mainly an industrial area, Lorraine is largely unspoiled and is popular with nature lovers and hikers. It's noted for its meandering rivers, rolling hills, wooded valleys, and delightful medieval towns and villages. Lorraine is famous for its Moselle wines and *quiche*, but regional cuisine also includes mouthwatering tarts, *clafoutis*, soufflés and gratins, and the local beer is highly regarded. Glass and crystal making are ancient traditions. Lorraine's main towns include Nancy (54), the regional capital, and Metz, and there's a wealth of picturesque villages, including Bussang, Ferrette, Le Hohwald, Saint-Amerin and Schirmeck, plus resort towns such as Masevaux and Plimbières-les-Bains. Lorraine has few foreign residents and is largely ignored by tourists and second homebuyers despite the relatively low cost of living and reasonable property prices. The region has good road access via the A4 and A31 motorways.

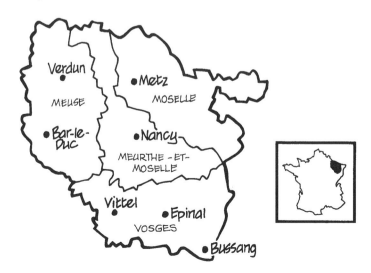

Alsace

Alsace is one of France's smallest regions containing just two departments: Bas-Rhin (67) and Haut-Rhin (68) – Lower and Upper Rhine. It's located in the extreme east of France bordering Germany, to which it has belonged at various times in its colourful history. Not surprisingly it has a Germanic feel, which is reflected in its architecture, cuisine, dress, dialects (German is still widely spoken), names and people (called Alsatians). Sandwiched between the Vosges mountains and the Rhine, Alsace is gloriously scenic and largely unspoiled, with delightful hills (cross-country skiing is a popular winter sport), dense forests, rich farmland and pretty vineyards. It's noted for its many picturesque villages, particularly on the Wine Road (*Route du Vin*) stretching from Marlenheim west of Strasbourg down to Thann beyond Mulhouse. Alsace is famous for its beer (such as Kronenbourg) and white wines. Perhaps surprisingly, Alsace has more Michelin restaurant stars than any other region of France!

The regional capital is Strasbourg (67), home of the European Parliament, the European Court and the European Commission on Human Rights. Other notable towns include Colmar and Mulhouse, a prominent industrial city. Property prices are higher than the average for France and there are few bargains to be found. Rundown or derelict rural properties for sale are rare in Alsace, where (unlike many other regions) there hasn't been a mass exodus from the farms and countryside. The region has excellent road connections with Paris, the south of France, Germany and Switzerland.

Franche-Comté

Franche-Comté (literally 'free country') contains the departments of Doubs (25), Jura (39), Haute-Saône (70) and the Territoire-de-Belfort (90). It's a little-known region in eastern France bordering Switzerland, with which it shares much of its architecture, cuisine and culture. It's known for cheeses such as Comté and Morbier, Jura wines, and Morteau and Montbéliard sausages. Franche-Comté is acclaimed for its beautiful, unspoiled scenery (more Swiss in appearance than French) and recalls a fairy-tale land where time has almost stood still. It's reputed to be the greenest region in France. Sandwiched between the Vosges range to the north and the Jura mountains to the south, the landscape consists of rolling cultivated fields, dense pine forests and rampart-like mountains. Although not as majestic as the Alps, the Jura mountains are more accessible and are a Mecca for nature lovers and winter sports fans. The Doubs and Loue valleys (noted for their timbered houses perched on stilts in the river) and the high valley of Ain are popular areas. The region's main towns include Belfort and Besançon (25), the regional capital on the river Doubs.

Franche-Comté is largely ignored by foreign tourists and homebuyers, although it has many attractions. Property prices are higher than the French average, although bargains can be found, particularly if you're seeking a winter holiday home. Besançon is served by the A36 motorway and has good connections with the centre and south of France, Germany and Switzerland via *TGV* (see map in **Appendix E**).

Centre-Val-de-Loire

The central region of France contains the departments of Cher (18), Eure-et-Loir (28), Indre (36), Indre-et-Loire (37), Loir-et-Cher (41) and Loiret (45), the Loire and its tributary, the Loir, giving their names to several of the departments. The Loire is France's longest river (1,020km/628mi), with its source in the Vivarais mountains (south of Saint-Etienne) and its outlet at Saint-Nazaire in the Pays de la Loire (see **Chapter 3**). It's considered to be the dividing line between the colder regions of northern France and the warmer south, although the change is gradual. The Loire valley is noted for its natural beauty and fertility, consisting of pleasant undulating woodland, lakes, rivers, orchards, and fields of maize and sunflowers (it's the market garden of France), as well as for its *châteaux*, widely considered to be among the most beautiful in the world. The principal *châteaux* are in Loir-et-Cher (Chambord, Chaumont and Chéverny) and neighbouring Indre-et-Loire (Azay-le-Rideau, Chenonceaux and Villandry, with its magnificent gardens).

The region's main towns include Blois, Bourges, Chartres, Orléans and Tours (37), the regional capital. In fact, these last two towns were recently rated the second and third-best places to live in France by *Le Point* magazine, although they rate rather lower according to the criteria selected by us (see

Appendix F). One of its most attractive areas is the old province of Berry (comprising the departments of Cher and Indre), whose ancient capital was the majestic city of Bourges.

The Loire valley is unspoiled by industry, mass tourism or a surfeit of holiday homes, although it's quite popular with retirees and second homeowners. Property prices vary considerably depending on the proximity to major towns, although they're generally well above the French average and bargains are rare. The region has excellent road connections via the A10, A11 and A71 motorways, which converge on Paris, as well as via the *TGV* from Paris to Poitiers and Bordeaux (see map in **Appendix E**).

Burgundy (Bourgogne)

Burgundy contains the departments of Côte-d'Or (21), Nièvre (58), Saône-et-Loire (71) and Yonne (89). The region has few industries, which means it's almost totally unspoiled and one of France's most beautiful and fertile areas (it has been dubbed the 'rural soul' of France). It's a timeless land where little has changed over the centuries and a haven of peace and serenity (particularly the Parc du Morvan at its heart). The name Burgundy is synonymous with magnificent wines such as Nuits-Saint-Georges, Meursault, Beaune, Puligny-Montrachet, Gevrey-Chambertin and Pouilly-Fuissé, grown on the 60km (37mi) Côte d'Or hillside, as well as fine cuisine, including *boeuf bourgignon* (made with Charollais beef), *coq au vin* (with Bresse chicken), Morvan ham

and snails, generally served with rich sauces, as well as *pain d'épices* ('spicy' bread) and *kir* (white wine with a dash of blackcurrant liqueur).

The region is also renowned for its many canals and canal boats, and has some 1,200km (750mi) of navigable waterways, including the Burgundy Canal and the rivers Saône and Yonne. Burgundy has a rich and colourful history (it was an independent kingdom for some 600 years), celebrated in numerous colourful festivals and pageants, and a wealth of Romanesque churches, cathedrals, medieval villages and historic towns. Its most important towns include Autun, Auxerre, Beaune, Chalon-sur-Saône, Dijon (21), famous for its mustard and the regional capital (and recently rated the fifth-best place to live in France by *Le Point* magazine – see **Appendix F**), Fontenay, Mâcon, Nevers, Paray-le-Monial and Vézelay.

Somewhat surprisingly, Burgundy isn't popular with foreign property buyers, perhaps because of its relative isolation, and there are few holiday and retirement homes there. It rarely features in international property magazines and, although the region has a wealth of beautiful *châteaux*, manor houses and watermills, these (and vineyards) are rarely on the market. Prices tend to be higher than average for France, but inexpensive, habitable village houses and farmhouses in need of restoration can be found in most areas. Burgundy is located just 100km (around 65mi) south of Paris and 80km (50mi) north of Lyons, and has excellent connections with both the north and south of France via the A6 and A31 motorways and the *TGV* (see map in **Appendix E**).

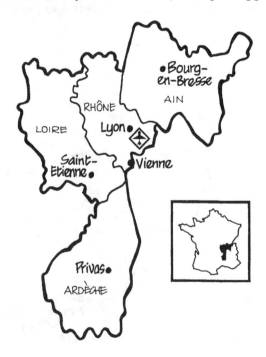

Rhône

The Rhône region is part of the larger Rhône-Alpes in the south-east of France. For details of the Alpine departments of Hautes-Alpes (05), Drôme (26), Isère (38), Savoie (73) and Haute-Savoie (74), see **Chapter 7**. The Rhône region contains the departments of Ain (01), Ardèche (07), Loire (42) and Rhône (69). Although largely unspoiled by development, the Rhône valley is one of France's major industrial regions. Lyons (69), which is the regional capital and France's second-largest city (the French spell it *Lyon*) as well as its gastronomic capital, has a beautiful medieval quarter. The Rhône river (whose source is high in the Swiss Alps) is a vital artery for river, road and rail traffic between the north and south of France.

The Rhône-Alpes is one of France's most scenic and beautiful regions with dense forests, lush pasture land, fast-flowing rivers, huge lakes, deep gorges and spectacular mountains, although these are mostly in the eastern part of the region (see **Chapter 7**). It's a land made for sports fans and those with a love of the outdoors, with superb summer (e.g. climbing, hiking, biking, canoeing and white-water rafting) and winter sports facilities, including some of the best skiing in the world in the Alps. Apart from Lyons, Rhône's major towns include Bourg-en-Bresse, Privas and Saint-Etienne.

The price of property in the Rhône-Alpes region as a whole is well above the average, although the most expensive areas are mostly in the Alps. Ardèche with its spectacular gorge is increasingly popular with foreign buyers and is consequently becoming more expensive. Like Franche-Comté, Rhône-Alpes is popular with the Swiss, many of whom live in the region and commute to their workplaces in Geneva and other Swiss cities. The region is noted for its extremes of temperature and is usually freezing in winter and hot in summer, and most pleasant in spring and autumn. The Rhône-Alpes has excellent road, rail and air connections and Lyons is just two hours from Paris by *TGV* (see map in **Appendix E**).

Corsica (Corse)

Containing the departments of Corse-du-Sud (2A) and Haute-Corse (2B), the island of Corsica covers an area of 8,721km^2 (3,367mi^2) with a coastline of around 1,000km (620mi). It's situated 160km (99mi) from France and 80km (50mi) from Italy, with which it has strong historical ties, having been an Italian possession until 1768, when France purchased it from the Genoese. Corsica is quite different from mainland France, not only in its geography but in its people, culture and customs. (Corsican men are reputed to be among the most chauvinistic in France – which is saying something!) The island even has its own language, Corsican, spoken regularly by around 60 per cent of the people, although it has no official status and French is also universally spoken and understood. There's a strong local identity (and independence movement) and Corsica enjoys a greater degree of autonomy than the mainland regions.

Corsica is sparsely populated with huge areas devoid of human life and has a stark, primitive beauty with superb beaches and picturesque hillside villages; it's considered by some to be the most beautiful Mediterranean island (it's known as the *Ile de Beauté*) and is a popular holiday destination (particularly the western coast). Mountains cover most of its surface, including some 200 peaks over 2,000m (6,500ft), the highest reaching over 2,700m (9,000ft) so that skiing is possible in the winter. Around half the island is covered in vegetation, including beech, chestnut and pine forests and the ubiquitous *maquis*, a dense growth of aromatic shrubs (heather and myrtle) and dark holm oak. Corsica also boasts some of Europe's most beautiful Romanesque art.

Tourism is the island's main industry (many French mainlanders holiday here), although it remains almost completely unspoiled and a haven for outdoor lovers (hikers and bikers) and those seeking peace and serenity. Not surprisingly, Corsica has a slow pace of life, which is epitomised by its ancient and spectacular mountain railway. The main towns include Ajaccio (the regional capital and birthplace of Napoleon), Bastia, Bonifacio, Calvi and Porto-Vecchio, all situated on the coast. It's popular with holiday homeowners, particularly Italians, and prices have risen in recent years following increased interest. It has, however, avoided the devastation wrought in many other Mediterranean islands by high-rise developments; buildings are restricted to two storeys and construction is forbidden close to beaches. Corsica has good air connections with France and most other European countries. Sardinia is only a short boat ride away.

ADVANTAGES & DISADVANTAGES

Nord-Pas-de-Calais

Frequent ferry services from Calais and Dunkerque and the Channel Tunnel make the region convenient for those living in south-east England. The *TGV* also provides a rapid link to Paris and Brussels. The region boasts sandy beaches with nearby golf courses, but inland the flat landscape is less inspiring. The climate is among the worst in France, not unlike that of the UK or Belgium, and property prices aren't among the cheapest of the ten regions considered in this chapter, although older houses are relatively inexpensive (see **Cost of Housing** on page 358). The region also suffers high unemployment and a high rate of new business failure.

Picardy

Along with Franche-Comté and Lorraine, Picardy is one of the cheapest regions in France for property. Both England in one direction and Paris in the other are accessible from most parts of the region, but it has little coastline and a rather featureless landscape. The climate is little better than in Nord-Pas-de-Calais.

Champagne-Ardenne

Conveniently placed for visiting Paris (and Disneyland), Champagne-Ardenne nevertheless offers reasonably priced property, but it suffers extremely cold winters and a large part of the region consists of monotonous chalk plains.

Lorraine

Lorraine is one of the cheapest regions in France, both for property and in terms of the cost of living, although the area around Metz is more expensive than the Nancy area. Like Alsace, it has many picturesque villages, but the weather is subject to sudden changes and extremes of temperature.

Alsace

Alsace boasts colourful towns and villages in the Germanic style and is one of the leading regions in France for economic growth. It enjoys (or suffers, depending on your point of view) hot summers and cold winters and is one of France's great wine regions. However, it's a long way from the sea and has poor air connections and, after Corsica, is the most expensive of the ten regions considered here for property, although the Mulhouse area is considerably cheaper than Colmar and Strasbourg. The crime rate is particularly high in and around Strasbourg, where vehicle burning has become a traditional part of the New Year 'festivities', and the city is liable to flooding.

Franche-Comté

Franche-Comté is one of the cheapest areas in France for property. It has attractive forest and mountain scenery and there is some skiing in the Vosges and Jura (the northern Alps aren't far away either). It's generally quiet, which may be an advantage or a disadvantage, and is a long way from the sea, although it has around 80 lakes, where there's a variety of watersports.

Burgundy

One of the great wine regions of France, Burgundy is predominantly rural and offers reasonably priced property. Rail and road connections are good and air links are improving (thanks to Buzz). Northern parts of the area are close to Paris and southern parts within reach of the Alps. It's widely tipped to be the most 'up-and-coming' region of France, although it may be rather unassuming for some.

Centre-Val-de-Loire

Architecturally one of the most interesting regions in France, with Chartres cathedral and the greatest of the Loire *châteaux*, Centre-Val-de-Loire also enjoys rapid *TGV* and motorway access from Paris and low-cost flights from London. Property is reasonably priced, except in the northern departments adjoining the Ile-de-France, and the climate is mild. Like Burgundy, it isn't a major economic centre but has few disadvantages unless you want hot summers or quick access to the coast.

Rhône

Strategically placed, just two hours from Paris and one hour from the Mediterranean coast and the northern Alps, Lyons is also a good place to find work, although the area may be too industrial for some tastes. The region is renowned for its food and includes Ardèche with its fabulous gorges and grottos. However, Lyons is relatively expensive and subject to horrendous traffic jams at holiday periods. The climate is mixed, although for some this will be an advantage.

Corsica

Corsica's main advantages are its great natural beauty, particularly inland, and superb climate. It's ideal for those seeking seclusion, but property is expensive, especially small apartments near the sea, and the island is relatively inaccessible (you may need to book your ferry passage well in advance). Coastal areas are crowded in summer and there are few employment opportunities. You may find it difficult to be accepted by Corsicans, who are renowned for their insularity, and the political future of Corsica is uncertain. A number of bombings are carried out each year by various Corsican terrorist groups; most of these are aimed at French government buildings, but non-Corsican property owners are also occasionally targeted, although there are rarely fatalities.

MAJOR TOWNS & PLACES OF INTEREST

Nord-Pas-de-Calais

Dunkerque (59): pop. 70,000; the third-largest commercial shipping port in France; has France's largest mining museum; ferries to Dover; near the Belgian border.

Lille (59): pop. 190,000 (excluding suburbs); second-largest city in northern France after Paris and the regional capital; a stylish, prosperous and vibrant city, with a unique cultural identity and no fewer than five universities (mainly business and engineering faculties); has a flamboyant old town and a revitalised city centre with new *TGV* station and other major developments; the industrial and commercial hub of region, with excellent road and rail connections with the rest of France and the UK, Belgium and Holland.

Arras (62): pop. 40,000 (80,000 including suburbs); the capital of Pas-de-Calais; historic and attractive town rich in museums, especially of fine arts.

Boulogne-sur-Mer (62): pop. 50,000; France's largest fishing port; national sealife centre (Nausicaa) with 800,000 visitors annually; 13th century ramparts around the upper town.

Saint-Omer (62): Attractive market town surrounded by the Audomarois Nature Reserve.

Le Touquet-Paris-Plage (62): pop. 5,000; an upmarket seaside resort (with a sandy beach over 1.5km/1mi long and a beautiful promenade). Horse racecourse and several golf courses nearby; attractive nearby fishing village of Etaples; high property prices.

Picardy

Laon (02): pop. 27,000; the capital of Aisne.

Saint-Quentin (02): pop. 59,000; a historic city on the Somme river with its 13th century Collégiale Saint Quentin cathedral; originally a Roman settlement and later an important battlefield of the first world war.

Beauvais (60): pop. 60,000; the capital of Oise; impressive, unfinished cathedral; airport.

Amiens (80): pop. 135,000; the capital of Somme; a university town, largely re-built after the second world war but with one of the finest Gothic cathedrals in France and picturesque Saint-Leu area.

Champagne-Ardenne

Charleville-Mézières (08): pop. 55,000; the capital of Ardennes.

Troyes (10): pop. 61,000; the capital of Aube; a university town (attached to the University of Reims); hosiery and mechanical industry; renowned for its *andouillette* (pig intestine) sausages.

Châlons-en-Champagne (51): pop. 47,000; the capital of Marne; a cathedral city.

Epernay (51): pop. 26,000 (40,000 including suburbs); Champagne Museum and the cellars (covering 14ha/35 acres) of Moët et Chandon among others.

Hautvilliers (51): pop. 900; with Benedictine Abbey; the place where Pierre Pérignon, a Benedictine monk in the 17th century, discovered how to put a fizz into the local wine, thus creating champagne.

Reims (51): pop. 190,000 (290,000 including suburbs); with a technological university and College of Art and Design; the 12th century cathedral is a fine example of Gothic architecture.

Chaumont (52): pop. 26,000; the capital of Haute-Marne; has a superb 19th century viaduct, 600m (2,000ft) long and over 50m (170ft) high.

Other: Extravagant basilica at l'Epine and two regional parks, Montagne de Reims and Forêt d'Orient.

Lorraine

Nancy (54): pop. 104,000; the capital of Meurthe-et-Moselle and former seat of the Dukes of Lorraine; fine 17th century architecture, especially in Place Stanislas, a World Heritage site.

Bar-le-Duc (55): pop. 17,000; the capital of Meuse; an industrial town (textiles, printing, machine tools, jam making, and food-research laboratories).

Metz (57): pop. 123,000; the capital of Moselle with a Gothic cathedral with the world's largest stained-glass windows, designed by Chagall; a university town and the largest river port in France; local industry includes Peugeot/Citroën car factories.

Verdun (55): pop. 21,000; war museum and nearby first world war battle fields; light industry.

Bussang (88): pop. 1,800; ski resort (one of the closest to Paris) and source of Moselle river.

Domrémy-la-Pucelle (88): pop. 170 and over 50,000 visitors a year; birthplace of Joan of Arc.

Epinal (88): pop. 36,000; the capital of Vosges; some light and heavy (metallurgy) industry.

Plombières-les-Bains (88): pop. 2,000; spa town.

Vittel (88): pop. 6,200; spa town with its renowned natural spring water.

Alsace

Strasbourg (67): pop. 270,000; the capital of Bas-Rhin and seat of the European Parliament; picturesque, animated, town centre with Germanic allure; a cathedral and university town and the second-largest river port in France (on the Ill and Rhine rivers); site of France's first urban 'eco-district'.

Colmar (68): pop. 67,000; the capital of Haut-Rhin; an attractive town with multi-coloured houses and an extremely picturesque old town and 'Venetian area' traversed by the Lauch river; an important artistic and cultural centre.

Mulhouse (68): pop. 110,00 (220,000 including suburbs); much more industrial than Colmar with a Peugeot car factory and national car and railway museums.

Riquewihr (68): pop. 1,200; features ancient houses and medieval walls and nearby Château de Haut-Koënigsburg (alt. 755m/2,475ft) with magnificent views.

Franche-Comté

Besançon (25): pop. 118,000; the capital of Doubs and birthplace of Victor Hugo; university town and the first official 'green' town in France; beautiful citadelle; Swiss influence evident in watch-making industry.

Lons-le-Saunier (39): pop. 19,000; the capital of Jura; a spa town with some industry, including the manufacture of spectacles. Ski resorts at Les Rousses (alt. 1,120m/3,675ft) dominated by La Dole mountain near the Swiss border and Lamoura (alt. 1,100m/3,610ft). Regional conservation area of Haut-Jura 146,000ha (360,000 acres), between 1,000 and 1,600m alt. (3,280 and 5,250ft).

Vesoul (70): pop. 18,000; the capital of Haute-Saône; Peugeot car factory. Ski resorts at La Planche-des-Belles-Filles (alt. 1,148m/3,765ft) and Belfahy (alt. 950m/3,115ft).

Belfort (90): pop. 50,000; the capital of Territoire-de-Belfort; an industrial town producing car components, railway equipment, electronic and computer goods.

Other: Le Corcusier's chapel at Ronchamp and Royal Saltworks at Arc-et-Senans.

Burgundy

Beaune (21): pop. 21,000; centre of the famous wine region with History of Wine Museum and splendid Hôtel-Dieu (15th century hospital).

Dijon (21): pop. 150,000; the capital of Côte-d'Or; the industrial centre of a mainly rural region; also a university and cathedral town and a major crossing point for motorway and rail routes.

Nevers (58): pop. 41,000; the capital of Nièvres.

Autun (71): pop. 17,000; Roman remains and a remarkable 12th century cathedral.

Mâcon (71): pop. 35,000; the capital of Saône-et-Loire; a cathedral town on banks of the Saône river and also a wine centre.

Chalon-sur-Saône (71): pop. 50,000; also noted for its wines.

Auxerre (89): pop. 38,000; the capital of Yonne.

Avallon (89): pop. 8,000; medieval, fortified town with panoramic view of the Cousin valley.

Vézelay (89): pop. 500; renowned medieval village of pilgrimage with 12th century basilica.

Centre-Val-de-Loire

Bourges (18): pop. 75,000; the capital of Cher, with a splendid Gothic cathedral, medieval houses and cobbled streets in the centre; industries include armaments.

Chartres (28): pop. 40,000; the capital of Eure-et-Loir; magnificent Gothic cathedral with unique stained-glass windows, widely considered to be the most beautiful in Europe and one of Christianity's great shrines; industries include cosmetics, electronics and mechanical engineering.

Châteauroux (36): pop. 50,000; the capital of Indre; industries include biscuit manufacture, ceramics and textiles.

Tours (37): pop. 133,000 (reputed to have the purest accent in France); the capital of Indre-et-Loire; a lively town with a Gothic cathedral; industries include aeronautics, electronics, mechanical and pharmaceutical products; nearby Loire *châteaux*, including Chenonceau and Villandry.

Blois (41): pop. 50,000; the capital of Loir-et-Cher; dominated by the castle and with its own and nearby *châteaux*, including Chambord and Cheverny; similar industries to Tours.

Orléans (45): pop. 114,000; the capital of Loiret; a lively cathedral town saved by Joan of Arc but heavily bombed in the second world war and largely rebuilt; various industries and nearby châteaux.

Rhône

Bourg-en-Bresse (01): pop. 41,000; the capital of Ain; some heavy industry (metallurgy, mechanical and lorry manufacture). Cross-country skiing at Brénod (alt. 1,100m/3,610ft), Giron (alt. 1,078m/3,535ft), Hotonnes (alt. 1,350m/4,430ft), Le Poizat (alt. 1,300m/4,265ft) and Mijoux-la-Faucille-Lélex (alt. 1,320m/4,330ft).

Privas (07): pop. 9,000; the capital of Ardèche, known for its *marrons glacés* (candied chestnuts); industries include textiles and weighing machine equipment. The Ardèche river valley is a natural conservation area offering superb canoeing. Ski resorts at Areilladou (alt. 1,448m/4,750ft), Borée (alt. 1,132m/3,710ft), Croix-de-Bauzon (alt. 1,511m/4,955ft) and Sainte-Eulalie (alt. 1,230m/4,035ft).

Saint-Etienne (42): pop. 183,000; the capital of Loire and the second-largest town in the area after Lyons, its great rival – not least in football; a university town (engineering and business faculties) and former mining area with various heavy and light industries. Some skiing at Le Bessat (alt. 1,170m/3,840ft) and Chalmazel (alt. 1,400m/4,590ft).

Charbonnières-les-Bains (69): pop. 4,000; a charming spa town.

Lyons (69): pop. around 1 million; the capital of Rhône and regional capital on the Saône and Rhône rivers; a university and cathedral city and one of the great gastronomic centres of France; has a huge modern shopping centre and pedestrian area; important electronic, chemical and mechanical industries and an important exhibition centre.

Corsica

Ajaccio (2A): pop. 53,000; the capital of Corse-du-Sud, a tourist centre and Napoleon's birthplace (almost every other bar is called Le Bonaparte); a cathedral town with an elegant crescent-shaped, palm-tree lined seafront.

Bonifacio (2A): pop. 2,500; a fishing port set on spectacular chalk cliffs facing Sardinia; the southernmost tip of Corsica.

Portovecchio (2A): pop. 10,000; a rare inlet on the comparatively straight eastern coastline.

Propriano (2A): pop. 3,000, one of several attractive fishing ports on the jagged west coast of Corsica, which has some beautiful creeks and inlets.

Bastia (2B): pop. 38,000; the capital of Haute-Corse; less exotic and more business-like than Ajaccio.

Note that population figures swell enormously in peak tourist season.

POPULATION

Approximate regional and departmental population figures, including numbers of foreign nationals with residence permits are shown below. For populations of towns, see **Major Towns & Places of Interest** above.

Nord-Pas-de-Calais

4 million, of which 45,500 Moroccans, 40,000 Algerians, 18,000 Portuguese, 15,500 Italians and 1,800 Britons. Aslo popular with Belgians and Dutch. The region's population is growing at well below the national average rate.

Nord (59): 2.6 million, of which 36,000 Moroccans, 35,000 Algerians, 16,500 Portuguese, 12,500 Italians and 940 Britons.

Pas-de-Calais (62): 1.4 million, of which 9,500 Moroccans, 5,000 Algerians, 3,000 Italians, 1,500 Portuguese and 870 Britons.

Picardy

1.9 million, of which 18,500 Portuguese, 18,000 Moroccans, 9,000 Algerians and 1,100 Britons. The region's population is growing at just below the national average rate.

Aisne (02): 550,000, of which 4,000 Portuguese, 3,500 Moroccans, 1,500 Algerians, 1,000 Spaniards, 650 Turks and 100 Britons.

Oise (60): 800,000, of which 11,500 Portuguese, 11,000 Moroccans, 6,000 Algerians, 3,000 from other African countries and 750 Britons.

Somme (80): 550,000, of which 3,500 Moroccans, 3,000 Portuguese, 1,500 Algerians, 1,200 from other African countries and 250 Britons.

Champagne-Ardenne

1.4 million, of which 15,000 Algerians, 14,000 Portuguese, 12,000 Moroccans and 375 Britons. The region is one of only three in France where the population is in decline (the others being the Auvergne and Limousin).

Ardennes (08): 300,000, of which 7,000 Algerians, 1,850 Italians, 1,850 Moroccans, 1,800 Portuguese and 45 Britons.

Aube (10): 300,000, of which 4,500 Portuguese, 4,000 Moroccans, 2,000 Algerians, 1,050 Spaniards, 1,000 Vietnamese, 900 Italians and 80 Britons.

Haute-Marne (52): 200,000, of which 1,800 Algerians, 1,200 Turks, 1,150 Portuguese, 1,150 Moroccans and 40 Britons.

Marne (51): 600,000, of which 6,550 Portuguese, 5,000 Moroccans, 4,200 Algerians, 1,500 from other African countries and 200 Britons.

Lorraine

2.3 million, of which 34,500 Italians, 29,000 Algerians, 22,000 Moroccans and 700 Britons. The region's population is virtually stagnant.

Meurthe-et-Moselle (54): 720,000, of which 9,000 Algerians, 8,500 Italians, 7,000 Moroccans, 6,000 Portuguese and 300 Britons.

Meuse (55): 195,000, of which 1,200 Turks, 1,000 Italians, 950 Portuguese, 900 Moroccans and 40 Britons.

Moselle (57): 1 million, of which 24,000 Italians, 18,500 Algerians, 10,900 Moroccans, 10,500 Turks and 280 Britons.

Vosges (88): 385,000, of which 5,000 Portuguese, 3,500 Turks, 3,200 Moroccans, 1,500 Algerians, 1,000 Italians and 100 Britons.

Alsace

1.7 million, of which 27,000 Turks, 19,000 Moroccans, 17,000 Algerians and 1,460 Britons. The region has the second-fastest growing population in France (after Languedoc-Roussillon – see **Chapter 6**).

Bas-Rhin (67): 1 million, of which 17,200 Turks, 11,400 Moroccans, 7,200 Portuguese, 5,700 Algerians and 930 Britons.

Haut-Rhin (68): 650,000, of which 9,800 Turks, 7,600 Moroccans, 11,300 Algerians and 530 Britons.

Franche-Comté

1.15 million, of which 11,400 Moroccans, 9,800 Turks, 8,700 Algerians, 7,600 Portuguese and 420 Britons. The region's population is growing at below the national average rate.

Doubs (25): 500,000, of which 5,000 Moroccans, 4,800 Algerians, 4,000 Turks, 3,000 Portuguese, 2,000 Spaniards and 170 Britons.

Jura (39): 250,000, of which 3,000 Turks, 2,500 Moroccans, 2,400 Portuguese, 1,200 Algerians, 600 Italians and 90 Britons.

Haute-Saône (70): 230,000, of which 2,800 Moroccans, 1,500 Portuguese, 1,000 Turks, 700 Algerians and 60 Britons.

Territoire-de-Belfort (90): 140,000, of which 2,000 Algerians, 1,800 Turks, 1,100 Moroccans, 600 Italians, 600 Portuguese and 100 Britons.

Burgundy

1.62 million, of which 22,000 Portuguese, 19,000 Moroccans, 9,550 Algerians and 900 Britons. The region's population is stagnant.

Côte-d-Or (21): 510,000, of which 8,300 Moroccans, 6,300 Portuguese, 3,500 Algerians, 2,000 Italians and 340 Britons.

Nièvre (58): 225,000, of which 2,100 Portuguese, 1,000 Moroccans, 400 Spaniards, 300 Turks and 80 Britons.

Saône-et-Loire (71): 550,000, of which 8,300 Portuguese, 5,100 Algerians, 3,800 Italians, 3,700 Moroccans and 270 Britons.

Yonne (89): 335,000, of which 6,000 Moroccans, 5,300 Portuguese, 1,600 Turks, 950 Algerians and 210 Britons.

Centre-Val-de-Loire

2.45 million, of which 43,000 Portuguese, 28,000 Moroccans, 12,000 Algerians, 12,000 Turks, 5,500 Spaniards, 3,200 Tunisians and 1,300 Britons. The region's population is growing at just below the national average rate.

Cher (18): 315,000, of which 4,800 Portuguese, 2,300 Moroccans, 2,000 Algerians, 950 Turks and 130 Britons.

Eure-et-Loir (28): 410,000, of which 8,200 Moroccans, 6,800 Portuguese, 2,500 Algerians, 2,500 Turks and 200 Britons.

Indre (36): 235,000, of which 1,100 Portuguese, 1,100 Moroccans, 500 Algerians and 110 Britons.

Indre-et-Loire (37): 555,000, of which 9,100 Portuguese, 3,600 Algerians, 2,800 Moroccans, 750 Spaniards and 420 Britons.

Loir-et-Cher (41): 315,000, of which 5,800 Portuguese, 2,700 Turks, 2,600 Moroccans, 700 Spaniards and 150 Britons.

Loiret (45): 620,000, of which 15,400 Portuguese, 11,000 Moroccans, 5,000 Turks, 3,200 Algerians and 280 Britons.

Rhône

The population region of Rhône-Alpes (including the departments discussed in **Chapter 7**) is growing at well above the national average rate.

Ain (01): 515,000, of which 8,000 Moroccans, 6,800 Portuguese, 6,500 Turks, 4,200 Algerians and 1,300 Britons.

Ardèche (07): 285,000, of which 2,000 Moroccans, 1,800 Algerians, 1,600 Portuguese, 1,000 Spaniards and 200 Britons.

Loire (42): 730,000, of which 16,500 Algerians, 8,500 Moroccans, 7,500 Portuguese, 6,000 Italians and 230 Britons.

Rhône (69): 1.6 million, of which 45,000 Algerians, 20,000 Portuguese, 20,000 Tunisians, 11,000 Italians and 1,500 Britons.

Corsica

260,000, of which 13,000 Moroccans, 3,000 Italians, 3,000 Portuguese, 2,300 Tunisians and 125 Britons. The region's population is growing at just above the national average rate, although the population of Ajaccio is declining faster than that of any other major town in France.

Corse-du-Sud (2A): 120,000, of which 5,900 Moroccans, 1,900 Portuguese, 1,800 Italians, 1,500 Tunisians and 65 Britons.

Haute-Corse (2B): 140,000, of which 7,100 Moroccans, 1,200 Italians, 1,100 Portuguese, 800 Tunisians and 60 Britons.

CLIMATE

Nord-Pas-de-Calais

The region experiences no extremes of temperature on account of the influence of the warm Gulf Stream flowing up the Channel from the North Atlantic, but the weather is changeable and often cloudy and wet. In fact Nord-Pas-de-Calais has the least sunshine of any part of France, with only 1,600 hours per year and around 120 days' rain annually. Particularly rainy areas are Artois, Haut-Boulonnais and Avenois. There's seldom snow or ice, although the hills of Ardennes, on the Belgian border, have some. The average for the region is 18 days of snow per year. Average maximum/minimum temperatures along the coast are around 20/14°C (56/67°F) in summer and 6/2°C (43/36°F) in winter.

Picardy

The climate of Picardy is similar to that of Nord-Pas-de-Calais (see above), although there's some continental influence, with greater variations in temperature between winter and summer in southern areas of the two inland departments, Aisne and Oise. The region enjoys around 1,660 hours of sunshine per year and it rains on around 120 days.

Champagne-Ardenne

Champagne experiences a continental climate with severe winter temperatures, sometimes as low as -15°C (5°F). Average annual sunshine is around 1,730 hours and average annual rainfall 600mm (24in) on 113 days of the year. Charleville-Mézières in Ardennes has the dubious distinction of having the least sunshine of any major town in France – a mere 1,440 hours annually.

Lorraine

Lorraine has a mixed continental and oceanic climate, the absence of high land around the Ile-de-France region acting as a corridor for westerly winds bringing rain. Days are often warm and sunny, but nights can be cold. (There may be a 20°C (36°F) variation between day and night temperatures.) The region experiences distinct seasons, although the weather can be very changeable with hot or cold, dry weather giving way to heavy rain. Average annual sunshine hours are around 1,650 and rainfall 760mm (30in) on 125 days (as many as 135 in parts of Vosges).

Alsace

As the region is protected from westerly winds by the Vosges mountains, Alsace has a continental climate with cold winters (60 to 70 days of frost per year) and hot, dry summers, with occasional storms. Average maximum/minimum summer temperatures are 25/13°C (77/55°F) and average winter temperatures around 1 to 2°C (34 to 36°F). Average annual rainfall is between 600 and 700mm (23.5 and 27.5in) on between 104 days (Colmar) and 123 days (Mulhouse) with Strasbourg having around 112 days' rain. The region is one of France's least sunny, with just 1,637 hours' sunshine per year in Strasbourg, 1,724 in Colmar and 1,768 in Mulhouse.

Franche-Comté

The climate of Franche-Comté varies between the plains, where it's mild, and the mountains, where it's humid and cold. There are corresponding variations in rainfall: between 700mm (27in) on the plains and 1,700mm (67in) in the mountains. Belfort (90) and Besançon (25) have around 1,100mm (43in) of rain annually and around 1,870 hours of sunshine. Average winter temperatures are around 2°C (36°F). Belfort has the dubious distinction of being the coldest and second-rainiest place in France: it rains on over 142 days in the year and the average annual temperature is a mere 9.3°C (48°F).

Burgundy

Despite its location, Burgundy's climate is predominantly oceanic with westerly winds bringing rain. Average annual rainfall is between 655mm (26in) on 115 days in Auxerre (89) and 815mm (32in) on 125 days in Nevers (58). Summers are usually hot (i.e. over 25°C/77°F during the day) and winters cold but sunny. The region enjoys between 1,758 (Auxerre) and 1,830 (Dijon) hours' sunshine per year. Not surprisingly, the mildest weather is in the most southern department, Saône-et-Loire (71). The Morvan mountains (in the centre of the region), which rise to over 600m (1,970ft) can experience sudden changes in weather.

Centre-Val-de-Loire

The climate of this region is similar to that of the Pays-de-la-Loire (see page 103), i.e. oceanic with moderate temperatures throughout the year and much less marked seasons than, for example, Alsace. Snow and ice are rare and the difference between average winter temperatures and average summer temperatures is just 14°C (25°F). Rainfall is between 580mm (23in) on 108 days in Chartres (28) and 725mm (28.5in) on 118 days in Bourges (18). The region enjoys between 1,750 (Chartres) and 1,845 (Blois) hours' sunshine per year.

Rhône

Rhône has a mainly continental climate, with temperatures approaching those of the Mediterranean coast in southern Ardèche. (The *Mistral* occasionally blows up the Rhône valley.) Average annual rainfall for the two largest towns in the region is 710mm on 99 days in Saint-Etienne (42) and 825mm (32.5in) on 107 days in Lyons (69). Bourg-en-Bresse (01) has as many as 126 days' rain and 1,787 hours' sunshine per year. Lyons has almost 2,000 hours of sunshine on average a year and average maximum/minimum summer temperatures of 27/15°C (81/59°F). Summer afternoon temperatures are almost always above 20°C (68°F) throughout the region. In winter, Lyons averages 5/-1°C (41/30°F).

Corsica

Not surprisingly, Corsica has a Mediterranean climate, with sudden storms in mountain areas. Ajaccio enjoys 2,735 hours of sunshine per year (Bastia around 2,655) and the island is often the hottest place in France, although temperatures rarely exceed 30°C (86°F) even in high summer. The sea temperature in July and August may reach 25°C (77°F). Average daytime January temperatures in both Ajaccio and Bastia are 9°C (48°F) and average annual rainfall is 645mm (25in) on 75 days in Ajaccio and 750mm (29in) on just 67 days in Bastia.

COST OF LIVING

Corsica is the most expensive of the ten regions considered in this chapter, on account of demand for property and scarcity of land, the cost of importing goods from the mainland, insufficient population to support competitive hypermarket chains and a fairly captive market (you cannot go far without leaving the island). The next most expensive region is **Alsace**, particularly around Strasbourg, where high-income MEPs push up the cost of living. Lyons has a similar effect on the **Rhône** region, which is the next most expensive. At the other end of the scale, **Bourgogne**, **Franche-Comté** and **Lorraine** are the three cheapest regions.

PROPERTY

Cost of Housing

The figures given below are average prices, and it should be borne in mind that particularly sought-after urban areas may be well in excess of these figures, particularly Strasbourg (which has some of the highest property prices in France after Paris), Lille and Lyons.

Apartments: The table below indicates comparative prices of new or recently built apartments and older apartments. Note that newer apartments tend to be larger than older ones; the average new/recent two-bedroom apartment is around 70m^2 and a three-bedroom flat around 80m^2, compared with around 65m^2 and 75m^2 for older apartments. The approximate average price per m^2 is indicated in brackets.

	New/Recent		Older	
	2-bedroom	3-bedroom	2-bedroom	3-bedroom
Nord-Pas-de-Calais	€117,000	€133,000	€75,000	€87,000
		(€1,666)		(€1,160)
Picardy	€103,000	€117,000	€71,000	€81,000
		(€1,467)		(€1,086)
Champagne-Ardenne	€100,000	€114,000	€67,000	€78,000
		(€1,425)		(€1,035)

Lorraine	€91,000	€104,000	€61,000	€70,000
		(€1,294)		(€939)
Alsace	€105,000	€120,000	€74,000	€86,000
		(€1,506)		(€1,141)
Franche-Comté	€85,000	€97,000	€59,000	€68,000
		(€1,210)		(€900)
Bourgogne	€95,000	€109,000	€64,000	€74,000
		(€1,364)		(€981)
Centre-Val-de-Loire	€106,000	€121,000	€65,000	€75,000
		(€1,514)		(€1,005)
Rhône	€100,000	€115,000	€64,000	€74,000
		(€1,435)		(€986)

Corsica is a special case. Two-bedroom apartments (both new and older) by the sea vary between 40 and 80m^2 and prices can vary from under €60,000 to over €100,000. Older two-bedroom apartments in a historic town measure between 60 and 75m^2 and cost from around €75,000 to €130,000. Three-bedroom apartments (both categories) tend to be much larger, from 90 to 105m^2, and cost from around €140,000 to €200,000.

Houses: Two-bedroom houses are rare, unless they're old village houses (perhaps with no garden, or just a yard) or recent maisonette-style houses in a block (perhaps terraced, where there may or may not be a small private garden). Therefore, prices are given only for three and four-bedroom houses in the same two categories as for apartments (see above). Average plot sizes are indicated in brackets.

	New/Recent		Older	
	3-bedroom	**4-bedroom**	**3-bedroom**	**4-bedroom**
Nord-Pas-de-Calais	€103,000	€129,000	€73,000	€92,000
		(725m^2)		(690m^2)
Picardy	€85,000	€107,000	€77,000	€97,000
		(985m^2)		(1,035m^2)
Champagne-Ardenne	€96,000	€120,000	€77,500	€97,000
		(800m^2)		(1,079m^2)
Lorraine	€98,000	€123,000	€78,000	€97,000
		(761m^2)		(1,014m^2)
Alsace	€125,000	€156,000	€110,000	€138,000
		(518m^2)		(853m^2)
Franche-Comté	€95,000	€119,000	€79,000	€99,000
		(967m^2)		(1,737m^2)

Bourgogne	€91,000 €113,000	€74,000	€92,000
	(1,048m^2)	(2,112m^2)	
Centre -Val-de-Loire	€90,000 €112,000	€80,000	€100,000
	(1,065m^2)	(2,368m^2)	
Rhône	€113,000 €142,000	€102,000	€127,000
	(568m^2)	(3,000m^2*)	

* Ardèche (07) often has extremely large plots, accounting for the high average figure for Rhône.

Corsica tends to offer three-bedroom houses (both categories) for around €200,000, with average plots around 1,500m^2, and four-bedroom houses for around €230,000, with similar size plots. A small two-bedroom house near the sea in Corsica can cost €110,000.

Land

Buying a plot and building a home is becoming an increasingly popular option in regions such as Nord-Pas-de-Calais, where there's now a shortage of rural properties for restoration. As with apartments and houses (see above), the following tables give average figures and it should be noted that the situation of a plot greatly affects the price. Note also that plots under 300m^2 should be checked for building restrictions. It will be noticed that plots over 1,000m^2 (around two-fifths of an acre) are generally cheaper than those between 600m^2 and 1,000m^2, which is partly because of demand and partly because larger plots are often isolated or in difficult terrain.

	Up to 600m^2	**600–1,000m^2**	**1,000–2,500m^2**
Nord-Pas-de-Calais	€23,000	€31,500	€29,000
Picardy	€21,000	€27,500	€22,000
Champagne-Ardenne	€20,000	€30,000	€23,500
Lorraine	€26,000	€35,500	€26,000
Alsace	€33,500	€55,000	€57,000
Franche-Comté	€13,000	€25,500	€25,000
Bourgogne	€17,000	€29,000	€19,000
Centre-Val-de-Loire	€21,000	€28,000	€22,000
Rhône*	€27,000	€44,000	€44,000

* Building land in the Rhône department (69) is considerably more expensive than in the other three departments, i.e. Ain (01), Ardèche (07) and Loire (42).

Corsica has few plots under 600m2 for sale. The average price of plots between 800 and 1,000m² is around €30,000. There's a wide variation in price according to situation (e.g. sea view) for plots between 1,000 and 2,500m², but the average is around €60,000.

Rental Accommodation

The table below gives an indication of monthly rental prices for apartments and houses in the ten regions. Where there's a large variation in apartment rental prices within a region, this is due to high rents in prestigious areas of major towns, such as Lille, Lyons, Reims, and Strasbourg. Short-term peak holiday period rentals (furnished) will cost about the same, **per week**.

	2-bed Apt	**3-bed Apt**	**3/4-bed House**
Nord-Pas-de-Calais	€ 280–€620	€380–€960	averages €760
Picardy	€ 550–€1,000	€600–€1,000+	averages €680
Champagne-Ardenne	€ 270–€800	€470–960	averages €870
Lorraine	€ 310–€760	€550–€880	averages €680
Alsace	€ 420–€600	€630–€1300	averages €1,000
Franche-Comté	€ 210–€640	€240–€830	averages €690
Bourgogne	€ 250–€680	€380–€850	averages €780
Centre-Val-de-Loire	€ 320–€700	€370–€770	averages €880
Rhône*	€ 300–€650	€380–€960	averages €970

* The department of Rhône (69) is considerably more expensive than the other departments in this region.

Corsica generally offers rental prices between those of Alsace and those of the Côte d'Azur (see page 271).

COMMUNICATIONS

The information below details communications by air between regional airports and the UK and Europe. For details of sea links between England and France, see **Sea** on page 81.

The Paris airports (see page 323) are accessible from most of **Picardy**, **Champagne-Ardenne**, **Burgundy** and **Centre-Val-de-Loire** as well as southern parts of **Nord-Pas-de-Calais**, offering flights to most world-wide destinations. Both Buzz and the recently merged EasyJet/Go fly to Paris from London area airports and also from other destinations in the UK and Europe.

Lyon-Saint-Exupéry is the other international airport with direct flights to and from several European destinations and is accessible from the **Rhône** region as well as southern parts of **Burgundy** and **Franche-Comté**. Go flies to Lyons direct from London Stansted, Air France from London Heathrow, and British Airways from Heathrow, Birmingham, Edinburgh and Manchester. Details of services to relevant regional aiports are given below. Note that there are no regular international flights to the airports at Amiens (**Picardy**), Reims and Troyes (**Champagne-Ardenne**) or Metz-Nancy (**Lorraine**). Details of all French airports and their services can be found on 🖳 www.aeroport.fr.

Nord-Pas-de-Calais

Lille airport (59) offers flights throughout France, and to and from Frankfurt, Munich and towns in Italy, Portugal, Spain and Switzerland, but no direct flights to and from the UK. There's a *TGV* connection to the city centre. Paris CDG is accessible from southern parts of the region.

Picardy

Beauvais airport (60) offers flights to Dublin, Shannon, Glasgow (Ryanair), Gothenburg, Stockholm, Malmo (Goodjet) and Parma (Ciaofly). Paris CDG is convenient for southern parts.

Alsace

Mulhouse-Basle airport (68) has direct flights, several times daily, to London Heathrow. Strasbourg airport (67) offers flights throughout France but no direct flights to the UK (change at Paris CDG for Heathrow and Stansted).

Franche-Comté

Dijon airport (see below) is convenient for the western departments and Mulhouse-Basle (see above) and airports in Switzerland for the east.

Burgundy

Dijon airport (21) is linked direct to London Stansted (Buzz). Paris Orly is convenient for northern parts (see above).

Centre-Val-de-Loire

Buzz offers direct flights from London Stansted to Tours airport (37). Paris Orly is accessible from Eure-et-Loir and Loiret, and Poitiers airport (see page 122) from Indre and Indre-et-Loire.

Rhône

For details of Lyon-Saint-Exupéry airport, see introduction above.

Corsica

There are no direct flights to Bastia or Calvi (Haute-Corse) from London or other European cities, but you must change at Marseilles or Nice, the latter airport also being the transit point for flights from the USA.

FURTHER INFORMATION

Useful Addresses

The following British Consulates or Honorary British Consuls cover the ten regions considered in this chapter:

- Consulate for the United Kingdom, 11, square Dutilleul, 59800 Lille (☎ 03.20.12.82.72)

- Honorary Consul for the United Kingdom, c/o Lemaire Frères et Fils, 30, rue l'Hermitte, BP 2/100, 59376 Dunkerque (☎ 03.28.66.11.98)

- Honorary Consul for the United Kingdom, 28, rue Saint jean, 62200 Boulogne-sur-Mer (☎ 03.21.87.16.80)

- Honorary Consul for the United Kingdom, 20, rue du Havre, 62100 Calais (☎ 03.21.96.33.76)

- Honorary Consul for the United Kingdom, 18, place Saint Michel, 80000 Amiens (☎ 03.22.72.08.48)

- Consulate for the United Kingdom, 24, rue Childebert, 69002 Lyon (☎ 04.72.77.81.70)

- Consulate for the United Kingdom, 24, avenue du Prado, 13006 Marseille (☎ 04.91.15.72.10). Responsible for Corsica.

Regional Tourist Offices

- Comité régional du Tourisme de **Nord-Pas-de-Calais**, 6, place Mendès France, 59800 Lille (☎ 03.20.14.57.57, 🖳 www.crt-nordpasdecalais.fr)

- Comité régional du Tourisme de **Picardie**, 3, rue Vincent Auriol, 80011 Amiens (☎ 03.22.22.33.66, 🖳 www.cr-picardie.fr)

- Comité régional du Tourisme de **Champagne-Ardenne**, 15, avenue du Maréchal Leclerc, BP 319, 51013 Châlons-en-Champagne (☎ 03.26.21. 85.80, 💻 www. tourisme-champagne-ardenne.com)

- Comité régional du Tourisme de Lorraine, Abbaye des Prémontrés, BP 97, 54704 Pont-à-Mousson (☎ 03.83 80 01 80, 💻 www.crt-lorraine.fr)

- Comité régional du Tourisme d'**Alsace**, 20A, rue Berthe Molly, 68000 Colmar (☎ 03.88.25.39.83, 💻 www.tourism-alsace.com)

- Comité régional du Tourisme de **Franche-Comt**é, La City, 4, rue Gabriel, Plançon, 25044 Besançon (☎ 03.81.25.08.08, 💻 www.franche-comte.org)

- Comité régional du Tourisme du **Centre-Val-de-Loire**, 37, avenue de Paris, 45000 Orléans (☎ 02.38.79 95 00, 💻 www.loirevalleytourism.com)

- Comité régional du Tourisme de **Bourgogne**, Conseil Régional, BP 1602, 21035 Dijon (☎ 03.80.28.02.80, 💻 www.bourgogne-tourisme.com)

- Comité régional du Tourisme de **Rhône-Alpes**, 104, route de Paris, 69260 Charbonnières-les-Bains (☎ 04.72.59.21.59, 💻 www.rhonealpes-tourisme.com)

- Agence de Tourisme de **Corse**, 17, Boulevard Roi Jérôme, BP 19, 20176 Ajaccio (☎ 04.95.51.77.77, 💻 www.visit-corsica.com)

Useful Publications

In addition to the national publications listed in **Appendix B**, the following regional and local publications will provide useful information:

- **Corse Matin**
- **La Voix du Nord**
- **Le Courrier picard**
- **Le Dauphiné libéré**
- **Le Journal de la Haute-Marne**
- **Le Populaire du Centre**
- **Le Républicain lorrain**

Useful Websites

See **Appendix C**.

Montenvers – The Alps

APPENDICES

APPENDIX A: USEFUL ADDRESSES

Embassies & Consulates

Embassies are located in the capital Paris and many countries also have consulates in other cities (British provincial consulates are listed on page 372). Embassies and consulates are listed in the yellow pages under 'Ambassades, Consulats et Autres Représentations Diplomatiques'. Note that many countries have more than one office in Paris. Before writing or calling you should telephone to confirm that you have the correct address.

Albania: 131, rue Pompe, 16e (☎ 01.45.53.51.32).

Algeria: 50, rue Lisbonne, 8e (☎ 01.53.93.20.20).

Angola: 19, avenue Foch, 16e (☎ 01.45.01.58.20).

Argentina: 6, rue Cimarosa, 16e (☎ 01.45.53.22.25).

Armenia: 9 rue Viète, 17e (☎ 01.42.12.98.00)

Australia: 4, rue Jean Rey, 15e (☎ 01.40.59.33.00).

Austria: 6, rue Fabert, 7e (☎ 01.45.56.97.86).

Bahrain: 3015 pl Etats-Unis, 16e (☎ 01.47.23.48.68).

Bangladesh: 5, sq Pétrarque, 16e (☎ 01.45.53.41.20).

Belgium: 9, rue Tilsitt, 17e (☎ 01.44.09.39.39).

Benin: 87, avenue Victor Hugo, 16e (☎ 01.45.00.98.82).

Bolivia: 12, avenue Président Kennedy, 16e (☎ 01.42.24.93.44).

Bosnia Herzegovenia: 194 rue Courcales, 17e (☎ 01.42.67.34.22)

Brazil: 34 Cours Albert 1er, 8e (☎ 01.45.61.63.00).

Brunei Darussalam: 4, rue Logelbach, 17e (☎ 01.42.67.49.47).

Bulgaria: 1, avenue Rapp, 7e (☎ 01.45.51.85.90).

Cambodia: 4 rue Adolphe Yvon, 16e (☎ 01.45.03.47.20)

Cameroon: 73, rue Auteuil, 16e (☎ 01.47.43.98.33).

Canada: 35, avenue Montaigne, 8e (☎ 01.44.43.29.16).

Central African Republic: 30, rue Perchamps, 16e (☎ 01.42.24.42.56).

Chad: 65, rue Belles Feuilles, 16e (☎ 01.45.53.36.75).

Chile: 2, avenue La Motte Picquet, 7e (☎ 01.44.18.59.60).

China: 11, avenue George V, 8e (☎ 01.47.23.36.77).

Colombia: 22, rue Elysée, 8e (☎ 01.42.65.46.08).

Comoros: 20, rue Marbeau, 16e (☎ 01.40.67.90.54).

Congo: 37 bis, rue Paul Valéry, 16e (☎ 01.45.00.68.57).

Costa Rica: 78, avenue Emile Zola, 15e (☎ 01.45.78.96.96).

Cote d'Ivoire: 102, avenue Raymond Poincaré, 16e (☎ 01.53.64.62.62).

Croacia: 79, avenue Georges Manbel, 16e (☎ 01.53.70.02.80)

Cyprus: 23, rue Galilée, 8e (☎ 01.47.20.86.28).

Czech Republic: 15, avenue Charles Floquet, 7e (☎ 01.40.65.13.00).

Cuba: 16, rue Presles, 15e (☎ 01.45.67.55.35).

Denmark: 77, avenue Marceau, 16e (☎ 01.44.31.21.21).

Djibouti: 26, rue Emile Menier, 16e (☎ 01.47.27.49.22).

Ecuador: 34, avenue Messine, 8e (☎ 01.42.56.22.59).

Egypt: 56, avenue Léna, 16e (☎ 01.53.67.88.30).

El Salvador: 12, rue Galilée, 16e (☎ 01.47.20.42.02).

Estonia: 14, boulevard Montmartre, 9e (☎ 01.48.01.00.22).

Ethiopia: 35, avenue Charles Floquet, 7e (☎ 01.47.83.83.95).

Finland: 2, rue Fabert, 7e (☎ 01.44.18.19.28).

Gabon: 26 bis, avenue Raphaël, 16e (☎ 01.44.30.22.60).

Gambia: 17, rue St Lazare, 8e (☎ 01.42.94.09.30).

Germany: 13, Ave F.D. Roosevelt, 8e (☎ 01.53.83.45.00).

Ghana: 8, villa Said, 16e (☎ 01.45.00.09.50).

Greece: 17, rue Auguste Vacquerie, 16e (☎ 01.47.23.72.28).

Guatemala: 73, rue Courcelles, 8e (☎ 01.42.27.78.63).

Guinea: 51, rue Faisanderie, 16e (☎ 01.47.04.81.48).

Guinea-Bissau: 94, rue St. Lazare, 9e (☎ 01.45.26.18.51).

Haiti: 10, rue Théodule Ribot, 17e (☎ 01.47.63.47.78).

Honduras: 8, rue Crevaux, 16e (☎ 01.47.55.86.43).

Hungary: 5 bis, sq Avenue Foch, 16e (☎ 01.45.00.41.59).

Iceland: 8, avenue Kléber , 16 (☎ 01.44.17.32.85).

India: 15, rue Alfred Dehodencq, 16e (☎ 01.40.58.70.70).

Indonesia: 49, rue Cortambert, 16e (☎ 01.45.03.07.60).

Iran: 4, avenue Léna, 16e (☎ 01.40.69.70.00).

Ireland: 41, rue Rude, 16e (☎ 01.44.17.67.00).

Israel: 3, rue Rabelais, 8e (☎ 01.40.76.55.00).

Italy: 51, rue Varenne, 7e (☎ 01.49.54.03.00).

Jamaica: 60, avenue Fich, 16e (☎ 01.45.00.62.25).

Japan: 7 avenue Hoche, 8e (☎ 01.48.88.62.00).

Kenya: 3, rue Cimarosa, 16e (☎ 01.45.53.35.00).

Korea: 125, rue Grenelle, 7e (☎ 01.47.53.01.01).

Kuwait: 2, rue Lubeck, 16e (☎ 01.47.23.54.25).

Laos: 74, avenue Raymond Poincaré, 16e (☎ 01.45.53.02.98).

Latvia: 6, Villa Saïd, 16e (☎ 01.53.64.58.10).

Lebanon: 42, rue Copernic, 16e (☎ 01.40.67.75.75).

Liberia: 12, pl Général Catroux, 17e (☎ 01.47.63.58.55).

Libya: 2, rue Charles Lamoureux, 16e (☎ 01.45.53.40.70).

Lithuania: 14, boulevard Montmartre, 9e (☎ 01.48.01.00.33).

Luxembourg: 33, avenue Rapp, 7e (☎ 01.45.55.13.37).

Madagascar: 4, avenue Raphaël, 16e (☎ 01.45.04.62.11).

Malawi: 20, rue Euler, 8e (☎ 01.40.70.18.46).

Malaysia: 32, rue Spontini, 16e (☎ 01.45.53.11.85).

Mali: 89, rue Cherche Midi, 6e (☎ 01.45.48.58.43).

Malta: 92, avenue Champs Elysées, 8e (☎ 01.45.62.53.01).

Mexico: 9, rue Longchamp, 16e (☎ 01.42.61.51.80).

Monaco: 22, boulevard Suchet, 16e (☎ 01.45.04.74.54).

Morocco: 35, rue Le Tasse, 16e (☎ 01.45.20.69.35).

Mozambique: 82, rue Laugier, 17e (☎ 01.47.64.91.32).

Myanmar: 60, rue Courcelles, 8e (☎ 01.42.25.56.95).

Nepal: 45 bis, rue Acacias, 17e (☎ 01.46.22.48.67).

Netherlands: 7, rue Eblé, 7e (☎ 01.40.62.34.66).

New Zealand: 7 ter, rue Léonard de Vinci, 16e (☎ 01.45.00.24.11).

Nicaragua: 34, avenue Bugeaud, 16e (☎ 01.44.05.90.42).

Niger: 154, rue Longchamp, 16e (☎ 01.45.04.80.60).

Nigeria: 173, avenue Victor Hugo, 16e (☎ 01.47.04.68.65).

Norway: 28, rue Bayard, 8e (☎ 01.53.67.04.00).

Oman: 50, avenue Léna, 16e (☎ 01.47.23.01.63).

Pakistan: 18, rue Lord Byron, 8e (☎ 01.45.62.23.32).

Panama: 145, avenue Suffren, 15e (☎ 01.47.83.23.32).

Paraguay: 1, rue St Dominique, 7e (☎ 01.42.22.85.05).

Peru: 50, avenue Kléber, 16e (☎ 01.53.70.42.00).

Poland: 1, rue Talleyrand, 7e (☎ 01.45.51.49.12).

Portugal: 3, rue Noisiel, 16e (☎ 01.47.27.35.29).

Qatar: 57, quai Orsay, 7e (☎ 01.45.51.90.71).

Romania: 3, rue Exposition, 7e (☎ 01.45.51.42.46).

Russia: 40, boulevard Lannes, 16e (☎ 01.45.04.05.50).

Rwanda: 12, rue Jadin, 17e (☎ 01.42.27.36.31).

San Marino: 21, rue Auguste Vacquerie, 16e (☎ 01.47.23.78.05).

Saudi Arabia: 5, avenue Hoche, 8e (☎ 01.47.66.02.06).

Senegal: 14, avenue Robert Schuman, 7e (☎ 01.47.05.39.45).

Seychelles: 51, rue Mozart, 16e (☎ 01.42.30.57.47).

Sierra Leone: 16, avenue Hoche, 8e (☎ 01.42.56.14.73).

Singapore: 12, sq Avenue Foch, 16e (☎ 01.45.00.33.61).

Somalia: 26, rue Dumont d'Urville, 16e (☎ 01.45.00.76.51).

South Africa: 59, quai Orsay, 7e (☎ 01.53.59.23.23).

Spain: 22, avenue Marceau, 8e (☎ 01.44.43.18.00).

Sri Lanka: 15, rue Astorg, 8e (☎ 01.42.66.35.01).

Sudan: 56, avenue Montaigne, 8e (☎ 01.42.25.55.73).

Sweden: 17, rue Barbet de Jouy, 7e (☎ 01.44.18.88.00).

Switzerland: 142, rue Grenelle, 7e (☎ 01.49.55.67.00).

Syria: 20, rue Vaneau, 7e (☎ 01.47.05.92.73).

Tanzania: 13, avenue Raymond Poincare, 16e (☎ 01.53.70.63.66).

Thailand:12, rue Lord Byron, 8e (☎ 01.42.89.89.44).

Togo: 15, rue Madrid, 8e (☎ 01.44.70.04.39).

Tunisia: 25, rue Barbet de Jouy, 7e (☎ 01.45.55.95.98).

Turkey: 16, avenue Lamballe, 16e (☎ 01.45.24.52.24).

Uganda: 13, avenue Raymond Poincaré, 16e (☎ 01.53.70.62.70).

United Arab Emirates: 3, rue Lota, 16e (☎ 01.45.53.94.04).

United Kingdom: 35, rue Fauberg St. Honoré, 8e (☎ 01.44.51.31.02).

United States of America: 2, rue St Florentin, 1e (☎ 01.43.12.23.47).

Uruguay: 15, rue Le Sueur, 16e (☎ 01.45.00.81.37).

Venezuela: 11, rue Copernic, 16e (☎ 01.45.53.29.98).

Vietnam: 62, rue Boileau, 16e (☎ 01.44.14.64.00).

Yemen: 25, rue Georges Bizet, 16e (☎ 01.47.23.61.76).

Yugoslavia (Republic of): 54, rue Faisanderie, 16e (☎ 01.40.72.24.24)

Zaire: 32, cours Albert, 1er, 8e (☎ 01.42.25.57.50).

Zambia: 34, avenue Messing, 8e (☎ 01.45.61.05.08).

Zimbabwe: 5, rue Tilsitt, 8e (☎ 01.53.81.90.10).

British Provincial Consulates

Amiens, British Consulate (Hon.), c/o Ecole Supérieure de Commerce, 18, place Saint Michel, 8000 Amiens (☎ 03.22.72.08.48).

Biarritz, British Consulate (Hon.), 7, boulevard Tauzin, 64200 Biarritz (☎ 05.59.24.21.40).

Bordeaux, British Consulate-General, 353, boulevard du Président Wilson, BP 91, 33073 Bordeaux (☎ 05.57.22.21.10).

Boulogne-sur-Mer, British Consulate (Hon.), c/o Cabinet Barron et Brun, 28, rue Saint Jean, 62200 Boulogne-sur-Mer (☎ 03.21.87.16.80).

Calais, British Consulate (Hon.), c/o P&O Stena Line, 20, rue du Havre, 62100 Calais (☎ 03.21.96.33.76).

Dinard, British Consulate (Hon.), La Hulotte, 8, boulevard des Maréchaux, 35800 Dinard (☎ 02.99.46.26.64).

Dunkerque, British Consulate (Hon.), c/o Lemaire Frères & Fils, 30, rue de l'Hermitte, BP 2/100, 59376 Dunkerque (☎ 03.28.66.11.98).

Le Havre, British Consulate (Hon.), c/o P&O European Ferries, 124, boulevard de Strasbourg, 76600 Le Havre (☎ 02.35.19.78.88).

Lille, British Consulate-General, 11, square Dutilleul, 59800 Lille (☎ 03.20.12.82.72).

Lyons, British Consulate-General, 24, rue Childebert, 69288 Lyon cedex 1 (☎ 04.72.77.81.70).

Marseilles, British Consulate-General, 24, avenue du Prado, 13006 Marseilles (☎ 04.91.15.72.10). Also deals with Monaco.

Nantes, British Consulate (Hon.), 16, boulevard Gabriel Giust'hau, BP 22026, 44020 Nantes cedex 1 (☎ 02.51.72.72.60).

Nice, British Consulate (Hon.), 26, avenue Notre Dame, 06000 Nice (☎ 04. 93.62.13.56). Also deals with Monaco.

Toulouse, British Consulate (Hon.), c/o Lucas Aerospace, Victoria Center, 20, chemin de Laporte, 31300 Toulouse (☎ 05.61.15.02.02).

Miscellaneous

British Council, 9, rue Constantine, 75340 Paris Cedex 07 (☎ 01.49. 55.73.00, 🖥 www.britishcouncil.fr). Has a lending library and an information section open to the public (for a fee).

British Institute in Paris, 11, rue Constantine, 75340 Paris Cedex 07 (☎ 01. 44.11.73.73). Provides courses in French language and culture.

British Tourist Authority, BP154-08, 75363 Paris Cedex 08 (☎ 01.58. 36.50.50, 🖥 www.visitbritain.com.fr). Note that the office isn't open to the public and information must be obtained by telephone or via the website.

French Consulate, 21 Cromwell Road, London SW7 2EN, UK (☎ 020-7073 1200, 🖥 www.ambafrance-uk.org)

Fédération française de Voile, 55, avenue Kléber, 75784 Paris cedex 16 (☎ 01.44.05.81.00)

Fédération française de la Randonée pédestre, 14, rue Riquet, 75019 Paris, (☎ 01.44.89.93.90)

France-British Chamber of Commerce & Industry, 3, rue Boissy d'Anglas, 75008 Paris (☎ 01.53.30.81.30, 🖥 www.francobritishchamber.com).

Intercontinental Church Society, 1 Athena Drive, Tachbrook Park, Warwick CV34 6NL, UK (☎ 01926-430347, ✉ enquiries@ics-uk.org). Publishes the *Directory of English-Speaking Churches Abroad* (around £4).

APPENDIX B: FURTHER READING

The lists contained in this appendix are only a selection of the hundreds of books written about France. In addition to the general and Paris guides listed below, there are also numerous guides covering individual regions of France. The publication title is followed by the author's name and the publisher's name (in brackets). Note that some titles may be out of print but may still be obtainable from book-shops and libraries. Books prefixed with an asterisk (*) are recommended by the author.

General Tourist Guides

*Allez France, Richard Binns (Chiltern House)

Berlitz Traveller's Guide France (Berlitz)

*Birnbaum's France, (Houghton Mifflin)

*The Blue Guide to France (A&C Black)

Collins Eurotunnel Weekend Guide (Harper Collins)

*Cruising French Waterways, Hugh McKnight (A&C Black)

Exploring France, Peter & Helen Titchmarsh (Jarrold)

Family France, Frank Barrett (Boxtree)

Fielding's France, Gary Krant (Fielding Morrow)

Fodor's Bed & Breakfast (Fodor)

*Franc-Wise France, Richard Binns (Chiltern House)

France, Emma Stanford (Independent Traveller's Guides)

France – Eyewitness (Dorling Kindersley)

French Gardens, Barbara Abbs (Sagapress)

*France: Landscape, Architecture, Tradition (Michelin)

France by Train, Simon Vickers (Random House)

*French Leave Encore, Richard Binns (Chiltern House)

*Frommers France (Prentice Hall Travel)

*Holiday Which? Guide to France, Adam Ruck (Consumers' Association and Hodder & Stoughton)

*Lets Go France (MacMillan)

Let's Go France (St Martin's Press)

*Lonely Planet: France (Lonely Planet)

***Mapaholics France**, Richard Binns (Chiltern House)

***Michelin Blue Guide to France**

***Michelin Green Guides**

Off The Beaten Track, France (Moorland Publishing)

On the Waterfront in France, Gill Charlton (Fontana)

***The Penguin Guide to France** (Penguin)

RAC Gault Millau 'The Best of France' (Andre Gayot)

***The Rough Guide to France**, Kate Baillie & Tim Salmon (Rough Guides)

Secret France (AA)

Slow Boat Through France, Hugh McKnight (David & Charles)

The Riches of France (St Martin's Press)

The Traveller in France (French Tourist Office, 178 Piccadilly, London W1J 2AL, ☎ 020-7491 7622, 🖳 www.franceguide.com)

Visitor's Guide France (Moorland)

Watersteps Through France, Bill & Laurel Cooper (Methuen)

Paris Guides

Blue Guide Paris (Black/Norton)

***David Gentleman's Paris** (Hodder & Stoughton)

Essential Paris, Susan Grossman (AA)

Eyewitness Travel Guide: Paris (Dorling Kindersley)

The Footloose Guide to Paris, Deidre Vine (Simon Price)

Guide to Impressionist Paris, Patty Lurie (Lilburne Press)

Lonely Planet: Paris (Lonely Planet)

Michael's Guide Paris (Inbal Travel)

Michelin City Plans, Paris

***Pauper's Paris**, Miles Turner (Pan)

Paris – Eyewitness, Alan Tillier (Dorling Kindersley)

Paris, Julian Green (Marion Boyars)

Paris, Vivienne Menkes-Ivry (Christopher Helm)

Paris Confidential, Joseph R. Yogerst (Roger Lascelles)

Paris for Free (or Extremely Cheap), Mark Beffart (Mustang)

Paris de Luxe: Place Vendôme, Alexis Gregory (Thames & Hudson)

*Paris Inside Out, David Applefield (Frank Books)

*Paris Mode d'Emploi/User's Guide (Paris Tourist Office)

Secret Gardens of Paris, Alexandria d'Arnoux & Bruno de Laboudère (Thames & Hudson)

*The Rough Guide to Paris (Rough Guides)

*Time Out Paris Guide (Penguin)

The Woman's Travel Guide Paris, Catherine Cullen (Virago Press)

Living & Working in France

The Blevins Franks Guide to Living in France, Bill Blevins & David Franks (Blevins Franks)

*A Bull by the Back Door, Anne Loader (Léonie Press)

The Dreamer's Guide to Living in France, John Hodgkinson (Breese Books)

Emplois d'Eté en France - Summer Employment in France (Vacation Work)

*An Englishman in the Midi, John P. Harris (BBC)

*Can We Afford the Bidet?, Elizabeth Morgan (Lennard Publishing)

*The Duck With a Dirty Laugh, Anne Loader (Léonie Press)

French Dirt, Richard Goodman (Pavilion Books)

French or Foe, Polly Platt (Culture Crossings)

The Grown Up's Guide to Living in France, Rosanne Knorr (Ten Speed Press)

Guide for US Citizens Residing in France (American Embassy, 2, rue St Florentin, 75382 Paris)

Guide to Education (AAWE Publications, BP127, 92154 Suresnes)

*How to Get a Job in France, Mark Hempshell (How To Books)

Home and Dry in France, George East (La Puce Publications)

At Home in France, Christopher Petkanas (Weidenfeld)

*A House in the Sunflowers, Ruth Silvestre (WH Allen)

Living as a British Expatriate in France (French Chamber of Commerce)

Living in France (AAWE Publications, BP127, 92154 Suresnes)

*More From an Englishman in the Midi, John P. Harris (BBC)

*A Normandy Tapestry, Alan Biggins (Kirkdale Books)

Paradise Found, Jim Keeble (Carnell)

*Perfume from Provence, Lady Fortescue (Black Swan)

*René & Me, George East (La Puce Publications)

*Some of My Best Friends are French, Colin Corder (Shelf Publishing)

*Sunset House, Lady Fortescue (Black Swan)

To Live in France, James Bentley

*Toujours Provence, Peter Mayle (Pan)

*Understanding France, John P. Harris (Papermac)

*A White House in Gascony, Rex Grixell (Victor Gollancz)

*Working in France, Carol Pineau and Maureen Kelly (Frank Books)

*A Year in Provence, Peter Mayle (Pan)

Property & Business

At Home in France, Christopher Petkanas (Weidenfeld and Nicolson)

At Home in France, Jane Hawking (Allegretto)

**Buying a Home in France, David Hampshire (Survival Books)

Buying Residential Property in France, Bertrand Defournier (French Chamber of Commerce)

Buying and Renovating Property in France, J. Kater Pollock (Flowerpoll)

Buying & Restoring Old Property in France, David Everett (Robert Hale)

English-French Building and Property Dictionary, J. Kater Pollock (Flowerpoll)

*French Country, Buchholz & Skolnik (Aurum Press)

*The French Farmhouse, Elsie Burch Donald (Little, Brown & Co.)

French Housing, Laws & Taxes, Frank Rutherford (Sprucehurst)

French Real Property and Succession Law, Henry Dyson (Robert Hale)

The French Room, Elizabeth Wilhide (Conran Otopus)

French Style, Suzanne Slesin and Stafford Dliff (Thames and Hudson)

The French Touch, Daphné de Saint Sauveur (Thames & Hudson)

Le Guide économique de la Normandie (PTC)

A Guide to Renovating Your Home in France, Janine Paul (199 Amyand Park Road, Twickenham, Middx. TW1 3HN)

Letting French Property Successfully, Stephen Smith & Charles Parkinson (PFK Publishing)

Maison Therapy, Alastair Simpson (New Horizon)

The Most Beautiful Villages of the Dordogne, James Bentley

Really Rural, Marie-France Boyer (Thames & Hudson)

Setting Up a Small Business in France (French Chamber of Commerce)

Traditional Houses of Rural France, Bill Laws (Collins & Brown)

Food & Wine

ABC of French Food, Len Deighton (Arrow)

The A-Z Gastronomique, Fay Sharman & Brian Chadwick (Papermac)

*Bistro Cooking, Patricia Wells

*Bocuse's Regional French Cooking, Paul Bocuse (Flammarion)

*Bon Appétit, Judith White (Peppercorn)

Brittany Gastronomique, Kate Whiteman (Conran Octopus)

Château Cuisine, Willan & Baker (Conran Octopus)

Cuisine Actuelle, Patricia Wells (MacMillan)

*Floyd on France, Keith Floyd (Michael Joseph).

*Floyd on Hangovers, Keith Floyd (Michael Joseph).

Food from France, Quentin Crewe & John Brunton (Ebury Press)

The Food Lover's Guide to Paris, Patricia Wells

*The Food Lover's Companion Guide to France, Marc & Kim Millon (Little, Brown)

The Food of France, Maria Villegas & Sarah Randell (Murdoch Books)

France: A Feast of Food and Wine, Roger Voss (Mitchell Beazley)

La France Gastronomique, Anne Willan (Pavilion)

France: The Vegetarian Table, Georgeanne Brennan (Chronicle)

The French Cheese Book, Major Pat Rance (Papermac)

*Le French Cookbook (Bay Books)

French Country Cuisine, Carole Clements & Elizabeth Wolf-Cohen (Lorenz Books)

*The French Food & Drink Dictionary, Robyn Wilson (Sphere)

French Vineyards: Complete Guide & Companion, Michael Busselle (Pavilion Books)

French Wines, Robert Joseph (Dorling Kindersley)

*Gault-Millau Guide de la France

*Les Routiers Guide to France (Alan Sutton)

*Les Meilleurs Restaurants 2002 Best Restaurants Provence E. Lallier and Richard Whiting (SARL Intermedia)

Mastering the Art of French Cooking, Simone Beck, Louisette Bertholle & Julia Child (Penguin)

*Michelin Red Guide France (Michelin)

Terence Conran's France, Terence Conran (Conran Octopus Books)

*The Pocket Guide to French Food and Wine, Tessa Youell & George Kimball (Carbery)

*The Taste of France, Robert Freson (Webb & Bower)

*Time Out Eating & Drinking in Paris (Penguin)

*Vegetarian France, Alex Burke & Alan Todd (Editions La Plage)

The Vineyards of France, Don Philpott (MPC)

*Wine Atlas of France, Hugh Johnson & Hubrecht Duijker (Mitchell Beazley)

The Wines of France, Clive Coates (Random Century)

Wining and Dining in France, Robin Neillands (Ashford, Buchan & Enright)

Woman of Taste, Pamela Vandyke Price (John Murray)

*Your Good Health: The Medicinal Benefits of Wine Drinking, Dr. E. Maury (Souvenir Press)

Miscellaneous

**The Alien's Guide to France, Jim Watson (Survival Books)

And God Created the French, Louis-Bernard Robitaille (RD)

*Cambridge Illustrated History: France, Colin Jones (Cambridge University Press)

The Complete Guide to Learning French in France - From Short Study Holidays to 'Gap Year' Breaks (Europa Pages)

***Cultural Atlas of France**, John Ardagh (Facts on File)

Cultural Misunderstandings: The French-American Experience, Raymonde Carrol (University of Chicago Press)

Dictionary of Contemporary France, Richard Alpin (Hodder & Stoughton)

Fragile Glory, Richard Bernstein (Bodley Head)

France, Clin Jones (CUP)

***France in the New Century: Portrait of a Changing Society**, J. Ardagh (Viking)

Francwise France, Harvey Elliot (Chiltern House)

French-American Guide (French-American Foundation, 54, boulevard Raspail, 75006 Paris)

***The French**, Theodore Zeldin (Harvill)

***Good Camps France**, Alan Rogers (Deneway Guides)

Le Guide officiel des Parcs d'Attractions (Guides Larivière)

Guide to Education (AAWE Publications, BP127, 92154 Suresnes)

***Hannibal's Footsteps**, Bernard Levin (Sceptre)

On the Brink – the Trouble with France, Jonathan Fenby (Little, Crown & Co.)

Postcards from France, Megan McNeill Libby (Harper Paperback)

Principles of French Law, John Bell, Sophie Boyron & Simon Whittaker (OUP)

Savoir Flair, Polly Platt (Culture Crossings)

Teach Yourself French Language, Life& Culture, Celia Dixie (Hodder & Stoughton)

The Identity of France, Fernand Braudel (Fontana)

The Legal Beagle Goes to France, Bill Thomas (Quiller)

The Making of Modern France - Politics, Ideology and Culture, Emmanuel Todd (Blackwell)

***The Man Who Broke Out of the Bank**, Miles Morland (Fontana)

Mapaholics' France, Harvey Elliot (Chiltern House)

The Nature Parks of France, Patrick Delaforce (Windrush Press)

***On The Brink**, Jonathan Fenby (Little Brown)

***Paris Chic**, Dominique Brabec & Eglé Salvy (Thames & Hudson)

Portraits of France (Hutchinson)

Searching for the New France, James Hollifield & George Ross (Routledge)

Taxation in France, Charles Parkinson (PFK Publishing)

Terence Conran's France (Conran Octopus)

That Sweet Enemy, Christopher Sinclair-Stevenson (Jonathan Cape)

Vital Issues (AAWE Publications, BP127, 92154 Suresnes)

Walking in France (Lonely Planet)

*Writers' France, John Ardagh (Hamish Hamilton)

*Xenophobe's Guide to the French, Nick Yapp & Michel Syrett (Ravette Books)

English-Language Newspapers & Magazines

Bonjour Magazine, Ash House South, Centre Road, New Ash Green, Kent DA3 8JF, UK (☎ 01474-871992, 💻 www.bonjourmagazine.com). Bi-monthly lifestyle/ property magazine.

Everything France Magazine, The Barn, Ladycross Farm, Hollow Lane, Dormansland, Surrey RH7 6PB, UK (☎ 01342-871727, 💻 www.efmag.co.uk, ✉ efmag@brooklandsgroup.com). Bi-monthly lifestyle magazine.

France Magazine, Cumberland House, Oriel Road, Cheltenham, Glos, GL50 1BB, UK (☎ 01242-216080, 💻 www.francemag.co.uk). Monthly lifestyle magazine.

France Review, La Feytaud, 24320 Coutures (☎ 05.53.90.49.76, 💻 www.france review.com). Bi-monthly magazine in French and English.

France-USA Contacts, FUSAC, 26 rue Bénard, 75014 Paris, France (☎ 01.56.53.54.54, 💻 www.fusac.fr). Free bi-weekly magazine.

French Property News, 6 Burgess Mews, London SW19 1UF, UK (☎ 020-8543 3113, 💻 www.French-property-news.com). Monthly property newspaper.

Focus on France, Outbound Publishing, 1 Commercial Road, Eastbourne, East Sussex BN21 3XQ, UK (☎ 01323-726040, ✉ outbounduk@aol.com).

Living France, Waterways World Ltd, The Well House, High Street, Burton-on-Trent, Staffordshire DE14 1JQ, UK (☎ 01283-742971, 💻 www.living france.com). Monthly lifestyle/property magazine.

The News, The News, SARL Brussac, 225 route d'Angoulème, BP4042, 24004 Perigueux, France (☎ 05.53.06.84.40, 💻 www.French-news.com). Monthly newspaper.

Paris Voice, 7, rue Papillon, 75009 Paris, France (☎ 01.47.70.45.05, 💻 www.parisvoice.com). Free weekly newspaper.

The Riviera Reporter, 56, chemin de Provence, 06250 Mougins, France (☎ 04.93.45.77.19, 🖳 www.riviera-reporter.com). Monthly free magazine.

The Riviera Times, 8 avenue Jean Moulin, 06340 Drap, France (☎ 04.93. 27.60.00, 🖳 www.rivieratimes.com).

French Property Magazines

Appel immo, 34399 Montpellier cedex 5 (☎ 04.99.74.74.65, 🖳 www.appelimmo.fr)

Le Journal des Particuliers, 40, rue du Docteur Roux, 75015 Paris (☎ 01.53.86.90.90, 🖳 www.journaldesparticuliers.com

L'Immobilier en France, 62–64, rue de Javel, 75015 Paris (☎ 01.56.77.56.77, 🖳 www.immobilierenfrance.com, ✉ ief@immobilierenfrance.com)

De Particulier à Particulier, 40, rue du docteur Roux, 75724 Paris cedex 15 (☎ 01.40.56.33.33, 🖳 www.pap.fr) – a weekly listing of private property advertisements, available at most news stands

APPENDIX C: USEFUL WEBSITES

There are dozens of expatriate websites and as the Internet increases in popularity the number grows by the day. Most information is useful, and websites generally offer free access, although some require a subscription or payment for services. Relocation and other companies specialising in expatriate services often have websites, although these may only provide information that a company is prepared to offer free of charge, which may be rather biased. However, there are plenty of volunteer sites run by expatriates providing practical information and tips. A particularly useful section found on most expatriate websites is the 'message board' or 'forum', where expatriates answer questions based on their experience and knowledge and offer an insight into what living and working in is *really* like.

Below is a list of websites not otherwise mentioned in the text. Note that websites are listed under headings in alphabetical order and the list is by no means definitive.

French Websites

General

- http://adminet.com – information about selected towns in France
- http://nucleaire.edf.fr – information about nuclear power stations in France
- www.abelcom.net – general information about France
- www.actualinfo.com – news
- www.admifrance.gouv.fr – includes links to all government ministry websites
- www.agence.francepresse.com – world news and information in English
- www.all-about-france.com – general information about France
- www.anglofrance.net – general information on France for English-speaking expatriates
- www.culture.fr – information about cultural events and activities
- www.diplomatic.fr/infopra/index – general information about life in France
- www.expatica.com – practical information for English-speaking expatriates; mainly Paris-orientated, but lots of useful general information as well
- www.finances.gouv.fr – economic information
- www.france.diplomatie – general information about France, including daily updated news

- 🖥 www.francealacarte.org.uk/education – information about education in France
- 🖥 www.franceguide.com – the French Tourist Office in London
- 🖥 www.franceguide.fr – tourist information
- 🖥 www.holidayfrance.org.uk – the British Association of Tour Operators to France
- 🖥 www.insee.fr – office of national statistics: population, unemployment, salaries, etc. (in English and French)
- 🖥 www.legifrance.gouv.fr – legal information
- 🖥 www.lepoint.fr – articles and surveys on all aspects of French life from the consumer magazine *Le Point*
- 🖥 www.leprogres.fr – general information
- 🖥 www.letudiant.fr – information for students
- 🖥 www.meteo.fr – weather and climate in France
- 🖥 www.pagesjaunes.fr – the French Yellow Pages
- 🖥 www.parisnotes.com – information about Paris
- 🖥 www.paris.alliancefrancaise.fr – the site of the Alliance Française
- 🖥 www.paris-touristoffice.com – tourist information
- 🖥 www.pratique.fr – practical information
- 🖥 www.service-public.fr – French Public Services; includes links to most important French government websites
- 🖥 www.sos-net.cu.org – general information

Amenities

- 🖥 www.amb-usa.fr/consul/guideoas/doc.pdf – a list of English-speaking doctors and hospitals
- 🖥 www.backspin.com – excellent guide to golf courses in France
- 🖥 www.cinefil.com – information about films showing in each area, with an indication of which films are being shown in the original language
- 🖥 www.cityvox.com – information about eating out, accommodation, foreign food shops, etc. in selected towns in France
- 🖥 www.eir.fr – Federation française d'Equitation for information on horse riding
- 🖥 www.equipyrene.com – Office of Pyrenean Equestrian Guides for information on horse riding
- 🖥 www.ffcanoe.assoc.fr – information on canoeing and kayaking

- www.ffgolf.org – the French golfing federation
- www.pavillonbleu.com – for a list of 'blue flag' beaches in France (awarded by the Foundation for European Education and Environment)
- www.quechoisir.org – reports and articles from the consumer magazine *Que Choisir*
- www.surfrider-europe.org – for details of 'black flag' (i.e. polluted) beaches in France (awarded by the Surfrider Foundation Europe)
- www.thalasso-france.com – for a list of balneology centres

Services

- www.apce.com – help for company founders
- www.ecis.org – European Council for International Schools
- www.europa-pages.com – list of language schools offering French courses
- www.paris.alliancefrancaise.fr

Property & Accommodation

- http://coast-country.com – Coast & Country; English estate agents on the Côte d'Azur
- www.aaterrains.com – information on buying land
- www.allobat.fr – building land for sale
- www.bonjour – property ads (from the *Comareg* free paper)
- www.construiresamaison.com – building land for sale
- www.entreparticuliers.com – property advertisements
- www.fnaim.com – French federation of estate agents
- www.foncia.fr – rental accommodation specialists
- www.frenchproperty.co.uk – French property search agents
- www.gites-de-france.fr – accommodation in *gîtes*
- www.green-acre.com – Green-Acres Services property agents
- www.immonot.com – property listed with *notaires* and information on buying
- www.immoprix.com – average property and building land sale prices by type, size, town, area, department and region

🖥 www.immostreet.com – properties for sale and rent; also has automatic calculator showing repayment amounts for mortgage purchases

🖥 www.journaldesparticuliers.com – advertisements in the French property magazine *Le Journal des Particuliers*

🖥 www.logic-immo.com – French estate agents' property advertisements

🖥 www.notaires.fr – property listed with *notaires* and information on buying

🖥 www.pap.fr – advertisements in the French property magazine *De Particulier à Particulier* (English-language version available)

🖥 www.seloger.com – properties for sale and rent plus quotations for insurance, removals and building work

🖥 www.terrain.fr – building land for sale and information on buying land

🖥 www.terrains-a-batir.com – building land for sale

🖥 www.vefuk.com – Vivre en France property agents

🖥 www.villagesetvillages.fr – building land for sale and information on buying land

Communications

🖥 www.aeroport.fr – details of and links to all French airports

🖥 www.airfrance.com – Air France

🖥 www.air-liberte.com – Air Liberté

🖥 www.britishairways.co.uk – British Airways

🖥 www.flybe.com – British European airline

🖥 www.flybmi.com – British Midland airline

🖥 www.brittanyferries.com – Brittany Ferries

🖥 www.buzzaway.com – Buzz airline (part of KLM)

🖥 www.condorferries.co.uk – Condor Ferries

🖥 www.easyjet.com – EasyJet airline

🖥 www.go-fly.com – Go airline (part of EasyJet)

🖥 www.hoverspeed.com – Hoverspeed fast ferries

🖥 www.norfolkline.com – Norfolkline ferries

🖥 www.poportsmouth.com – P&O Portsmouth ferries

🖥 www.posl.com – P&O Stena ferries

🖥 www.raileurope.co.uk – Eurostar/*TGV* link

- www.ryanair.com – Ryanair
- www.seafrance.com – Sea France ferries
- www.transmancheferries.com – Transmanche ferries
- www.autoroutes.fr – information about French motorways and tolls
- www.autoroutes.fr – information about French motorways
- www.bison-fute.equipement.gouv.fr – French road traffic reports
- www.eurolines.co.uk – Eurolines coaches
- www.eurostar.com – Eurostar rail services
- www.eurotunnel.com – Eurotunnel
- www.frenchmotorail.com – Motorail
- www.gobycoach.com – National Express coaches
- www.iti.fr – road route planning through France
- www.rac.co.uk – Royal Automobile Club (RAC) /
- www.raileurope.com – Rail Europe
- www.ratp.fr – Parisian regional transport authority
- www.sncf.fr – French national railways
- www.theaa.co.uk – Automobile Association (AA)
- www.transbus.org – information about tramways in France

Employment

- www.anpe.fr – French national employment agency
- www.apec.asso.fr – Association Pour l'Emploi de Cadres (for senior management positions)
- www.cadremploi.fr and www.cadresonline.com – for executive or managerial positions
- www.cybersearch.fr (for business and trade, computing, industry, tourism and accounting jobs)
- www.keljob.com – job search portal

General Websites

Australia Shop (www.australia.shop.com). Expatriate shopping for homesick Australians.

British Expatriates (⌨ www.britishexpat.com and www.ukworldwide.com). Two sites designed to keep British expatriates in touch with events in and information about the UK.

Direct Moving (⌨ www.directmoving.com). General expatriate information, tips and advice, and numerous links.

Escape Artist (⌨ www.escapeartist.com). One of the most comprehensive expatriate sites, including resources, links and directories covering most expatriate destinations. You can also subscribe to the free monthly online expatriate magazine, *Escape from America*.

ExpatAccess (⌨ www.expataccess.com). Aimed at those planning to move abroad, with free moving guides.

ExpatBoards (⌨ www.expatboards.com). A comprehensive site for expatriates, with popular discussion boards and special areas for Britons and Americans.

Expat Exchange (⌨ www.expatexchange.com). Reportedly the largest online 'community' for English-speaking expatriates, including articles on relocation and a question and answer facility.

Expat Forum (⌨ www.expatforum.com). Provides cost of living comparisons as well as over 20 country-specific forums.

Expat Mums (⌨ www.expat-moms.com). Information for expatriate mothers.

Expat Network (⌨ www.expatnetwork.com). The UK's leading expatriate website, which is essentially an employment network for expatriates, although it also includes numerous support services and a monthly online magazine, *Nexus*.

Expat Shopping (⌨ www.expatshopping.com). Order your favourite foods from home.

Expat World (⌨ www.expatworld.net). Information for American and British expatriates, including a subscription newsletter.

Expatriate Experts (⌨ www.expatexpert.com). Run by expatriate expert Robin Pascoe, providing advice and support.

Global People (⌨ www.peoplegoingglobal.com). Includes country-specific information with a particular emphasis on social and political issues.

Living Abroad (⌨ www.livingabroad.com). Includes an extensive list of country profiles, which are available only on payment.

Outpost Information Centre (⌨ www.outpostexpat.nl). Contains extensive country-specific information and links operated by the Shell Petroleum Company for its expatriate workers, but available to everyone.

Real Post Reports (🖥 www.realpostreports.com). Includes relocation services, recommended reading lists and 'real-life' stories written by expatriates in cities throughout the world.

SaveWealth Travel (🖥 www.savewealth.com/travel/warnings). Travel information and warnings.

Trade Partners (🖥 www.tradepartners.gov.uk). A UK government-sponsored site providing trade and investment (and general) information about most countries, including the USA.

The Travel Doctor (🖥 www.tmvc.com.au/info10.html). Includes a country by country vaccination guide.

Travelfinder (🖥 www.travelfinder.com/twarn/travel_warnings.html). Travel information with warnings about danger areas.

World Health Organization (🖥 www.who.int). Health information.

The World Press (🖥 www.theworldpress.com). Links to media sites in practically every country in the world's media.

World Travel Guide (🖥 www.wtgonline.com). A general website for world travellers and expatriates.

Yankee Doodle (🖥 www.yankeedoodleiow.com). Import American products.

Websites for British Expatriates

British Expatriates (🖥 www.britishexpat.com and www.ukworldwide.com). These websites keep British expatriates in touch with events and information in the United Kingdom.

Trade Partners (🖥 www.tradepartners.gov.uk). A government-sponsored website whose main aim is to provide trade and investment information for most countries. Even if you aren't intending to do business, the information is comprehensive and up to date.

Websites for Women

Career Women (🖥 www.womenconnect.com). Contains career opportunities for women abroad plus a wealth of other useful information.

Expatriate Mothers (🖥 http://expatmoms.tripod.com). Help and advice on how to survive as a mother on relocation.

Spouse Abroad (🖥 www.expatspouse.com). Information about careers and working abroad. You need to register and subscribe.

Women Abroad (💻 www.womanabroad.com). Advice on careers, expatriate skills and the family abroad. Opportunity to subscribe to a monthly magazine of the same name.

Worldwise Directory (💻 www.suzylamplugh.org/worldwise). Run by the Suzy Lamplugh charity for personal safety, the site provides practical information about a number of countries with special emphasis on safety, particularly for women.

APPENDIX D: WEIGHTS & MEASURES

France uses the metric system of measurement. Nationals of a few countries (including the Americans and British) who are more familiar with the imperial system of measurement will find the tables on the following pages useful. Some comparisons shown are only approximate, but are close enough for most everyday uses. In addition to the variety of measurement systems used, clothes sizes often vary considerably with the manufacturer (as we all know only too well). Try all clothes on before buying and don't be afraid to return something if, when you try it on at home, you decide it doesn't fit (most shops will exchange goods or give a refund).

Women's Clothes

Continental	34	36	38	40	42	44	46	48	50	52
UK	8	10	12	14	16	18	20	22	24	26
USA	6	8	10	12	14	16	18	20	22	24

Pullovers

	Women's						Men's					
Continental	40	42	44	46	48	50	44	46	48	50	52	54
UK	34	36	38	40	42	44	34	36	38	40	42	44
USA	34	36	38	40	42	44	sm	medium		large		xl

Note: sm = small, xl = extra large

Men's Shirts

Continental	36	37	38	39	40	41	42	43	44	46
UK/USA	14	14	15	15	16	16	17	17	18	-

Men's Underwear

Continental	5	6	7	8	9	10
UK	34	36	38	40	42	44
USA	small	medium		large	extra large	

Children's Clothes

Continental	92	104	116	128	140	152
UK	16/18	20/22	24/26	28/30	32/34	36/38
USA	2	4	6	8	10	12

Children's Shoes

Continental	18	19	20	21	22	23	24	25	26	27	28	29	30	31	32
UK/USA	2	3	4	4	5	6	7	7	8	9	10	11	11	12	13

Continental	33	34	35	36	37	38
UK/USA	1	2	2	3	4	5

Shoes (Women's and Men's)

Continental	35	35	36	37	37	38	39	39	40	40	41	42	42	43	44	44
UK	2	3	3	4	4	5	5	6	6	7	7	8	8	9	9	10
USA	4	4	5	5	6	6	7	7	8	8	9	9	10	10	11	11

Weight

Avoirdupois	Metric	Metric	Avoirdupois
1 oz	28.35 g	1 g	0.035 oz
1 pound*	454 g	100 g	3.5 oz
1 cwt	50.8 kg	250 g	9 oz
1 ton	1,016 kg	500 g	18 oz
1 tonne	2,205 pounds	1 kg	2.2 pounds

* A metric 'pound' is 500g, g = gramme, kg = kilogramme

Length

British/US	Metric	Metric	British/US
1 inch	2.54 cm	1 cm	0.39 inch
1 foot	30.48 cm	1 m	3 feet 3.25 inches
1 yard	91.44 cm	1 km	0.62 mile
1 mile	1.6 km	8 km	5 miles

Note: cm = centimetre, m = metre, km = kilometre

Capacity

Imperial	Metric	Metric	Imperial
1 pint (USA)	0.47 litre	1 litre	1.76 UK pints
1 pint (UK)	0.57 litre	1 litre	0.26 US gallons
1 gallon (USA)	3.78 litre	1 litre	0.22 UK gallon
1 gallon (UK)	4.54 litre	1 litre	35.21 fluid oz

Area

British/US	Metric	Metric	British/US
1 square inch	0.45 sq. cm	1 sq. cm	0.15 sq. inches
1 square foot	0.09 sq. m	1 sq. m	10.76 sq. feet
1 square yard	0.84 sq. m	1 sq. m	1.2 sq. yards
1 acre	0.4 hectares	1 hectare	2.47 acres
1 square mile	259 hectares	1 sq. km	0.39 sq. mile

Temperature

° Celsius	° Fahrenheit	
0	32	freezing point of water
5	41	
10	50	
15	59	
20	68	
25	77	
30	86	
35	95	
40	104	

Note: The boiling point of water is 100°C / 212°F.

Oven Temperature

Gas	Electric	
	°F	°C
–	225–250	110–120
1	275	140
2	300	150
3	325	160
4	350	180
5	375	190
6	400	200
7	425	220
8	450	230
9	475	240

For a quick conversion, the Celsius temperature is approximately half the Fahrenheit temperature.

Temperature Conversion

Celsius to Fahrenheit: multiply by 9, divide by 5 and add 32.
Fahrenheit to Celsius: subtract 32, multiply by 5 and divide by 9.

Body Temperature

Normal body temperature (if you're alive and well) is 98.4° Fahrenheit, which equals 37° Celsius.

APPENDIX E: MAPS

The map opposite shows the 22 regions and 96 departments of France (excluding overseas territories), which are listed below. The departments are (mostly) numbered alphabetically from 01 to 89. Departments 91 to 95 come under the Ile-de-France region, which also includes Ville de Paris (75), Seine-et-Marne (77) and Yvelines (78), shown in detail opposite. Corsica consists of two departments, 2A and 2B.

01 Ain	32 Gers	64 Pyrénées-Atlantiques
02 Aisne	33 Gironde	65 Hautes-Pyrénées
2A Corse-du-Sud	34 Hérault	66 Pyrénées-Orientales
2B Haute Corse	35 Ille-et-Vilaine	67 Bas-Rhin
03 Allier	36 Indre	68 Haut-Rhin
04 Alpes-de-Hte-Provence	37 Indre-et-Loire	69 Rhône
05 Hautes-Alpes	38 Isère	70 Haute-Saône
06 Alpes-Maritimes	39 Jura	71 Saône-et-Loire
07 Ardèche	40 Landes	72 Sarthe
08 Ardennes	41 Loir-et-Cher	73 Savoie
09 Ariège	42 Loire	74 Haute-Savoie
10 Aube	43 Haute-Loire	75 Paris
11 Aude	44 Loire-Atlantique	76 Seine
12 Aveyron	45 Loiret	77 Seine-Maritime
13 Bouches-du-Rhône	46 Lot	78 Yvelines
14 Calvados	47 Lot-et-Garonne	79 Deux-Sèvres
15 Cantal	48 Lozère	80 Somme
16 Charente	49 Maine-et-Loire	81 Tarn
17 Charent-Maritime	50 Manche	82 Tarn-et-Garonne
18 Cher	51 Marne	83 Var
19 Corrèze	52 Haute-Marne	84 Vaucluse
21 Côte-d'Or	53 Mayenne	85 Vendée
22 Côte-d'Armor	54 Meurthe-et-Moselle	86 Vienne
23 Creuse	55 Meuse	87 Haute-Vienne
24 Dordogne	56 Morbihan	88 Vosges
25 Doubs	57 Moselle	89 Yonne
26 Drôme	58 Nièvre	90 Territoire de Belfort
27 Eure	59 Nord	91 Essonne
28 Eure-et-Loir	60 Oise	92 Hauts-de-Seine
29 Finistère	61 Orne	93 Seine-Saint-Denis
30 Gard	62 Pas-de-Calais	94 Val-de-Marne
31 Haute-Garonne	63 Puy-de-Dôme	95 Val-d'Oise

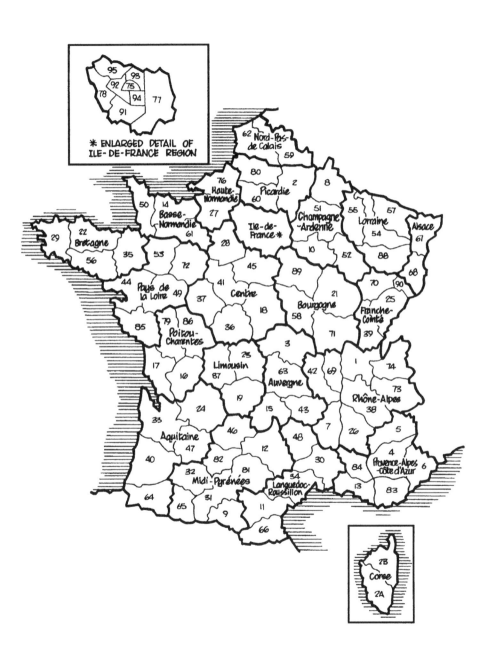

The map below shows the high-speed train (*train à grande vitesse/TGV*) network. Thick lines indicate special track on which trains can run at up to 300kph (187mph); on the rest of the network, trains are restricted to around 200kph (122mph).

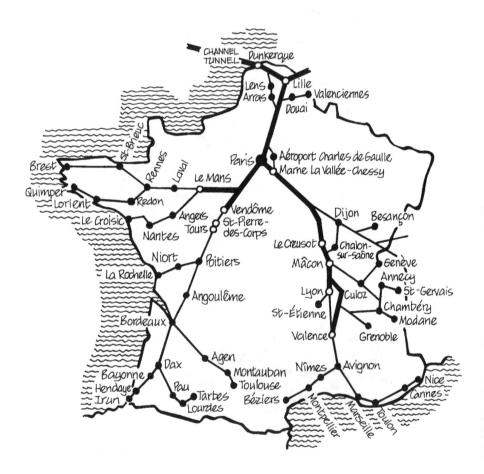

APPENDIX F: MAJOR TOWN RATING

The table below is derived from a nationwide survey of 100 of the largest cities and towns in France published in January 2002 by *Le Point* magazine. Towns are rated in seven categories, each rating consisting of several criteria, as follows:

Cost: The four criteria for evaluation were the cost per m² of resale property between 1st April 2000 and 31st March 2001, the rate of *taxe d'habitation* and *taxe foncière* (the two property taxes levied in France), and the cost (per cubic metre) of mains water.

Accommodation: The five criteria were the percentage of property owners in the town, the percentage of family homes, the percentage of properties without a bath or shower, the percentage of vacant properties, and the percentage of new properties (built during 2000).

Work: The nine criteria were the unemployment rate (in 1999), the unemployment rate among inhabitants under 25, the percentage of long-term unemployed, the percentage of employed people, the percentage of women in employment, the percentage of employed people who work in the town itself, the percentage of new businesses (in 2000) that have failed, the average annual salary of workers (in 1999), and the percentage of jobs created between December 1999 and December 2000.

Safety: The nine criteria were the number of crimes per 1,000 inhabitants in 2000 and the increase or decrease in crime between 1998 and 2000, the number of people killed and injured on the roads per 1,000 inhabitants in 2000, the number of times the town has been flooded since 1982 and whether or not the town has published a flood-prevention plan, whether or not there's a nuclear power station or reprocessing plant within 50km (30mi) of the town, the number of high-risk factories in the town, whether or not the town has a major incinerating plant, and the number of areas of high pollution.

Health: The six criteria were the child mortality rate (1996–98), the percentage of inhabitants dying of lung cancer, the rate of alcohol-related illnesses, the rate of coronary thrombosis, the suicide rate (1996–98) and the overall death rate in proportion to the average age of the population.

Leisure: The nine criteria were the number of state-owned museums, whether or not the town has a state-run theatre and a dance centre, the number of listed buildings, the number of library books borrowed, magazines sold and cinema visits per inhabitant, the number of Michelin-starred restaurants, and the percentage of students in the town (1999–2000).

Economy: The four criteria were the growth or decline in the town's population, the extent to which the town's population is ageing, the rate at which people are being attracted to the town, and the rate at which workers are being attracted to the town (all measured by comparing the national censuses of 1990 and 1999).

The lower the figure, the higher the rating in each category, the total figure for all categories giving an overall rating for France's main towns, which are listed in descending order of preference in the table below. (Note that the ranking below doesn't match that given by **Le Point**, which included two further categories: the average wealth of each town's inhabitants, and its 'pleasantness', which was evaluated according to whether it was accessible by *TGV*, its proximity to the sea and to the nearest ski resort, the amount of sunshine and rain it experienced and its average annual temperature, the percentage of employees who walked to work, the extent of the public transport network, and the amount of green space and cycle track and the number of clubs and associations per inhabitant. **Le Point**'s ranking is given for comparison.) Full details of the survey can be found (in French) on 🖳 www.le point.com.

Rank & Town	Dept.	Cost	Accom.	Work	Safety	Leisure	Health	Econ.	*Le Point* Total	*Rank*
1 La Roche-sur-Yon	85	23	3	13	31	47	45	23	185	8
2 Vannes	56	78	11	8	6	30	54	4	191	11
3 Laval	53	32	16	12	10	72	11	46	199	15
4 Quimper	29	33	7	20	41	22	48	31	202	31
5 Orléans	45	62	47	5	43	26	23	6	212	2
6 Dijon	21	72	66	6	24	5	9	33	215	5
7 Albi	81	21	9	22	17	61	13	82	225	28
8 Poitiers	86	36	82	22	44	3	34	15	236	17
9 Gap	05	55	2	16	1	70	39	57	240	19
10 Rennes	35	80	53	2	65	9	22	14	245	4
11 Besançon	25	43	69	17	39	8	30	41	247	13
11 Montpellier	34	48	46	59	51	17	17	9	247	9
13 Aix-en-Provence	13	88	45	28	44	19	3	22	249	1
14 Toulouse	31	53	51	21	91	13	6	19	254	12
15 Cholet	49	14	1	55	16	90	2	77	255	24
15 Nantes	44	76	25	25	74	18	26	11	255	6
17 Blois	41	40	35	45	28	31	28	56	263	38
18 Caen	14	45	85	31	53	5	25	29	273	10
18 Chambéry	73	52	31	24	67	40	27	32	273	20
20 Rueil-Malmaison	92	99	27	18	11	99	18	2	274	26
21 Tours	37	60	58	43	57	11	16	37	282	3
22 Versailles	78	97	76	14	8	25	46	21	287	22
23 Angers	49	56	69	53	36	11	55	16	296	7
24 Bourg-en-Bresse	01	29	37	39	78	44	12	59	298	56

Rank & Town	Dept.	Cost	Accom.	Work	Safety	Leisure	Health	Econ.	Total	*Le Point Rank*
25 Angoulême	**16**	4	72	71	20	37	62	35	**301**	*55*
26 Boulogne-Billancourt	**92**	93	84	3	18	86	5	13	**302**	*25*
27 Périgueux	**24**	58	80	50	3	50	19	45	**305**	*51*
28 Niort	**79**	20	22	30	59	70	32	73	**306**	*33*
29 Lyons	**69**	74	99	9	92	4	13	17	**308**	*14*
30 Créteil	**94**	92	23	15	52	65	36	27	**310**	*58*
31 Annecy	**74**	91	19	7	81	35	50	28	**311**	*18*
31 Evry	**91**	71	51	4	71	82	31	1	**311**	*74*
33 Limoges	**87**	31	63	35	30	20	57	84	**320**	*42*
33 Tarbes	**65**	8	43	90	5	52	51	71	**320**	*54*
35 Agen	**47**	19	63	66	48	77	6	44	**323**	*63*
35 Chartres	**28**	81	33	19	33	45	88	24	**323**	*34*
37 St-Germain-en-Laye	**78**	98	83	10	2	54	60	18	**325**	*32*
38 Pau	**64**	28	55	54	22	46	53	68	**326**	*43*
39 Metz	**57**	61	42	40	87	14	63	20	**327**	*23*
39 St-Brieuc	**22**	39	40	63	14	57	76	38	**327**	*60*
41 Nancy	**54**	50	98	33	64	7	71	7	**330**	*21*
42 Villeurbanne	**69**	44	71	38	48	92	29	11	**333**	*49*
43 Bordeaux	**33**	54	91	26	93	2	43	25	**334**	*27*
44 Montauban	**82**	38	6	36	69	66	40	81	**336**	*73*
44 St-Nazaire	**44**	51	4	60	13	76	58	74	**336**	*69*
46 Bourges	**18**	34	39	43	55	21	61	85	**338**	*59*
47 Grenoble	**38**	75	73	48	76	22	8	38	**340**	*16*
47 Valence	**26**	11	32	72	70	28	70	57	**340**	*46*
49 Nîmes	**30**	22	30	76	85	50	15	63	**341**	*41*
50 Brest	**29**	16	20	67	63	52	78	49	**345**	*37*
51 Arles	**13**	17	17	73	23	87	37	92	**346**	*80*
52 Neuilly-sur-Seine	**92**	100	79	11	7	95	4	52	**348**	*39*
53 Castres	**81**	2	8	56	56	90	52	93	**357**	*72*
54 Clermont-Ferrand	**63**	35	88	41	46	28	74	46	**358**	*40*
55 Colmar	**68**	65	44	29	38	34	95	53	**358**	*53*
56 Bayonne	**64**	67	35	75	27	36	72	50	**362**	*50*
56 Compiègne	**60**	68	38	42	61	62	65	26	**362**	*61*
58 La Rochelle	**17**	86	59	61	93	10	24	33	**366**	*47*
58 St-Malo	**35**	87	5	34	26	55	89	70	**366**	*68*

Rank & Town	Dept.	Cost	Accom.	Work	Safety	Leisure	Health	Econ.	*Le Point* **Total** *Rank*	
60 Epinal	**88**	18	62	51	19	88	69	62	**369**	*62*
61 Valenciennes	**59**	57	54	79	42	39	91	8	**370**	*64*
62 Brive-la-Gaillarde	**19**	15	29	64	66	78	38	89	**379**	*82*
63 Auxerre	**89**	37	61	49	73	33	63	64	**380**	*84*
64 Beauvais	**60**	27	48	65	34	56	97	54	**381**	*66*
64 Reims	**51**	77	56	52	40	38	67	51	**381**	*45*
66 Avignon	**84**	25	23	94	98	26	49	67	**382**	*76*
66 Melun	**77**	89	77	32	25	72	82	5	**382**	*67*
66 Paris	**75**	96	100	1	88	1	20	76	**382**	*36*
69 Carcassonne	**11**	5	10	88	77	81	44	78	**383**	*79*
70 Montluçon	**03**	1	68	89	4	68	56	98	**384**	*70*
71 Dunkerque	**59**	42	18	69	50	63	84	59	**385**	*86*
71 Nevers	**58**	9	75	58	21	75	75	72	**385**	*90*
73 Rouen	**76**	66	92	37	75	15	93	9	**387**	*30*
74 Perpignan	**66**	7	34	99	54	42	66	87	**389**	*48*
75 Le Mans	**72**	41	15	47	83	84	41	79	**390**	*29*
76 Antibes	**06**	95	13	57	79	82	1	65	**392**	*52*
77 Ajaccio	**2A**	82	14	62	29	74	47	95	**403**	*87*
78 Sarcelles	**95**	49	28	97	9	100	85	42	**410**	*96*
79 Bastia	**2B**	83	12	85	32	98	21	89	**420**	*85*
80 Belfort	**90**	79	74	78	35	48	79	36	**429**	*81*
81 Vichy	**03**	10	97	91	15	67	86	68	**434**	*88*
82 Lille	**59**	73	96	81	72	16	100	3	**441**	*71*
82 St-Etienne	**42**	6	89	83	62	69	33	99	**441**	*57*
82 Strasbourg	**67**	84	93	27	100	24	73	40	**441**	*44*
85 St-Quentin	**02**	12	50	95	12	96	94	86	**445**	*91*
86 Charleville-Mézières	**08**	24	59	74	57	80	77	79	**450**	*97*
87 Nice	**06**	90	80	46	97	32	10	96	**451**	*35*
88 Troyes	**10**	26	94	86	60	58	99	30	**453**	*92*
89 Chalon-sur-Saône	**71**	13	86	68	68	64	80	83	**462**	*89*
90 Mulhouse	**68**	30	90	70	96	41	83	54	**464**	*78*
91 Toulon	**83**	47	66	92	47	93	35	94	**474**	*65*
92 Béziers	**34**	3	41	96	90	94	58	97	**479**	*94*
93 Marseilles	**13**	69	65	81	95	43	42	91	**486**	*75*
94 Sète	**34**	59	26	98	37	89	90	99	**498**	*98*

Rank & Town	Dept.	Cost	Accom.	Work	Safety	Leisure	Health	Econ.	Total	*Le Point Rank*
95 Calais	**62**	63	21	100	84	85	81	65	**499**	*95*
96 Amiens	**80**	64	78	76	80	59	97	59	**513**	*83*
96 Cannes	**06**	94	57	84	86	49	68	75	**513**	*77*
98 Le Havre	**76**	46	48	93	89	79	96	88	**539**	*93*
99 St-Denis	**93**	85	95	80	98	59	86	48	**551**	*100*
100 Corbeil-Essonnes	**91**	70	86	86	82	97	92	43	**556**	*99*

INDEX

T

W

BUYING A HOME IN FRANCE

Buying a Home in France is essential reading for anyone planning to purchase property in France and is designed to guide you through the jungle and make it a pleasant and enjoyable experience. Most importantly, it's packed with vital information to help you avoid the sort of disasters that can turn your dream home into a nightmare! Topics covered include:

- Avoiding problems
- Choosing the region
- Finding the right home & location
- Estate agents
- Finance, mortgages & taxes
- Home security
- Utilities, heating & air-conditioning
- Moving house & settling in
- Renting & letting
- Permits & visas
- Travelling & communications
- Health & insurance
- Renting a car & driving
- Retirement & starting a business
- And much, much more!

Buying a Home in France is the most comprehensive and up-to-date source of information available about buying property in France. Whether you want a detached house, townhouse or apartment, a holiday or a permanent home, this book will help make your dreams come true.

Buy this book and save yourself time, trouble and money!

Order your copies today by phone, fax, mail or e-mail from: Survival Books, PO Box 146, Wetherby, West Yorks. LS23 6XZ, United Kingdom (☎/▤ +44 (0)1937-843523, ✉ orders@survivalbooks.net, 💻 www.survivalbooks.net).

ORDER FORM

ALIEN'S GUIDES / BEST PLACES / BUYING A HOME / WINES

Qty.	Title	Price (incl. p&p)*			Total
		UK	Europe	World	
	The Alien's Guide to Britain	£5.95	£6.95	£8.45	
	The Alien's Guide to France	£5.95	£6.95	£8.45	
	The Best Places to Buy a Home in France	£13.95	£15.95	£19.45	
	The Best Places to Buy a Home in Spain	£13.45	£14.95	£16.95	
	Buying a Home Abroad	£13.45	£14.95	£16.95	
	Buying a Home in Britain	£11.45	£12.95	£14.95	
	Buying a Home in Florida	£13.45	£14.95	£16.95	
	Buying a Home in France	£13.45	£14.95	£16.95	
	Buying a Home in Greece & Cyprus	£13.45	£14.95	£16.95	
	Buying a Home in Ireland	£11.45	£12.95	£14.95	
	Buying a Home in Italy	£13.45	£14.95	£16.95	
	Buying a Home in Portugal	£13.45	£14.95	£16.95	
	Buying a Home in Spain	£13.45	£14.95	£16.95	
	How to Avoid Holiday & Travel Disasters	£13.45	£14.95	£16.95	
	Maintaining & Renovating Your French Home	Autumn 2003			
	Rioja and its Wines	£11.45	£12.95	£14.95	
	The Wines of Spain	£15.95	£18.45	£21.95	
				Total	

Order your copies today by phone, fax, mail or e-mail from: Survival Books, PO Box 146, Wetherby, West Yorks. LS23 6XZ, UK (☎/▤ +44 (0)1937-843523, ✉ orders@survivalbooks.net, ▢ www.survivalbooks.net). If you aren't entirely satisfied, simply return them to us within 14 days for a full and unconditional refund.

Cheque enclosed/please charge my Delta/Mastercard/Switch/Visa* card

Card No. _ _ _ _   _ _ _ _   _ _ _ _   _ _ _ _

Expiry date _____   **Issue number (Switch only)** _____

Signature _____   **Tel. No.** _____

NAME _____

ADDRESS _____

_____

_____

* Delete as applicable (price includes postage – airmail for Europe/world).

LIVING AND WORKING IN FRANCE

Living and Working in France is essential reading for anyone planning to spend some time in France including holiday-home owners, retirees, visitors, business people, migrants, students and even extraterrestrials! It's packed with over 400 pages of important and useful information designed to help you **avoid costly mistakes and save both time and money.** Topics covered include how to:

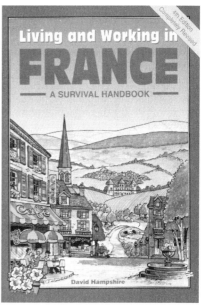

- Find a job with a good salary & conditions
- Obtain a residence permit
- Avoid and overcome problems
- Find your dream home
- Get the best education for your family
- Make the best use of public transport
- Endure motoring in France
- Obtain the best health treatment
- Stretch your euros further
- Make the most of your leisure time
- Enjoy the French sporting life
- Find the best shopping bargains
- Insure yourself against most eventualities
- Use post office and telephone services
- Do numerous other things not listed above

Living and Working in France is the most comprehensive and up-to-date source of practical information available about everyday life in France. It isn't, however, a boring text book, but an interesting and entertaining guide written in a highly readable style.

Buy this book and discover what it's *really* like to live and work in France.

Order your copies today by phone, fax, mail or e-mail from: Survival Books, PO Box 146, Wetherby, West Yorks. LS23 6XZ, United Kingdom (☎/▤ +44 (0)1937-843523, ✉ orders@survivalbooks.net, 💻 www.survivalbooks.net).

ORDER FORM

LIVING & WORKING SERIES / RETIRING ABROAD

Qty.	Title	Price (incl. p&p)*			Total
		UK	Europe	World	
	Living & Working Abroad	£16.95	£18.95	£22.45	
	Living & Working in America	£14.95	£16.95	£20.45	
	Living & Working in Australia	£14.95	£16.95	£20.45	
	Living & Working in Britain	£14.95	£16.95	£20.45	
	Living & Working in Canada	£16.95	£18.95	£22.45	
	Living & Working in the Far East	Winter 2003			
	Living & Working in France	£14.95	£16.95	£20.45	
	Living & Working in Germany	£16.95	£18.95	£22.45	
	Living & Working in the Gulf States & Saudi Arabia	£16.95	£18.95	£22.45	
	Living & Working in Holland, Belgium & Luxembourg	£14.95	£16.95	£20.45	
	Living & Working in Ireland	£14.95	£16.95	£20.45	
	Living & Working in Italy	£14.95	£16.95	£20.45	
	Living & Working in London	£11.45	£12.95	£14.95	
	Living & Working in New Zealand	£14.95	£16.95	£20.45	
	Living & Working in Spain	£14.95	£16.95	£20.45	
	Living & Working in Switzerland	£14.95	£16.95	£20.45	
	Retiring Abroad	£14.95	£16.95	£20.45	
				Total	

Order your copies today by phone, fax, mail or e-mail from: Survival Books, PO Box 146, Wetherby, West Yorks. LS23 6XZ, UK (☎/🖨 +44 (0)1937-843523, ✉ orders@survivalbooks.net, 🖳 www.survivalbooks.net). If you aren't entirely satisfied, simply return them to us within 14 days for a full and unconditional refund.

Cheque enclosed/please charge my Delta/Mastercard/Switch/Visa* card

Card No. _ _ _ _   _ _ _ _   _ _ _ _   _ _ _ _

Expiry date _____ **Issue number (Switch only)** _____

Signature _____ **Tel. No.** _____

NAME _____

ADDRESS _____

_____

_____

* Delete as applicable (price includes postage – airmail for Europe/world).

NOTES

NOTES

NOTES